THE CATHOLIC IMAGINATION
IN AMERICAN LITERATURE

THE
CATHOLIC
IMAGINATION

IN AMERICAN
LITERATURE

ROSS LABRIE

UNIVERSITY OF MISSOURI PRESS

COLUMBIA AND LONDON

Library of Congress Cataloging-in-Publication Data
Labrie, Ross.
    The Catholic imagination in American literature / Ross Labrie.
       p.   cm.
    Includes bibliographical references and index.
    ISBN 0-8262-1110-0 (alk. paper)
    1. American literature—Catholic authors—History and criticism.
2. Christian literature, American—History and criticism.
3. Christianity and literature—United States—History.
4. Catholics—United States—Intellectual life.   5. Catholic Church—
In literature.   6. Catholics in literature.   I. Title.
PS153.C3L33   1997
810.9'9222—dc21   96-37254
                                                        CIP

∞ ™ This paper meets the requirements of the
American National Standard for Permanence of Paper
for Printed Library Materials, Z39.48, 1984.

Designer: Stephanie Foley
Typesetter: BOOKCOMP
Printer and binder: Thomson-Shore, Inc.
Typefaces: Copperplate Gothic and Palatino

For credits, see page 305.

Publication of this book has had the generous assistance
of the Clifford Willard Gaylord Foundation.

In memory of Ernest Powers Labrie (1940–1995)

Contents

VIII   CONTENTS

PREFACE

THIS STUDY OF Catholic writing in the United States has three underlying principles. It deals with authors who represent high intellectual and artistic achievement, it considers only authors who were practicing Roman Catholics, and it focuses only on literary works that center on Catholic belief and spirituality. In this way, the book fills a distinct place in the criticism of American literature. Separate chapters have been devoted to the work of each of the writers in an effort to bring out both the unity and the rich diversity of Catholic American writing while recognizing the distinctiveness of the individual authors whose works have been examined. In an effort to align the writing considered with the history of the church, I have arranged the authors in chronological sequence.

While this is not intended to be an exhaustive study, it is meant to cover significant and representative writing in the field. I acknowledge, though, that there will always be some disagreement about the selection of authors in the case of a broad study of this sort. While there is a presumed agreement about the high literary standing of nearly all of the authors included, I have attempted to make the case for literary excellence in one or two instances, as in that of Ralph McInerny, for example—though McInerny has already received respectful analysis from critics such as Anita Gandolfo. Moreover, in the last chapter I touch briefly on some recent Catholic writing in an attempt to see the direction ahead. Throughout this study I have chosen to discuss works that meet the criteria set out above, but in one or two cases there is simply too much writing to consider within the bounds of a single chapter. What I have done, in the case of Thomas Merton, for example, whose output was enormous, is to select from among the writings those works that best illustrate the *kind* of Catholic writer he was.

In an introductory chapter I attempt to delineate the nature of the Catholic imagination and sensibility and to link this discussion to the more general question of the relationship between Catholicism and art. In a concluding chapter I look at the significance of the corpus of Catholic American writing in the period from 1940 to 1980, regarding this literature as a distinct field of study comparable, for example, to that of Jewish American literature in the same period.

I am grateful to the Social Sciences and Humanities Research Council of Canada for the financial support that enabled me to travel to special-collection libraries in different parts of the United States in order to look at the papers and especially the unpublished correspondence of most of the writers considered in this study. I am especially grateful to Patricia Willis, curator of American literature at the Beinecke Library, Yale; James Lewis, curator of the Houghton Reading Room at Harvard; Jean Preston, curator of manuscripts at Princeton; James Tyler of the Olin Library at Cornell; Teri Rinns of the Bancroft Library at the University of California at Berkeley; and Dr. Robert Daggy, curator of the Merton Center at Bellarmine College. Finally, I would like to thank those in the interlibrary loan division of the Main Library at the University of British Columbia for their generous assistance.

THE CATHOLIC IMAGINATION
IN AMERICAN LITERATURE

THE CATHOLIC IMAGINATION

ALTHOUGH SINCE 1850 Roman Catholics have been the largest single religious denomination in the United States, representing slightly more than one-fifth of the population, they have also been the subject historically of what Andrew Greeley called, not without a measure of hyperbole, the "last remaining unexposed prejudice in American life." Similarly, the historian James Hennesey concluded that one of the consequences of the immense immigration of Catholics into the United States in the nineteenth century was to intensify the "latent anti-Catholic sentiment" that other Americans had inherited from the original English colonists. The fiction writer J. F. Powers, in an interview with Donald McDonald, recalled growing up as a Catholic, excluded from the American mainstream, and remembered his southern Illinois town as distinctly Protestant with the "best people" in town being Protestants. Likewise, Flannery O'Connor remembered growing up as a Catholic in the South and her imagination having been "molded" by a culture that was traditionally Protestant.[1] The consciousness of being different from the cultural majority in America has, in general, colored the imaginations of Catholic novelists and poets.

Nevertheless, Flannery O'Connor finally regarded her region's Protestant culture as fortuitous, arguing that her contact with evangelical

---

1. Greeley, *An Ugly Little Secret: Anti-Catholicism in North America*, 1; Hennesey, *American Catholics: A History of the Roman Catholic Community in the United States*; McDonald, "Interview with J. F. Powers," 88; O'Connor, *Mystery and Manners*, 196.

Protestantism provided her with a more concrete and experiential understanding of religion than had been the case with the abstract and
somewhat legalistic Catholicism that had come down to her, virtually intact, from the sixteenth-century Council of Trent. The sociologist Andrew
Greeley also argued that the social and political experience of Catholics
in the United States was superior to that of the old-world, hierarchical,
often Catholic countries from which most of them had originated, adding
that in his view the dominant Catholic theorists of the twentieth century concluded that although Catholicism could coexist with a variety
of political regimes, there is a "special affinity" between Catholic social
theory and liberal democracies of the American kind. For this reason,
perhaps, after the first quarter of this century Catholics in the United
States tended, according to the historian Philip Gleason, to become much
more "Americanized" in their outlook. An example is the assertion by
Thomas Merton that he and his fellow Trappists were "at the same time
Cistercians and Americans," a combination that made them approach
their work aggressively, like a "college football team taking the field."[2]

Drawing on the traditions of the early church, as well as Scripture,
Catholicism has tended to emphasize not only the Word of God but also the
sacraments. Because of this, Catholics regard the world in a sacramental
manner, as a place charged with the creative and providential activity of
God. The theologian David Tracy explained that in the Catholic view of
things, the "entire world, the ordinary in all its variety," is theologically
envisioned as a sacrament emanating from Christ, who in turn is viewed
as a "paradigmatic clue to humanity and nature alike." Similarly, in his
essay "Poetry and Contemplation: A Reappraisal," the monk and poet
Thomas Merton observed that to the Christian poet the "whole world
and all the incidents of life tend to be sacraments—signs of God, signs of
His love working in the world."[3]

Thus, although Catholics perceive the world as flawed because of the
effects of original sin, they also see it as retaining some of the inherent
goodness that originated in its creation by God, and in this way their
view obviously differs from that of many Protestants, especially those in
the Calvinistic tradition. The distinction was articulated by Merton, who
described Aldous Huxley in *The Seven Storey Mountain* as discarding his
family's materialism in favor of the "old Protestant groove" of making the

2. Greeley, *The Catholic Myth*, 309; Gleason, *Keeping the Faith: American Catholicism
Past and Present*, 65; Merton, *The Sign of Jonas*, 41.
3. Tracy, *The Analogical Imagination: Christian Theology and the Culture of Pluralism*,
413; Merton, *The Literary Essays of Thomas Merton*, 345.

"material creation evil of itself." The poet William Everson, who wrote also under the name of Brother Antoninus, drew a distinction between Catholicism, which he wrote had a "sense of immediate physical contact with God through the sacraments," and Protestantism, which separated the physical world and God. So, too, the poet Allen Tate, in his essay "The Angelic Imagination," reflected a Catholic viewpoint in recoiling from what he called a Cartesian tendency in romanticism, which unfortunately detached the imagination from the realities of the physical world.[4]

Catholic writers such as Merton and Daniel Berrigan exhibit a clear attraction to the natural world in their writings, attempting thereby not only to search for God in nature but also, by perceiving nature through the eyes of Christ and the church, to explore how best to interpret both nature and themselves. Because of this openness to the world, the Catholic tradition, as Greeley noted, saw no harm in appropriating whatever was deemed as good, even in paganism, so long as what was appropriated was reinterpreted to have a "solidly Catholic meaning." Catholicism has also, in spite of the shadow of Galileo, ultimately been hospitable, especially in recent years, to the findings of science, including evolution, which many Catholic theologians have integrated into the theology of Creation. Both Pope Pius XII in 1950 in the encyclical *Humani Generis* and Pope John Paul II in 1996 in a communication to the Pontifical Academy of Sciences declared the theory of evolution to be compatible with the Christian faith. The aspects of evolution that involve predation and violent competition have generally been assimilated by Catholic philosophers and theologians into the Thomist view of the imperfection of Creation, a matter quite distinct from the Fall, which Catholics see as centered on the moral behavior of human beings. Some Catholic theologians, such as the Dominican theologian Raymond Nogar, regret the fact that it took one hundred years of "tedious research and discipline" to mend the breakdown in communication between the "evolutionary views of Darwin, Spencer and Huxley, and the world of Christian thought." For theologians such as Nogar and his more famous predecessor, the Jesuit anthropologist Teilhard de Chardin, evolution does not undermine the idea of a created, cosmic order but does, rather, refine it: "Not only is there a magnificent order in and among things," Nogar argues, but because of evolution "there is an unimaginable dynamic and developmental order in their history."[5] Thus, Catholics, without being pantheistic, regard the

4. Merton, *Seven Storey Mountain*, 186; Ruth Teiser, "Brother Antoninus: Poet, Printer, and Religious: An Interview," 57; Tate, *Collected Essays*, 444.

5. Greeley, *Catholic Myth*, 274; Nogar, *The Lord of the Absurd*, 38, 67.

sacred as continuous with the secular and as somehow involved in the secular, though this involvement is always seen as subject to the final interpretation of the church.

The Catholic Church's view of nature has traditionally been a balanced one, conceding the evil and imperfection that are part of nature and part of human beings, who are themselves part of nature. Saint Thomas Aquinas argued that in God's seeking to create a world in which there was a multiplicity of beings and in which freedom was possible, some imperfection or lack of development was inevitable. At the same time, Catholic philosophers and theologians, such as Cornelius Hagerty, have traditionally asserted the qualitative distinctiveness of human life and of the human soul in contrast to the rest of nature. Animals, Hagerty observed, are fundamentally instinctual and thus "not free," whereas human beings can "know abstract, universal good and, therefore, can see advantages and shortcomings in all particular goods." From the point of view of Catholic doctrine, the distinction between the physical and moral worlds has been aptly commented on by Bishop Donald Wuerl, who observed that while the created world has always been essentially "limited and imperfect," God created men and women in the beginning in a state of "holiness, freedom, and peace." In its sinfulness and sorrow, Wuerl added, the world mirrors the "frailty and malice of creatures who resist their Creator God." On the other hand, because of the "grandeur" and "grace" that yet penetrate the world, it continues to reflect, at least in part, the "boundless goodness of God."[6] Furthermore, the Catholic view has traditionally been that while the original fall from grace inflicted a wound upon human beings, leading them toward concupiscence—the inclination toward evil—human nature has not been totally corrupted and is capable of acts of natural virtue, even if the acts require an infusion of the grace of Christ in order to become habitual and in order to be meritorious in terms of eternal salvation.

Steeped in the doctrine of the communion of saints, traditional Catholicism has celebrated the relationship between the faithful on earth with Mary, the mother of God, and with the saints, whose images until recently have adorned most Catholic churches. The presence of the images of saints in Catholic churches in North America has diminished since the Second Vatican Council, although statues of Mary are still commonly seen. Holding to the doctrine of the incarnation of Christ, Catholics regard matter,

6. Aquinas, *On the Truth of the Catholic Faith: Summa Contra Gentiles*, bk. 3, chap. 71, 237–44; Hagerty, *The Problem of Evil*, 121; Wuerl, *The Catholic Catechism*, 39–40, 43.

and especially human nature, as having been permanently transformed by Christ in spite of the residual attrition of the Fall; thus, they live in hope, believing that God's grace is offered to all. As Stephen Happel and David Tracy point out, Catholics, again in contrast to those in the Calvinistic tradition, expect no assurance here on earth that they have been saved; rather, they must "trust in God's presence and promises in the past, their loving interpretation of that past in the present, and their discerning hope for God's Grace in their future."[7]

Catholicism's relatively positive view of nature, including the venerable doctrine that grace builds on nature, has made Catholic writers open to some parts of nature that other Christian writers have eschewed. Allen Tate, Caroline Gordon, Thomas Merton, and William Everson, for example, were all interested in the subconscious, and in dreams particularly, as an area of potential spiritual activity and significance. Tate and Gordon were especially interested in the religious applicability of the work of Carl Jung. Even Jacques Maritain, an orthodox Catholic philosopher, described poetic insight as germinating in the "spiritual unconscious." Not all Catholics, however, have been as positive as Maritain about the subconscious and other aspects of nature. The American Catholic Church, for example, which until recently was dominated by bishops and clergy of Irish background, has had a strong element of Jansenism. Indeed, according to the historian Philip Gleason, the Irish are frequently thought to have imbued the American church with "sexual puritanism" in addition to strains of cultural "separatism, authoritarianism," and a tendency toward anti-intellectualism.[8]

While there are romantic elements in the works of some twentieth-century Catholic American writers, notably Thomas Merton and William Everson, the Catholic view of nature, especially in the last hundred years, has been more rational than romantic. In 1879, Pope Leo XIII elevated Saint Thomas Aquinas to a position of special authority in the church. A follower of Aristotle, Aquinas attempted in the thirteenth century to merge the thinking of the Greek philosopher with Christian theology. As a theologian and philosopher, Aquinas was rational and realistic in his approach. Even if not part of a scientific culture, Aquinas emphasized that knowledge began with the senses. In the mid-nineteenth century, Orestes Brownson, who had earlier been part of the transcendentalist movement, accepted the thought of Aquinas and medieval scholasticism

7. Happel and Tracy, *A Catholic Vision*, 186.
8. Maritain, *Creative Intuition in Art and Poetry*, 115; Gleason, *Keeping the Faith*, 64.

and assured his readers that human beings had been made rational by God precisely so that they could, by the exercise of reason and the assistance of grace, have the power to control their passions and conform to the law of God. The Catholic novelist and professor of philosophy Ralph McInerny noted that for Aquinas, human beings, in spite of their fallen natures, were not simply "propelled into conjugation" like beasts but were given the power to act "consciously, responsibly" and to foresee and provide for consequences. For Aquinas nature was, as McInerny put it, a "promulgated rational ordination" by the Creator, designed to enhance the common good.[9]

In *The Rights of Man and Natural Law*, Jacques Maritain set forth the view about natural law that has dominated American Catholic thought for the past one hundred years, describing it as an order that human reason can discover and according to which the human will "must act in order to attune itself to the necessary ends of the human being."[10] In this way, nature is seen to have associated with it certain ends that can be identified by reason and that have been implanted by God, including those related to sexuality. This particular application of what has traditionally been called "natural law" underlay, for example, the momentous 1968 decision of Pope Paul VI to reaffirm the ban against artificial contraception on the grounds that it directly impeded the divinely implanted, "natural" ends of the sexual organs. The storm of controversy surrounding that decision reflected the gradual waning of the authority of the norm of natural law and of Thomism following Vatican II.

As Ralph McInerny recently observed in speaking of Catholic universities, within the Catholic tradition faith and reason "complement and reinforce one another." The Catholic philosopher and theologian Hugo Meynell has argued that the most cogent reason for believing in the existence of God is the "openness of the universe to investigation by the human mind." Operating on the basis of what he calls "rational theism," Meynell concludes that the intelligibility of the universe to "enquiring minds" is the best evidence that the universe is "itself due to mind."[11]

Arnold Sparr has noted that Thomism occupied a privileged place in the thinking of twentieth-century Catholic American writers because of the

---

9. Brownson, *The Works of Orestes A. Brownson*, 18:458; McInerny, *St. Thomas Aquinas*, 67, 63.
10. Maritain, *Rights of Man*, 61.
11. Theodore Hesburgh, ed., *The Challenge and Promise of a Catholic University*, 185; Meynell, *Is Christianity True?* 3, 4.

influence of European philosophers such as Jacques Maritain and Etienne Gilson who "creatively adapted the thought of Thomas Aquinas to modern times." The realistic epistemology that characterized Thomist thought and thereby the Catholic sensibility has led to a distaste among Catholic writers for the nominalism in some contemporary literary theory—as in deconstructionism, for example—a distaste shared even by recent Catholic writers (such as Mary Gordon) who are otherwise at odds with what they regard as persistent reactionary tendencies in Catholicism. Catholic writers on the whole sympathize with critics like George Steiner, who in his book *Real Presences* affirmed the writer's ability to communicate experience, thought, and feeling. A somewhat apocalyptic but essentially reliable example of the resistance of Catholic writers to literary theories such as deconstructionism can be found in Ralph McInerny's novel *The Search Committee*, where Rogerson, the disaffected central character, recalling Yeats's dark vision of the Second Coming of Christ, reflects dourly at one point: "Foucault. Derrida. The apostles of deconstructionism. The slouching was over now, the monster had occupied Bethlehem and everywhere else, iconoclasm was the only remaining art form."[12]

One of the problematic aspects of Thomist thought is the relegation of art, along with ethics, to the lower epistemological level of the practical intellect. On the highest level in Aquinas's view was the speculative intellect, whose sole purpose was to arrive at truth. For this reason, modern Thomist philosophers such as Maritain have attempted to bring out the speculative aspects of the artist's, particularly the Christian artist's, work. It has to be conceded, however, that the Catholic Church's traditional assessment of the artist has been marginal at best, far behind the value that, certainly in the last four hundred years, has been given to theological doctrine, metaphysics, and ethics. In this connection, Flannery O'Connor observed that during the last four or five hundred years, the Catholic Church overemphasized the abstract and consequently "impoverished" the imaginations of Catholics as well as their "capacity for prophetic insight," the latter a quality that she gratefully found present in the evangelical Protestantism of the South.[13]

O'Connor's remarks about excessive abstractionism are ironic, to say the least, when one considers that she is discussing a church that holds a sacramental view of life. No doubt the need of the Catholic Church to

12. Sparr, *To Promote, Defend, and Redeem: The Catholic Literary Revival and the Cultural Transformation of American Catholicism*, xiii; McInerny, *Search Committee*, 87.
13. O'Connor, *Mystery and Manners*, 203.

define itself following the Reformation intensified its penchant for the abstract. Historically, however, the church has tended to value art for its didactic usefulness, whether in the case of the windows of Chartres or the *Paradiso* of Dante, and one cannot help but feel that the absence of interest in a Catholic aesthetics has reflected either condescension or distrust on the part of the church hierarchy toward the artist.

However, in recent years, apart from the useful work done by Maritain, the Catholic theologian Hans Urs von Balthasar has called attention to the need to complement the visions of the true and the good, as aspects of God, with the vision of the beautiful. Although von Balthasar cautioned against any merely anthropomorphic or romantic exploration of the transcendental beauty of God, some Catholic writers have had no hesitation in doing so. William Everson, for example, described beauty as the "blood of God." Similarly, using Platonic language in an evident effort to secure the sort of ethereal atmosphere for the discussion of divine beauty that von Balthasar would later advocate, Orestes Brownson defined art, in an article on Catholic "secular" (nonreligious) literature, as the expression of the "true under the form of the beautiful."[14] The presence of Platonism in von Balthasar, who won the respect of Rome, may indicate a softening of the church's strict allegiance to Thomism in recent years. At the same time, the Catholic Church's primary view of the deposit of faith has consistently been to see it as a reality principle, and an admission that that reality may be beautiful has always been regarded as a secondary consideration. On the whole, this is a balance that the Catholic writers discussed in this study endorse—even Thomas Merton, who felt that the church had given insufficient attention to the aesthetic dimensions of the faith.

Respect for the hierarchical structure and authority of the church has been, until recently, a salient feature of American Catholicism, as Anita Gandolfo noted. Although proclaimed only in the second half of the nineteenth century, the doctrine of papal infallibility was designed to provide a measure of certainty with respect to the fundamentals of the faith, a certainty that Catholics believe was guaranteed by the promised arrival of the Holy Spirit on Pentecost and by the transmission of Holy Orders in a line that stretches back to the apostles. The complementary hierarchical division of the church, which dates from Constantine and paralleled the organization of the Roman Empire, led to the establishment of three tiers of authority: bishops, priests, and laity, with the duties of

14. Balthasar, foreword to *The Glory of the Lord: A Theological Aesthetics*; Everson, *The Excesses of God*, 140; Brownson, *Works*, 19:303–4.

each carefully articulated. In spite of the mellowing of the organizational church following the Second Vatican Council, this is still essentially the structure of the hierarchy. The force of this hierarchical arrangement has been registered in the work of some Catholic American writers more than others, but it is always at least implicitly present in the writing. The stamp of the principle of ecclesiastical hierarchy can be felt in Andrew Greeley's jaundiced recollection of the typical parish priest of the 1940s and 1950s: "The pastor was everything. You were a valet to the pastor. You were a serf. You did his bidding."[15] Similar testimony can be found in the fiction of J. F. Powers, all of it provided by a writer who was a faithful son of the church. However, there can be no doubt that, since the 1960s especially, the tensions between the Catholic hierarchy and American Catholics have been more pronounced, particularly as some Catholic writers—including Thomas Merton, Daniel Berrigan, William Everson, and Mary Gordon—awakened to their inherited, and largely Protestant, American individualism.

Although American writers, because of the individualism emphasized by their culture, are more prone than most other nationals to challenge hierarchical models of authority, it is worth pointing out that the nature of the church itself allows for the possibility of some ambivalence on the part of Catholics in thinking about ecclesiastical hierarchy. This is because the church is viewed by Catholics as both the divinely ordained, spotless bride of Christ, incorporating Christ's mind and spirit through the ages, while also being a very human and fallible institution caught up in the temporal sphere. While these two aspects of the church are inseparable in actuality, they present different faces of religion at times to Catholic writers, who often take the measure of the gap between the divinely supported spiritual authority of the church and the practices and character of its clerical leaders.

Earlier in the century, in part as an antidote to the modern tendency toward secular humanism, many Catholic writers came to perceive the medieval world as an ideal society for the church. As Philip Gleason has pointed out, scholastic philosophy, principally that of Saint Thomas Aquinas, was part of this attraction to medievalism in that it ruled out the possibility that the "passage of time and changing circumstances might require any *essential* modification" of Saint Thomas's synthesis of natural knowledge and supernatural revelation. "Truth was truth and remained

---

15. Gandolfo, *Testing the Faith: The New Catholic Fiction in America*, 5; Ronald Pasquariello, *Conversations with Andrew Greeley*, 38.

the same, despite changing outward circumstances."[16] The problem historically, however, was that the medieval paradigm fostered the continuation of hierarchically organized political structures that, in retrospect and in comparison with Protestant nations, can be regarded only as reactionary. Those Catholics who favored medievalism rejected modernist tendencies, such as the new historicism that revolutionized biblical scholarship in the late nineteenth century. Apart from the luster given to medieval life in this century by scholars such as Jacques Maritain, Christopher Dawson, and Anton Pegis, many literary artists were attracted to the medieval paradigm, or a variation on it, by the desire for a society in which there was a unity and hierarchy of traditional Western values.

One finds elements of nostalgia for such a paradigm in Thomas Merton and Allen Tate, who were both attracted to agrarianism and who bristled at modern technological culture. Moreover, although medieval society was rigidly hierarchical, it could be viewed as centering on the local community. As Andrew Greeley explained, Catholic social theory in the last hundred years, as articulated in papal encyclicals and texts of moral theology, has espoused decentralization—not unlike Jeffersonian democracy—in focusing on the local community, indeed on the family itself, as the essential nucleus of a healthy society. Catholic theology, spurred by the Pauline doctrine of the Mystical Body of Christ, is remarkably communal in contrast to the emphasis in Protestantism upon the individual's relationship with God. The communal action of grace, defined in the doctrines of the Mystical Body of Christ and the communion of saints, is especially evident in the works of Orestes Brownson, Thomas Merton, Walker Percy, Caroline Gordon, and Daniel Berrigan.

The strong Catholic interest in social unity, both here and in the life hereafter, has traditionally rooted itself in the morality of interpersonal relationships. On the other hand, papal encyclicals, from the time of Leo XIII in the late nineteenth century, have begun to analyze the structural causes underlying social injustice, always with the assumption that although societies, like individuals, are flawed with inherent evils, moral improvement is nevertheless attainable. As Andrew Greeley has suggested, this would seem to distinguish Catholic social theory yet again from that of Calvinism, which held a more pessimistic view of social reform, perceiving the world at large as saturated with sin. Reviewing the Catholic social theory promulgated in the last century, Greeley concluded it made the fundamental assumption that one fosters social order by an

16. Gleason, *Keeping the Faith*, 27.

appeal to "humankind's cooperative disposition," rather than by force or by "Hobbesian constraints."[17]

Greeley has been particularly perceptive in linking Catholic social theory with the doctrine of the Incarnation. According to him, because Catholics picture God as present both in Creation and in humanity, because of the intervention of Christ into history, they will therefore be more likely to support social change in the hope that this will result in a fuller imprint of God on society.[18] In this light, one can perhaps better understand the readiness of many Catholics to shape the whole of society on issues such as abortion, in the belief that the incorporation of Catholic values will benefit the whole of society by transforming the world into the likeness of Christ and thus perfecting it, not only in a religious sense but also in accord with the fulfillment of its own nature. Orestes Brownson, Robert Lowell, Daniel Berrigan, Walker Percy, Thomas Merton, and other Catholic writers used their writing, at least in part, to call attention to the discrepancies they perceived between political and social policy and the moral ideals upheld by their faith. The classical Catholic emphasis on the necessity for faith *and* good works, as opposed to Luther's insistence upon justification by faith alone, has animated the social criticism of a number of Catholic novelists and poets of this century.

In terms of a Catholic social outlook, no one has had a more profound effect on the Catholic American writers of the twentieth century than Dorothy Day, the founder, along with the French peasant intellectual Peter Maurin, of the Catholic Worker movement. In the 1930s, Day, a journalist and single mother, set up the first of a number of settlement houses and farm retreats that sought to bridge the gap between the Catholic middle class, especially students and teachers, and the poor. Day's influence upon Thomas Merton, Daniel Berrigan, Flannery O'Connor, Allen Tate, Caroline Gordon, and William Everson was immense, both in person and through the pages of her penny-a-copy newspaper, the *Catholic Worker*. Furthermore, Day, more than anyone else, moved the American church toward the left during the 1930s through her writings and protests, attracting support for exploited workers and struggling labor unions. The effects of this shift from a traditional American Catholic social conservatism toward the left were manifold, including the movement of the church itself more into the political mainstream, as Jay Dolan has suggested.[19]

17. Greeley, *Catholic Myth*, 258–59.
18. Ibid., 47.
19. Dolan, *The American Catholic Experience*, 407.

A controversial part of Catholic social thought has been the role of women. On the one hand, the role of Mary as the mother of God, together with the example of formidable female saints such as Teresa of Avila, have elevated the image of women in the church, as has been recognized by Catholic feminist writers such as Mary Gordon. In this connection, according to Carl Jung, the psychological windfall produced by the 1950 papal proclamation of the Assumption of Mary into Heaven was profound. The new dogma affirmed that Mary as the "Bride is united with the Son in the heavenly bridal chamber, and as Sophia (Wisdom) she is united with the Godhead. Thus the feminine principle is brought into immediate proximity with the masculine Trinity."[20]

It is not at all clear, however, that the restiveness of many contemporary Catholic feminist writers is related to the role of Mary or any of the female saints. Rather, it stems from the gulf between the altered role of women in contemporary American society and the still rather modest power offered to women in the church. Furthermore, what has provoked a number of American Catholic feminists is the further disparity between what they perceive as the relatively subordinate role accorded to women in the church and the lofty ideals of human dignity that have been enshrined in encyclicals and in official texts articulating the Catholic social vision. As Catholic fiction writers such as Mary Gordon have attested, the struggle for the rights of women in the church is far from being settled amid the unprecedented departure by women from religious orders that has characterized the American Catholic church in the last thirty years, a far larger exodus than the defection of Catholic clergy in the 1960s and 1970s.

There can be no doubt that the face of the American church has altered appreciably from the 1940s when the lives of American Catholics were characterized for the most part by personal piety and an unquestioning loyalty to ecclesiastical authority. Definitive change came with the Second Vatican Council in the early 1960s. A prominent feature of this international gathering was its dedication to ecumenism, based upon a professed desire by Rome for a closer unity with certain other Christian churches, particularly the Christian Orthodox churches. As a result of the ecumenical spirit of Vatican II, there was a shift in Catholic writing and ritual toward an emphasis on biblically based descriptions of the church's mission and activity. Furthermore, in contrast to the 1869–1870 First Vatican Council, which emphasized papal infallibility, the Second Vatican Council emphasized the collegial role of the bishops, who together with

20. Jung, *Memories, Dreams, Reflections*, 202, n. 2.

the laity made up the people of God as the council chose to designate the church. The effect of the council on American Catholicism was immediate and revolutionary, as novelists such as J. F. Powers, Walker Percy, Mary Gordon, and Ralph McInerny have vividly documented. The fiction and poetry written by American Catholics in the 1960s and 1970s reflected the flux of a church that seemed no longer certain of its mission and increasingly at odds with itself.

As Philip Gleason has stated, among certain elements of the Catholic intelligentsia, the enthusiasm for what was modern and secular reached "near-euphoric levels" in the early sixties.[21] In some respects the changes were subtle, though far reaching, as in the substitution of the forward altar (with the priest facing God at the head of his people) by the Communion table (with the priest surrounded by the congregation). While the new Liturgy generated feelings of unity and involvement among the laity, it also drained some of the transcendental atmosphere that had accompanied the earlier ritual, as writers such as Mary Gordon and Ralph McInerny have attested. Moreover, the support by the Second Vatican Council for the sovereignty of the individual conscience had the sudden and unintended effect of moving millions of American Catholics to consider their own views on such issues as birth control, abortion, the ethics of war, and the duties of citizens toward government.

As Flannery O'Connor observed, the Catholic writer inevitably used his or her "whole personality" to write, in contrast to the scientist in whom it would be possible to "disregard large parts of the personality" in scientific discourse. The distinction between science and religion hinges, as Northrop Frye has indicated, on the moral and imaginative vision of the artist, who is likely to be concerned not only with the actual world but also with the world that human beings might want to live in. The direction of both the arts and religion, as Frye has noted, is not linked with the accumulation of knowledge but rather with a movement "upward from where we stand" through which the actual is compared with the possible.[22]

Certainly the tendency of artists to apply such vertical criteria to experience and history has been the subject of comment by a number of Catholic American writers. For example, the poet William Everson observed that in art we see things "under the aspect of eternity." The novelist Paul

21. Gleason, *Keeping the Faith*, 32.
22. O'Connor, *Mystery and Manners*, 155–56; Frye, "Humanities in a New World," 27.

Horgan, in a 1941 letter to his longtime literary agent and friend, Virginia Rice, expressed the view that significant art was "derived from belief" and "from morality." In connection with the application of morality to literature, Allen Tate, in his essay "To Whom Is the Poet Responsible?" credited literature with preserving the "knowledge of evil." Flannery O'Connor noted that in her case, religious belief was the "engine" that made "perception operate." Generalizing on the basis of her experience as a writer of fiction, Caroline Gordon observed in a little-known piece that the writing of "serious fiction" was, in essence, a "religious act," in that the artist was moved to imitate God as Creator. Echoing these sentiments, the narrator of Ralph McInerny's novel *Connolly's Life*, a lapsed Catholic who appears to reflect the author's view of the relationship between art and religion, confides that the only "substitute" that he had found for his lost faith was in creating the "tidy arrangement of imagined incidents in fiction."[23]

In a collection of forewords and afterwords to his books, William Everson described the poet as possessing a kind of "divine proclivity." Everson was particularly insistent and eloquent about this aspect of the artist's vocation:

> Man ritualizes, always, in order to step out of the tyranny of the temporal, which is death, and make life new. Wherever he pauses in order to abolish time, he enacts the original gesture of creation, enters the order of sacrality, which is life. . . . In his act of creation, he ritualizes the character of chaos, makes time "real" by holding it at bay. It is in this that he is a priest.
>
> But it is through time that the poet compels reality into the substance of his form. His words, material elements, have all the character of chaos until his act ordains them to permanence.[24]

In his essay "Louis Zukofsky—The Paradise Ear," Thomas Merton described the artist's creativity as a kind of recovery of Eden: "Not that the poet comes up with a report that he, an unusual man, has found his own way back into Eden: but the living line and the generative association, the new sound, the music, the structure, are somehow grounded in a

23. Everson, *Birth of a Poet: The Santa Cruz Meditations*, 74; Horgan to Rice, November 26, 1941, Horgan Collection, Yale Collection of American Literature, Beinecke Rare Book and Manuscript Library, Yale University; Tate, *Collected Essays*, 407; O'Connor, *Mystery and Manners*, 109; Gordon, "The Art and Mystery of Faith," 56; McInerny, *Connolly's Life*, 219.

24. Everson, *On Writing the Waterbirds and Other Presentations: Collected Forewords and Afterwords, 1935–1981*, 66; Everson, *Excesses of God*, 104.

renewal of vision and hearing so that he who reads and understands recognizes that here is a new start, a new creation. Here the world gets another chance."[25]

Perhaps the strongest linking of religion and art set forth by a Catholic writer in the United States was articulated by Orestes Brownson in his novel *Charles Elwood, or the Infidel Converted:*

> There is no radical difference between this inspiration proper to the poet, and that of the prophet. The poet is inspired by God under the aspect of love, beauty, joy, sorrow, liberty, heroism; the prophet is inspired by God under the aspect of Sovereign, Father, Preserver, or Redeemer, and is moved by a sense of obedience, piety, sanctity, goodness. But in both it is one and the same God that inspires. The true poet utters as infallible truth in relation to the subject-matter of his song, as the prophet. The poems of the one are as authoritative, as far as they go, as the other's prophecies. Poetry . . . is the out-speaking of the Divinity, and embraces elements of universal truth.[26]

Put in yet another way, Paul Horgan contended that when aesthetic perception reached its "fullest realization," it was "akin to man's religious vision, whatever form this may take." The intimacy of art and religion was most paradoxically underlined by Allen Tate, who indicated that since his whole effort as a poet had involved the "incarnation of reality in language," this had prepared him for and indeed led him toward religion in general and Catholicism in particular with its sacramental view of reality.[27]

In addition to sharing a holistic approach to experience, both literature and religion have generally been viewed by Catholic writers as involving the fundamental pursuits of meaning and wisdom. Flannery O'Connor described this pursuit as a desire to "penetrate the surface of reality and to find in each thing the spirit which makes it itself and holds the world together." In this connection, Jacques Maritain argued that artists were capable of the sort of wisdom that strengthened an artistic work even while they led immoral lives. The creative intuition that allowed the artist to do this, which he described as an aesthetic "innocence," was of an ontological rather than a moral order.[28]

25. Merton, *Literary Essays,* 128.
26. Brownson, *Works,* 4:291–92.
27. Horgan, *Approaches to Writing,* 15; Everson, *Excesses of God,* 27; Michael Millgate, "An Interview with Allen Tate," 31.
28. O'Connor, *Mystery and Manners,* 168; Maritain, *Creative Intuition,* 374–76.

While Catholic writers share a belief in immortality, such as that set forth by Rogerson in Ralph McInerny's novel *The Search Committee* when he reflects that what we do now "determines what we will be forever," the exigencies of art direct the attention of the writer to this world rather than the next. Flannery O'Connor called particular attention to this in noting that if the Catholic writer hoped to reveal supernatural "mysteries," he or she would have to do so by "truthfully" portraying the data of experience. By submitting to the reality of this world, O'Connor believed, the artist, if receptive enough, would discover the author of Creation and convey the resonance of this discovery to the reader. Such a transmission through art is characteristically done not directly but through symbolism. Northrop Frye drew attention to the mutual reliance on symbol and metaphor by both art and religion, explaining that the attempt of religious language to express elusive spiritual realities had led to the extensive use of metaphor in scriptural writings.[29] A similar sort of case might be made in connection with the artist, whose task often involves the description of that which cannot literally be seen but can often be conveyed only through the description of something that can be seen.

A central and potentially thorny question concerning Catholic imaginative writing is that of didacticism. The matter is raised, for example, in Caroline Gordon's story "Emmanuele! Emmanuele!" in which, after Heyward proclaims that the artist's first duty is to himself, Pleyol, who appears to have Gordon's support, responds that an artist's first duty is the "same as any other man's—to serve, praise, and worship God." A number of twentieth-century Catholic intellectuals, including Jacques Maritain, have argued that the Christian artist should not preach in his or her art but should, rather, live a fully Christian life and in that way the art, which could be on any subject, would be purified. Indeed, Maritain contended that art in its own domain was sovereign and should not be hindered by any external pressures to conform to so-called higher virtues of the mind and spirit. Maritain, who had a considerable influence on Flannery O'Connor, Allen Tate, Caroline Gordon, Robert Lowell, and Thomas Merton, asserted that both the artist and the theologian were involved in the pursuit of wisdom, the success of which pursuit would, after all, affect the value of the art object. A similar point was made by Umberto Eco in his study of Saint Thomas Aquinas's aesthetic philosophy: "When considered in the world of ends as a whole, the idol does not fit

---

29. McInerny, *Search Committee*, 91; O'Connor, *Mystery and Manners*, 150; see Frye, *The Double Vision: Language and Meaning in Religion*, 17.

harmoniously, but provokes imbalance and disquiet. It is adequate to the transmission of falsehood, but inadequate to mankind and to what is good. . . . The idol may be beautiful in color and proportion, but it does not fit in with the harmony of the universe."[30] In other words, even the skillfully crafted work of art is capable of being flawed by a lack of wisdom, which in Aquinas's view took precedence over the relatively subordinate issue of moral correctness.

The scorning of didacticism can be observed in the remarks of a number of Catholic American writers, as in Thomas Merton, who in a piece titled "Message to Poets" asserted that the artist should preach nothing, "not even his own autonomy." On the other hand, Mary Gordon, in an autobiographical essay titled "Getting Here from There," recalled that in the American church in which she grew up, art for art's sake was as foreign as the idea of a "Moslem heaven," that the life of the mind was not regarded as an end in itself but as a service to God. Evidently irritated by this sort of memory, Gordon, unlike other writers considered in this study, rejected the overlapping of art and religion, conceding that although such an overlapping might exist in the case of particular works, it need not.[31] There would seem to be some merit to Gordon's characterization of the church's attitude toward the doctrine of art for art's sake. Throughout *Art and Scholasticism*, for example, Jacques Maritain makes it amply clear that art for art's sake is an idolatrous, secular dogma, the substitution of a relatively narrow, aesthetic divinity for a more comprehensive Christian God.

In his well-known essay "Inside the Whale," George Orwell observed in 1940 that the atmosphere of orthodoxy was inimical to art, especially to the novel, which he defined as the most anarchical form of literature, a "Protestant" form of art that necessarily issued from an autonomous mind. In such a light, Catholic literature might seem to be a contradiction in terms. Nonetheless, just as one is aware of Protestant writers who have been straight-jacketed by religious ideology, so too one is aware of Catholic writers who are not. Furthermore, there are Catholic authors who sometimes sound as if they are determined to shape their art in the light of religious convictions and who, in the practice of their art, instinctively throw such baggage overboard. Such a writer is the novelist J. F. Powers, who agreed with Allen Tate that the writer must re-create

---

30. Gordon, *The Collected Stories of Caroline Gordon*, 337; Eco, *The Aesthetics of Thomas Aquinas*, 187.
31. Merton, *Literary Essays*, 378; Gordon, *Good Boys and Dead Girls*, 171.

the image of humanity for the age and "propagate" norms by which the reader could distinguish the false from the true.[32] Anyone familiar with the subtle ironies of either Powers's fiction or Tate's poetry would hesitate to accuse either of them of sacrificing their art to didacticism.

In Paul Horgan's fiction, the protagonists, especially in the Richard trilogy, act according to inner narrative exigencies that have little directly to do with the faith of the author; but, nonetheless, in a letter to Virginia Rice in 1951, Horgan took pains to alert her to the implicitly Catholic atmosphere of his story "Parma Violets." Expressing this sort of view even more strongly, the English novelist Bruce Marshall noted that the Catholic fiction writer could write about "murder in Baluchistan or chorus girls in the Folies Bergères," provided that he or she included the supernatural "screen" behind the characters. Marshall cautioned, however, that the writer must avoid distorting experience in order to illustrate a moral. Putting the issue more pointedly, Flannery O'Connor wrote that the Catholic writer whose judgment failed in matters of art could not expect to be believed in matters of religion.[33] The risk of didacticism is clearly present in the case of Catholic writers, and it would seem that the stronger the faith of the writer, the greater the risk. Even in the face of disclaimers, such as the one above from Flannery O'Connor, there does at times appear to be a didactic pressure behind her work, notably in the conversion scenes of tales such as *The Violent Bear It Away* and "The Artificial Nigger."

In a thoughtful article, Peter Hebblethwaite, while conceding that the Catholic writer will inevitably be guided by his or her beliefs, added that what would most concern the writer was the fit between his or her imaginative perception of experience and "what faith proposes."[34] Clearly, for the writer who is a believer, the temptation to distort experience in order to accommodate a religious vision must at least be taken into account by both writer and reader, as it must be in the case of any writer whose point of view has been shaped by a powerful ideology. The best writers will be those who test their ideologies against experience, something that Catholic writers, with their incarnational theology and consequent dedication to the world, ought to, in theory at least, be prepared to do. In these writers, the fiction and poetry will often end with a lingering, unresolved air of complexity—even if the moral foundations of the universe have

32. Orwell, "Inside the Whale," 518; Powers, "And of the Author as a Responsible Storyteller," 3.
33. Horgan to Rice, September 24, 1951; Marshall, "The Responsibilities of the Catholic Novelist," 169; O'Connor, *Mystery and Manners*, 190.
34. Hebblethwaite, "How Catholic Is the Catholic Novel?" 678.

been made adequately clear to the reader. In adhering to the world as sacrament, Catholic writers have, whether deliberately or not, committed themselves to reality in whatever unwelcome and inconsistent form it might appear, in the expectation that God, the epitome and ultimate author of all reality, will thereby somehow be present.

ORESTES BROWNSON

(1803-1876)

CONVERT AND EX-TRANSCENDENTALIST, Orestes Brownson portrayed Catholicism in his essays and fiction in a buoyant and even triumphant form. Applying his newly acquired Thomist learning, he criticized his fellow transcendentalist Emerson for celebrating Creation while leaving the Creator out of his cosmology, endorsing what Brownson regarded as naturalism. The essence of American transcendentalism, Brownson argued, was an assertion of the superiority of imagination and feeling over reason, a view that he could not accept. Though he derided the nonrationality of transcendentalism, Brownson nonetheless retained from his earlier Unitarian and transcendentalist background a vestigial belief in the importance of intuition, which he felt enabled the intellect to adopt a faith in God. Recalling the primum mobile arguments for the existence of God adduced by Aristotle and Saint Thomas Aquinas, Brownson contended in his essay "Dignity of Human Reason" that one had to inevitably factor in a fundamental intuition of the "Intelligible, the infinite, the necessary, the perfect" as well as the reality of logic and meaning themselves.[1]

Brownson's customary confidence in writing about Catholicism is striking, given the dominance of Protestantism in nineteenth-century America.

1. Brownson, *Works*, 1:443–44.

In addition, American Catholicism had a relatively low intellectual profile, in part because American Catholics in the nineteenth century had been drawn largely from immigrant stock. Furthermore, the hegemony of the Irish in the episcopacy over other ethnic groups such as the Italians and Germans (since the Irish came to the United States speaking English) was unfortunate. Irish Catholics had for centuries been denied the right to education by their English rulers. In any case, in looking at the American scene Brownson regretted that in his reading of history he could find no epoch, as he put it in his essay "Catholic Polemics," in which the "directors of the Catholic world" manifested so "great a dread of intellect." This was, he concluded, because of a widespread fear among the American Catholic hierarchy that "he who thinks will think heretically."[2]

In direct opposition to the prevailing Catholic practice of building parochial schools in order to separate students from the cultural mainstream, Brownson urged that Catholics should integrate themselves into the intellectual and political life of the United States, arguing that American democracy offered an ideal environment for the practice of religion, certainly superior, he added, to that which existed in the Catholic countries of the world. In the same way, although Brownson admired the Greek and Roman contributions to Western civilization, he judged the Greco-Roman world, in his *The American Republic*, limited by its approval of slavery. Nevertheless, in the same work, Brownson, mirroring the prejudices of his age and church, argued that the ideal of equality was applicable only within one's gender, that God had made man the "head of the woman."[3]

All the same, recognizing that American democratic principles arose out of a Protestant tradition, Brownson contended that this reflected a respect for human freedom that ought to have been found within Catholic countries but had been suppressed beneath the weight of old-world politics. Furthermore, unlike a number of Catholic writers of both the nineteenth and the twentieth centuries, Brownson disliked the nostalgic medievalism of Catholic culture, the tendency to center on the Middle Ages as a high point in the development of Western culture, concluding that this tendency focused Catholic education on the past and created an inappropriate indifference toward the present.

Anticipating the pronouncements of the Second Vatican Council in the early 1960s, Brownson advocated a full participation by American Catholics in the political and social affairs of their country in an effort

2. Ibid., 20:112.
3. Ibid., 18:185.

to incorporate into society Catholic ideas of truth and justice, not in a sectarian manner but in a universal sense with the good of the whole society in mind. Taking the long view of Catholic culture, rather than what he regarded as the insular outlook of many nineteenth-century American Catholics, Brownson maintained that Catholic thought was fundamentally realistic and insightful about the nature of human be-ings, both individually and collectively, and that a state informed by the principles of Catholic morality could only benefit thereby. At the same time, Brownson supported the American Constitutional division between church and state, largely because it secured religious freedom, believing that although church and state were both ultimately subject to God, they nevertheless operated in distinct and different spheres.

In *The American Republic*, Brownson contended that the United States had been chosen by God for the realization of a great moral purpose, the creation of a society that would reconcile the need for public order and for the public good with the freedom of the individual conscience. Dismayed by the historical practice of authoritarianism in Catholic coun-tries, Brownson, always as American as he was Catholic, argued in a noteworthy essay titled "Civil and Religious Freedom," that the spirit of Christ was the spirit of liberty and that God governed the world by moral suasion, "never by physical force." In addition, well ahead of his time, Brownson affirmed the power of the laity and criticized the tone of any official pronouncements that created a picture of the church as rigidly hierarchical. Catholic theology of the day, Brownson observed in an 1862 essay titled "Lacordaire and Catholic Progress," often left the impression that the people seemed to "count for nothing in the church, as formerly they counted for nothing in the state."[4] In his eloquent appeal to American democratic ideals against the entrenched hierarchical practices of the Catholic Church, Brownson anticipated Catholic writers of the 1960s such as Thomas Merton and Daniel Berrigan.

Brownson's attraction to Catholicism was based in part on his reserva-tions about other philosophical and religious systems that he had studied. He believed that humanitarianism, for example, lost sight of individ-ual rights in its abstract and amorphous focus on humanity, while the Calvinist—"with his brother Jansenist"—sacrificed the rights and dignity of nature in order to emphasize God's "freedom" in dispensing grace.[5] So firm was Brownson's belief in the illumination cast by Catholic philosophy

4. Ibid., 20:321; ibid., 272.
5. Ibid., 18:90.

and theology that he felt that Catholicism and science could never really be in conflict and that when there was an apparent conflict it resulted from either an imperfect understanding of science or a weak theology.

Recognizing, however, that scientists were increasingly observed to be undermining religious truth, Brownson concluded in his essay "Science and the Sciences" that many scientists, "whether in or out of the Church," had "no philosophy" as "our pretended philosophers" had "no theology."[6] Thus, with breadth of understanding ever his goal, Brownson objected to scientists relying on the scientific method as an exclusive and sufficient description of reality. Instead of recommending that scientists stick to their instruments, however, leaving philosophy and theology to others, he urged scientists to widen their range of knowledge and vision.

At the root of Brownson's convictions was always the belief that Catholic philosophy and theology expressed reality. His reasoning was set forth in *The Convert,* an autobiographical novel written in 1857 that somewhat resembled Newman's *Apologia Pro Vita Sua,* which had appeared in 1846. "If Catholicity be from God," Brownson reflected, "it does and must conform to the first principles of things, to the order of reality, to the laws of life or intelligence; and hence, a philosophy which conforms to the same order will conform to Catholicity."[7] In this way, Brownson believed that, although America had developed politically from a Protestant tradition, it had also, he believed, fortuitously embodied fundamental principles of Catholic social philosophy as articulated by Saint Thomas Aquinas.

While Brownson generally took the high ground in defending both Catholicism and Christianity against secularist tendencies in nineteenth-century science and philosophy, he could be unabashedly sectarian at times. In his essay "Newman's Development of Christian Doctrine," for example, he declared that the church must "precede" the Scriptures in importance, a clear challenge to Protestant thought, which Brownson based on his belief that only on the authority of the church could the "inspiration" of Scripture be guaranteed.[8] Reflecting Catholic theology, Brownson argued that Christianity was a living religion, given directly and orally to humanity by Christ, with Scripture coming into play following the death of Christ after the church had already been established.

6. Ibid., 9:264.
7. Ibid., 5:173.
8. Ibid., 14:22.

In an essay titled "Emerson's Prose Works," Brownson was even of-
fensive in his characterization of Protestantism, calling it "narrow, superficial, unintellectual, vague, indefinite, sectarian," a view that would
appear to be at odds with his earlier valuing of the Protestant tradition
for its contribution to the development of democracy.[9] The scathing tone
and spirit of partisanship in this passage reflect the role that Brownson
assumed in his later writings of being an apologist for Catholicism in
America in a way that was analogous to Newman's role in England, where
Catholicism was also not part of the cultural mainstream. Whether in his
fiction, autobiographical writings, or in the journals he edited—*The Boston
Quarterly Review* (which he edited from 1838 to 1842) and *Brownson's
Quarterly Review* (which he edited from 1844 to 1864 and from 1873 to
1875)—Brownson's policy was to attack on all fronts.

While Brownson acknowledged the distinguished spiritual and theological writings that English-speaking Catholic writers of his time had
produced, he nonetheless lamented the lack of Catholic creative literature.
In his essay "Catholicity and Literature," he argued that a distinguished
novel or poem by a Catholic author would do more to attract the respect of
other Americans than yet another theological treatise or polemical tract,
"however able or learned." Brownson's two novels, *Charles Elwood* and
The Spirit-Rapper, were designed to meet this perceived need. While in
retrospect these novels seem uncomfortably polemical, Brownson apparently did not regard them as primarily didactic. He observed in his
1849 essay "Catholic Secular Literature" that Catholic novelists and poets
should not surrender to didacticism but should create the sort of art
that Beethoven, Haydn, and Mozart produced, art that was "instructive"
by virtue of the "moral power" it stimulated, the "lofty thoughts" it
contained, and the "tone and direction" it imparted to the "whole interior
man."[10] Whatever his own practice might have been, Brownson's splendid
articulation of a rationale for the Catholic creative artist has never been
surpassed.

Charles Elwood, or the Infidel Converted, which appeared in 1840, foreshadowed Brownson's entry into the Catholic Church. Exhibiting thin
characterization and a slight plot, the novel offers little development of
its central situation, except perhaps for the discovery by Elwood that he
had been a Christian all along even if he had thought of himself as an
atheist or, as he would now be called, an agnostic. From a literary point

9. Ibid., 3:433.
10. Ibid., 18:461; ibid., 19:304.

of view, the best features of *Charles Elwood* are to be found in the first half of the novel where Brownson focuses on the efforts of Elwood's fellow townspeople to convert him and, failing that, to ostracize him. In spite of Elwood's inoffensive behavior and willingness to enter into religious discussion, he is virtually treated as a pariah, and even his fiancée is urged to drop her association with him.

While such narrative detail helps to fill out Brownson's canvas so that the novel is more than a thinly disguised polemic, nevertheless, structurally, *Charles Elwood* is basically composed of a series of debates. In these debates the protagonist, skeptical at the outset, engages in discussion with religious spokesmen in the community until he is finally won over by the excellent Mr. Morton. Unfortunately, the long statements made by some of the characters more nearly resemble tracts than dialogue, a literary affliction that is particularly obvious in the second half of the novel. Nonetheless, the debates, as in a play by Bernard Shaw, are often interesting in their own right. It is noteworthy that the Christian apologists who rely solely on faith or reason are equally unsuccessful in convincing Elwood. The reason that Morton is successful is that he possesses both a fine reason and a sensitive intuitive faculty, both of which Brownson believed were integral to mature religious consciousness. The debates at times resemble those that occur at the beginning of *The Scarlet Letter*, and in fact Brownson's Mr. Wilson somewhat recalls the character by the same name in Hawthorne's novel.

Beginning as an empirical reformer and a follower of John Locke, Elwood eventually concedes that reform based on "enlightened self-interest" failed in general to move anyone to beneficial social action and that some measure of sacrifice was required.[11] While Elwood eventually accepts Christianity as a perfect model for moral idealism and social reform, he moves from that relatively empirical position to a theocratic faith based ultimately upon intuition, which he defines as an "intelligence that knows God immediately" and an inherent capacity to recognize God everywhere (187). While in this passage Brownson clung to a transcendentalist reliance on intuition, he thought of intuition as consistent with reason and as a reality-centered faculty.

As an intellectual document, *Charles Elwood* is given dramatic tension and complexity by the author's alternating defenses and criticisms of Catholicism. For example, having arrived at the doorstep of Christianity, Elwood, aided by Mr. Howard, is persuaded that Protestantism is not a

---

11. Ibid., 4:225, subsequently cited in the text parenthetically.

religion in itself but merely "what has been retained of Catholicism" (232). Brownson's partiality toward Catholicism is also manifested in Morton's attack against the supposition that the Bible is a sufficient basis on which to accept Christianity since what is inevitably required in a Christian church, he argues, is an authority to interpret the teachings of Jesus. Though the polemical tone wears at times, Brownson's exposure of Christian failings, including those of the Catholic Church, is acute. Particularly singled out for criticism is the tendency of all the Christian churches to conventionalize the thinking of their members. Mr. Howard, for example, notes dryly that while the churches demanded freedom from state interference, they were usually reluctant to accord such freedom to their members. On the level of argument at least, Brownson vividly captures the contrast between the churches' elevated, authoritative proclamations of faith and the lower-level, often unrelated conformity that has marked religious culture, a theme that would be taken up in the twentieth century by Catholic writers such as J. F. Powers and Daniel Berrigan. Similarly, the shabby treatment afforded Elwood by Christians contrasts sharply with the gospel of love in which they purport to believe. In this manner, Brownson gradually builds up a dramatic tautness between an idealized Christian philosophical and theological tradition, stretching back to the moral majesty of its founder, and the corruption of that tradition, which is all too visible to someone like Elwood who is not a part of it.

In spite of its discursiveness, *Charles Elwood* contains some richly evocative and affecting passages—such as that in which Elwood recalls the religious feelings that stirred within him as an orphan: "Religion I had loved from my infancy. In my loneliness, in my solitary wanderings, it had been my companion and my support. . . . When I was thrown upon the world at a tender age without a friend, and left to buffet my way unaided, unencouraged, and felt myself cut off from all communication with my kind, I could hold sweet and mysterious communion with the Father of men" (197). Sensitive and poignant, the passage undoubtedly reflects something of Brownson's own experiences as an orphan.

The novel is also strengthened by its moments of psychological insight. Some examples include the trenchant exposition of the contrasting moral effects that conversion produced on different types of people and the candid admission of the limits of religious faith when the death of a loved one "breaks in upon the soul." The immortality of the soul is at that moment "assented to rather than believed," observes Elwood, and "believed rather than lived" (221). Such passages fill out the novel as a drama of experience in addition to its being a trial of ideas. Furthermore, although Brownson does not provide a great deal of physical description, what there is is often pithy and memorable. His account of the inquiry meeting, attended by those who wanted to assess and deepen their faith, is a case in point:

> Here was the old man of threescore and ten, with whitened head, palsied arm, and broken frame, bewailing a misspent life, and trembling with fearful apprehension of a judgment to come. By his side was the boy with chubby face and flaxen locks, his bright blue eyes swollen with weeping for sins he had not yet learned even by name. A little further on was a middle-aged man, his strong athletic frame writhing and contorting under a guilty conscience. I turned with horror from his countenance, which bore witness that the fires of hell were doing their strange work within. (192–93)

Because of the austerely imagined and semiallegorical collection of figures suspended between material and immaterial worlds, one is again reminded of Hawthorne. In this scene, Brownson clearly wanted to bring out the relative coolness of Protestant spirituality, which he would later contrast with the warmer Catholic doctrine of the communion of saints.

Also reminiscent of Hawthorne is Brownson's fondness for spare, aphoristic phrasing. At one point Elwood observes, for example, that we "value those opinions the most for which we pay the dearest" (178). Reflective of the gray tones of the novel, the wit is of a caustic sort, as in Elwood's rejoinder to Mr. Wilson that the biblical forbiddance against casting pearls before swine was an "unnecessary prohibition" in his case (218). While such dialogue sharpens the novel's edges, one cannot help but feel that the atmosphere is sterner and more astringent than it should have been in a work that was meant to recommend religion. The reason appears to have been that Brownson, having moved to a position that was so much against the currents of his time and of his own intellectual circle, felt the need before all else to defend that position.

The Spirit-Rapper, which appeared in 1854, was in every respect a superior novel to *Charles Elwood*. In his second novel, Brownson paid a good deal of attention to the development of characterization, incident, and dialogue, and although the novel contains a considerable amount of discussion, it is generally subordinated to and integrated with the exigencies of the narrative (with the exception of the middle section of the novel in which Brownson reviews political events in Europe from 1843 to 1850). A satiric novel directed at the occult spiritualism that became so prominent in the mid-nineteenth century, *The Spirit-Rapper* reflects Brownson's view that demonic and absurd religions in various forms would inevitably fill a void left by the abandonment of Christianity.

Although Brownson's imagination was clearly tinged with gravity, he brought many scenes to life by infusing them with a dry irony. One example is his portrayal of the meetings of the philanthropists, whose support of political freedom for black Americans is revealed as ludicrously incompatible with the custom of excluding them from their meetings. Employing a wider canvas than he had in *Charles Elwood*, Brownson introduces a number of topics that are not strictly of a religious nature, though in retrospect they all acquire a religious relevancy due to Brownson's careful interweaving of his major themes. Brownson ridicules the optimistic nineteenth-century idea of progress, for example, on the rational grounds that the idea is absurd without a goal by which to evaluate progress, a goal that the novel makes evident must ultimately be teleological.

As in *Charles Elwood*, Brownson centers the novel in a narrator whose initial skepticism lends authority to his eventual conversion. In his dedication to the physical sciences and in his disdain for vagueness, the unnamed narrator of *The Spirit-Rapper* resembles one of Poe's fastidious storytellers. He is certainly a more full-blooded character than Charles Elwood. Moreover, in contrast to the earlier novel, *The Spirit-Rapper* more successfully integrates the discussions of theological and philosophical issues with the life of the narrator/protagonist, who has an evil aptitude for manipulating others. Thus, the novel's central theme—that the demonic will masquerade as the secular in any society that abandons Christianity—is depicted both on an intellectual and on a narrative level.

Brownson's darkly satirical rendering of the narrator's seduction and enslavement of Priscilla, which so blatantly contradicts his professed feminist ideals, is principally portrayed not as hypocrisy but as a sign of the narrator's having succumbed to the temptations of sexual power. On the other hand, Brownson incisively reveals the narrator's apparent helplessness to free himself from his hold over Priscilla, an ironic undercutting of the narrator's scientific rationalism. Furthermore, Priscilla herself, an eloquent exponent of female autonomy, is ironically reduced to pathos by the passion that has overtaken her. In this way, Brownson constructed a pattern of psychic layering that reveals the complexities of behavior that underlie the relative simplicity of the logical debates taking place at the surface of the novel.

Brownson's satire on the bizarre religious practices that had emerged in the mid-nineteenth century is given depth, as is always the case in his work, by the colorful use of historical perspective. The latter days of the Roman Empire are cited as a period in which, following the decline of the "natural" religion of Rome, magicians from Asia and Africa flocked to the eternal city. The historical vignette illustrates Brownson's thesis that there is no such thing as a religious vacuum, that religious awareness is so deeply etched in the soul that no amount of rationalism can supplant it. To illustrate this latter point, which relates directly to the narrator of *The Spirit-Rapper*, Brownson focuses on the eighteenth century, when, in the words of the narrator, there had never been a "fairer chance for rooting out Christianity," a reference to the scandalous corruption of the clergy and the naturalistic philosophy that pervaded both school and court.[12] In spite of the subsequent antireligious, Napoleonic revolution that swept Europe, however, the narrator is forced to concede that by 1850, religion of one kind or another was back in vogue. With persistent logic, Brownson moves the narrator ever closer to an acceptance of the fact that, if it is impossible to root out the religious impulse, one had best find a religion worthy of it.

In the ending of *The Spirit-Rapper*, Brownson turns what had been a moral tale into one of tragedy. Ironically, just at the moment when the narrator recognizes that his power over Priscilla has vanished, he is suddenly murdered by her husband, who misunderstands the true situation. Nevertheless, Brownson underlines the fact that it is the narrator who initiated the process that led to what turns out to be a fatal stabbing, a tragic process that proceeds with a logic of its own. The narrator's final suffering is integrated into a sustained analysis of the problem of pain. Brownson's attempt to justify the ways of God to man brings out his Catholic trust in reason. The fact that the argument is presented by Mr. Merton, a Protestant, may have been due to the fact that Brownson thought the words of a Protestant in mid-nineteenth-century America would carry more authority. In any case, Merton puts the theme eloquently, arguing that natural evils are within the control of Satan and permitted by God in order to give human beings the opportunity to choose God at a moment when that choice has not been made easy.

While Merton's intellectualizing risks overshadowing the novel's dramatic conclusion, the narrator's story is ably developed. Moreover, most of the other characters are vividly depicted, including the anarchist, Hobbs, with his long, uncombed hair and gray, patched frock coat, leather trousers, red waistcoat, and red bandanna handkerchief. Dialogue is also more animated and convincing than in *Charles Elwood*, as can be seen in the pointed remarks by the transcendentalist Edgerton, as he regards the common ignorance of nature: "No one trusts to nature. None are satisfied with wild flowers or native forests. All seek an artificial garden. They will

---

12. Ibid., 9:135, subsequently cited in the text parenthetically.

not hear the robin sing unless it is shut up in a cage. The rich undress of nature is an offence, and she must be decked out in the latest fashion of Paris or London, and copy the grimaces of a French dancing-master, or lisp like an Andalusian beauty, before they will open their hearts to her magic power" (56). Though set in the formal, antithetical prose style of the age, the passage resonates with a motivational force and particularity that bring out the character of its speaker, as is generally the case in this novel.

If in some respects Brownson's writing seems dated, particularly in his fondness for polemics, which has also caused the reputations of Catholic writers such as Chesterton and Belloc to fade in recent years, he is significant for the clarity, vigor, and, at times, imaginative invention with which he set forth the case for Catholicism. Nevertheless, although steadfast in his defense of Catholic orthodoxy, Brownson was scathing in his attacks upon the insularity and anti-intellectualism of the Catholic Church in America, administered by bishops with what seemed to Brownson to be meager intellectual agendas. In so doing, Brownson set the pattern for the writing by Catholic American authors that would follow in the twentieth century. A number of these writers would contrast the inherited treasures of Catholic intellectual culture abroad with the relative thinness of Catholic culture in America.

The sorts of objections that Brownson raised against many of the Catholic practices of the mid-nineteenth century would be raised by twentieth-century writers such as Robert Lowell, Allen Tate, and Thomas Merton, all of whom bridled not against the authority of the historical church but against the regimented and ossified version of the church that confronted them in everyday life. Orestes Brownson's particular contribution was to give this conflict a distinctly rational shape. Brownson belonged to an older rhetorical tradition that valued not only truth but also the detailed and often fastidious reasoning that led to that truth. That twentieth-century readers may have lost the taste, and perhaps the aptitude, for such writing may well not, in the final analysis, be belittling to Brownson.

In two essential respects Brownson cogently placed Catholic writers in their paradoxical relationship with American society. First, Brownson drew attention to the hiatus that existed between the hierarchical and authoritarian structure of Catholicism—a structure that, with some important modifications, he affirmed—and the democratic character of American society, which he also affirmed. In the intersection between these two forces, Brownson argued, Catholic American writers would find their distinctive subject matter. Brownson also affirmed the right, indeed the need, for Catholic American writers, by virtue of what he regarded as their encompassing knowledge into the nature and purpose of human life, to offer insight of a universal kind to the whole society. In both of these respects, he anticipated the shape and character of the significant Catholic American fiction and poetry that would be written in the twentieth century.

CAROLINE GORDON
(1895-1981)

IF ONE WERE to rank Catholic American writers on the strength of their faith, Caroline Gordon, rather like her good friend Flannery O'Connor, would be near or at the top. In an article titled "Letters to a Monk," written in 1964, she wrote that she had come to believe that there was only one plot, the "scheme of Redemption," only one author, the "Holy Ghost," and only one book, "made up of His revelations—even if we get hold of only one page at a time." Upon converting to Catholicism in 1947, Gordon felt that she was transferring her primary allegiance from art to the church. Walter Sullivan has noted that Caroline Gordon's faith stood out in contrast with that of other intellectual American Catholics, including Allen Tate, to whom she had been married since 1924. Nevertheless, in a 1957 letter to Tate, Gordon acknowledged his role in introducing her to Catholicism, recalling an incident when the two of them first came to New York in the 1920s and Tate had unexpectedly suggested that they go into a Catholic church to pray.[1]

By 1930 Gordon wrote to Sally Tate Wood with what appeared to be an exuberant faith, light-humoredly exhorting all her acquaintances to

---

1. Gordon, "Letters to a Monk," 10; Gordon to Tate, Tate-Gordon Collection, Manuscripts Division, Department of Rare Books and Special Collections, Princeton University Libraries. Unless otherwise indicated, letters from Caroline Gordon are from this collection.

"turn Catholic at once." In a little-known talk given at the University of Minnesota in 1953 called "The Art and Mystery of Faith," Gordon noted that two events helped to move her definitively toward the Catholic Church, the first an encounter with a pious, middle-aged woman in Rouen, France, whose robust faith was untroubled by her evident poverty, and the second a crucial meeting with Dorothy Day, whose unsentimental depth of faith touched Gordon. Gordon had met Dorothy Day when Day had been a journalist in New York City, prior to Day's conversion and subsequent founding of the Catholic Worker movement in the 1930s.[2]

As conservative a southerner as Tate was, Gordon shared his agrarian outlook and his heightened consciousness of the moral responsibility of the artist. As the two moved through various academic institutions in the 1940s and 1950s, they made friends with a number of Catholic writers, including Robert Lowell, Flannery O'Connor, J. F. Powers, and Walker Percy. Writing to Robert Lowell from Princeton in 1956, for example, Gordon announced proudly that she had a "new pupil," Walker Percy, "Will Percy's nephew. Came to me around Christmas time out of two Nazareths: Sewanee and Greenville, Mississippi."[3]

Moving about the country, Gordon became aware of the cultural diversity of American Catholicism and became used to contrasting the Irish-dominated Catholicism of the East with, as was also pointed up in J. F. Powers's fiction, the German and Polish influence in the West and Midwest. As with many pre–Vatican II converts, Gordon resented many of the changes that altered the Catholic Church in the 1960s. In a letter to Chauncey Stillman in which she described a trip to the University of Dallas in 1973, for example, she observed that she was pleased to see nuns in traditional habits, "real nuns, not the kind that run around in tweed suits, getting married!" Similarly, writing to Ashley Brown in the summer of 1963, Gordon recalled liking Thomas Merton's "cutting his way back to the mediaeval" era in *The Seven Storey Mountain,* an age, she added, in which faith was "more easily possible." The Tates' admiration for and friendship with the distinguished Thomist philosopher Jacques Maritain and his wife, Raissa, helped to deepen their loyalty to traditional Catholicism as opposed to many of the ecumenically inspired changes in Liturgy and outlook that followed Vatican II. In a letter to Maritain in

2. Gordon to Wood, June 21, 1930, published in Gordon, *The Southern Mandarins: Letters of Caroline Gordon to Sally Wood, 1924–1937,* 52; Gordon, "Art and Mystery," 59–62.
3. Gordon to Lowell, Lowell Collection, Houghton Library, Harvard University.

October 1969, Gordon said that she was glad she had entered the church when she did and that the "new theology" had left her "baffled." She was especially anxious about the Protestant-sounding deference in Vatican II to the primacy of the individual conscience, as opposed to the long-standing emphasis in Catholicism upon ecclesiastical authority and unity.[4]

It was Caroline Gordon's love of the doctrine of the community of saints that led her to seek the companionship of other intellectual Catholics such as Dorothy Day, who in a striking way lived out the Gospels in her work among the poor and the exploited. Like Day, Gordon was attracted to asceticism, both in the disciplined practices of her daily life and in the spirituality that informs her fiction. In particular, she was wary about the tendency of some post–Vatican II theological opinion that sought to celebrate the sacredness of sexual love, and in this respect she clearly differs from writers such as William Everson. In literary and theological notes sent in the early 1970s to her grandson, Allen Tate Wood, she warned of the danger of spiritual love degenerating into a merely sensual love if the eye were not "kept fixed on the blood of Christ crucified." Along with Flannery O'Connor, Caroline Gordon possessed an acute sense of the value of suffering, not only in a personal sense but in a cultural one as well. She noted on one occasion that southerners—and southern writers in particular—had the advantage of living in a culture that had been deepened by having experienced defeat.[5]

Gordon's conception of evil is essentially Thomist and reality oriented; in other words, she tends to perceive evil not as a romantically mysterious and perhaps tantalizing abyss but rather as the metaphysical absence of a good that ought to be there. In Gordon's short story "Emmanuele! Emmanuele!" (published in 1954), Robert Heyward, the American academic who had attached himself to a great French writer, conjectures that the artist is one who "goes down into the abyss for the sake of his fellow men." His interlocutor, Raoul Pleyol, replies discerningly, from Gordon's point of view, that such an artist will have "spent his life for nothing. There is nothing at the bottom of the abyss."[6] Similarly, Heyward himself comes to the conclusion that his literary idol, Guillaume Fay, has no life of his own but only a vicarious existence through his good wife.

---

4. Gordon to Stillman, January 29, 1973; Gordon to Brown, July 23, 1963; Gordon to Maritain, October 25, 1969.
5. Gordon, literary and theological notes to her grandson, Wood, Tate-Gordon Collection, Manuscripts Division, Department of Rare Books and Special Collections, Princeton University Libraries; see O'Connor, *Conversations with Flannery O'Connor*, 66.
6. Gordon, *Collected Stories*, 338.

While Gordon's sense of evil is acute, she was not a Manichaean or Jansenist Catholic and was thus wary about the theology of Catholic novelists such as Mauriac, Bernanos, and Greene, as she wrote in a letter to Walker Percy in 1952. Gordon's embrace of incarnational theology and her dislike of Calvinist thought are evident everywhere in her work. Possessed of a particular interest in both theological argument and theological history, she sometimes made these the focus of her fiction—as in the 1977 short story "A Walk with the Accuser." In that tale, Gordon portrays Calvin as both cunningly subtle and dangerously malicious in getting rid of a theological rival. In a letter to Ashley Brown in December 1963 she dismissed Calvin's conception of nature as unsubstantial, merely a "painted backdrop." Like Tate, Gordon felt that whatever was still valuable in Western culture and in moral standards clung to the Christianity that remained as a residue in the culture that followed the twentieth-century decline in formal religious practice. Thus, she argued that even many ostensibly agnostic twentieth-century novels reflected something of a Christian outlook in unconsciously adopting the nineteenth-century "Christian" plot of redemption.[7]

Gordon confided to Flannery O'Connor that she loved the incarnational cosmology of Catholicism that, in spite of its hierarchical structure, left her free to "use her eyes" and to "accept what she saw for the first time." Furnished with an orderly and meaningful picture of the world, Gordon felt relieved of the burden felt by other writers who, as she wrote to Walker Percy in 1951, were forced to set up a "new heaven and a new earth."[8] Nonetheless, like Allen Tate, she insisted on the need for Catholic writers to adopt high formalist standards of craftsmanship and attempted, along with Tate, to set up a workshop for Catholic writers in the early 1950s, a project that was, for various reasons, never realized. Alert to the dangers posed by ideology, Gordon believed that the novelist should avoid incorporating too much thought into the work, thus drying it up, but should instead attempt to embody this thought subliminally in narrative action.

As in the cases of Allen Tate and Robert Lowell, Gordon's formalism derived in part from her schooling in classical literature. In a letter written

7. Gordon to Brown, St. Lucy's Day, December 13, 1963; Gordon, "Some Readings and Misreadings," 384–85.

8. Remark about Gordon quoted in a letter from O'Connor to John Lynch, November 6, 1955, Lynch Collection, Yale Collection of American Literature, Beinecke Rare Book and Manuscript Library, Yale University, reprinted in O'Connor, *The Habit of Being*, 114; Gordon to Percy, December 18, 1951, Percy Collection, Southern Historical Collection, Library of the University of North Carolina at Chapel Hill.

to Ashley Brown in 1957 she said that Greek and Roman literature had had more influence on her as a fiction writer than any later literary influences she had been subject to. Eileen Simpson, a literary acquaintance, recalled that Gordon felt a "mixture of pity and scorn" for writers who had not studied Greek as well as Latin. In Gordon's later fiction, particularly in *The Glory of Hera,* the classicism merged with her interest in Jung, whose insights about the subconscious were not only much more hospitable to religion than Freud's but also, in Gordon's view, far less narrow. As the psychiatrist George Crenfew in Gordon's novel *The Malefactors* observes, the trouble with Freud was that he "never got around to but one myth," that connected to sexuality (276). Gordon's liberal interweaving of Jungian and Christian motifs can be observed both in her fiction and in her correspondence. For example, in a 1977 letter to Benjamin Toledano, she compared the Jungian, archetypal symbol of the "Ouroboras, the serpent which bites off its own tail," with the Christian serpent that "lies beneath our path." More than writers such as William Everson or Thomas Merton, though, Gordon was alert to the dangers of an unbridled Jungianism, arguing in a letter to Jacques Maritain in 1956, for example, that the artist's unconscious could easily be mistaken for "something going on in Plato's cave," for a glimpse, in other words, however indirect, of ultimate reality. Thus, while Gordon's characters rely a good deal on dreams and the flow of unsolicited memories in order to see their way, these dreams and memories are accepted as valid only when they mesh with the Christian perceptions of reality that pervade the fiction. This may help to explain the crucial role of the dream in Tom Claiborne's conversion in *The Malefactors,* an incident that critics such as Robert Brinkmeyer have otherwise found wanting in plausibility.[9]

Brinkmeyer has vividly and appreciatively shown that Gordon's Catholic fiction dawned in the short story "The Presence." He is less sanguine about Gordon's Catholic novels, though, and there may be some usefulness in attempting to bring out the aesthetic value of these works. The novels that most clearly embody Gordon's Catholicism are *The Strange Children* (published in 1951), *The Malefactors* (published in 1956), and *The Glory of Hera* (published in 1972). Both *The Strange Children* and *The Malefactors* are examples of romans à clef, with the child who acts as the point-of-view character in *The Strange Children,* for example, resembling

---

9. Gordon to Brown; Simpson, *Poets in Their Youth,* 200; Gordon, *Malefactors,* 276, subsequently cited in the text parenthetically; Gordon to Toledano, October 31, 1977; Gordon to Maritain, April 19, 1956; see Brinkmeyer, *Three Catholic Writers of the Modern South,* 110.

the Tates' daughter, Nancy, while the parents bear some resemblance to the Tates themselves. Nonetheless, in this novel as well as in *The Malefactors,* it would be rash to place too much weight upon biographical sources. Vera in *The Malefactors,* for example, unlike Caroline Gordon herself, has only a marginal intellectual life.

The title of *The Strange Children* is taken from Psalm 144: "Rid me, and deliver me from the hand of strange children, whose mouth speaketh vanity." In this context, all the characters are portrayed as strange children. Even Lucy, who otherwise has Gordon's support, appears to have been made somewhat strange by the adults around her. The title appears to have been intended to project God's view of humanity and therefore, from Gordon's point of view, provide us with an unusually objective view of ourselves. The word *strange* appears repeatedly in the novel. At one point, for example, Lucy hears Isabel talked about as a "strange lady," while, later on, Jenny, the cook, calls Kevin Reardon "that strange gentleman."[10] Even God's strangeness becomes an issue when the eccentric Uncle Fill wonders how one can come to accept the apparently capricious and occasionally destructive God of the Old Testament.

With considerable skill, Gordon focuses on the strangeness of two characters—Isabel and Kevin Reardon—both of whom are caught vividly in the mirror of Lucy's consciousness. The two are given antithetical colors by Gordon, rather suggestive of the sort of fairy tale that would engage Lucy's imagination. Isabel is fair and Kevin dark, complementing Lucy's contrasting impressions of them when she first meets them. As time goes on, however, their symbolic roles are neatly reversed. Even before the denouement, however, Lucy is aware of flecks of strangeness in Isabel's behavior. At one point, coming back from a stroll with Kevin, Lucy is suddenly troubled by the voice of Isabel coming from the open upper window of the house, a voice that made the child think unaccountably that Isabel was "not a grown woman who could take care of herself but a child who might leap out of the window and tumble to the ground" (111). Kevin Reardon's strangeness stems from his intensely held Catholicism and from his brooding relationship with his past, which is crowned by a car accident in France that included a strange vision of the Blessed Virgin.

Technically, the novel is Jamesian in its impressionistic reliance upon a central point-of-view character. Commenting on Gordon's debt to James, Rose Ann Fraistat noted Gordon's habit of freezing significant moments of perception in order to emphasize those occasions when "phenomenal

---

10. Gordon, *Strange Children,* 32, 169, subsequently cited in the text parenthetically.

and noumenal realities are fused."[11] Gordon's skill in this respect is considerable. While, for example, the Catholic Church plays no role in Lucy's upbringing, the child at one point has a curious perception of a distant steeple cross as no larger than a "bent pin" (13). Parenthetically inserted into the text, the passing image, so precisely inscribed, clings to the mind. Similarly, when Lucy mulls over Kevin Reardon's offer to buy her a pony, she is again puzzled by his mysteriousness, concluding simply that he "knew something that she didn't know," an open-ended reflection that eventually draws her toward religious consciousness (258).

Gordon's use of Jamesian indirection combines with a sensitive description of Lucy's intuitive powers to reveal the child's startled, fresh awareness of human sexuality, the power of which she is shown to feel even if she lacks specific knowledge. Drawn by curiosity, for example, she persuades Jenny to accompany her to the woods where she suspects that Tubby and Isabel are having sexual relations, and although she doesn't see all, she sees enough, as in James's fiction, to guess the rest. Furthermore, as with James's characters, she is precociously imaginative: "How did you know that another body lay under his? It was the eyes, she thought" (220). Gordon's skillful use of impressionism is particularly evident, as has already been intimated, in her enlarging of moments of perception, coloring them softly with symbolic overtones. For example, fleeing from the scene in which she sees Isabel and Tubby in the woods, Lucy "brushed against the blackberry briars as she went; she half paused once, noting abstractedly how darkly green they grew. Only a few minutes ago they had been speckled with light, but the sun had left the ravine; it was later than she had thought. Her fingers tingled. She raised her hand and saw a drop of blood oozing where a briar had pierced her finger, and let the hand fall again at her side" (219). With an unerring touch, Gordon subtly registers the moment of shock while gently conveying overtones of a fall from innocence (the thorn and blood), all the while keeping a steady eye on the realistic progress of the physical action.

A more pronounced symbolic technique, again integrated with the impressionistic format, is the Jungian use of the tale of Undine to parallel the momentous change in Lucy's experience. Just after the discovery of Isabel and Tubby, for example, Lucy opens her favorite book at the place where the knight goes in search of Bertalda in the Black Valley. Approaching the white shape of a woman lying near him on the ground, he leans over her only to discover in a flash of lightning a "hideous and wasted countenance" (233). With dramatic economy, the Gothic language

---

11. Fraistat, *Caroline Gordon as Novelist and Woman of Letters*, 146.

from *Undine* signals Lucy's upset state and anticipates the madness that will later be seen in Isabel. The story of Undine provides Lucy's childhood experience with mythic ramifications, widening and deepening the circle of meaning without breaking the circumference of the point-of-view method. As *Undine* is the archetypal story of a water nymph who longs to acquire a human soul, so in a sense is Lucy's drama and so also is Isabel's, her story ending as sorrowfully as Undine's. Lucy does acquire a human soul, though, as the novel shows. It is not only that she acquires experience but also that she develops a moral and religious consciousness, largely through the relationship with Kevin Reardon that offsets the bland and superficial knowledge of life she has acquired from her parents.

The Strange Children is a novel of identity and initiation, as can be observed in the following scene in which Lucy catches sight of herself in the mirror following her theft of Kevin Reardon's crucifix:

> As she replaced the lid she became aware that somebody was watching her in the mirror. She stood still to meet the strict gaze. The girl had on a yellow dress. There was a green ribbon in her long, light brown hair, but she had not known that her own eyes could hold such an expression. She stared back. The expression in the grey eyes did not change. It was as if the girl in the mirror did not know that it was she, Lucy Lewis, who was looking back at her. (103)

Like Undine staring up at the world from the ocean depths, the guilty, mirrored Lucy looks back at a more familiar Lucy, who has evasively concealed from herself the moral significance of what she has just done. The scene is beautifully fashioned to convey profound action and meaning without a trace of authorial intrusiveness.

Although Gordon has said she had not read *What Maisie Knew* when she wrote *The Strange Children*, she was certainly familiar with James's writing and used the impressionistic method deftly to bring out the powerlessness of her young reflector character's situation. This is evident, for example, in the scene in which Tubby first arrives:

> "You haven't forgotten *Uncle Tubby?*" he asked.
>   Lucy murmured something and stood with her eyes downcast. The blades of grass were airier than feathers and had a rosy tint in the sun. One of the fragile blades was bending double under the weight of a butterfly that had just alighted on it. The butterfly's body was blue-black, its wings yellow, ornamented with purple dots. (19)

Startled by the sudden appearance of Tubby, Lucy feels a fright that prevents her from answering immediately but instead transfers her attention to her surroundings. With its beauty, the natural scene in turn lifts the pressure from her so that she is then prepared to answer. The sensitivity and technical skill of Gordon are apparent everywhere in her handling of point of view in this scene. The parallel with James's Maisie is especially visible when Lucy's father, Stephen, accuses her bitterly of "always hanging around, listening to grown people talk. What," he asks exasperatedly, "are we going to *do* with you?" (230).

Using the technique of indirection, Gordon points up the detached parenting by the Lewises of their gifted child. On one occasion, for example, looking down the hill at the sharecropper MacDonough family, Gordon reveals Lucy as ironically envying the very poverty that forces them all to sleep in one bed. Members of the Holy Rollers, a fundamentalist sect, the MacDonoughs symbolize the hazards of a valid faith within an irrational religious culture. While the MacDonoughs misread a scriptural passage that they believe authorizes their putting themselves in danger of snakebite, for example, they nevertheless stir genuine religious consciousness in Lucy—as when they paint a huge rock with the warning: PREPARE TO MEET THY GOD. The significance of the message is emphasized for Lucy by the curious fact that, although ivy grew all over the rock, it mysteriously never grew over the letters, a nice touch that awakens Lucy's religious curiosity without overtaxing the reader's ability to believe.

In line with her own novelistic theories, Gordon's development of Lucy's characterization is always pinned to action, more than is the case in James's fiction, as in Lucy's return of the crucifix to Kevin Reardon. When she finally returns it to him, it takes on an unforeseen luster: "In the hands and the feet, the rubies, gleaming darkly, rounded like drops of blood that might spill to the floor. Light shone from the eyes; a paler light on the white brow under the clotted curls" (300). Gordon handles the scene deftly on many levels at once. On the psychological level she shows the child's relief at returning the crucifix, revealing as well the existence of a conscience within her, though Lucy is herself unaware of this nuance at this juncture. On the symbolic level the scene is one of many that employ the symbolism of light and darkness, here linking beauty and sacrificial love.

As Gordon named her principal character after the saint of light, Santa Lucia, whose feast occurs in the darkest period of the year, Lucy is, then, a light out of the darkness, and this connects her symbolically with Kevin Reardon, whose dark eyes emit an intense light. Auxiliary images abound. For example, when Lucy follows Kevin into the small Catholic church where he goes to confession, she catches a glimpse through the briefly opened door of a darkness but then of something "bright" that "glinted through the gloom" (272). At times, the light imagery is interwoven with water imagery, as in Lucy's view of Kevin's eyes, which were the "darkest eyes she had ever seen, yet full of light—the deepest well will brim with light when one leans to look into it" (128–29).

While Isabel and Tubby are associated with a superficial play of light, the symbols are used ambiguously throughout until the characters are finally enveloped in a symbolic darkness. While at one point Tubby's eyes appear "bright," for example, he is described as "dazed," like a person who had just "come to the surface after swimming under water," a suggestive image that concisely conveys an ominous blindness in addition to replaying the tragic Undine motif (148). Blond and bright, Isabel glitters through much of the novel only to collapse in the darkness of madness. Her connection with water imagery, like Tubby's, is also ambiguous since, while her early book of poetry, *The Water-Bearer*, was, according to Stephen Lewis, her finest work, she had fallen into a decline afterward. Even Lucy's parents, Stephen and Sarah, are depicted as locked in a spiritual wasteland, as the child herself perceives, having forgotten the "dark water" of their subconscious and intuitive natures, which Lucy herself, another Undine, is in the midst of experiencing (265). Significantly, Lucy's mother, Sarah, seeing the dry patches of grass around her house, exclaims: *"If only I had water"* (234). The other character most conspicuously associated with water and light symbolism is Uncle Fill, who sits in front of a cave through which water flows, ignoring its spiritual meaning while engaging in endless, sterile, theological disputation. The contrast between the symbolic evocativeness of the scene and the man's obliviousness is one of the comic high points of the novel and a sign of Gordon's mastery of diverse moods and narrative textures.

Gordon's superb creation of atmosphere is seen in her evocation of a mood of hushed quiet, torn by images of violence and death associated with both the present and the past. While the images of death from the past are obviously not as immediate in their effect, their grotesqueness often makes them at least equally as memorable as those in the present. Examples include both the photograph of the twelve-year-old boy, propped up in death so that his picture could be taken, and the recurrent face of Captain Green, clubbed to death in his wheelchair at the end of the Civil War by a confused black servant. While the symbols of death and violence are ubiquitous in *The Strange Children*, they are offset by other more restorative symbols, including the sycamore tree that had apparently been struck by lightning. However, because of the snakes inhabiting its decaying mass, the sycamore tree and the nature that it represents do not symbolize final spiritual destinations; instead, nature is seen as a way station, beautiful in itself at times and indicative of a higher beauty beyond itself. The same sort of note of intermediacy is struck with Kevin Reardon, who, Lucy observes, while listening intently to what others say to him, appears all the time to be thinking about something else. Much more than in writers such as Thomas Merton or William Everson, Caroline Gordon stressed the transcendentalism of God rather than the divine immanence in nature. Moreover, when grace flows to human beings in Gordon's fiction, it characteristically flows through human beings rather than through nature, though Gordon does not present a negative view of nature. In Gordon's writings, nature is integrated with human history as part of an overall myth that culminates in a vision of God, even if only an oblique one, such as that diffused through Kevin Reardon.

With her Jungian/Catholic background, Gordon was used to interpreting history in terms of heroic archetypes. Not unlike Daniel Berrigan, Gordon found in the lives of the saints the sense that history was made by heroic individuals. Thus, over the mantel at the Lewises' house is a portrait of Stonewall Jackson (about whom Allen Tate had written extensively), "blue-eyed, black-bearded, his uniform without stain or wrinkle" (11). Contrasted with Stonewall Jackson is Stephen Lewis, who spends his days searching for new details about the Civil War while living his life on a purely mundane level. Kevin Reardon, on the other hand, had been a genuine hero in World War II, having been decorated for bravery, though the experience, given his subsequent religious conversion, is one he would rather forget.

The seamless integration of the Jungian and Christian elements in Gordon's thought can be seen in the way in which she unites the father/son archetype, exemplified in Tubby McCallum and Kevin Reardon, with the religious motif of the extended search for the perfect father, a search that in Gordon's view would eventually lead one to God. Thus, Kevin Reardon begins his search for identity by living in his father's house and by adopting his father's religion. Significantly, the natural, archetypal need of the son to be accepted by the father is given spiritual significance by Gordon instead of being rejected as pagan, another sign of her incarnational theology. At the same time, the flow of dreams and symbols from the subconscious is affirmed only when it leads toward Catholic orthodoxy.

The Strange Children is such a rich novel in both themes and form that it is a pity Gordon chose to end it with Stephen Lewis's sententious reflections, including the pat observation that all men "die on the same day: the day on which their appointed task is finished" (303). It is not at all clear why Gordon shifted the point of view from Lucy to her father at the end, but the change is unfortunate. Up to that point the book is remarkably pleasing in its skillful maintenance of the classical unities of time and place and in its structural and stylistic rendering of a significant series of events and their consequences. Suspended over that fine web is the haunting and uncertain consciousness of a girl who, in spite of being isolated from any but a superficial experience of life by her background, discovers through a fortuitous encounter that life may be a more searching yet more final process than she had thought.

In *The Malefactors*, Caroline Gordon once again relies on scenic impressionism, centering on three principal settings: Blencker's Brook, New York, and Mary Farm. Although the governing point of view is given to an adult, Tom Claiborne, Gordon wrote to Ashley Brown in 1956 that she thought of Claiborne, "being a poet," as sharing some of the innocence of Lucy in *The Strange Children*. In the same letter, Gordon indicated that she was proud of the way in which she had extended the novel's theater of consciousness by including in her cast a saint, a madman, and three persons who are dead: a poet, a painter, and another man who is a "great sinner."[12] She contended that these personae, removed from the usual categories of human life, brought knowledge into the novel that Claiborne would not possess. Furthermore, she was pleased with her merging of the Jungian underground of the novel with its realistic surfaces, as in Catherine Pollard's continuation with Tom Claiborne of a conversation that had begun in a dream. Though she makes extensive use of dreams in the novel, Gordon obviously had reservations about the cul-de-sac that an unmediated reliance on the subconscious could lead to, as can be seen in her negative portrait of the painter Carlo Vincent, whom she based on the surrealist painter Giorgio de Chirico.

Although one can recognize the originals for a number of the characters in *The Malefactors*, including Tom Claiborne (Allen Tate), Horne Watts (Hart Crane), Catherine Pollard (Dorothy Day), and Joseph Tardieu (Peter Maurin), they are presented as part of what Flannery O'Connor aptly described as a fictional study of religious conversion.[13] However, Tom Claiborne's conversion is a Jungian narrative as well, as the novel's epigraph, taken from Jacques Maritain's essay "The Frontiers of Poetry," indicates: "It is for Adam to interpret the voices that Eve hears." Maritain was describing the balance that ought to obtain between the creative and analytical intelligence, but Gordon thought of the quotation as also representing the desirable balance between the animus and the anima,

12. Gordon to Brown.
13. See O'Connor, *The Presence of Grace and Other Book Reviews*, 16.

which she portrays the overly cerebral Claiborne as having to attain before regaining his creative powers.

Even though Cynthia Vail, for example, as her name implies, is a specious personality, she does have the salutary effect of opening up the affective and intuitive side of Claiborne's nature. The depth of her effect on him is indicated in the recurrent dream of the underground cavern, a dream that arises just prior to his first sexual encounter with her. No longer a detached observer in the dream, Claiborne (whose name reminds the reader, if not Claiborne himself, of his earthly roots) finds himself, carried now by passion, "plunged deep" in the waves where at a fortuitous moment he could see a "cavern yawning" on the riverbank (134). The erotic nature of the imagery makes the passage seem more Freudian than Jungian, although the satiric portrayal in the novel of the psychologist, Marcia Crenfew, ought to give the Freudian critic pause. Nonetheless, it must be remembered that Gordon's reservations about Freud were not based on the perception that he was wrong but rather that he was narrow. Thus, Claiborne's new openness to women (and thus to his own anima) is not limited to the sexual but extended to the spiritual in his eventual reconciliation with Vera and also in his response to Catherine Pollard, who embodies the anima on a religious level. He finds himself as much moved by Catherine kneeling before the wooden statue of Saint Ciannic as by Vera's selfless praying in Clermont for the dying Leontine.

With considerable skill Gordon uses natural symbols, often the product of dreams or of spontaneous imaginings, to illuminate Claiborne's inner struggles throughout the novel. Drawing on her knowledge of classical mythology, for example, Gordon associates Cynthia Vail with the moon. Under her influence, Claiborne recalls there being something about the sun as a "light by day and the moon by night. Could it be the other way around? A man seeking to travel by day by the light of the moon?" (212). The matter is a critical one. While Claiborne must open himself to the anima, he is not meant to live exclusively in its light but rather in a state of balance between the rational/analytical and the creative/affective sides of his nature.

Fire symbolism emerges powerfully in the scene in which Claiborne angrily resents Vera's delaying of their travels through France in order to obtain holy water from a shrine for Leontine. In a hotel in Clermont, Claiborne looks out at the hot hills nearby and sees "flames spill over the lip of the old crater until the whole horizon was one fiery ring in which gigantic shapes moved among heaving mounds, rocky crags, columns of granite or black basalt tossed in air, and knew that the fires that had shaped that whole country were still raging underground" (97). Like the magma that produced the craters of the Auvergne region, the anger of the domineering animus burns on beneath the level of Claiborne's arid consciousness.

The recurring dream of the cavern, however, which connects with the real-life, youthful adventure of Claiborne and his cousin George Crenfew, finally precipitates an overthrow of the animus following the disastrous party organized by Cynthia in New York. Switching to a first-person narration in order to capture the immediacy and intensity of Claiborne's emotional crisis, Gordon shows him in the dream running after some men in the cavern, one of whom is his father. Looking down into the cavern, Claiborne sees the two men far below, their legs sprawled wide, "each head, now only a grinning skull, lying at a little distance from the neck from which it had just been severed and I turned to the man and he grinned too, and put up his hand to tear his own head off and fling it over the cliff" (270–71). The two men are Carlo Vincent and Horne Watts, both suicides, who narcissistically discarded life for art and of whom Claiborne is still jealous at some subconscious level. The man who threatens to take off his head (a recurrent motif in Allen Tate's poetry) is Claiborne's father, who leads his son into understanding what he must do in order to overcome the sterility that has overtaken his life—the trimming of his self-conscious intellectualism. As in *The Strange Children*, the father/son archetype is used skillfully by Gordon; she leaves it uncertain as to whether or not the beneficent appearance of Claiborne's father is a wish-fulfillment dream or a moment of grace.

In the healing interview with George Crenfew, which is filled with stories from Greek mythology, Claiborne recovers a sense of the sort of inner balance that, on a purely natural level, he ought to possess. Here, one sees Gordon's belief that the ancient Greeks reached a degree of wisdom just short of the Christian revelation, a theme that she developed later in *The Glory of Hera*. The entry into the supernatural occurs within the domain of Catherine Pollard, the "saint" whom Gordon placed in the novel. Significantly, Catherine's world encompasses both contemplation and social action. In this way, she incorporates a Jungian balance of sorts within the religious sphere. Similarly, Vera achieves a desirable balance with her suntanned skin (which contrasts with Cynthia's marble look) and her religious devotion.

The Jungian balance between the animus and the anima is paralleled in the novel by that between the natural and the supernatural with the two joined ideally in the figure of Christ, the God-man. Gordon's positive rendering of nature, stronger than in *The Strange Children*, shows up in various ways, as in the important scene at Blencker's Brook when Claiborne shows Catherine Pollard the statue of Saint Ciannic on his property. On their way to that statue, though, they pass a bronze statue (titled *France*) by a famous sculptor, and this serves as a foil to the statue of the saint. The bronze statue is of a woman a little larger than life, who seemed to be "marching toward them, hands outstretched" (78). Apart from the stylized, rather vague abstractionism of the statue, its bronze finish signals an attempt to elude mortality. Saint Ciannic, on the other hand, more particularly depicted, is described as clothed in a "ragged gown" with his head "inclined forward and one leg crossed over the other" (79). He stretches out his hand to something at his knee, a stag, which, as legend had it, came regularly to hold his book in its antlers. The wood from which the statue was carved has wormholes, and plants that had begun to cover the pedestal have begun to reach over the seated figure. Decay, death, and the natural cycle are all subsumed in the symbol of sanctity before which Catherine Pollard sinks to her knees.

Ironically, Tom Claiborne takes a Manichaean position (parallel to his excessive intellectualism) in a conversation about animals in which he asks Catherine Pollard:

> "Don't the psychologists say that when we have an excessive love for animals we are worshiping the animal in our own nature?"
> "I don't know," she said. "There's an Italian proverb that says that the man who isn't kind to beasts will not be kind to Christians either." (80)

If one accepts Tom Claiborne as representing Allen Tate, the scene is paradoxical, since Tate opposed angelism, the separation of soul from body, in all his writings. However, Tate was afflicted with the sort of creative block in the 1940s and 1950s that Gordon describes, a block that inhibited the creation of poetry in particular as opposed to the essays that continued to flow from the rational, conscious part of his mind.

Gordon's affirmation of nature in the novel is unreserved as long as nature can be perceived as part of divine design. In the above scene, for example, just after Catherine Pollard declared that Saint Ciannic, dead for seven hundred years, was more alive than ever in the twentieth century, the Claibornes' dog leaps into a hedge and returns with a woodchuck in its jaws, having given the animal a "savage shake" in order to break its neck (83). The Darwinian implications are clear. Gordon takes the scene further, however, when Catherine, who had initially been shocked by the killing, asks for the woodchuck so that it can be used as food for the poor. A theme of acceptance prevails here. For whatever mysterious reasons, God is assumed by both Pollard and Gordon to have made a world of predators and prey; what matters with respect to salvation is not this given circumstance—about which one can do nothing—but rather one's response to the needs of other human beings. At bottom, Catherine Pollard's faith, like Gordon's perhaps, is crystalline in its simplicity, like that of the people of Chiapas, Mexico, among whom Gordon chose to live out her final years. Nevertheless, if Gordon's faith was simple, her mind was not, or she would not have included the woodchuck scene. In the intersection between that scene with its Darwinian implications and the demands of faith lies the Christian drama in Gordon's fiction.

While the symbolism of the copper beech is a transparent reminder to Claiborne of his place in nature, the bull symbol is considerably more complex. Initially, the live young bull that Vera had bred is presented as a substitute for unsatisfied marital and maternal needs. Later, though, the bull symbol becomes associated with the story of Saint Eustache, the Christian Roman general who, along with his family, suffered martyrdom by being burned to death within a brass bull. The symbol thus evolves from its sexual, psychological meaning to a symbol of heroic, sacrificial love. For Gordon, this sort of symbolic evolution is consistent with her view that nature exists in a continuum that spirals upward toward God. In contrast to a writer such as William Everson, who shared her interest in Jung, Gordon adjusts her vision of nature by measuring it against revelation, rather than, as Everson tends to do, attempting to add to revelation by probing nature for evidence of the divine.

As in *The Strange Children*, Gordon incorporates comedy in *The Malefactors* as if to broaden the novel's range of vision. For example, there is the case of Sister Immaculate, the old Irish nun who is doing a study of the similarities between Horne Watts's (Hart Crane's) poetry and that of Saint Catherine of Siena. While Gordon, who knew Crane well, believed that there were clear Christian elements in his poetry, she points up the comedy of the old nun's attempts to paint all of culture with a Catholic brush. The incident shades into something more serious and significant, however, when Catherine Pollard overcomes Claiborne's last defenses in telling him that she has been praying for the soul of Horne Watts since she first heard of his suicide. With its tender enactment of spiritual love, the scene brings to life the doctrine of the communion of saints, one of Gordon's favorite Catholic beliefs.

While the ending of *The Malefactors* may be somewhat predictable, the novel as a whole powerfully portrays the struggle of an intelligent man who, contrary to all his cautionary instincts, sees that he must abase himself in faith if he is to escape the narcissistic cell of the ego. His drama is recounted by Gordon with a depth of learning and a quiet subtlety that draw the reader's admiration throughout. As for Gordon's technical skill, that has, it is to be hoped, been amply demonstrated. Like the fiction of Henry James that Gordon so much admired, *The Malefactors* will reward the refined attention of those who can discern its value.

In *The Glory of Hera*, Gordon unites classical, Jungian, and Christian motifs in an attempt to extend even further her depiction of the transformation of human experience by the Incarnation. In November 1963, Gordon wrote to Ashley Brown that in her view there was "no gap between paganism and Christianity" but that Christianity was distinguished from all other religions by its "historicity," the involvement of God in human affairs. What she admired in the Greeks was their openness to the supernatural. The ancient Greeks, she asserted, might not "recognize the supernatural at first glance, but they were trained from infancy to realize that they might encounter one of its manifestations at any moment." In the same essay, Gordon indicated that she had devoted much of her life to the study of the hero. In 1968, for example, she wrote to Jacques Maritain that she was still struggling with Heracles as the "proto-type of the Christian soul." In a subsequent letter to Maritain, written sometime in 1969 or 1970, she observed that Heracles was the only one of the Greek heroes who "went to heaven" because he had honored a female virgin. In a letter to Ashley Brown written in the fall of 1961, she had observed that in certain narrative moments, Heracles could be regarded as a "fore-runner of Christ."[14] Moreover, as the title of the novel implies, Gordon's portrayal of Hera as partially parallel to the Virgin Mary was an attempt to bring out the feminist sides of both the Greek and the Christian archetypes. For this reason, Gordon's Hera is given considerably more moral dignity than her original in Hesiod, and Hera's tormenting of Heracles is largely passed over.

As has been suggested, Gordon in *The Glory of Hera* departed from Hesiod in reconstructing the myth of Heracles as an archetype of Christ. She also presents an altered Zeus, who desires to save mankind and who discovers in the depths of his unconscious a desire to unite mankind with the divine. Gordon's Heracles points the way to Christ by acting in obedience to the will of both Zeus and Hera, who together make up the Jungian balance of male and female in the divine. The relationship

14. Gordon to Brown, November 5, 1963; Gordon, "Cock-Crow," 563; Gordon to Maritain, February 11, 1968; Gordon to Maritain, (1969–1970); Gordon to Brown, November 15, 1961.

expresses Gordon's rejection of Prometheus as the only answer to the tension perceived by the Greeks between the gods and humanity. While allusions to the Old and New Testament abound in *The Glory of Hera*, strengthening Gordon's theme of the spiritual continuity between the ancient Greek and the Judeo/Christian traditions, Heracles falls far short of being a type of Christ, especially in the scenes in which he is depicted as a slave to instinctual violence. Gordon creates a large synaptic gap between the Greek and the Christian dispensations, allowing for the vigorous intervention of God to perfect the hero who will at last adequately mediate between the divine and the human.

Somewhat dry and desultory in its copious detailing of Greek mythology (particularly in the first half of the novel), *The Glory of Hera*, while an interesting experiment from an intellectual point of view, lacks the emotional power that Gordon had achieved in her earlier fiction. In *The Strange Children*, but particularly in *The Malefactors*, Gordon had set the anxious shape of her own circumstances into the context of her Catholic beliefs with poignant persuasiveness. Unlike the writings of Walker Percy, Thomas Merton, and Daniel Berrigan, Gordon's writings are not issue oriented; rather, they focus, nearer to home, on the contradictions and deceptions that clutter the lives of those whose religious commitment is otherwise strong and clear-minded. Unlike Allen Tate, whose faith was largely a matter of introspective analysis, Gordon's fiction centers on the fruitful interaction of those Catholics who, like Kevin Reardon in *The Strange Children* and Catherine Pollard in *The Malefactors*, live their faith in an orthodox, sacrificial, yet social spirit. Furthermore, while in Mary Gordon's fiction the doctrine of the community of saints operates as a deadening weight upon the central characters, in Caroline Gordon's world it bears the very shape of rescue.

ALLEN TATE (1899-1979)

I N 1956, ALLEN Tate wrote to his wife, Caroline Gordon, complaining that there had not been a study by a Catholic critic of him as a Catholic poet. Although Tate formally became a Catholic only in 1950, he thought of his writing as having reflected a Catholic outlook for most of his career. Early in 1929, for example, he wrote to his fellow Fugitive poet, Donald Davidson, saying that he was "more and more headed toward Catholicism," adding that he particularly valued the Catholic Church's emphasis on the "authority of dogma" as a bulwark against naturalism and against moral vagueness. Furthermore, in *I'll Take My Stand*, the famous collection of essays on agrarianism to which Tate had contributed, he argued that the failure of the South to embrace Catholicism had been a serious error. He reaffirmed this view in 1952 in a letter to Catholic (and southerner) Walker Percy, arguing that the South had "no tradition without the Church." While Tate's position represents a simplification of history, it did reflect both the depth of his attachment to Catholic ideas and his painful consciousness of what he saw as a portentous shortcoming in southern culture.[1]

1. Tate to Gordon, January 24, 1956, Tate-Gordon Collection, Manuscripts Division, Department of Rare Books and Special Collections, Princeton University Libraries. Unless otherwise indicated, letters from Tate are from this collection; see Davidson and Tate, *The Literary Correspondence of Donald Davidson and Allen Tate,* 223–24; Tate to Percy, January 1, 1952, Percy Collection, Southern Historical Collection, Library of the University of North Carolina at Chapel Hill.

By the 1920s, as Robert Brinkmeyer has suggested, three principal interests had established themselves in Tate's mind: order and community in the South, Roman Catholicism, and modernism. Indeed, as early as 1927, the poet John Gould Fletcher, after meeting Tate, came away feeling that Tate was under the influence of an ascetic "medieval Catholicism." In 1951, Tate wrote to Cleanth Brooks that he had finally done "what I should have done and what I don't know why I didn't do, years ago: I have joined the Catholic Church." Tate's delay in formally entering the Catholic Church can probably best be seen as evidence of a scrupulous tendency to weigh and reweigh everything. When Tate finally entered the Catholic Church in 1950, Jacques Maritain remarked dryly that if Tate had delayed any longer, he would have been "committing a sin against the Holy Ghost."[2]

Seen in retrospect, Tate's poetry and essays, from the 1920s forward, seem markedly Catholic in character. Reflecting Tate's reading in Aquinas, Augustine, Dante, and Maritain—Maritain became Tate's godfather upon his formally entering the church—the writing reflects both a spiritual search and a prophetic denunciation of a society whose naturalism and accompanying materialism would, Tate believed, cause its disintegration. Referring to the Catholic historian Christopher Dawson in the introduction to Robert Lowell's *Land of Unlikeness*, for example, Tate warned of the link between twentieth-century materialism and spiritual decay. More particularly, writing in a *Partisan Review* survey titled "Religion and the Intellectuals," Tate argued that twentieth-century culture was impoverished due to a failure to "possess and be possessed by a controlling sense of the presence of redemptive powers." In the same article, Tate distinguished sharply between formal religious belief and the twentieth-century revival of interest in myth, which he dismissed as a retreat by naturalists to a "plane where the idea of transcendence can be entertained as a pleasant rhetorical diversion."[3]

From the beginning, Tate's approach to Catholicism had been intellectual, following the cerebral tradition of European and particularly French Catholicism rather than the relatively pious tradition of Irish American Catholicism. He saw Catholicism as freeing the mind, not limiting it, and he attacked the Catholic Church when he perceived it to be attempting to exceed its authority, as he did in a letter to the *New York Times* in 1951

2. Brinkmeyer, *Three Catholic Writers*, 6; Fletcher, *The Autobiography of John Gould Fletcher*, 350; Tate to Brooks, January 20, 1951; Maritain's remarks are quoted in Walter Sullivan, *Allen Tate: A Recollection*, 110.

3. Tate, "Religion and Intellectuals," 251, 253.

in which he took issue with Cardinal Spellman's attempt to ban a film. Tate contended that while the Catholic Church had the right to publish a censorship list for the use of the faithful, it had no right to trespass into the area of civil jurisdiction.

In spite of his attraction to Roman Catholicism on intellectual grounds, Tate, like Robert Lowell, had been strongly attracted to the church by the figure of Mary, and he regretted, as he wrote to Caroline Gordon in the fall of 1963, the Second Vatican Council's voting to "play down" the importance of Mary in an effort to improve ecumenical relations. In an attempt to raise the intellectual profile of Catholicism in the United States, Tate and Gordon attempted in 1953 to organize a school of writers, which would be conducted "under Catholic auspices and in a Catholic atmosphere," as Tate put it in a letter to Robert Lowell in the spring of 1953, adding that Dorothy Day had agreed to let them hold the school at one of the Catholic Worker farms.[4]

In the 1950s, while Tate followed ascetic practices such as the reading of the prayers of the Divine Office, ordinarily done only by the clergy, he also manifested a sexual promiscuity that led to his divorce (for the second time) from Caroline Gordon in 1959. In his subsequent marriages to Isabella Gardner, in 1959, and Helen Heinz, in 1967, he technically cut himself off from the sacraments, although he continued to attend Mass, though not regularly, and to think of himself as a Catholic until his death in 1979. In this connection, Tate's friend Walter Sullivan said that "never once in his life" had Tate ceased to believe in the Catholic faith.[5]

In the 1950s, Tate and Gordon arrived at a synthesis of Jungian psychoanalysis and Catholic theology that allowed each to draw on dreams and archetypal symbolism in their work. Writing to Gordon in January 1958, Tate declared that what Saint Catherine of Siena believed about spiritual love was the "mystical equivalent of Jung." It would seem that Tate's interest in Jung was in part an attempt to mitigate the cerebralism of his approach to both art and religion. In a March 1958 letter to Gordon, Tate emphasized the value of Jung in illuminating some deeper aspects of theology, saying at one point that Jung had given him more insight into the *experience* of the Trinity, as distinguished from the intellectual formulation of that doctrine, than any other writer.[6]

4. Tate to Gordon, November 12, 1963; Tate to Lowell, April 11, 1953, Lowell Collection, Houghton Library, Harvard University.

5. Sullivan, *Allen Tate,* 37.

6. Tate to Gordon, January 31, 1958; Tate to Gordon, March 8, 1958.

The intellectualism of Tate's approach to Catholicism, prominent in both his essays and his poetry, is what distinguishes his contribution to Catholic American writing. Dismissing Faulkner's novel *A Fable* in 1962, for example, he described the work as contrived in "theological ignorance." In an essay about Emily Dickinson, he maintained that religion benefited society (even in the case of Puritanism), providing a "heroic proportion" and a "tragic mode" to the experience of the individual—a hierarchical norm by which to judge the flow of history.[7] Tate regarded religion as the great unifying force in society—although he conceded that it tended to wilt, as John Crowe Ransom also observed, in modern industrial conditions when nature was subjugated and lost much of its mystery.

In the tradition of poet-critics such as Arnold and Eliot, Tate fashioned a criticism in which he synthesized perceptions about art and society. His particular emphasis was to stress the role of the critic as philosophical realist in the Thomist and Aristotelian tradition, and in this respect he resembles Ivor Winters, for whom Tate had great respect. Tate argued that the literary critic mediated between imagination and philosophical reasoning, and his central thesis was that modern thought, following Descartes, had degenerated into a Manichaean division of the world into intellect and matter. In an important essay titled "The Angelic Imagination," he called this phenomenon "angelism" and contended, as had Jacques Maritain, whom Tate in part relied on, that if we take nothing but our intellects to the top of the Platonic ladder, we "shall see nothing when we get there."[8]

In "The Man of Letters in the Modern World," Tate argued that angelism produced a mechanized view of nature, at odds with the "eternal society of the communion of the human spirit," a cultural blindness that led to an impotent and "shadowy political philosophy" in modern literature that extended from Proust to Faulkner. We are disciples of Pascal, Tate wrote, "the merits of whose Redeemer were privately available but could not affect the operation of the power-state." Tate emphasized the effect of science on the decay of religion and social unity in his essay "Religion and the Old South." From the Renaissance to the present, he noted, scientific philosophers had chosen to discard traditional "mystical" spirits and symbols, which were judged to be superfluous in describing natural phenomena, finally dispensing with the soul itself. In contrast to

7. Tate, *Memoirs and Opinions*, 84; Tate, *Collected Essays*, 199.
8. Tate, *Collected Essays*, 454.

the narrow empiricism of science, Tate added, religion had directed its attention to the "whole" horse, the "horse cropping the blue-grass on the lawn." As Robert Brinkmeyer has observed, Tate came to realize that the Cartesian dilemma that separated matter from spirit and subject from object had been addressed by Catholicism, as it, in its centering of itself in the Incarnation, metaphysically reconciled the pairs of opposites that Descartes had divided.[9]

For Tate a significant part of the holistic approach taken by religion, particularly by medieval Christianity, was its unblinking consciousness of evil, which he regarded as the most valuable contribution of Catholicism to the modern age, where he witnessed evil being explained out of existence by scientist and neoscientist alike. In this respect, in an essay titled "To Whom Is the Poet Responsible?" he acknowledged the usefulness not only of religion but also of poetry in thwarting the attempt to "purify ourselves of the knowledge of evil."[10]

Tate perceived the decline of Western culture and the disintegration of traditional religious symbolism as interwoven. Since the eighteenth century, he argued, symbolism had tended to become merely historical and analytical, cut off from the religious roots that related human beings to their place in the scheme of things and that had also provided them with a moral framework. In this situation the writer was forced to reimagine even symbols of a traditional kind, integrating these with the experience of his characters and thus creating a fresh cosmology and symbolic landscape with the production of each literary work.[11]

Tate was attracted to Catholicism because of its incarnational theology, which he saw as reconciling thought and matter and thus overcoming the Cartesian hiatus. Thus, he admired Saint Augustine's parallel studies of the cities of God and man because they established the continuity between political and theological worlds whereby the earthly city could be judged by the heavenly ideal. Even in American society Tate felt that the same sort of analogy was still possible by applying the ideals of Jeffersonian democracy to contemporary American society. He felt, though, that America had become an abstraction governed by a mechanical cosmology that brought about social fragmentation. Ironically, while honoring the example provided by Augustine and Dante, Tate cautioned in his essay "The Symbolic Imagination" that modern Catholic writing, from Francis

9. Tate, "Man of Letters," in *Collected Essays*, 381–82; Tate, "Religion and the Old South," in *Collected Essays*, 313, 306; Brinkmeyer, *Three Catholic Writers*, 63.
10. Tate, *Collected Essays*, 407.
11. See Allen Tate and Carolyn Gordon, eds., *The House of Fiction*, 633.

Thompson to Robert Lowell, was in danger of losing the "gift for concrete experience" and of sinking into the angelism that had come to characterize the mainstream of American culture and literature.[12]

As a remedy for the Cartesian impasse that American writers had constructed, Tate affirmed not only traditional Catholic thought but also a healthy provincialism, a connection to one's immediate surroundings, reminiscent in some respects of William Carlos Williams but tied in Tate's case to a more ambitious theological scheme. Thus, he approved of Joyce's Irish provincialism, which nonetheless, as he explained in a letter to Lincoln Kirstein, still offered "certain truths" that were "common to the mainstream of European culture." At the same time, in an essay titled "The New Provincialism," Tate cautioned against a merely secular provincialism, which looked to material welfare and legal justice as solutions to social fragmentation. Instead, he called for a return to the "classical-Christian world," based upon a "regional consciousness," a formulation that reflected the amalgam of Catholicism and southern culture in his own life.[13]

In addition to their profundity, Tate's essays are remarkable in twentieth-century American literature for their limpid and reasoned organization, as is amply evident if one places them next to the essays of Ezra Pound, William Carlos Williams, or even Wallace Stevens, whose thought as a group, even if original and distinguished, often *appears* to be more rational than it is. Even Eliot's essays, with their rather dated neoscientific language, appear at times to be more affected and awkward than Tate's. Grounded in Thomist and Aristotelian philosophy, Tate proceeded by definition and logic to set out issues clearly, believing that his function might well be to uphold the standards of polemical discussion in a period when he felt that standards were falling.

If Tate lamented the contemporary cleavage between information and understanding, and between action and intelligence, he counted on the critic's precision in language to at least sort out the elements of this cultural malaise. Similarly, in contrast to the imagist manifesto, he counted on the poet to include the expression of abstract ideas in his writing—though he objected to didacticism. Poetry was best suited, he wrote in the preface to *Reactionary Essays on Poetry and Ideas,* to the testing of ideas by experience. In spite of the rational tenor of Tate's criticism, the essays are sometimes softened by an attractive, religiously inspired compassion, as

12. Tate, *Collected Essays,* 414.
13. Tate to Kirstein, February 6, 1933; Tate, *Collected Essays,* 291–92.

can be seen in his remarks about Hart Crane in *The Forlorn Demon:* "There is a Christian commonplace," he wrote, "which says that God does not despise conditions. Out of the desperate conditions" of Crane's life, which included "almost unimaginable horrors of depravity and perversity of will," Tate observed, Crane produced in the end a "shining *exemplum* of uncompromising human dignity: his poetry."[14]

While Tate's sympathy reflected his earlier friendship with Crane and while he respected the architectural strength of Crane's poetry, he was not in sympathy with the romanticism underlying that poetry. As Robert Dupree observed, Tate disliked the tendency in romanticism to "segregate the truth of the heart from that of the mind." Beginning with Poe, Tate contended, romanticism had undermined American literature by dividing the world into sensation and unanchored mysticism—another version of angelism. In "The Angelic Imagination," Tate maintained that Poe's romantic exaltation of the imagination in its "Cartesian vacuum" had severed both the relationship between nature and consciousness and the relationship between literature and life. In a review of Crane's late-romantic poem *The Bridge,* Tate observed that this severance was all too manifest. Crane had incorporated in his poem a "sentimental muddle" of Whitman, Anderson, and Williams raised to the level of a "vague and transcendental reality." While Crane thus aspired to religious consciousness, Tate saw him as failing to produce a coherent structure of religious ideas, and he was especially critical of Crane's attempt to create myth, arguing that genuine myth arose from broad, communal experience: "It is still a nice problem among higher critics," Tate added, whether the authors of the Gospels were deliberate mythmakers or whether their minds were "simply constructed that way; but the evidence favors the latter."[15] Tate's allusion to the divinely created seeds in the psyche that underlie archetypal expression reflects the sort of mingling of Jungian and Christian elements that one encounters in some other Catholic American writers such as Caroline Gordon, Thomas Merton, Paul Horgan, and William Everson.

In Dante, Tate found a poet who reflected a Thomist approach to experience and who demonstrated the analogies present in common, realistically described physical experience that led to an approximate understanding of higher spiritual realities. Tate also leaned toward neoclassicism because of what he regarded as its underlying realism, which

14. Tate, *Collected Essays,* xv, 532.
15. Dupree, *Allen Tate and the Augustinian Imagination,* xiv; Tate, *Collected Essays,* 444; Tate, *The Poetry Reviews of Allan Tate, 1924–1944* 103, 102.

included its moderation. He praised some of Laura Riding's early poetry, for example, for its restrained diction and theme and its fine lucidity. In a discussion (within an essay about John Crowe Ransom) of nineteenth-century poetry, he further elaborated on the advantages of classicism—its precision, objectivity, humility, and restraint—in contrast to the romantic infinite in which the "megalomania of man rhetorically participates." What distinguishes Tate's neoclassicism is the moral coloring that is so often a part of his thought. Even the quality of irony, for example, which is so ubiquitous in his own poetry, is given moral significance, as in a review of T. S. Eliot's poetry where irony is associated with the virtue of humility.[16]

Stylistically, Tate's poetry, with its conscious dedication to tension as its underlying constructional principle, is markedly metaphysical. Replete with dark conceits and bleak ironies, the poems of the 1920s and 1930s focus on Tate's disaffection with naturalism, which is offset by religious allusions that bring to bear a contrasting set of forgotten ideals. For example, "Last Days of Alice," one of Tate's most brilliant poems, contrasts the abstractionism or angelism of contemporary culture—here associated with Alice's frozen and innocent vision behind the looking glass—with incarnational Christianity:

> —We too back to the world shall never pass
> Through the shattered door, a dumb shade-harried crowd
> Being all infinite, function depth and mass
> Without figure, a mathematical shroud
> Hurled at the air—blessed without sin!
> O God of our flesh, return us to Your wrath,
> Let us be evil could we enter in
> Your grace, and falter on the stony path![17]

Composed of alternating rhymed quatrains, a reflection of Tate's formalism, the poem wittily yokes the innocent heroine of the story by the mathematician, Lewis Carroll, with the mathematical abstractionism that Tate perceived as having sterilized twentieth-century culture. Implicitly invoking Keats's Grecian urn poem as well, Tate silhouettes not only the spiritual death of American society but its consummate ennui as well. In contrast, the speaker pleads with God to permit him to be allowed to

16. Tate, "Laura Riding," in *Poetry Reviews*, 54; Tate, "John Crowe Ransom," in *Poetry Reviews*, 23; Tate, "T. S. Eliot," in *Poetry Reviews*, 109.

17. Tate, *Collected Poems, 1919–1976*, 39. All subsequent quotations of Tate's poetry are from this volume and are cited parenthetically in the text.

return to a world in time, where failure and evil are again possible and where the forgiving grace of God also then becomes possible.

In a poem appropriately titled "The Ivory Tower," Tate launches a withering attack upon the abstractionism of contemporary culture:

> Let us begin to understand the argument.
> There is a solution to everything: Science.
> Separate those evils strictly social
> From other evils that are eventually social.
> It ends in all evils being social. (83)

In Tate's view, since the loss of the concept of sin had led to the loss of the concept of evil, a substantive morality, he felt, could not survive the decline of the Christian cosmology. Thus, in the poem "To a Romantic Novelist," Tate queried ironically:

> And what's the bother about sin?
> It doesn't matter so
> Whether a woman's unchaste.
> Talk to Trimalchio. (8)

In the poem "Causerie," one sees the conjunction of Tate's prophetic disdain for his society with his ironic sense that God—so needed by the modern world—is so silent within it. Tate takes up the theme not of a world without God but of a world with a merely latent Christ within it, like an unopened seed:

> Year after year the blood of Christ will sleep
> In the holy tree, the branches sagged without bloom
> Till the plant overflowing the stale vegetation
> In May the creek swells with the anemone,
> The Lord God wastes his substance towards the ocean. (14)

The daring of the image of God's waste, here seen not only as a river but also as an onanistic flow of divine semen, is typical of Tate's bracing metaphysical style.

Passionately, Tate calls for the return of an age of faith:

> In Christ we have lived, on the flood of Christ borne up,
> Who now is a precipitate flood of silence,
> We a drenched wreck off an imponderable shore. (14–15)

The poem rises to a marginal hope in its final overlay of the images of the tree of Eden and the cross of Calvary:

> . . . whence the impulse
> To lust for the apple of apples on Christ's tree,
> To desire in the eye, to penetrate your sleep,
> Perhaps to catch in unexpected leaves
> The light incentive of your absolute suspicion?
> Over the mountains, the last barrier, you'd spill
> These relics of your sires in a pool of sleep,
> The sun being drained. (15)

Teeming with paradox and interwoven motifs, the passage is a good example of Tate's formal complexity, even if he here uses a relatively free verse. The unexpected turning toward Christ contrasts with an earlier section of the poem in which Tate considered, not unsympathetically, the religious skepticism of some of his friends, such as Ransom and Warren, a skepticism that is represented here by the word "suspicion." The tree conceit, which holds the stanza together, also brings the theme of religious consciousness forward past the historic threshold of the cross to modern humanity's curiosity about religious consciousness. The image of spillage recalls the earlier image of divine "wastage," but here the context proves a positive one in which cerebral objections, symbolized by the sun, give way to a "pool of sleep," a fertile image of religious reawakening. The poem brims with puns, as with the phrase "absolute suspicion," which can mean either a complete agnosticism or an incomplete but residual and marginally hopeful suspicion of the absolute. Moreover, structurally, the poem is marked by a number of dramatic and unexpected reversals, as in the movement away from the initial image of the grave (reminiscent of Tate's "Ode to the Confederate Dead") toward the image of "Christ's tree."

In a poem titled "Homily," written in 1925, to which Tate appended an epigraph from the New Testament ("If thine eye offend thee, pluck it out"), the poet hints at one of the salient causes of modern unbelief in the image of the "close vermiculate crease" (4). The speaker calls for a stemming of the cerebral self-consciousness that had eroded religious consciousness in the twentieth century, a somewhat paradoxical stance, perhaps, for an intellectual poet such as Tate to adopt. Interwoven with the Christian themes is language that is specifically Catholic, as in the reference to the doctrine of the Immaculate Conception in "The Meaning of Life" and in the references to the Virgin Mary and to the community of saints in the "Sonnet to Beauty."

One of the most interesting of the poems from the 1930s is "The Cross," a poem whose dense symbols have a mysterious suggestiveness in contrast to the complex lucidity of Tate's accustomed metaphysical style. In the poem, which is set in quatrains joined together in a single stanza, the speaker focuses starkly on Calvary with the image of the "day-sky" of "moonless black," which symbolizes the self-imposed darkness of irreligious modern America (33). The cross is pictured as an emblem of love whose function is to end death for Christians, who, like "young wolves" that have "tasted blood," will hunger thereafter for the new dispensation of eternal life. With its savagery the image of the wolves is so unexpected that it catches the reader off guard. The effect is intensified at the end of the poem when the wolf returns in pursuit of the stag, "charged both at heel and head," signifying that the latent religious consciousness of humanity has been undermined by skepticism (head) and by materialism (heel). Apart from the images of the wolves, the picture of the modern world as an infernal "world-destroying pit" gives the poem an unsettling resonance that extends past its immediate theme to that of a complex, underlying malaise. Even if one as an individual were to attain belief, it would seem, the destructiveness of modern culture would envelop the believer. Moreover, Tate's neoclassicism precluded his turning to nature for any reassuring signs of a divine immanence.

In the first sonnet of the "Sonnets at Christmas" (both in the Italian style), Tate looks askance at those who enjoy Christmas as a secular holiday while he struggles cheerlessly with the religious significance of the day:

> But I must kneel again unto the Dead
> While Christmas bells of paper white and red,
> Figured with boys and girls spilt from a sled,
> Ring out the silence I am nourished by. (103)

Exhibiting a fine play of mind, Tate contrasts his own Christmas, whose tranquility is evoked by the silent bells among his Christmas decorations, with the boisterous, secular celebrations elsewhere. Tellingly, the word *nourished*, with its positive connotations, nicely undercuts the implied picture of the speaker as merely a religious recluse. Even the reference to the "Dead," while far from positive, suggests a suitable starting point for religious consciousness.

In the second sonnet there is again the image of bells, though this poem opens with less measured solemnity than the first sonnet and is more intimate and expressive in tone and rhythm: "Ah, Christ, I love you rings to the wild sky" (103). The mood quickly turns toward the penitential, however, as Tate recalls a factual incident from his Kentucky childhood in which a black boy was punished for something he himself had done, a guilt that reaches into his Christmas meditation, altering the atmosphere so that it approximates that which one might associate with Good Friday. A central image in the poem, though, the "Ancient crackle of Christ's deep gaze," compassionately implies that, if Christ's look is painful to the speaker, it also answers his profound need for spiritual recognition and forgiveness.

The poetic sequel, "More Sonnets at Christmas," composed in 1942, comprises four sonnets, again in the Italian mode, in which the social implications of Christianity are explored more than they had been in the earlier sonnets. Set against World War II, which Tate approached with an attitude of Christian nonviolence—an attitude he passed on to Robert Lowell, whom he had befriended in the 1930s—Tate looked back over the period between the two sets of sonnets, regretful that he had vacillated about formally entering the church. "Ten years," he wrote ruefully, were "time enough to be dismayed / By mummy Christ, head crammed between his knees" (104). Christ is portrayed as a mummy because he has been made so by the "dithering" poet.

Forcing himself to consider a more external and active world in order to overcome his introspective malaise, Tate then thinks about the bombers over Europe:

> . . . stroke
> By stroke, up to the frazzled sun to hear
> Sun-ghostlings whisper: Yes, the capital yoke—
> Remove it and there's not a ghost to fear
> This crucial day, whose decapitate joke
> Languidly winds into the inner ear. (104)

Incorporating the recurrent and deliberately ambiguous image of decapitation as a symbol both of the removal of Christ as the moral head of society and of the need to attenuate reflexiveness, Tate nevertheless shows the folly of a plunge into the active sphere as a relief from excessive cerebration. Characteristically, there is a meticulous, stylistic play on words, not only through the rhyming of "yoke" and "joke" but also through the implicit identifying of "capital" and "decapitate"—with the word *capital* referring not only to the head but also to the mortal punishment that will overtake those who kill in war.

In the second poem from "More Sonnets at Christmas," Tate's asceticism is evident as he takes aim not only at the war but also at the materialism that would otherwise prevail in peacetime. The images are stinging as Tate parodies what he conceives to be the wartime version of the American dream:

> . . . pray most fixedly
> For the cold martial progress of your star,
> With thoughts of commerce and society,
> Well-milked Chinese, Negroes who cannot sing,
> The Huns gelded and feeding in a ring. (105)

The ironic conjunction of "martial progress" and the Christmas "star" illustrates Tate's sense of the savagely un-Christian depths to which America had sunk. The intensity of Tate's anger matches that of Robert Lowell's war poetry, though Tate is not so apocalyptic, keeping his vision always neoclassically within the middle range.

The third of the set of Christmas sonnets connects with the earlier group of sonnets in which Tate recalled the incident about the black boy who had been wrongly whipped in his stead, an obsessive memory that acquired additional poignancy when Tate learned that the black boy, now a young man, had been killed in the war. The painful individual memory is generalized by being interfused with memories connected with the American dream and American involvement in the war:

> Nobody said that he could be a plumber,
> Carpenter, clerk, bus-driver, bombardier;
> Let little boys go into violent slumber,
> Aegean squall and squalor where their fear
> Is of an enemy in remote oceans
> Unstalked by Christ: these are the better notions. (105)

One senses that, with his predilection for punning, Tate here intended the reader to hear the word *nations* as well as the word *notions*. The better nations, morally speaking, may well be those that are not Christian.

Although his vantage point was clearly religious, Tate found himself at odds with the contemporary behavior of the Christian church, as can be seen in the fourth sonnet. There, churchgoers are called "Plato's Christians in the cave," hoodwinked by the government ("your master's ease") into a "Mild-mannered" cooperation (106):

> . . . the nave
> Gives back the cheated and light dividend
> So long sequestered; now, new-rich, you'll spend
> Flesh for reality inside a stone
> Whose light obstruction, like a gossamer bone,
> Dead or still living, will not break or bend. (105)

The lines are skillfully wrought. Apart from the pun on "nave," Americans, devoted to commerce, are visualized in the central conceit as having bartered the lives of their young in order to acquire a sense of reality, whose symbol is the grave. Tate's poem is an unbending rebuke of an ideological dream about the nature and morality of war. The motif of "light" is especially well handled—initially a pure Platonism, then a "light obstruction" as the reality of war begins to filter through, then the "gossamer bone," a subtle mingling of lingering illusion and slowly dawning horror as the actuality of war gradually emerges.

Two of the most conspicuously Catholic poems of the 1940s, at the end of which decade Tate formally entered the Catholic Church, are "Winter Mask" and "Seasons of the Soul," the latter being one of Tate's most significant works. "Winter Mask" reveals the extent of Tate's reading of Dante, especially visible in the re-creation of the Count Ugolino episode from the *Inferno* in which the Count and Archbishop Ruggieri are frozen together as a punishment for treachery, the sin of cold blood:

> Both damned in eternal ice,
> The traitor become the boor
> Who had led his friend to slaughter,
> Now bites his head—not nice,
> The food that he lives for. (112)

The ironic, cannibalistic bonding of the two men, whom treachery had divided in life, is crowned by a witty, parenthetical tone ("not nice") whose offhandedness contrasts incongruously with the grim fate depicted. The Dantean prototype provided Tate with a Catholic cosmology that exceeded the restrained emotional and imaginative limits of neoclassicist art.

Organized around a seasonal cycle that in some respects recalls Eliot's *Four Quartets*, "Seasons of the Soul" also relies upon Dantean motifs, including the epigraph from book 13 of the *Inferno:* "Then I stretched forth my hand a little and pulled a twig from a large thorn and the trunk cried: 'Why do you tear me?' " While much of the poem centers on the war, the epigraph extends Tate's condemnation, similar to Lowell's, of the war's assault upon the ecology of the world. Such is the effect of his striking image of France in 1944:

> It was a gentle sun
> When, at the June solstice
> Green France was overrun
> With caterpillar feet. (115)

The montage of industrialized tanks and a plague of caterpillars reaffirms the agrarian values of Tate's earlier essays, as does the insistent, predatory imagery of "jaws" in the poem. Moreover, the dynamism of the symbols underscores the surge of activity of the summer season, a season of the body rather than of the soul, which is represented by the eye.

The first section concludes with a scene, re-created from the *Inferno,* in which Dante and Virgil see a centaur, a summer creature that, although mixing human and animal traits, symbolizes the physical:

> Stopping, they saw in the narrow
> Light a centaur pause
> And gaze, then his astounded
> Beard, with a notched arrow,
> Part back upon his jaws. (116)

Again, the primitive and predatory aspects of the centaur—notably the jaw—are emphasized in Tate's portrait of the soul caught in an inhospitable season when it is likely to be overrun by the physical.

In the autumn section, another version of hell is offered, based upon the desolate emptying of the landscape. Here Tate recalls a recurrent dream in which he finds himself in the empty hall of a closed house. He encounters his father and mother, both dead, who don't recognize him and who fail to recognize each other, a sign in part, perhaps, of their difficult marriage. Reminiscent of the wandering dead in Dante, the figures are given added dramatic value through Tate's sensitive use of sound—as in the following lines:

> I counted along the wall
> Door after closed door
> Through which a shade might slide
> To the cold and empty hall. (116)

While the sibilant *s*s generate the prevailing and unsettling silence of the house, the assonant vowels convey a haunting quality, which is present even in the word "hall" where the final *l*s cause the short *a* to do what it does not ordinarily do—to echo.

The "Winter" section of the poem paradoxically centers on sexuality, perhaps because the frigidity and aridity of winter promote sexual desire, and, appropriately, the figure of Venus dominates this section of the poem:

> Goddess sea-born and bright,
> Return into the sea
> Where eddying twilight
> Gathers upon your people—
> Cold goddess, hear our plea!

Leave the burnt earth, Venus,
For the drying God above,
Hanged in his windy steeple,
No longer bears for us
The living wound of love. (118)

The appeal to Venus to return to the sea reflects the speaker's desperate reflection that, if Christianity has perished (the windy steeple), perhaps a return to a pagan religion might be preferable. Such a move is clearly impossible, though, and the speaker is left stranded amid contemporary sordidness, symbolized by the shark.

In this section of the poem Tate powerfully merges the seasonal motif with the theme of modern lust:

Eternal winters blow
Shivering flakes, and shove
Bodies that wheel and drop—
Cold soot upon the snow
Their livid wound of love. (119)

In addition to his tempering of erotic feeling through the "wound of love" refrain, Tate drains any erotic suggestiveness that these lines might otherwise have through the image of semen as cold soot upon the snow.

In the final "Spring" section of the sequence Tate relies upon the holy figures of Saint Monica, the mother of Saint Augustine, as well as that of the Virgin Mary, to be symbolic counterweights to the earlier ugly depiction of contemporary love:

Come, mother, and lean
At the window with your son
And gaze through its light frame
These fifteen centuries
Upon the shirking scene
Where men, blind, go lame. (121)

Saint Monica, the "mother of silences," wipes away the unsatisfactory memory of the "livid wound of love" from the winter section.

While spring brings back memories of youthful vigor, including sexual vigor, such memories are not, after all, sufficient for the speaker in the poem. Thus, the sexual pun on dying gives way to a desire for a more spiritual death:

Speak, that we may hear;
Listen, while we confess

That we conceal our fear;
Regard us, while the eye
Discerns by sight or guess
Whether, as sheep foregather
Upon their crooked knees,
We have begun to die. (122)

Addressed to the "mother of silences," the speaker's prayer, here associated with the "sheep" who are Christ's followers, expresses a longing
for a death to oneself, now fully credible, given the poem's disaffected
review of modern life. In its spiritual ripeness "Seasons of the Soul"
represents a watershed in Tate's Catholic poetry. Gone at last are the inner
tensions that issued from Tate's guilty procrastination in the sight of God.
While he had much to feel guilty about, especially in the sexual area,
the guilt he experienced now was as a full-blooded believer. Ironically,
Tate's suspended state had allowed him to decry sexual sordidness from
a privileged, somewhat detached and not uncomfortable vantage point.
As a Catholic, however, his moral perceptions would become heavier and
more mortifying, devoid of the intellectual suspense that had animated
the earlier journey of faith.

Nevertheless, the poems of the 1950s, which followed Tate's formal
entrance into the church, are no less impressive, even if his output diminished during the decade. In "The Maimed Man," Tate returns to the dense
and surreal symbolism of earlier poems such as "The Cross." However,
the poem exhibits a rational neoclassical and Christian superstructure that
offsets the underlying surrealism with its mysterious motifs and feelings.
The dominant classical symbols of laurel (reason) and myrtle (passion)
parallel the two Christian symbols of Eve and Mary (sin and redemption),
both conveying the struggle of reason and passion within the speaker.
Typical of the poems of the 1950s, Tate adopts a tight tercet stanza in which
the sound ending the second line becomes the dominant rhyming sound
of the succeeding stanza. The rhythm follows a loose iambic pattern.

"The Maimed Man" is heavy with guilt, a reflection perhaps of the
tension between Tate's orthodoxy and piety and his concupiscence. Such
a reading is reinforced by the speaker's being described as "Witching for
water in a waste of shame," which recalls Shakespeare's famous sonnet
about lust. The guilt is resolved symbolically in the disturbing figure of
the maimed man, who initially appears in a dream but who later looms
out of the speaker's own mirror as a scarecrowlike apparition:

. . . one day I whirled
Towards a suggesting presence in my room
And saw in the waving mirror (glass swirled

By old blowers) a black trunk without bloom—
    Body that once had moved my face and feet.
    My secret was his father, I his tomb. (130)

In this, the poem's nadir, the speaker confronts his moral ugliness and guilt and the eternal death that lies before him because of his unconfessed "secret."

Seeing himself as "God's image made uncouth," the speaker slowly rises out of his guilty, subjective vortex into an external world of natural time. Having escaped the bottomless depths of the psyche, a "half-hell," the speaker is capable, through the Incarnation, of entering a world of redemption and thus prays to the Virgin Mary for the return of an earlier, less sullied and more hopeful self:

Now take him, Virgin Muse, up the deeper stream:
    As a lost bee returning to the hive,
    Cell after honeyed cell of sounding dream—

Swimmer of noonday, lean for the perfect dive
    To the dead Mother's face, whose subtile down
    You had not seen take amber light alive. (131)

The first mother, Eve, dead through original sin, is polarized with the figure of Mary, the "Virgin Muse," a reconciling of classical and Catholic motifs.

Although Tate has been criticized by some for not having a good ear, one is struck by the success of lines such as "Cell after honeyed cell of sounding dreams," whose soft consonants and easy vowels (the significant exception being "sounding") evoke the trance in which the speaker has been held for much of his life. The poem's rich obscurity stems both from Tate's desire to continue to hide the guilty secret that is at its center and also because he clearly wanted to dramatize the murky psychological ambivalence of a sinner whose desire for change is mitigated by his clinging attachment to sin.

In "The Swimmers," which appeared in 1956, Tate adopted a narrative format, an unusual step in itself, in which he recalled an episode from his youth in the South. A black man had been lynched by some of Tate's fellow townspeople before the sheriff could arrive to prevent it. In the actual event the black man had murdered his landlord in the midst of an argument, but Tate suppresses this aspect of the tale in order to focus on the boy observer's awakening to the latent brutality of society. Stylistically, the poem is framed in concrete, rather imagistic language, again unusual for Tate, who tended to regard imagistic poetry, in and of itself, as superficial. As in the best imagistic poetry, though, Tate's descriptions carry their

themes within, making additional comment, however lyrical, superfluous. Structurally, Tate regarded the poem as incorporating the "archetype
of death and resurrection," as he wrote to Caroline Gordon in February
1956, a further indication of the merging of Jungian and Christian elements
in his thought in the 1950s.

The references to Christian archetypes are trenchantly set forth:

> Peering, I heard the hooves come down the hill.
>> The posse passed, twelve horse; the leader's face
>> Was worn as limestone on an ancient sill. (133)

Ironically resembling the twelve apostles with the black man/Christ as
their leader, the members of the lynch mob are pictured as betraying
their nominally Christian identity—("Jesus-Christers unmembered and
unmade") in deadly pursuit of their black, Christ-like victim (133). The
southern Fundamentalists who make up the vigilante group are depicted
as causing the death of Christ again in "dirty shame." Since they act
quickly and in relative secrecy, they are "unremembered"; more telling,
they are "unmade" by their acts, reduced to what Tate perceived as a
barbaric level, below that of nonbelievers.

The most innovative and symbolically important, though relatively
unobtrusive, section of "The Swimmers" is the stanza in which the boy
witness stares down at the pool that he had hoped to enter as an escape
from the summer heat:

> I gazed at its reticulated shade
>
> Recoiling in blue fear, and felt it roll
>> Over my ears and eyes and lift my hair
>> Like seaweed tossing on a sunk atoll.
>
> I rose again. Borne on the copper air
>> A distant voice green as a funeral wreath
>> Against a grave: 'That dead nigger there' (133)

Although the boy's entry into the water is psychological and vicarious
rather than actual, he is described as experiencing a resurrection of sorts,
having been initiated into violence and death. The basis for his sense of
being resurrected is never explained, but is presumably linked with his
lonely vigil at the end of the poem where he emerges as the only one in
the town to stand beside the black man's corpse. Tate is careful, however,
in structuring the above passage, to juxtapose the moment of resurrection
with the prosaic utterance of the sheriff in discovering the body. In this
way the resurrectional motif is prevented from rupturing the narrative

verisimilitude—although the event obviously had its effect in shaping the morally sensitive adult that Tate was to become.

"The Buried Lake," which is also set in tercets, centers on a holy female figure parallel to that of Saint Monica in "Seasons of the Soul"—in this case Santa Lucia or Saint Lucy, the "Lady of light." As her feast day falls in mid-December, Santa Lucia is also associated with Christmas and with the light associated with that important day. Since Santa Lucia is associated with curing blindness, "The Buried Lake" may be seen as a votive poem in which the speaker prays for such a cure.

With its archetypal associations, the title of the poem reflects Tate's interest in Jung. The speaker encounters the buried lake in a dream as a "sullen spectrum," a manifestation of the unconscious that not even the dreamer can fathom (136). In the dream he proceeds along the shore of the lake to a "pinched hotel" where a sick dog "coughed out a sickly cark / To let me in" (137). Seeing no one inside, he realizes nevertheless that he is there to play the violin—though he is cautioned by a small dancing girl not to play it: "She locked the fiddle up and was not there. / I mourned the death of youth without a word" (137). While Tate in his youth had been told that he lacked the talent to play the violin, the scene obviously conveys more than this disappointment, as the otherwise disconnected line about vanished youth suggests.

In Tate's Jungian typology, such images as the violin communicate much more than they appear to, in part because of autobiographical resonances that are only hinted at but also because their function is to be mysterious, quasi-universal keys to experience and trailing chords of memory whose overall contents are meant only to be approximated in favor of a more general tale of humanity's collective, religious unconscious. In a more practical sense, by relying on his dreams and memories as material for his poems in the 1950s, Tate attempted to overcome the writer's block that had all but staunched his poetic creativity.

Drifting onto Tate's dream stage in "The Buried Lake" comes the empirical philosopher John Locke, a contrasting, prickly presence—at odds, basically, with Tate's theism—who offsets sharply the poem's pervasive and melancholy surrealism. Following Locke, though, is the vision of a mysterious, stately woman, a figure from Tate's rose garden of the past, who causes indistinct remembrances of a no-longer-attainable love. The poem slowly descends into an inferno as the speaker decapitates the stately lady, whose head metamorphoses into that of Christ before sinking into hell where the "Head of God had sped / On the third day" (139). The severed second person of the Trinity, then, is interfused with Tate's own obsessive archetypes in this novel picturing of the harrowing of hell.

From this point on, the prevailing motifs are those of light and darkness in the somber December that Tate saw as the twentieth century. The poem is Tate's dark night of the soul:

> Deprived, poured stinging dark on cold delight
>> And multitudinous whined invisible bees;
>> All grace being lost. (139)

Toward the end, however, in answer to the speaker's anguished prayer, the poem becomes suffused with light:

> . . . light Lucy, light of heart—

> Light choir upon my shoulder, speaking Dove
>> The dream is over and the dark expired.
>> I knew that I had known enduring love. (140)

While the dove image applies to Saint Lucy, it also inevitably invokes the presence of the Holy Ghost, the third person of the divine Trinity, here symbolizing the integration of that Trinity, as it were, following the earlier grisly image of descent. This sort of radiance is unusual in Tate's poetry, which is otherwise relentlessly austere.

More than other twentieth-century Catholic American writers—such as Robert Lowell, for example—Tate was uncompromisingly philosophical in his view of Catholicism as a reality principle. Whatever the moral imperfections of the man, the intellectual fastidiousness that characterized his outlook as a poet and essayist together with the subtlety and refinement of his art distinguish him from all others. While Tate's poetry is intellectually consistent with his prose, in the poetry he used his imagination to reveal the psyche in its nonlogical, subconscious activities, even though this did not easily mesh with his Thomist framework. In the 1950s, in particular, Tate showed his openness to experience by probing the images of the subconscious for clues to his own nature and, with the aid of Jungian analysis, to being itself. If Tate's poems lack the consolation to be found in the poetry of writers such as Thomas Merton and William Everson, they are nonetheless astringent in their drawing of all things to God. Moreover, considering Tate's respect for rationalism, one is struck by his ability, finally, to submit himself before the ineffable—as in the characterization of Saint Lucy in "The Buried Lake"—in an eloquent admission of the limits of reason.

In 1954, Tate delivered a lecture to the Third International Congress for Peace and Christian Civilization in Florence. In that lecture he considered the state of contemporary American society in relation to Christianity and argued that the Jeffersonian democratic ideals that had animated American political idealism had been stripped of their Christian underpinning. In Jefferson's time, Tate noted, the "Christian sanction was still so powerful that men could take for granted its effectiveness in the political order." In the contemporary period, on the other hand, there had developed a "radical split" between the secular and the spiritual in American life, such that it was considered "dangerous to liberty" to entertain the idea of an "avowedly Christian culture."[18]

The result, in the view of writers such as Tate and Walker Percy, was a rampant materialism that has eroded the spiritual dimensions of the American ideology of individualism. In 1929, in a letter to Donald Davidson, Tate contended that the fragmentation and dilution of dogma evident in contemporary Protestantism would weaken its ability to withstand the dismissive exclusion of religion from American culture, leading to the domination of American culture by a "monistic," naturalistic science. In such a morass, Tate added, metaphysics and morality would become merely "private and irresponsible."[19] Tate's attack against this cultural malaise, in essays that are among the most judicious and polished in modern American literature, was to emphasize the stature and dignity conferred upon human beings by traditional Christianity and by Catholicism in particular through the doctrine of the Incarnation. In his poetry, Tate characteristically portrayed with measured but unforgettable anguish the betrayal—by himself as well as by twentieth-century American culture— of that gift of dignity to humanity.

18. Tate, "Christ and the Unicorn," 176, 177.
19. Davidson and Tate, *Literary Correspondence*, 224.

PAUL HORGAN

(1903-1995)

A S A CATHOLIC novelist and short story writer, Paul Horgan is noteworthy for his depiction of goodness, that ostensibly blandest of all fictionalized subjects. In a letter to Sean O'Faolain, written in 1966, Horgan observed that "goodness, heroism, patience, humility" were subjects that were as real and as suitable for the writer of fiction as more "fashionable and negative" ones. Horgan also once wrote that since suffering was "generic," while joy was "particular," it was easier to depict than joy. Horgan is not an ingenuous writer, and he was not inclined to overlook evil in his fiction. In this connection, as he explained in an introduction to the poetry of Witter Bynner, the "private sin" of the writer would surface in print sooner or later, and, fittingly so, he added, since the artist must represent "diverse" human nature.[1]

Moreover, grounded in Catholic incarnational theology, Horgan's conception of the good made ample room for the physical aspects of experience. The body, he wrote in an important essay, is the "vessel" of our being, the "agent of our love," our opportunity to know the beautiful. It is also our medium of "pain and joy" and of our "perpetuation through conjugal union," as well as being the source of our idea of the self and its "place in

1. Horgan to O'Faolain, May 22, 1966, Horgan Collection, Yale Collection of American Literature, Beinecke Rare Book and Manuscript Library, Yale University; Horgan, *Approaches to Writing*, 152; Horgan, "Critical Essay," 290.

nature." The body is the "temple," Horgan concluded, that one inhabits as both "votary and priest."[2] While the temple image recalls the scriptural admonition that the followers of Christ were temples of the Holy Spirit, both the image and the language surrounding it also suggest a temple to natural beauty. The ambiguity is expressive in a writer who, especially in novels such as *Whitewater,* straddled Catholicism and romanticism.

A Catholic all his life, Horgan dedicated his writing to honoring the "Creator of all life" and to seeking the "memory" of the first Creation in the "core of man's awareness." As Robert Gish observed, Horgan's outlook is that of a Christian humanist. In his celebrated biography of Archbishop Lamy of Santa Fe, for example, Horgan meticulously brought out Lamy's essential goodness, "of which probably he was mostly unaware," as Horgan stated in accepting the Campion Award in the 1950s. Similarly, in commenting on the art of N. C. Wyeth, Horgan paid tribute to the painter's wholesome rendering of the dignity of all things and praised the harmony illuminated by the artist between "God's inscrutable designs and our daily course on earth." Underlying Horgan's interest in the subject of goodness was a pervasive religious consciousness that he discussed in a letter to Virginia Rice in 1951: "I do not want to seem to be parading my Catholicism. And yet it is an integral and vital element in all my work, the most determining, I should imagine, even in my satirical efforts, and still present when not explicit."[3]

In addition to the high moral ground that Horgan attempted to cover, he exhibited an almost Jamesian respect for manners. In a book edited by Horgan about the English writer Maurice Baring, Horgan singled out Baring's "manners" as a Catholic apologist, which he contrasted with those of other English Catholic writers, including Chesterton, Greene, and Waugh. Horgan praised Baring's respect for opinions other than his own and his scrupulous echoing of the "sceptical world's case against the Catholic Church," a feature of Horgan's own writing. Baring, according to Horgan, believed that although religious faith eventually became inescapable, it was often, in worldly terms, a "catastrophe," even if a necessary one.[4]

Juxtaposed with Horgan's firm religious faith was a punctilious sensitivity to matters of both form and fact. In 1942, he wrote to Helen McAfee

---

2. Horgan, "The Abdication of the Artist," 269.
3. Horgan, "A Writer's Discipline," 32–35; Gish, *Paul Horgan,* 75–76; Horgan, Campion Award acceptance speech, May 2, 1957, Horgan Collection, Yale Collection of American Literature, Beinecke Rare Book and Manuscript Library, Yale University; Horgan, *N. C. Wyeth,* 12; Horgan to Rice, September 4, 1951.
4. Horgan, introduction to *Maurice Baring Restored,* 41, 42.

of the *Yale Review* that he had reinserted phrasing that had been edited out of a story because, he explained, it was "exact and true to what the alfalfa field in the sunlight appears to do." Even in those writings that drew almost exclusively upon Horgan's imagination, he maintained a meticulous respect for the way things actually looked and felt. In reflecting on the process of writing, for example, he affirmed the value of revision in achieving a "purity of expression" that can arise "only from exactitude."[5]

Horgan's fiction is characteristically enriched by precise descriptive detail. For example, in his 1955 *The Saintmaker's Christmas Eve*, which chronicles the ordeal of a nineteenth-century sculptor who delivers a statue to a remote New Mexican church for Christmas, Horgan describes a local custom that, though seemingly inconsequential, freshens the story immeasurably while anchoring it brightly in its historical setting:

> The church was decorated with fresh pine boughs. New candles were waiting in profusion to be lighted. The saint's niche in the altar was outlined with bright paper flowers and more paper flowers were arranged in bouquets. Did he know where the paper came from to make them? At Taos, during the fair last October, crockery from China, brought across the Pacific Ocean to Mexico, and shipped north in the yearly wagon train, had been unpacked from straw hampers. Every dish and cup was wrapped in Chinese paper—yellow, blue, pink, or green, and when an article was displayed, the paper was thrown on the ground. People of this town had earnestly gathered the rumpled little sheets and had brought them home to fashion for tonight.[6]

The patient placement of the detail about the paper flowers captures forever a distinctive but easily overlooked custom of the American Southwest while deftly underlining the faith of the settlers, a narrative rendering of grace building upon a nature already suffused with dignity.

The short fiction in his 1954 *Humble Powers*, the subsequent novels in the Richard trilogy, and his 1979 *Whitewater* are Horgan's chief contribution to Catholic American fiction. By far the strongest of the tales in *Humble Powers* is "The Devil in the Desert," which centers on an old French missionary, Father Louis Bellefontaine, who for thirty years had brought the sacraments and the Mass to Catholics scattered through the Southwest. Though the priest is too old to continue these arduous journeys, he craftily blocks his young religious superior's attempt to prevent him from setting out on what becomes his final circuit. At the heart of the story is Horgan's

5. Horgan to McAfee, April 3, 1942; Horgan, "Reflections on the Act of Writing," 4.
6. Horgan, *Saintmaker's Christmas Eve*, 64–65.

moral probing of the simple priest, who embodies the "humble powers" alluded to in the book's title.

Horgan's descriptive power can be observed in the scene in which Father Louis is bitten by a large rattlesnake, and in a delirious episode before dying, imagines himself talking to the snake as Satan. The debate with Satan arises not merely from fancy but also from the humiliating realization that the rattlesnake has ended the priest's attempts to prolong his usefulness, a recognition that is made more painful by the conscious- ness that in all probability no other priest will follow. The power of the scene derives not simply from the moral profundity of the debate but also from the beauty of the natural setting, which is inextricably linked with its deadliness. Horgan's language is wonderfully expressive in this respect. The scene in which the missionary dies is described as imbued with a "lacy shade" cast by tall bushes in which little "coins of light" fall over the priest through "intricate branches." Even in striking, the snake, which had approached "flowing in a dry glitter," is depicted as turning dust into "liquid light" as its coils lash the recumbent body of the priest.[7] Completing Horgan's harshly beautiful portrait of nature is the lulling music of the cicadas, which ironically help to conceal the sound of the approaching rattlesnake. If the created beauty of the world draws one to nature, Horgan appears to imply, the world is not, after all, one's final abode, and is in fact a test of one's ability to transcend the natural.

Horgan's astuteness in characterization is evident in the way in which he shows that Father Louis, now that the struggle to go on is over, yields with relief to his impending death, absolved by it both of his own imperfections and of his priestly mission. Imperceptibly, Horgan shifts the debate from the issue of the blocked course of the missionary's life to the power of evil. Facing evil literally, Father Louis concedes the paradoxical necessity of evil, which "must be done to death over and over again, with every act of life," for only by such acts, the old priest reflects, can "more life be made" (43).

Throughout the silent debate with the snake, Horgan shows Father Louis as displaying an insight that far surpasses his modest education, as can be seen in the following exchange:

> "Goodness is often performed without the slightest knowledge of
> its doing. But evil is always known."
> "Yes, I think more people know me than the other thing."

---

7. Horgan, *Humble Powers*, 37–39. All subsequent references to "The Devil in the Desert" are cited parenthetically in the text.

"But don't congratulate yourself upon that," said Father Louis, "for it always means one of your unaccountable defeats when you are known." (46)

Intuitively, with the inherent wisdom of his humanity behind him and with the grace of God in him—for it is doubtful that his limited education would have provided the knowledge—Father Louis articulates the Thomist idea that evil only attracts by appearing as a good and that, correspondingly, when it is recognized as evil, it loses its power.

Summing up his argument concerning the eventual triumph of good over evil, Father Louis refutes the snake's assumption of victory over him by arguing that, while the snake had prematurely ended his life, it did so only with the permission of God: "At these words the snake with the speed of lightning knew convulsion in its dread coils and with mouth wide open and fangs exposed struck again and again at the earth where the dust rose like particles of gold and silver" (48). The final imagery of gold and silver reinforces the motif of the marriage of beauty and evil, which is the result, theologically, not of the monopoly of evil over beauty but rather of the involvement of evil in matter, whose beauty nonetheless still bears the stamp of its creator. Horgan here silhouettes his Catholic consciousness of the moral neutrality of nature and of matter, which are only given moral significance by human engagement with them.

"To the Castle," a story in *Humble Powers* about the Allied advance through Italy in World War II, focuses on a Catholic chaplain who gives his life for a soldier who had earlier scorned the chaplain's relatively insulated participation in the war. What gives the story its narrative élan, however, is the unexpectedly comic language used to describe the chaplain as he runs to place his body between the soldier's and the enemy fire: "He ran to Gates, making a picture of supreme gaiety, if you looked at it abstractly beyond the connotation of what the machine-gun bullets had already done and were still trying to do. His dancing flight, his arms hugged to his side in their pumping motions, his twinkling legs, his bare head shining without its too-heavy helmet, made a hilarious defiance of the intelligence behind the machine gun on the platform below."[8] The novelty of the diction in part reflects the point of view of the witnessing officer, but is also a reflection of the author's imaginative perception of the chaplain's pious detachment from life, his affronting of the fearful power of death. It is a mark of Horgan's quiet realism, however, that he registers incisively

8. Ibid., 184. All subsequent references to "To the Castle" are cited parenthetically in the text.

the "hot spatter" of the machine gun bullets that found the chaplain and "packed him with death" (185).

Horgan had served as an intelligence officer, stationed in Washington, during World War II and was convinced that the Allied effort was morally justified. In the case of the Vietnam War, however, he wrote to Wilfrid Sheed in 1964 that, although he would not sign Sheed's antiwar petition, he would act independently to make his opposition to the war known to those who were in a position to influence public policy. In a subsequent letter, written to Virginia Rice in 1968, however, he observed pessimistically that those who violently suppressed political freedom had a "terrible advantage" over those who hesitated to use "force and killing."[9] On the whole, Horgan leaned toward the traditional Augustinian philosophy of the just war rather than the newer, nonviolent philosophy espoused by Catholic writers such as Robert Lowell, William Everson, Thomas Merton, and Daniel Berrigan, all of whom had been influenced by Dorothy Day.

Horgan's ambivalence is mirrored in "To The Castle," in which (although the Allied advance appears to have his moral support) the setting and symbolism nevertheless subtly undermine the justification for the war. The central symbol in this respect is the ancient castle that had been used as a fortress on and off through the centuries and was now manned by German soldiers: "There it sat under its eighth century of sky, the castle, alive once more with defenders, blindly restored to its first purpose, and rising across my path with its requirement of duty, beautiful, impossible, and brutally appealing" (168). The complexity of Horgan's moral vision here reflects not only his association with the military but also his tendency to weigh all sides. Because of this balance in his writing, his fiction is sometimes lacking in drama and force; what it lacks in these respects, however, it tends to make up for in discrimination and complexity, in shading and subtlety.

In the Richard trilogy—which includes *Things as They Are* (published in 1964), *Everything to Live For* (published in 1968), and *The Thin Mountain Air* (published in 1977)—Horgan wrote a connected series of novels depicting the maturation of a young man from his earliest years until his twenties, with a brief final view of him in middle age. While the three novels involve discrete plots and sets of characters, Horgan said that he regarded the novels as essentially one story. In each of the novels the point of view is calibrated to match Richard's age and experience. Like Horgan, Richard comes from an Irish and German Catholic background.

9. Horgan to Sheed, September 7, 1964; Horgan to Rice, summer 1968.

Another autobiographical inclusion is the bifocal setting, the northeastern United States (with its urban, sophisticated atmosphere) and the natural grandeur of the Southwest (where Horgan, like Richard, was forced to move when his father developed tuberculosis). It is noteworthy that we are never given Richard's last name, a sign of his representative value as one who measures off the stages of life. The impression is amplified by the epigraph for *Things as They Are,* which is taken from Sir Thomas Browne's *Religio Medici,* in which Browne speaks of lives that are lived over and over again.

In *Things as They Are,* which focuses on Richard's earliest years, the point of view is shared between the older Richard and his youthful self. Horgan's depiction of affluent Americans is somewhat reminiscent of Henry James and Edith Wharton. As in James's fiction, the impact of wealth is shown to have turned America into a plutocracy of sorts, a theme that is developed in *Everything to Live For.* In spite of his grandfather's restraint and modesty regarding the family's position, Richard is part of a social class that feels money has bestowed on them an extraordinary measure of freedom—only to discover the limits of that freedom in time.

Contrasted with the second and third volume of the trilogy, whose narrative strands are more sustained, *Things as They Are* is rather episodic and in this way symbolic of a child's view, which tends to center on incident. The incident of the alcoholic tramp is a case in point. While the man ludicrously exposes himself before Richard and the housekeeper, what Richard remembers of the event is the cruelty of the adults around him in punishing the man: "He tried to become a ball like a bear asleep in the zoo against the cold of winter, but they pulled his arms away from his head and between their hands they punched his head back and forth. They knocked his knees down from protecting his loins and kicked him there until he screamed silently."[10] Beginning with the simile of the bear, appropriate to a child's viewpoint, the passage traces the buildup of horror in Richard as he now sees not his own cruelty, which he had earlier discovered in his drowning of a kitten, but the cruelty of the adult world around him whose goodness he had unconsciously taken for granted. By objectifying evil in this way so that the young Richard does not feel its dark pleasures, Horgan deftly shows how the child can more easily arrive at a moral judgment of it.

Horgan also develops the slow awakening of moral consciousness in Richard through a series of episodes, including that of a mentally retarded

---

10. Horgan, *Things As They Are,* 28, subsequently cited in the text parenthetically.

boy neglectfully allowed to die of infection. A surge of moral consciousness follows Richard's learning, late in the novel, that his father's business
partner had treacherously entered into a partnership with another man.
What Horgan subtly exposes through the incident is the way in which evil
can attach itself to good. Thus, as the business partner deliberately and
crudely breaks up the friendship with Richard's father, Horgan shows
how the two families close ranks out of a loyalty that, good in itself,
nonetheless promotes evil in this instance.

Horgan's success in *Things as They Are* lies in his refined exploration of
the subtle and ambiguous interfusion of innocence and evil in childhood.
Balanced against the growth of conscience in Richard, for example, is the
undertow of childhood egoism. In spite of his later estimation of his Uncle
Dylan as a dullard, for example, Richard recalls having viewed the man
as simply his Aunt Bunch's husband. As such, he recalls, he "belonged
to my world, as she belonged," and, as long as they "remained fixed, any
relationships were accepted" (224).

Through the antiphonal structuring of *Things as They Are* Horgan juxtaposes the child's tenacious need for stability against those elements
that undermine it—principally, death. While the death that most engages
Richard's consciousness is his grandfather's, Horgan shows Richard's
initial encounter with the face of death as coming with the collapse of
the iceman's horse:

> one eye that I could see was open. A fly walked across it and there
> was no blink. His teeth gaped apart letting his long tongue lie out on
> the street. His body seemed twice as big and heavy as before. . . . From
> under his belly flooded a pool of pale yellow fluid—his urine—and
> from beneath his tail flowed the last of his excrement, in which I could
> see oats.
> . . . I imagined Grosspa's heavy death, with his open eye, and his
> loss of his fluids, and his sameness and his difference all mingled, and
> I wept for him at last, and for myself if I should die, and for my ardent
> mother and my sovereign father, and for the iceman's old horse, and
> for everyone. (142–43)

Delicately chosen, the words capture the overlapping consciousnesses of
Richard's boyish sensibility and the mature vision of the retrospective
adult, who treads carefully through his memories, trying not to obscure
his past by overlaying it with sophistication.

Raising the scale of pain and difficulty as his young protagonist passes
through childhood, Horgan centers finally on the most abject death of all,
the suicide of Richard's Uncle Fritz, who had been diverted from a priestly

vocation by family responsibilities and who had mourned the loss of his vocation ever after:

> In habiliments out of the stock of a theatrical costumer, Uncle Fritz was lying in state on his hotel bed, wearing a bishop's mitre, and a scarlet chasuble over alb and cassock, and a pair of gold-embroidered scarlet gloves. His hands were folded upon his breast and on his right ring-finger his large amethyst edged with diamonds had now become a bishop's ring. Over his face was a faint smile, even though his brows were drawn upward in shadowy sorrow. (94)

With elegant symmetry, Horgan sets off Fritz's failed vocation against the momentous church vigil in which Richard attempts to have God reveal to him whether or not he has a vocation. The sequence contains some of Horgan's best writing and is a literary monument of sorts in terms of the depiction of this kind of experience. Sitting in the dark and cold, Richard has, instead of a vision of God beckoning, a vision of hell:

> You could see in the red glass how the fires of Hell always looked, except that this glass was only one little pool of fiery light, and those fires were everywhere all about you. You could not count the bodies of the damned. In their legions, they were thrown upon each other, fixed in writhen positions upon red-hot rocks, and they were naked, men and women alike, as you had seen in your grandfather's copy of Dante's *Inferno* with plates by Gustave Doré. (184)

Balancing the two viewpoints of his central character, Horgan has the older Richard provide a retroactive stability by tracing his childhood vision to his grandfather's copy of the *Inferno*, but he yields to the sovereignty of the child's experience and to the perception that no amount of subsequent religious understanding will ever replace the terror of the night in church.

At the climax of Richard's vision, when the lips of Jesus, as the Infant of Prague, move at last, Horgan floods the scene with irony. Arresting the moving figure of the dead bishop atop his sarcophagus, the Infant of Prague assures Richard that the dead would stay dead, that though he had courted the dead in search of his destiny, God would not come to bring terror. Ironically, in the midst of his fright, Richard forgets to ask the speaking statue about his vocation, and the vision fades. The Gothic rendering of the scene hangs over the whole novel, dwarfing, in its emotional intensity, other aspects of the protagonist's development in much the same way as the death of the iceman's horse comes to dominate Richard's concept of death. In this way, Horgan silhouettes the extraordinary power of the imagination, by which Richard's subconscious experience far outweighs his conscious religious life. In contrast to Richard's night vision, for example, incidents such as the attempt by a Baptist woman to wean him away from Catholicism appear comparatively superficial.

The only other episode to sink as deeply into Richard's psyche is his preadolescent sexual attraction to his Aunt Bunch, whose full lips, "ever so delicate in their scrolling," arouse feelings which he will only later recognize (221). Given the various erotic relationships in which this aunt becomes involved, including one with Richard's father, Richard's possessive, sexual attraction to her in youth is portrayed in retrospect as both ironic and appropriate, a rite of passage subtly connected not only to the development of his male identity but also, through Aunt Bunch's connection with his father, to the continuity and similarity of life, which is the heart of Horgan's theme in the Richard trilogy. Without breaking the membrane of his young protagonist's consciousness through authorial intrusion, Horgan reveals in *Things as They Are* the primal psychic matter of youth, which ties humanity to both nature and to God, from whose prolific creational hand all had been derived.

In *Everything to Live For,* Horgan depicts the adolescence of his protagonist. The setting shifts to eastern Pennsylvania, where Richard spends the summer visiting with wealthy relatives. The novel exhibits a dramatic unity of place and time since the central events are clustered about the July 4 holiday, thus inviting the reader to contrast the aristocratic lives of the Chittendens with the egalitarian ideals that had marked the founding of the American Republic. Another important aspect of the setting is the season—summer—symbolic of Richard's age, a motif that is beautifully developed by Horgan in a lyrical style that pervades this second novel of the trilogy.

Horgan skillfully plays off the foreground summer setting against the autumnal motif associated with the inner lives of the Chittendens, especially with Max. In Max's diary, discovered after his suicide, Richard reads: *"when I see the death of the year transpire in such glory, why do I hesitate? Must I await my own autumn?"*[11] The autumnal motif is double-edged and reaches a paradoxical conclusion in the novel when the first chill and misty winds stimulate Richard's fundamental attachment to life as he begins to feel "zest for the season" (214).

While the aristocratic life of the Chittendens is portrayed as an ironic affront to republican ideals, Horgan, like James before him, uses the monumental architecture of the Chittenden estate and the Chittenden art

11. Horgan, *Everything to Live For,* 209, subsequently cited in the text parenthetically.

collection to suggest a level of civilization uncharacteristic of American culture: "On its crest was a heat-grayed fieldstone house. It had many wide chimneys rising from a great central temple which threw out long wings leading to lesser temples at each end. There was an impression of white columns and three browlike pediments at middle and ends. Woods broke up against the crest of the hill like great waves, leaving the top clear, except for formal planting" (8). Apart from the classical overtones of the temple image, suggestive of a refined but pagan beauty, the metaphor of the waves suggests that the house and its location were designed as a statement of triumph over nature, an ironic symbol in the case of the Chittendens, who are overwhelmed by nature from within, if not from without.

While Horgan's social views were rather conservative, he does take pains to expose the danger the Chittendens posed to America. In a letter written to Helen McAfee in 1931 from Clarksville, Tennessee, an area one associates with the agrarianism of writers such as Allen Tate, Horgan wrote that he preferred the historical stability of the South, where land stayed in the family for generations and there was respect for the "ancient ideas of responsibility to labor" and for the "importance of fixity in institutions."[12] The Chittendens, however, are described as oblivious of the needs of labor. Alexander Chittenden's father had blocked the development of limestone quarries in the area, not through any agrarian ideal, but simply through selfishness. In his default in administering his wealth and in thus looking out for those who were dependent on him, Alexander Chittenden is portrayed as little better. The example of Byron, who had a highly developed social conscience, in addition to high aesthetic standards, is recalled repeatedly in the novel in contrast to the ineffectualness of Alexander Chittenden.

Using a Gothic style, which is, however, on this occasion reflexively parodied, as in the titles of the Gothic thrillers turned out by the Chittenden librarian, Horgan depicts the elder Chittendens as barely clinging to life and as living insulated, futile lives that ineluctably draw their son, Max, toward death. Horgan blends aristocratic and Gothic motifs throughout the novel to underline his social and psychological themes. Marietta's setting fire to Max in childhood, for example, springs from her resentment that Max, dressed in a " 'long royal robe of red crepe paper,' " would not permit her to " 'be the queen' " (25). In the quarry lake at night, when Richard fears that Max may be drowned, he feels like a "prisoner

---

12. Horgan to McAfee, December 15, 1931.

in a palatial dungeon" (142). As the above passage implies, Horgan balances his outer and inner narratives by extending the aristocratic motif to Richard, who, in being invited to stay on at Newstead, feels a "treacherous lick of excitement," as if he had been "summoned to Court in France before the Revolution" (109).

The force of Richard's temptation arises not only from the Chittenden wealth but also from their representing a dominant American strain, the Protestant tradition, in contrast to his own minority position as a Catholic from upper New York State. He quickly becomes aware at Newstead that as a Catholic he is tolerated rather than accepted, though this merely intensifies his desire to identify with his surroundings. Ironically, Richard's Catholicism is precisely what Alicia Chittenden values in him in her struggle to save her son, Max. Horgan brings this out in a conversation between Alicia and Richard in which Richard says of Max:

> "But he knows much more than I do."
> "Perhaps—but what he knows isn't as good as what you know."
> "I don't know what that is."
> "How to live with what God has given you." (110–11)

Juxtaposed with Richard's desire to become one of the Chittendens, the passage is suffused with irony. All the same, Richard is moved to reflect gratefully on the immaterial riches of his own family, in particular on his parents' modest acceptance of life and the attrition that is inevitably a part of it, "sustained by their belief in the forgiveness of sin and their faith in the attainment of heaven" (111).

There are two other noteworthy incidents in the novel related to Catholicism. When, as a child, Max had been seriously ill, his nanny, a pious French Catholic, had secretly baptized him. When he got well, Max tells Richard stiffly, he washed it off with soap. The incident is interesting, not because of its sacramental significance, as might have been the case in Flannery O'Connor's fiction, but rather because of its psychological ramifications, its disclosing of Max's fundamentally closed nature, his narrow and ultimately desolate independence and isolation. This isolation is clearly hardened, though, by his guilt for his mother's grotesque injury. Moreover, convinced that forgiveness is impossible in his case, he doesn't seek it. Horgan subtly and circumspectly shows that beneath Max's rebellious behavior lies a spiritual despair that has an embittered pride at its core. Max symbolizes the reason that despair has been classically described in Catholic moral theology as the unforgivable sin, because the despairing soul does not seek forgiveness.

The subplot involving Max's sister, Lina, includes a further Catholic strand. Because of his susceptibility to the persuasiveness of the Chittenden point of view, Richard comes to perceive Lina, the wife of a minor Italian nobleman, as having been diverted from her proper course by her brief affair with and then forced marriage to the young Italian. If one accepts the Chittenden view of her, she became a Catholic in order to become part of her husband's family. While the reader is given little direct evidence of her situation, it would seem that she is happy and indeed that in leaving Newstead she escaped the sort of fate that overtakes her brother. Certainly, there are incestuous overtones in Horgan's portrayal of the relationship between Lina and her father that parallel the oedipal relationship between Max and his mother. An attendant irony is that apparently Lina's husband's appearance resembles her father's as a young man.

The reader is led to infer that Lina's Catholicism has taken root when she donates the Chittenden estate to an order of monks. With his eye ever on irony, however, Horgan details the tasteless renovation of the great house into a subdivided workshop and dormitory for married couples' retreats. The cultural devastation is vividly conveyed: "The library became the assembly hall of the Marriage Counseling Conference, where group retreats were held, and films were shown dramatizing marital problems which were used as a basis for seminar discussions" (212). Like Allen Tate, Caroline Gordon, Ralph McInerny, and Mary Gordon, Horgan bristled at the banality of some aspects of American Catholicism during the 1960s.

In *Everything to Live For,* as in much of Horgan's work, Catholicism is present not simply as a focus of action or ideas but as an undercurrent that shapes our view of everything else. This is true, for example, of the central symbolic episode in the novel, the night blooming of the cereus flower. As Alexander Chittenden has been reduced to a vicarious life as a student of Byron, so has his wife been reduced intellectually and spiritually to presiding over an absurd horticultural vigil. Furthermore, the vicariousness of Alicia's experience is given a sexual coloring by her son, who comments on the phallic appearance of the cereus plant. Moreover, with evocative phrasing Horgan succeeds in depicting the vigil, here seen from Richard's viewpoint, as a parody of religious experience: "We were at a small round table in a pool of lantern light. Behind us the high glass wall of the Crystal Palace rose to its pinnacles and domes and slopes like an iceberg. The lights within, reflecting off the airy greenery under the vault, had a greenish-blue cast, and turned the air into a likeness of underwater distances" (164).

The otherworldly light described is followed by the opening of the flower, which is in turn given religious significance through white petals that reveal a "mystery solved at last" and a "blessing" (172). The mingled, sexual aspects of the scene surface in Alicia as, in ecstasy, she feels "like the Cereus opening." The episode, which contains some of Horgan's most brilliant writing, absorbs all the witnesses, including Richard, who, afterward, finds it difficult to return to a conventional scale of time: "How," he wonders, does one "withdraw from a sacrament?" (173). Balanced delicately between the sacred and the sexual, and between self-consciousness and genuine emotional understanding, the effect of the incident is to lead Max and his mother to a momentary reconciliation.

Horgan also uses the scene to foreshadow Richard's later lovemaking with Marietta, his formal initiation as a sexual being. At that moment he feels himself to be the cereus plant, and after the "long sleep of neutral preparation," he feels himself falling through darkness until he enters the "kingdom of earth" (190). Horgan's masterful phrasing transforms the cereus incident into the imaginative center of his novel. In addition, a Catholic balance is implicit in Horgan's rendering of sexuality, which in the light of the Incarnation is fundamentally affirmed by the Catholic Church as a good even if regarded as illicit outside of marriage. Horgan's depiction of unmarried sex, for example, is viewed as a lesser evil in comparison with the destructive narcissism of the Chittendens.

In *The Thin Mountain Air*, the final novel in the trilogy, Richard is in his early twenties, and one has a greater sense in this novel of the larger public world that surrounds him. His father, for example, is depicted as prominently involved in New York State politics within the Democratic Party, a traditional choice for American Catholics. The tone of *The Thin Mountain Air* is appreciably more philosophical and settled than the earlier novels in the trilogy and the language appropriately a little less imaginative.

Attracted to the political idealism of Woodrow Wilson, about whom he hopes to write, Richard's father combines a highly moral political ideology with a strong religious spirit. Although Richard's father frequently attends weekday Mass and Communion, he avoids organizations like the Knights of Columbus. Horgan, like Robert Lowell, shows the intellectual Catholic in America as ill at ease with the cultural and social aspects of Irish American Catholicism. This elitist strain is also evident in Richard's attaching of himself to the touring Earl of Saint Brides and his family, who display the sort of aristocratic Catholicism portrayed in Evelyn Waugh's *Brideshead Revisited*. Polarized with this relatively sophisticated eastern setting, however, is the vast landscape of the Southwest with its natural grandeur.

A mood of melancholy is ubiquitous in *The Thin Mountain Air*, flooding both major settings, a foreshadowing of the death of Richard's father in New Mexico. Even in the East, the reader encounters the image of "piled leaves to be burned along the curbstones."[13] The opening somber atmosphere becomes heightened as Richard's father is diagnosed as having tuberculosis, and Richard suddenly realizes the changes this will produce in his own life:

> I began to say a prayer for us all, which summoned up images of the past, even from my earliest childhood, in the company of saints, sacraments, and guardian angels; the banks of lighted candles at Mass far away where the figures at the altar moved in all their gold and color representing powers which had nothing to do with hardness, but with hope, and a way to hope. Yes, I said, yes, God's will be done—but it was my will I was praying about. (41)

In contrast to the earlier parts of the trilogy, one notices Horgan's developing of self-consciousness and a salutary skepticism in his protagonist, all the while showing the continuation of his faith. When his father is dying, for example, Richard finds himself spontaneously confessing his sins to God in an attempt to stem the encroachment of death.

The panorama of the Southwest provides a theater of action whose monumental scale dwarfs the human beings who move across it. Thus, the plateau whose thin air ironically contributes to the death of Richard's father also appears as a luminous landscape containing miles of "diamond-clear light" and crusts of black lava that, against the horizon, resemble the "man-made deities of Egypt which seemed to become natural earth forms" (267). The creational grandeur coexists with the strong religious and particularly Catholic character of the Southwest, a reminder of the time when Catholic missionaries from various parts of the world were a prominent part of its history. Richard's father, for example, finds himself in a convalescent hospital operated by nuns who had arrived in the nineteenth century. The nuns, Richard notes, "established an early intimacy with us all," so that when he and his mother came daily to visit his father they were welcomed "as if we belonged to their family, as in their professional eyes and actual faith we did" (73).

While the Southwest is a more egalitarian setting than the East, Horgan makes it clear that a considerable social stratification had nonetheless set in. An oligarchy of white Protestant Americans who had supplanted Spanish landowners is portrayed as having effected a transition that led

---

13. Horgan, *Thin Mountain Air*, 6, subsequently cited in the text parenthetically.

to the original Indians in the area becoming strangers in their own land. Horgan offsets this bleak social picture, however, with one of his most attractive and powerful fictional figures, Don Elizario, a wealthy Mexican American landowner who, despite being an absolute ruler of sorts, has an agrarian philosophy and administers his affairs with dignity and fairness. The characterization of Don Elizario is an accomplished piece of writing in which Horgan depicts natural nobility interfused with aristocratic habits. The characterization of Don Elizario is enhanced by the respect he receives from the evangelical Christian, Tom Agee, who is Elizario's foreman. Agee, who shares Don Elizario's agrarian outlook, has also had his "values" sharpened through having to survive in the harsh landscape (143). Like Don Elizario, he himself has come, rather like the Egyptian monuments cited earlier, to resemble a part of the landscape.

Essentially, *The Thin Mountain Air* is a novelistic rite of passage in which the protagonist endures the death of not just one father but two. Memories of the sudden murder of Don Elizario are thus interwoven with those of the slow death of Richard's father. Furthermore, Horgan underlines the unity and symmetry of Richard's journey by having him return for his father's funeral Mass to the cathedral in the East where he had experienced the night of terror and vision in the first book of the trilogy. His entry into manhood is made possible, however, not simply by the death of the fathers in his life but also by the disclosure by Richard's father of an earlier adulterous affair. The confession from father to son frees the son from the paralyzing effects of his own sense of unworthiness so that he can become more actively involved in life, as his father had been. With such archetypal themes, Horgan once again brings out the universal aspects of Richard's story. The death and rebirth motif inevitably suggests the exemplary death of Christ and the incarnational theology that reaches into every aspect of Horgan's novel.

A major symbol in the novel, Niagara Falls, adds further to the archetypal design of *The Thin Mountain Air*. A symbol of the evolutionary journey of all life, the falls represent the "illimitable reservoir of past humanity" as well as the fall into death—conservation and entropy (287). Poised over the abyss between the flow of life and the plunge into death is the struggle for survival, a theme that Horgan embraces as readily as that of faith. For Horgan, faith builds on Darwin, and the theme of survival is portrayed frequently in the novel, as in the unforgettable description of the sheep-dipping trough:

> They must swim to live, all seventy-five feet of its length. They cannot scramble out of the dip over the sides, which are sheer, and eight feet deep. Struggling to keep their heads above the surface of the foul dip,

> the sheep make a continuous bleat. Their shorn legs lash, they survive by sheer terror and instinct. But not an inch of their skins is spared the treatment of the dip, for men with long poles which end in Y-shaped prongs are stationed at intervals on each side of the dip, and with their prongs, the men push every animal under the surface as it passes them. The sheep struggle against each other, tightly packed, choking and crying, lashing the dip mixture to spray which scatters upon the men. (178)

The syntactic suspension of clauses and phrases that mirrors the frantic ordeal of the sheep points up Horgan's stylistic mastery. With its broad scope and modulated styles, the Richard trilogy is Horgan's most distinguished work. With his eye on both the possibilities and the limits of virtue, Horgan convincingly traced not only the stages of growth but also the ascent of moral consciousness from the atavistic depths of the natural to the limned periphery of the supernatural.

While *Whitewater* is not a novel whose subject matter is peculiarly Catholic, it does eloquently embody Horgan's continuing interest in the theme of goodness. The scene in which a competitive team calls off a track meet following the tragic death of the opposing team's star athlete is a case in point:

> In the face of such goodness of spirit on the part of feared and hated rivals, many teachers, parents, and students of Belvedere felt in their hearts the sentiment of the psalmist, "Oh, grave where is thy victory," and the rest, and some even spoke the words, and felt their eyes smart. If they could not openly admit to the power of the psalm with its ancient feeling, they rubbed their eyes and exclaimed impatiently against the way the dust out of the sky pressed its way everywhere, even into your eyes, dust hauled up from the earth, their substance and their end.[14]

Characteristically, Horgan relates the goodness felt not only to the vision of the psalmist but also, in the concluding reference to the villagers' "substance" and "end," to his own Catholic conception of the good earth.

Filtered through the viewpoint of Phillipson Durham, Horgan constructs a historical axis in which the past and present of Whitewater are divided temporally into the lives of those who lived there before and after the flood and divided spatially into the lives lived above the water and below. In a modernist rendering of his setting, Horgan shows the past to be as fictive as it is real, beginning with Phillipson Durham's classroom

---

14. Horgan, *Whitewater*, 219, subsequently cited in the text parenthetically.

observation that the life that is mirrored on the surface of a lake can add another dimension to what is looked at, allowing one to see it in a "pure but dislocated way." Durham goes on to suggest that the mirrored perception resembles the past, "about which there is so much to learn and remember," while the present remains less open to analysis because of our "simply living" in it (3–4).

While the past may offer us another view of experience, it is subject, Horgan implies, not only to misunderstanding but to manipulation as well. Such is the effect of Durham's demand that Guy DeLacy destroy the erotic correspondence between Ben Grossman and Tom Bob Gately. Durham's motives are conspicuously moral, the attempt to save the reputation of a good and now dead man and to protect the marriage and reputation of a second man. Nonetheless, Durham's demand involves a conscious reshaping of the past, even if for a good end. In this way, Horgan hints at the subtler limits of human goodness, even as he affirms the virtue of his protagonist's action. In another part of the novel, Horgan suggests that it is not only moral interference that can restructure our view of the past but a moral reinterpretation of it can have a similar effect as well. Such is the case with Judge Cochran, who abandons his biography of Napoleon, based upon his revised sense of the French leader as a shabby "swindler," similar to Hitler and Stalin, who, out of vanity, destroyed the lives of millions (96).

Ever symmetrical in his structuring, Horgan shows that just as the present shapes our view of the past, so has the past shaped our view of the present. Hence, the suicide of Ben Grossman, eventually given a legendary status within Whitewater, foreshadows other such deaths, including that of Marilee Underwood. Similarly, the scars of Phillipson Durham's past, his ill-fated love of Marilee and involvement in the death of Billy Breedlove, are visible in his emotionally tepid, even if professionally successful, progress through middle age. Nevertheless, with considerable skill, Horgan contrasts the deterministic overtones of the relationship between past and present with the transcendentalism of religion and art. Staring at a painting by Manet in the Cochran house, Phillipson Durham is struck by the way in which the painting took the observer "farthest away, into its own existence" (88). While the scene in the painting and, indeed, the painting of that scene are an inexorable part of the past, they are also lifted from it through the timelessness of art.

Horgan's handling of the transcendentalism of religion, and particularly of Catholicism, is complex since he contrasts the moral ugliness of a number of his Catholic characters with the exceptional goodness of a young priest and a non-Catholic woman who embody the novel's spiritual idealism. Advised of the death of Billy Breedlove, for example, Mrs. Underwood, a Catholic, cannot conceal her relief. While one of the two priests in Whitewater, Father Judson, is sympathetically portrayed by Horgan, the other is portrayed as a rigid and tyrannical legalist who would have refused burial in consecrated ground for Marilee Underwood and would certainly not have permitted a memorial Mass to be said for Billy, a non-Catholic.

In contrast to Father Elmansdorffer's hollow priesthood, Father Judson, prodded by Marilee's mother to put a stop to the relationship between her daughter and Billy Breedlove, yields before the love that Marilee exhibits and, filled with misgivings, kneels down at the altar in prayer for the girl "who was helpless to help herself" (86). Even more highlighted by Horgan is the goodness of Thyra Doolittle, a woman of no particular religious background who is Tom Bob Gately's mistress. In spite of her nonreligious status, Horgan elevates her characterization by infusing it with theological language. Following her abortion, for example, Thyra is described as doing her best to "expiate" that "unborn death" by helping others (307). Similarly, apprehensive about the fate of Marilee Underwood, she tells Phillipson about the girl's pregnancy in the hope that he would be the very one to "redeem everything" (306). When Tom Bob Gately becomes helplessly bedridden after a stroke and is returned to the vindictive hands of his wife, Thyra is portrayed wandering desperately into a Catholic Church:

> She knew Catholics believed that when the red lamp was burning it meant God was there in the tabernacle. She knelt in the last pew and prayed through her shaking bones, in an act of love.
> "Oh God, You know I don't belong here, and I know I have no right to be heard, but oh, God in heaven, please, please, let him die" (278).

This presentation of Thyra's implicit faith, more sublime than anyone else's in the novel, silhouettes Horgan's open-ended religious conscious-ness. The characterization of Thyra is not ecumenical since that would imply the coming together of ecclesiastical organizations; it is universal, the touching of an individual soul by God, which Horgan, like Flannery O'Connor, doubtlessly regarded as a reflection of the Catholic doctrine of the baptism of desire.

Horgan's antithetical presentation of true and false religion continues to the end of the novel where Phillipson Durham attends a memorial Mass for his mother in the university chapel: "The human yet impersonal love of the tremendous words which he followed in his missal seemed to him to image eternity; and he was exalted in the thought of his mother received into unending light. Only such a reward could justify her life. He bent his head and felt that he understood the act of prayer" (330). Immediately following this exalted moment, Durham is accosted by the priest who said the Mass in the largely empty chapel, and the feeling of sublimity dissipates as the priest crudely attempts to recruit him into the priesthood.

If one compares the ending of *Whitewater* with the earlier fiction, one cannot help but be struck by the darkening of Horgan's vision of the church. In contrast with the heroic, religious figures in *Humble Powers*, for example, the church in *Whitewater* is portrayed, often satirically, as mundane and uninspired. Nevertheless, the religious idealism that absorbed Horgan throughout his career continued to burn beneath the surface—as is shown in the characterizations of Father Judson and Thyra Doolittle. Rather like Phillipson Durham, though, Horgan depicts heroism and intensity as part of a perception of the past, in somewhat the same way as the present citizens of Whitewater regard their underwater ancestors as superior people. The past in Horgan's fiction, though, includes not only the heroic missionaries of the American Southwest but also, as has been seen, a less conspicuous social history, which is exemplified in the unfolding of individual lives that begin with the psychic fires of childhood. Immersed in history, Horgan's writings portray how the mystery of God, never to be forgotten, is first encountered.

6

WILLIAM EVERSON/
BROTHER ANTONINUS
(1912-1994)

T HE CALIFORNIA POET William Everson, who wrote under the
name Brother Antoninus while he was a Dominican lay brother,
worked toward a synthesis of Catholicism and pantheistic romanticism. Exhibiting a sacral sense of landscape in the 1940s, Everson later
evolved toward a sacral sense of personhood, centered in Christ. As he
explained in a letter to Robert Bly, personhood gradually took precedence
in his thought over the immanence of the divine in nature, though both
remained salient aspects of his thought and art throughout his career.
Everson came to perceive Christ as the epitome of divine immanence,
with the rest of nature following along, as it were.[1]

In one sense the effect of Catholicism, to which he had converted in
the 1940s, had been to free him from having to overload nature with
significance, as he explained to an interviewer in 1975. Even in the early
years of his life in the monastery, though, Everson was only marginally
restrained in his attitude toward nature, as can be seen in the following
extract from a letter to the poet Kenneth Rexroth: "To the Christian, Nature
is merely the veil that is between the Bridegroom and the Bride; it is

---

1. Everson to Bly, May 22, 1964, Everson Collection, Bancroft Library, University
of California at Berkeley.

stripped aside for the naked act of love." While he points in the direction of a higher mystical love flowing from God to humanity through the personhood of Christ, his sense of the enchantment of nature is apparent in the letter. Focused ecstatically upon the doctrine of the Incarnation, Everson perceived nature, particularly in its local and concrete reality, as the "force" through which "God participates in the whole," as he expressed it in *Birth of a Poet*. Putting it in yet another way, Albert Gelpi observed that Everson surrendered to "primal experience" until at last it "yielded him the Christian mystery."[2] While for Everson nature represented divinity as the "other" in an external sense, it also represented divinity working in the mysterious depths of the psyche.

In its ruggedness, Everson's romanticism resembles that of Robinson Jeffers. "Ineradicable," wrote Everson in an essay titled "The Tragic Vision," was Jeffers's consciousness of original sin—even if sin was viewed as a "past evolutionary mishap." Also drawn from Jeffers was Everson's association of violence with nature. Violence, Everson wrote in *The Excesses of God*, is part of a "dynamic of change" that in its higher registers can be considered as a tension between the sacred and the profane. In a 1966 letter to the poet William Stafford, Everson related the violence in his own poetry to his preoccupation with the Crucifixion, a violence that resulted when "organic wholes" collided with a "reality that exceeds them."[3]

Everson construed the solution to the problem of violence to be found in the cross of Christ. In an important essay titled "Dionysus and the Beat Generation," Everson contended that on the cross one sees a symbol of a perfect synthesis between body and soul, instinct and intelligence, eros and agape.[4] Everson conceived of Christ on the cross as the uniquely successful example of a nexus between incompleteness and wholeness. For this reason, the figure of Christ is always a dynamic one in Everson, who associated the figure and influence of Christ with an insistent, insurgent force in Western culture. In this respect, Everson's poetry has much in common with that of Thomas Merton and Daniel Berrigan, both of whom wrote to him from time to time expressing their admiration for his poetry.

In Everson's writings, suffering is presented as a form of violence that is a prerequisite to mystical intuition. Everson derived this view not only

2. Everson, "A Conversation with William Everson," 8; Everson to Rexroth, January 15, 1954; Everson, *Birth of a Poet*, 165; Gelpi, "Everson/Antoninus: Contending with the Shadow."

3. Everson, *Earth Poetry*, 90; Everson, *Excesses of God*, 68; Everson to Stafford, September 24, 1966.

4. Everson, *Earth Poetry*, 24.

from his reading of Christian authors but also from his reading of Robinson Jeffers. In "The Tragic Vision," Everson described Jeffers as using pain, "as does the Christian poet," as the "primary separating agent" between the ego and God. Through such suffering the temporarily liberated soul could see God. Everson's emphasis on the revolutionary character of Christ and on the relationship between suffering and mystical awareness underlay the monastic poems of the 1950s. While his conversion dated from a Christmas Mass in 1948 in which he had an overwhelming consciousness of God's presence in the Eucharist, he also indicated in an interview in 1975 that, if it had not been for the pacifism of Dorothy Day at a time when he himself was being punished as a conscientious objector, his life might have taken a different course.[5]

The impact of Everson's admiration for Jeffers and of his ingrained romanticism led him at times to visualize a God of an almost Nietzschean kind, "beyond good and absolutely beyond evil," transcending every attribute that human beings could predicate of God. The dynamic nature of Everson's approach reflected a Dionysian view of experience: It was not Dionysus, he once observed, who crucified Christ, but a "rational Apollonian Roman governor" and his "religious counterpart," the high priest. Perceiving twentieth-century culture as reflecting a conflict between Apollonian and Dionysian forces, typified by the tensions within both Catholic and Protestant churches, he doubted the capacity of "fallen man" to formulate a cultural reconciliation between the two—unlike Nietzsche—arguing that only in the tragedy of Calvary was a "final catharsis" achieved. In a letter written to Harry Stiehl in 1958, Everson divided American literature into that written by Apollonian (James) and Dionysian (Whitman) writers, arguing that such cleavages were inevitable, as were the attendant hostilities, unless dissolved by the encompassing perspective of the Catholic faith.[6]

Reflecting on the poetry of T. S. Eliot, in a letter written to Lewis Hill in 1954, Everson regretted the influence on Eliot of the French, whom Everson regarded as part of the Apollonian tradition. In an unpublished essay, he also regretted the effort of Catholic poets such as Allen Tate to intellectualize their writing and to detach themselves from contemporary experience in order to return artificially to the "phantasm-character of medieval man." Feeling alienated from the minimalist style of a number of

5. Ibid., 91; Everson, "Conversation with Everson," 3.
6. Everson, *Excesses of God,* 56; Everson, *Earth Poetry,* 23, 26; Everson to Stiehl, January 6, 1958.

academic poets, Everson looked toward the Beat poets of the San Francisco renaissance. Though he did not share the agnosticism and liberal lifestyle of the Beats, he was welcomed by Kenneth Rexroth, who regarded him as "probably the most profoundly moving and durable" of the poets of the San Francisco renaissance.[7]

In accord with Beat poetics, Everson described his poetry as more of a process than a matter of formal construction. Nevertheless, he also favored a more oratorical tradition than the academic poets and felt free to use techniques like anaphora to amplify feeling. Although Everson is capable of achieving a fine imagistic precision, nonetheless, as he noted in a letter to Thomas McDonnell in 1961, he generally preferred to push past the objects and creatures in his poems to the absolute. At the same time, rather like Thomas Merton, Everson felt that being a poet was incompatible with the call to mysticism. In a letter to William Lynch in 1962 he observed that the mystic was happier than the poet and the philosopher because the mystic did not seek to formalize or to conceptualize his consciousness of unity with God but rather sought only to have his human nature "completely activated in beatitude." Everson thought of mysticism as arising from an anxiety produced by the soul's inner awareness that it did not possess the power to sustain its own existence.[8]

The only significant advance in mystical experience that Everson felt had occurred since the time of Saint John of the Cross or Saint Ignatius of Loyola had been the insights into the soul provided by depth psychology, by Jung especially. At the same time, in a letter written to Lewis Hill in 1954, Everson resisted the efforts of some twentieth-century writers to water down "supernatural reality" for the sake of "common intellectual ground," not because he felt alienated or aloof from contemporary thought but because he felt that the only way to achieve mystical union with God was to "whet" consciousness through fasting, penance, prayer, and "by far the most important, the sacraments." Later, Everson spoke more cautiously about mysticism, arguing in an unpublished manuscript about Whitman that while there was always some mysticism in sanctity, mysticism did not require sanctity.[9]

Although Everson tended to be more doctrinally orthodox in his views in the 1950s than he was in later years, he always affirmed the mythic value of religion. Not unlike Caroline Gordon and Thomas Merton, Everson

7. Everson to Hill, April 1, 1954; Everson, "Is the Modern Sensibility Defective?"; Rexroth, "San Francisco Letter," 8–9.
8. Everson to McDonnell, June 16, 1961; Everson to Lynch, April 14, 1962.
9. Everson to Hill, April 1954; Everson, "Whitman's Mysticism," 6.

emphasized the centrality of the Promethean archetype as a symbol of pre-Christian Western civilization, observing in a letter to Frederic Carpenter in 1968 that Christ was the "ultimate solution" to the Promethean problem, adding that even if Jesus were judged by some not to be the Redeemer, the world would inevitably be "waiting for the one who will do the same thing." In composing, Everson noted in *The Excesses of God*, the poet was also linked to myth, the "primal mythic ritual of creation." In *Birth of a Poet*, Everson stressed the importance of the poet as mythic shaman in a "flat," democratic, "non-hierarchical" society in which the ordeal of the hero comes under greater and greater stress since he has to take the place of the "whole hierarchy that isn't there." In the anarchy of values that inevitably befalls democratic societies, the poet, as Whitman and Stevens had maintained, becomes the priest, and like the priest speaks under the "aspect of eternity."[10]

In the 1950s Everson came to believe that one of the aspects of eternity lay buried in the underlying psychic archetypes that were universally present, according to Jung, in the mind. He was strengthened in this belief by his relationship with Father Victor White, the British Dominican theologian who came as a visitor to Everson's Oakland, California, priory in 1956. Father White, the author of *God and the Unconscious*, had known and studied Jung, and he had formulated the sort of accommodation between Christianity and depth psychology that would mark Everson's outlook more and more prominently after the mid-1950s. Apart from recognizing the depths of the psyche as a pristine area of divine creativity, Everson felt liberated by the discovery of the "anima," the female principle in himself, as can be seen in poems such as "The Encounter" and "Annul in Me My Manhood."

That Everson's commitment to Jung preceded his meeting with Victor White is clear from his correspondence—even if that meeting intensified his position. As early as 1950, for example, he had written to Naomi Burton-Stone saying that he was planning some autobiographical writing involving a synthesis of Jungean psychology and Thomist metaphysics. As late as 1960, Everson, in an unpublished manuscript, restated the Thomist/Jungian poles of his outlook, adding, however, that he regarded himself as Freudian in his emphasis on individual experience. While Everson relied on Thomist philosophy for general metaphysical knowledge, in an essay titled "The Presence of the Poet" he indicated that he used Jung

---

10. Everson to Carpenter, July 22, 1968; Everson, *Excesses of God*, 105; Everson, *Birth of a Poet*, 94, 127.

to supplement that knowledge in yielding insight into the "infra-rational" areas of being where neither Aquinas nor most Christian poets, including Hopkins, he felt, had ventured.[11]

Given the branching of Everson's thinking into such exotic areas, as well as the sexual candor that was to mark his work, he was continuously surprised by the ease with which ecclesiastical censors accepted his manuscripts. In retrospect, he marveled at the freedom that his order had granted him, even in the case of *The Rose of Solitude*, which drew fire from many Catholic commentators. Even after he ceased being a Dominican lay brother in 1969, Everson looked back on his years as a monk with the feeling that, as he had expressed it in 1956 in a lengthy autobiographical narrative called *Prodigious Thrust*, published in 1996, the monastic years had been an "extraordinarily stabilizing force" in his life.[12]

Published under his religious name of Brother Antoninus, *The Crooked Lines of God*, published in 1954, reflected in its title Everson's startled sense of having been lifted by his vocation out of a habitual, passionate contact with women into the life of a celibate monk. Thus, the poems tend to reflect his bewildered consciousness of his state. Even before his entry into the religious life, the oddity of his situation had struck him during the year when he worked in Maurin House, one of Dorothy Day's Catholic houses of hospitality for the poor. In "Hospice of the Word," the speaker wonders about the appropriateness of the shabby house for the poor as a setting in which human beings were implicitly invited to feel their spiritual link with God, who to Everson was perfect beauty:

> In the ventless room,
> Over the beds at the hour of rising,
> Hangs now the smother and stench of the crude flesh;
> And at the grimed sink
> We fill the basin of our mutual use,
> Where our forty faces, rinsed daily,
> Leaves each its common trace.[13]

On subsequent reflection the speaker concludes that the shabby rooms of Maurin House were a more suitable site for the presence of God than the houses of the rich:

11. Everson to Burton-Stone, June 21, 1950; Everson, "The Artist and the Religious Life," 1; Everson, *Earth Poetry*, 115.

12. Everson, *Prodigious Thrust*, 20.

13. Everson, *The Veritable Years, 1949–1966*, 88. All subsequent quotations from Everson's poetry are from this volume and are cited parenthetically in the text.

For in the crucible of revulsion
Love is made whole. St. Francis
Ran on gooseflesh toward the leper's sore
He saw his God. (89)

Anchored solidly in its physical details, the poem reaches a high point of paradox and wit in the image of Saint Francis running toward the leper's sore, thereby undercutting the speaker's earlier mood of aesthetic discomfort.

Everson explored the unnaturalness of his calling as a lay brother in "The Falling of the Grain," a poem that juxtaposes spiritual asceticism, or death of the body, with sexual "dying":

Wrapped to the branch the runner
Rings its yearly span.
Man is made for the woman.
And woman for the man. (53)

The balladlike quatrains reinforce the notion that the speaker, in adopting celibacy and asceticism, is going against the wisdom and practice of the ages. The second stanza makes the theme even more pronounced with its graphic, phallic imagery:

Stalk of the weed is stiffened,
And stands, and will be dried.
But the Word of God is prior;
It may not be denied. (53)

While the alternating rhyme unites the stanza, the imagery and tone divide it, dramatizing the hierarchy between nature and God.

The middle of "The Falling of the Grain" breaks into free verse as the speaker relies on the goodness of God to see him through the mysterious journey he has undertaken:

Only the flawed of heart foul Him.
Only the blind, a fist pitched at the sky,
A mouth smoky with imprecation;
Or that sullen hutch of the heart's embittered brood,
Like the serpent's egg
Hatched out in the breast. (55)

While the speaker adopts a pious stance, the tautness of the tone and imagery stem the loosening effect of the free verse. The violence of the image of the "fist pitched at the sky," for example, which recalls Marianne Moore's well-known poem about the armadillo, suggests a Promethean undercurrent that is only partially alleviated by the speaker's submission to God. The same might be said of the infernal image of the mouth, "smoky with imprecation."

The resolution of the underlying tension occurs when the motif of blood replaces that of the seed as a symbol of spiritual fertility. Drawing on his own expert knowledge as a bookbinder, Everson recalled the blood that spurted when the binder, "too rough with the needle," pierced his hand, letting blood fall onto the book, resulting in the rejection of the marred leaf. The blood of renunciatory suffering, both in himself and in Christ, is presented as of a different order, and the speaker prays that the book of his life may be

> Quenched in that brighter Blood,
> Which burns, and is the true
> Letter of life,
> And pure on the page
> Makes up the rare
> Rubrication of the Word. (58–59)

With a deft projection of ambiguity, Everson implies that the rubrication of the word is rare in more than one sense. For one thing, pages with blood on them are usually discarded; more important, though, the living of the Word of God, which leads to suffering and even death, is rare indeed. Finally, the red coloring recalls the medieval illumination of Scripture, which Everson had earlier attempted to emulate in the production of his Psalter.

At the end, the poem returns to the balladlike stanzas and seed motif with which it opened, bringing it full circle:

> And all creation will gather its glory up
> Out of the clouded winter-frigid womb;
> And the sudden Eye will swell with the gift of sight,
> And split the tomb. (61)

The return of the seed image, even in its sublimated form as the eye of faith that will overcome death, indicates the profound feeling of continuity that, in spite of the tension in the poem, characterized Everson's passage from the secular to the religious state. Implicit in the seed motif is its earlier sexual significance, a sign that Everson was not at war with his earlier sexual life but committed to transcending it.

Similarly, Everson, as Brother Antoninus, attempted to come to terms with his earlier pantheism without rejecting it outright, as in "The Screed of the Flesh":

> As the greyhound runs, as the jackrabbit runs in the jimson;
> As the kestrel flies, as the swamphawk flies on the tules;
> As the falcon stoops in the dawn, as the owl strikes in the
>   dusk;
> I flew, but I never knew the face of the Light that I flew in. (63)

While drinking in these natural scenes, the speaker nevertheless registers a distinct theistic awareness in the image of the "face of the Light," the capitalized letter being especially significant here. A further source of detachment arises from nature's contentment with death:

> As the earth wants back the ash of the
>   grass in the smoking fields of October,
> When the sun-struck face of the hill is
>   burnt to make for the pastures of spring;
> As the earth wants back the black on the
>   rocks when the hill is burnt for pasture. (65)

The precision of the imagery, which gives the poem a fine luster, reflected Everson's ready knowledge of natural detail, gained in part from his early years on a farm. Furthermore, the long, measured lines with their embedded repetitions convey an oratorical amplitude that is characteristic of Everson, whose sweeping vision lent itself to a wavelike expansiveness.

In "The Screed of the Sand," Everson retrospectively confronted his earlier romantic dependence upon the heart, visualizing it somewhat contemptuously as a sandstorm sweeping the "vineyard at year's change" (72). While the heart brought emotional excitement, Everson came to believe, it failed to bring wisdom; God, on the other hand, is described as bringing rain that comes "far" and "deep" from a place eyes "never have looked on" (72). Everson's revisionary distrust of the inward gaze is accompanied by a cautionary, unromantic recognition of the effects of sin in "The Screed of the Frost."

In poems such as "Peter Martyr" and "Triptych for the Living," Everson manifested his pleasure with Catholic incarnational theology, which he saw as tracing a continuum from the natural to the supernatural in a manner that paralleled his own ascent from pantheism to monasticism. One of the most successful of his devotional poems is "A Canticle to the Waterbirds," which first appeared in Dorothy Day's newspaper, the *Catholic Worker*, in 1952. During the period of the poem's composition, Everson recalled, he could not have been in a less literary frame of mind since he had been immersed in a discipline of "unmitigated prayer."[14]

---

14. Everson, *On Writing the Waterbirds*, 66.

Philosophically stratified in viewpoint—as opposed to Everson's earlier anarchic pantheism—the poem presents the waterbirds as representing a different level of being from either God or humanity, yet as instinctively carrying out God's secret purposes. It is noteworthy that the speaker in the poem seems serenely unconcerned with the Darwinian pattern that dictates the life and death of the birds:

> Wholly in Providence you spring, and when you
>   die you look on death in clarity unflinched,
> Go down, a clutch of feather ragged upon the brush;
> Or drop on water where you briefly lived, found food,
> And now yourselves made food for His deep current-
>   keeping fish, and then are gone:
> Is left but the pinion-feather spinning a bit on the uproil
> Where lately the dorsal cut clear air. (85)

There is no questioning here as to what kind of God would create a world in which predation was the rule; Everson's reading of Jeffers had already predisposed him to accept such a God. The new element in Everson's picturing of divinity is the providential character of God, accepted here on faith as touching both the birds and, implicitly, Everson himself. The rationale provided for God's creation of the animals is that they were designed to symbolize creaturehood to humanity, thereby illustrating the obedience that God wants from free human beings and that, by contrast, is biologically encoded in animals.

The related theme of humanity's dominion over the things of the earth is taken up in "The Making of the Cross," one of Everson's better poems. Grounded in vividly exact images of the natural world, the poem dwells on the origin of the materials that went into the making of Christ's cross:

> Rough fir, hauled from the hills. . . . that tree went over
> Bladed down with a double-bitted axe; was snaked with winches;
> The wedge split it; hewn with the adze
> It lay to season toward its use.
>
> So too with the nails: milleniums under the earth,
> Pure ore; chunked out with picks; the nail-shape
> Struck in the pelt-lunged forge, tonged to a cask,
> And the wait against that work. (32)

With a patient and observant eye, Everson depicts first the neutrality and then the useful goodness of the wood and iron as well as the ironic, destructive purpose that lies before these materials, all of this conveyed through orderly language that symbolizes the workmanlike behavior that human beings are capable of even in the performance of savage deeds.

Anticipating the later poetry of erotic mysticism, though more delicately crafted than much of the later work, is the long poem "The Mate-
Flight of Eagles." Although the poem is ostensibly set in Palestine, the
eagle imagery suggests an American landscape, thus integrating Everson's primary subject, the Crucifixion, with his own environment. The
first section, "A Savagery of Love," begins with a portrayal of violence
and sexual passion in the superimposed images of the mating eagles and
the cross. The eagles in turn are linked with Mary Magdalene, to whom the
poem is dedicated, who symbolizes both sexuality and suffering as well
as a higher spiritual love. The violence of Everson's symbols reaches an
outer limit of sorts when the soldier's lance, driven into the side of Christ
at Calvary, is compared with the phallic advance of the groom toward
the bride, the wound of love inextricably entwined with the wound of
suffering and sacrifice:

> Beautiful,
> Clean,
> A movement matchless and sublime
> As the glide of a dancer,
> Homes to its perfect place. (99)

These beautifully fashioned lines capture Everson's ecstatic sense of the
triumph of Christ's pain and of God's love for humanity. Reciprocally, the
passionate and swift mating of the eagles symbolizes the soul's mysticism, the "grappling of the soul in its God" (100). The radical violence
of the conjoined symbols served to provide mystical experience with
a dynamism that Everson felt other poetic renderings of it had lacked.
Repeatedly, the image of the phallus striking against the hymen becomes
the archetype of religious consciousness. The archetype is raised to represent salvation history itself in the image of the cross of Calvary tearing
a "hole in the sky," a literal reference to the scripturally recorded opening
up of the heavens as well as a bold, implicit use of the cross as phallic
symbol (101).

In the second and larger section of the poem, which opens with a
passage from Saint John's Gospel—containing the central motifs of spirit,
water, and blood—Everson generates a diversity of poetic formats, united
by a refrain, to further develop his polarized themes of pristine creation
and human depravity:

> Adam's old intransigence
> Fishhooks down time
> To jerk the God-man on the wristed nail. (102)

The writing is incisive: the word *fishhook,* for example, precisely evokes the compelling temptation of sin down through the ages, just as the word *wristed* captures the recoiling, atoning action of Christ's pierced wrist on the cross.

In the second section, the cross once again becomes the symbolic nexus of a driving world of physical generation and a supernatural, sacrificial love:

> Tall on his Tree of Life
> His gritted gasp, the long
> Life-going, pants its full pang,
> And breathes into earth's lung.
> The seedcake of his kiss
> Is tongued in the Beloved's lips,
> Given in the Lover's gift. (104)

The image of the seedcake nicely merges the continuing erotic motif with the spiritual rejuvenation of Creation effected by the cross, as the divine seed is infused into the female earth and female human soul, a Jungian touch.

In the second section of "The Mate-Flight of Eagles," narrative and expository materials are skillfully interwoven with lyrical elements, producing a richer texture than in the earlier part. The cry of the refrain ("Come, my beloved"), for example, tenderly depicts the sterile earth awaiting the coming of Christ in a manner that recalls Whitman's famous image of the hermit thrush:

> And everywhere that music,
> Where the moon-mad bird,
> High on the pepper tree,
> The mocker,
> Broke all night his tortured heart,
> Broke his love-tormented song,
> Tossing himself in the moon-drenched air,
> The mad song of that love. (106)

Anaphora and gerund generate a sense of the continuous present that allows the cross to permeate all time. Also reminiscent of Whitman is the use of apostrophe ("O mystery! Deep fragrance / Of the disrobing earth") as the poet recalls his earlier pantheistic search for God (107). The language melts under the touch of the speaker's remembrance:

> Shuff-stoned, soft through shade
> Slupped, of the wet-worked world.

> Sought so to quench all ardor up,
> Shining, in shapes
> Froth-forthed of earth,
> Nor yet to find, shape-slack. (108)

The invented, sibilant words evoke the nonconceptualized beauty of the earth that had drawn Everson's affection as a young man at the beginning of his journey to God. Everson depicts Christ as a dynamic fertility god in whose fervid embrace the "birth-panged earth / Hurls and uproils" (112). Even more striking is the symbolizing of the speaker's soul as a hymen breached by Christ: "Christ-crossed I bleed. / I am One" (116). Through its arresting juxtaposition of symbols the poem marks a high-water mark in Everson's poetry.

Although published only after he had left the Dominican order, Everson believed that the long poem "River-Root," published in 1957, reflected an orthodox faith in spite of the sexual explicitness that had caused him to delay its publication. Centered on the lawful sexual union of husband and wife (a reminder of Everson's earlier married state), the poem consecrates sexual energy in a way that Everson felt that Beat poets such as Ginsberg, who affirmed unlimited freedom, did not, and in a manner that challenged Aquinas's polarizing of sexuality and contemplation. The poem is bound together by the priapic symbol of the river that both unites male and female and carries them in an upward spiral to the love of God while allowing them to keep in contact with the subterranean biological and psychic worlds that move them toward love. In this sense, there is no Platonic thinning out of eros as the experience of agape is felt, but rather at the peak of the lovers' awareness an affinity with both heaven and earth is experienced.

The long, expansive lines teem with a panoply of animal life:

> Deep down under
> The snapping turtle sulks in his cutbank hole. Over his head
> Bigmouth bass break water for joy. Far back on the bayou
> One bull frog swells his organ-note gong: the syllable of desire
> Booms over the bog.
> And the River runs. (131)

Crowning this pageant of creation is the sexual union of husband and wife, which Everson describes in slow, sensual detail. As the speaker experiences an inner wholeness in contemplating the cross in the first section of the poem, so do the man and women in a love that evolves into a spiritual union as the two become aware of the majesty of Creation:

> For over the bed
> Spirit hovers, and in their flesh
> Spirit exults, and at the tips of their fingers
> An angelic rejoicing, and where the phallos
> Dips in the woman, in the flow of the woman on
>   the phallos-shaft,
> The dark God listens. (140–41)

Though one can appreciate the concept at the heart of the poem, the power of Everson's portrayal of sexuality weights the lovers' contact with the divine toward a gratitude for the gift of life rather than toward mystical knowledge. Nevertheless, the language is carefully modulated to evoke sexual pleasure while connecting it with larger aspects of Creation.

While he wore the habit of a Dominican lay brother, Everson exhibited complex and, some might say, antithetical attitudes toward the physical world. If on the one hand he wrote poetry that related sexuality to divinity, his view of his own vocation as a monk was strenuously ascetical at times. In 1956, for example, he temporarily left the priory when his fellow Dominicans installed television, the last straw, he felt, in a gradual relaxing of the rules. Moreover, in spite of Everson's lapse into an affair in the 1960s (which was recorded in *The Rose of Solitude*), he was conservative in outlook, writing to Frank Sheed in 1957, for example, about his opposition to "liberal intellectual Catholics." In August 1957 he wrote to Father Victor White to complain that the three traditional elements of the Dominican way of life—study, liturgy, and monastic observance—were being eroded. In an earlier letter to Victor White, who had become his spiritual advisor, Everson also wondered about the harmfulness of his public poetry readings, which undermined the solitariness of his contemplative vocation.[15]

Even after leaving the Dominicans in 1969 in order to marry, an action that, as a lay brother, presented Everson with relatively few complications, he objected to those who wanted to allow the clergy to marry. While conceding that celibacy was not inherent in the archetype of the priest, he argued in an unpublished essay on celibacy that it conferred an important "added dimension," separating the priest from the secular society around him. In a wider context he objected, in another unpublished essay, to the "aesthetic of skepticism" embedded in modernism, contending that for this reason both religion and politics were ill served

---

15. Everson to Sheed, June 4, 1957; Everson to White, August 10, 1957; ibid., June 4, 1957.

by modernist thought and that both spheres demanded "affirmative passion."[16]

Everson's scrupulosity can be seen in the introduction to *The Hazards of Holiness*, published in 1960, in which he cautioned that many a saint and many a mystic had mistaken the devil for Christ, and Christ for the devil. What hope, then, he wondered, for the religious poet who sought to register his spiritual wrestlings and terror? On the other hand, as Everson explained in a letter written in 1958 to Paul Carroll, the editor of *The Chicago Review,* he had come increasingly to regard evil as that which had to be encountered and passed through on the soul's journey to God.[17] *The Hazards of Holiness* is Everson's dark night of the soul, reflecting in part the tension between the sexual promptings of his nature and his celibate vows. The greatest despair, however, issued not from Everson's desire to be purified of sin but rather from his fearful consciousness of the withdrawal of God, as can be seen in "A Siege of Silence":

> What storms of the dredgèd deep
> Your absence lets, the rock-croppage mind,
> Kelp-girthed, sunken under swell,
> All seas of the unislanded soul
> Typhooned, hurricaned to hell! (167)

With its violent images, augmented by Everson's extensive use of the caesura, the passage all too vividly conveys the picture of a soul in torment.

One of the most unsettling of the dark night poems is "A Frost Lay White in California." In an unpublished manuscript titled "Poetry and the Dark Night of the Soul," Everson said that, although the poem dealt with the aridity of the soul, it did so in the final "resolving stages of acceptance and assimilation" rather than in the initial stages in which the "terrors of the opened unconscious" threatened to "swamp" the ego. The title conveys the central dichotomy of the poem—with frost symbolizing coldness, rigidity, and aridity while the California landscape otherwise evokes an impression of warmth and fertility. The poem is framed dramatically as a dialogue between the soul and God (with God's voice represented in italics). The setting is the Dominican chapel at night in the coldest time of the year where the speaker is determined to encounter God, who is

16. Everson, "Letter on Clerical Celibacy"; Everson, "Rhetoric and the Poetry of Protest."
17. Everson, *On Writing the Waterbirds,* 46; Everson to Carroll, April 19, 1958.

revealed as the unconscious: *"I am that void behind your eyes"* (182). The most arresting language in the poem is that in which the voice of God approaches Everson, seductively, as a woman, courting the soul, and then as a dog, abased before the speaker, who has ironically felt abandoned by God. The effect is paradoxically to turn the speaker, as dawn arrives, toward the world of Creation and toward that holy human history in which God had been immanent:

> The light woke in the windows.
> One by one the saints existed,
> The swords of their martyrdom healed in their hands.
> The linnet opened his voice;
> He blistered his throat on the seethe of that rapture. (185)

Employing a pathetic fallacy, Everson concluded his poem with the falling of rain, symbolizing the end of the soul's aridity:

> Into the frost,
> Into the frozen crotches of the bush,
> Into the feather of the singing bird.
>
> Across the stuttering mouths of those seeds;
> Against the sob of my tongue. (186)

On the one hand, while Everson celebrated the divinity that is embedded in nature, even in granite in one of the poems, he also affirmed the explanatory power of the transcendental God, whose voice is audible through Scripture, the church, and through mystical communication. While the dark creative hand of God is *felt* in nature, nature is mute. Revelation and mysticism are thus perceived as the roads to a further illumination of reality. A third route is that through dreams and the subconscious, the Freudian/Jungian landscape that is intermediate between the dark, instinctual movement of nature and the meaning conveyed by intelligent life. In "The Song the Body Dreamed in the Spirit's Mad Behest," Everson attempted to reconcile the natural and supernatural poles of his thinking by creating a violent incarnational theology in which God plunges into the soul with all of the sexual appetite of an ancient Greek deity. The effect is once again mixed, with the reader quickly caught up in the surging of the eroticism but finally unconvinced about its representation of mystical union. More persuasive are poems such as "All the Way to Heaven," in which the speaker wrestles, in vain it often seems, against the enemy within:

> Man walks: a demon
> Smirks, crouches
> On his shoulder,
> Clots his ear.
>
> Man sleeps: a demon
> Hulks, debouches
>
> In his brain. (165)

Here the subconscious, now seen from an ascetical perspective, reeks with sinful contents. The choppy rhythm and blunt, grotesque images all too readily convey the weight of sin on the soul in a way that recalls the truncated lyrics of Stephen Crane. The poem ends with an abject confession of Satan's power over the speaker: "I bear thy obscene vision in my breast / And tread thy mill with staves upon my neck!" (166) Thus, the antithesis between a Freudian, guilt-ridden picture of the subconscious and a Jungian/religious view of it alternate in Everson's poems as he attempts to reconcile a vigorous monastic spirituality with a lingering romanticism.

One of the most conspicuous reconciling symbols in *The Hazards of Holiness* is that of the Blessed Virgin, possibly because through her virginity and fruitful womb she united the otherwise opposed elements of a sensuous naturalism and spiritual transcendence. The "Canticle to the Great Mother of God" and "Who Is She That Looketh Forth as the Morning," written in the late 1960s while Everson still wore the habit, are examples of Everson's tribute to Mary. Set in traditional quatrains with end-stopped, alternating rhymes, the second long poem to Mary contrasts with the looser Whitmanesque dilation of the "Canticle to the Great Mother of God." In both poems the sea is used as the matrix for Mary's appearance, evoking the image of Venus as a sensual archetype and conveying the blue color, which is customarily associated with Mary. Though the sea imagery shows Mary as immersed in nature, she is also depicted in "Who Is She That Looketh Forth as the Morning" as magisterially in control of it:

> Lips glitter prophecies in waterlight,
> Chromatic glints, bright oceanic flame,
> Presaging triumphs and the doom of kings;
> They sigh submission when she breathes their name.

The image of "waterlight" beautifully captures the simultaneously immanent and transcendent aspects of Mary with its blending of temporal and ethereal nuances.

The carefully modulated shift from the portrayal of Mary in an orthodox context to the portrayal of her as a Jungian archetype is effected in a novel manner through the creation of a Gothic atmosphere:

> Upon a night of geysers by a sea
> When the dead lay listening in their soundless pall,
> And angels, fallen, shrilled the monody,
> Strophe on strophe of their ancient gall.

The surreal language, amplified by the long, haunting vowels, prepares the reader for a view of Mary arising out of the ocean of the unconscious. Furthermore, as is often the case in Gothic fiction a sexual undercurrent is embedded in the surrealism:

> Prey of the lightning flash she dropped, consumed,
> A votive-victim and a sacred feast;
> Spun to the black and leopard-throated wind,
> The Spirit cupped her like a roaring beast.

Everson's depiction of the insemination of Mary by the Holy Spirit more nearly resembles the union of Leda and Zeus than any familiarly Catholic version of that mysterious dogma. What Everson wanted to establish was the seamless relationship between Creator and creature, the one the image of the other, so that God can be perceived to be as readily existent in matter as in spirit or, in terms of the figure of Christ, in matter/spirit. The problem again, though, is that, from a religious perspective, while Everson's language is original and boldly imaginative, it is so largely in its depiction of physical passion. Everson's descriptions of spiritual (rather than psychological) states are comparatively attenuated in comparison with writers such as Thomas Merton or Flannery O'Connor. Furthermore, even seen as a subconscious drama involving the animus and the anima, the divine impregnation of Mary is rendered largely from a male point of view.

After the early 1960s, Everson turned increasingly toward non-Christian themes, reverting in the poetry written after 1969 to an ecologically sensitive version of his early pantheistic romanticism. In his poem "The Poet is Dead," for example, which appeared in the early sixties, Everson confided to Lee Bartlett that what astonished him was that there was "not a Christian concept in the poem." Even though, as late as 1981 in *Birth of a Poet,* Everson declared himself a Christian poet, he meant this in a general sense connected with his continuing celebration of the glory of Creation and the Creator.[18] Thus, when he claimed that his 1967 *The Rose of Solitude,* which centered on his affair with a Mexican American woman in the early 1960s, was a poem of Christian mysticism, one is bound to have reservations. Furthermore, while in depicting the theme of *felix culpa* in that poem Everson described the unfolding of his guilt and subsequent spiritual renewal with evident sincerity, he did so without the coiled tension and dense craftsmanship that had marked the poems of the 1950s.

In retrospect, it is the Catholic poems of Brother Antoninus, largely contained in *The Crooked Lines of God* and *The Hazards of Holiness,* that represent Everson's most impressive work. Charged with a romantic emotion derived from Jeffers, the poems show the poet straining to lift himself into a teleological order that would equal his ecstatic level of feeling. Intellectually, the union of monastic spirituality and Jungianism enabled Everson (and Allen Tate and Caroline Gordon) to synthesize fresh approaches to mystical awareness. The poems are convincing as poetry and are often heightened by fine workmanship. As spiritual documents, ironically, what one remembers about Everson's poetry is the passion, and, even when the poet fails to reach higher ground, one remembers vividly the striving that, in the best poems, allows the uplifted face of the soul to shine through the form.

18. Bartlett, *William Everson: The Life of Brother Antoninus,* 192; Everson, *Birth of a Poet,* 19.

7

THOMAS MERTON

(1915-1968)

L IKE WILLIAM EVERSON, Thomas Merton, a monk and poet, intuitively sought a rapprochement of sorts between Catholicism and romanticism—although Merton was far less focused on sexuality than Everson. Drawn toward the writings of William Blake in his university years (Merton confided in *The Seven Storey Mountain* that reading Blake had led him into the Catholic Church), Merton, like Blake, celebrated the beauty of Creation as evidence of the presence of the divine in the world. More particular, though, as George Kilcourse has perceptively observed, in Merton's reading of Blake, nature was not "intelligible" until it was "transfigured in Christ." While for Wordsworth, Merton argued in his master's thesis about Blake, nature was "God's greatest and most important creation," for Blake nature was only the "hem of God's garment." Nevertheless, with characteristic balance, Merton observed in an essay titled "Blake and the New Theology" that although Blake's God was "present and immanent in his creation," God was still the Creator and not simply the "creation process." The distinction is a crucial one in understanding Merton's straddling of romantic and Christian thought.[1]

Michael Higgins has rightly viewed Blake as the formative influence on Merton's poetic vision. In *The Seven Storey Mountain*, Merton characterized

1. Kilcourse, *Ace of Freedoms: Thomas Merton's Christ*, 46; Merton, *Literary Essays,* 451, 9.

Blake's distinctiveness as a romantic as lying in his rebellion against "literalism and naturalism" in art and in the "moral order." Significantly, Merton referred to Blake's rebellion as that of the "saints," noting that Blake had once described Catholicism as the only religion that "really taught the love of God." The observation is typical of the partiality of *The Seven Storey Mountain* in which Merton, writing in the first flowering of his life as a Trappist monk, sought to assimilate and thereby to justify the parts of his earlier thought that lay beyond the perimeter of the church's teaching.[2]

Throughout his writings Merton balanced himself between a Neoplatonic and Thomist reading of the world. For example, he declared himself captivated by the "superb moral and poetic beauty" of Plato's Phaedo, enthralled by this "purifying music of which my spirit has need" but with which, he added tellingly, his mind did "not agree." As a priest his mind had been formed by Thomism, and he always valued Saint Thomas Aquinas's *"turning to the world,"* to the concrete reality of the universe in contrast to the tendency of Platonism to leave the palpable world behind in a spiritual ascent.[3]

The romanticism of Merton's thought is apparent in his centering of experience and meaning within individual consciousness and in turn within the imagination, a distinct sign of romanticism according to literary historian Lilian Furst. Furthermore, Merton's uniting of mystical and artistic experience on the basis of the "intuitive perception" that underlies each, as he put it in *The Seven Storey Mountain*, exemplifies what Furst refers to as the capacity of the imagination in romantic thought to seek out hidden "correspondences" between things. In his essay "Rain and the Rhinoceros," Merton described the artist's goal as the reaching of the "intimate, that is ontological, sources of life which cannot be clearly apprehended in themselves by any concept, but which, once intuited, can be made accessible to all in symbolic and imaginative celebration."[4] The statement is a quintessential example of the union of romanticism and Catholicism in Merton with its insistent retention of the "ontological," the Thomist reality principle, in connection with the imaginative and intuitive effusions of consciousness.

Like the American romantics of the nineteenth century, Merton was greatly attracted, particularly in his later writings, to Asian religious thought, especially for its emphasis upon consciousness. Merton regarded

2. Higgins, "A Study of the Influence of William Blake on Thomas Merton," 378; Merton, *Seven Storey Mountain*, 203, 190.

3. Merton, *Conjectures of a Guilty Bystander*, 46, 185.

4. Furst, *Romanticism in Perspective*, 56, 58, 112; Merton, *Seven Storey Mountain*, 202; Furst, *Romanticism in Perspective*, 126; Merton, *Literary Essays*, 30.

Christianity as focused upon action, particularly salvific action, and in contrast he thought Buddhism much more developed as a religion in its *understanding* of religious experience. Merton celebrated the capacity of "pure consciousness" to accept things fully, in "complete oneness with them," looking "out of them" as though fulfilling the role of consciousness "not for itself only but *for them also.*" The remark recalls Emerson's famous image of the mind as a transparent eyeball through which all of being passes, and in the same volume Merton praised the work of Emerson and Thoreau in opening American culture to Eastern mysticism.[5]

The connection between Merton and Thoreau is all the more convincing when one recalls that both writers sought a balance between the active and the contemplative, and specifically between social protest and spiritual and aesthetic contemplation. While Dennis McInerny initiated the inquiry into Merton's debt to the American romantics, much has yet to be added to that discussion. Writing to Henry Miller in 1962, for example, Merton declared that Thoreau was "one of the only reasons" that he became an American citizen, and he was pleased that Miller had compared him to American transcendentalists such as Emerson and Thoreau, adding that he would try to be worthy of the comparison.[6]

Not only did Merton characterize Thoreau's gift to America as "incomparable" but the whole course of his life would in significant respects parallel that of Thoreau, especially when he moved into a woodland hermitage in the 1960s. Indeed, he confided wryly in 1967 in his essay "Day of a Stranger" that he had been accused of "living in the woods like Thoreau instead of living in the desert like St. John the Baptist," an accusation that he does not deny. What he does do is redefine the spiritual life so that it resembles a paradigm that Emerson and Thoreau might have embraced: "Up here in the woods is seen the New Testament: that is to say, the wind comes through the trees and you breathe it." Merton's continuous urging of the need to simplify recalls similar sage advice by Thoreau throughout *Walden.* In *Raids on the Unspeakable,* Merton wrote that "only he who has the simplest and most natural needs can be considered to be without needs, since the only needs he has are real ones." In *The Sign of Jonas,* Merton quoted the passage in *Walden* in which Thoreau recalled that he had gone to live in the woods in order to confront *"only the essential facts of life."*[7]

5. Merton, *Mystics and Zen Masters,* 245, 69.
6. Merton to Miller, August 7, 1962, quoted in Merton, *The Courage for Truth: The Letters of Thomas Merton to Writers,* 277.
7. Merton, *Conjectures,* 277; Merton, "Day of a Stranger," 211, 214; Merton, *Raids on the Unspeakable,* 23; Merton, *Sign of Jonas,* 316.

114 THE CATHOLIC IMAGINATION IN AMERICAN LITERATURE

If some of the aspects of Merton's thought were Thomist, his romanticism can be seen in his resistance to a predominantly ratiocinative
approach to contemplative spirituality, which he increasingly came to
think of in an intuitive rather than in a systematic and theological manner.
In *Conjectures of a Guilty Bystander,* for example, Merton confided that at
moments he experienced a "flash of Zen" in the "midst of the Church" but
that such experiences were often foreshortened by "reasoning too much
about everything." Since romantic thought in both England and America
derived in part from Kant, the romantics tended to posit the legitimacy of
certain kinds of a priori perceptions. From Merton's mystical and romantic
perspective, all that existed was intuitively perceived as part of the dance
of life, as he visualized it, echoing Yeats, in the incandescent ending of his
1961 *New Seeds of Contemplation.* Similarly, in a letter to Marco Pallis in 1965,
Merton argued that the division between the natural and supernatural
in religion was "misleading and unsatisfactory." The letter signaled a
turnaround for Merton from an earlier letter to Aldous Huxley in 1958
in which he had contended that Huxley ought to have distinguished
experience that was essentially *"aesthetic and natural"* from that which was
"mystical and supernatural."[8] While Merton's initial romanticism, which
predated his entry into the monastery, was somewhat crimped during the
1940s and early 1950s by his desire to center himself on the church, as he
grew older his romanticism reasserted itself, especially in the post–Vatican
II liberalism of the 1960s.

Romantic primitivism is evident everywhere in Merton's thought. For
example, in the lecture he gave at the Abbey of Gethsemani on Faulkner's
novel *The Wild Palms,* he identified the primitive characters as the ones
who were aware of the "nature of things" in contrast to the mechanical
existences lived by the "more civilized" characters. Romantic primitivism
can also be observed in his celebration of the child, as in an essay on the
poet Louis Zukofsky in which he described the speech of the child as
"paradise speech." This romantic motif was Christianized when Merton,
in speaking of Karl Barth, declared that though Barth had matured into a
great Protestant theologian, Christ had remained a "child" in him.[9]

The most memorable poem in *Emblems for a Season of Fury* is "Grace's
House," which focuses on the sublimity and primacy of the child's vision.
The occasion for the poem was Merton's receiving of a child's drawing

8. Merton, *Conjectures,* 136; Merton to Pallis, Easter 1965, published in Merton, *The Hidden Ground of Love: The Letters of Thomas Merton on Religious Experience and Social Concerns,* 470; Merton to Huxley, November 27, 1958, in ibid., 437.
9. Merton, *Literary Essays,* 524, 130; Merton, *Conjectures,* 4.

of her house. Her name, Grace, along with the simple sketch, had a suggestive effect on Merton's imagination:

> Where all the grass lives
> And all the animals are aware!
> The huge sun, bigger than the house
> Stands and streams with life in the east
> While in the west a thunder cloud
> Moves away forever.

Looking at the Edenic landscape before him, Merton experienced intimations of immortality, as had Wordsworth before him, in addition to noting sorrowfully the distance back to the sacred and primal world of childhood. "Alas," he noted, looking at the drawing, there was "no road to Grace's house!"[10]

In following Blake, Merton strove to recover, here on earth, the consciousness of the unity that had been "shattered by the 'knowledge of good and evil.'" Reconciling his adherence to both romantic primitivism and Catholicism, Merton declared in the preface to an Argentine edition of his writings that his Catholicism dated from the "beginning of the world" when the first human being emerged in the "image of Christ." In a 1958 essay titled "Poetry and Contemplation: A Reappraisal," Merton associated the recovery of paradise and a renewed contact with God with the exercise of creativity. On another occasion, in an essay called "Louis Zukofsky—the Paradise Ear," he maintained that all "valid" poetry, that which generated "imaginative life," was a kind of "recovery of paradise." Similarly, in discussing the writings of Boris Pasternak in an essay titled "The Pasternak Affair," and in particular his character Zhivago, Merton identified the artist, specifically, as one who can evoke the primal experience of paradise: "It is as artist, symbolist, and prophet that Zhivago stands most radically in opposition to Soviet society. He himself is a man of Eden, of Paradise. He is Adam, and therefore also, in some sense, Christ." The inclusion of Christ at the end of this passage about the artist reflects Merton's perception that creativity, preeminently, links the divine and human worlds—as in Christ's re-creation of human nature.[11]

---

10. Merton, *The Collected Poems of Thomas Merton*, 331. All subsequent quotations from Merton's poetry are from this volume and are cited parenthetically in the text as *CP*.

11. Merton, *Zen and the Birds of Appetite*, 117; Merton, *Honorable Reader*, 41; Merton, *Literary Essays*, 345; ibid., 128; ibid., 47.

The idea that the artist's imagination might be used to restore the fallen world to its pristine, Edenic state was one that Merton had encountered in Blake, particularly in Blake's "Vision of the Last Judgment," where Blake described his painting as an attempt to restore the "Golden Age." In writing about the poetry of Edwin Muir, Merton again emphasized the Edenic consciousness of the poet, who "follows Adam and reverifies the names given to creatures by his first father." For Merton, paradise was the recovery of the consciousness of the state in which humanity had been originally created. At one point he wrote ecstatically that paradise was "all around us" and that the "sword" had been "taken away" though "we do not know it." Evil in Merton seems distinctly Rousseauesque at times, a darkness connected with the outer, "false" selves of human beings rather than with their deeper, inner, solitary lives. The false or collective selves of human beings were those that Merton identified with technological society, which he felt erased the face of Creation, the face that human beings needed in order to discover both their authentic being and God. Furthermore, Merton did not dignify the ascendancy of technology in the twentieth century by calling it rational; instead, he asserted in *Conjectures of a Guilty Bystander*, technology represented the triumph of the "rule of *quantity.*"[12]

The following scene from *Conjectures of a Guilty Bystander*—a sudden, joyous recognition by Merton of the beauty of his fellow human beings, an experience that unexpectedly arose out of a visit to Louisville—illustrates his belief in the presence of a hidden, unspotted area of the human soul:

> I suddenly saw the secret beauty of their hearts, the depth of their hearts where neither sin nor desire nor self-knowledge can reach, the core of their reality, the person that each one is in God's eyes. If only they could all see themselves as they really *are.* . . . At the center of our being is a point of nothingness which is untouched by sin and by illusion, a point of pure truth, a point or spark which belongs entirely to God.[13]

For Merton, contemplative solitude made one aware of the ground of being, as Paul Tillich expressed it, "that ground," Merton wrote, in which all being "hears and knows itself." In his essay "Rain and the Rhinoceros," Merton, while conceding that we must begin life in the "social womb," argued that our higher destiny was to be born out of this womb into the self through contemplative solitude. The sound of the rain is described as

12. Blake, *Complete Writings,* 605; Merton, *Literary Essays,* 29; Merton, *Conjectures,* 64.
13. Merton, *Conjectures,* 142.

"wonderful, unintelligible, perfectly innocent speech" and is contrasted with the "noises of cities, of people," of the "greed of machinery that does not sleep." In a sense, not only is society rejected here but so is the language of society. For this reason, the poet represents an alternative to the debased language of the group, an attempt to begin over again, to seek the voice of the primal, that which still bears the imprint of the divine hand. The connection between nature and paradise is made over and over in Merton's work, as in *The Monastic Journey,* published in 1963, in which he speaks of the monk's call to "wilderness and paradise." Similarly, in *Opening the Bible,* which was published in 1970, Merton contrasts the perversity of "civilized and rationalistic man, caught in the web of purely abstract time" with the concrete and natural time in which Faulkner's admirable character Dilsey in *The Sound and the Fury* lives.[14]

Although in his master's thesis Merton argued that Blake, unlike Wordsworth, did not idolize nature, there is a tendency in Merton's writings to perceive the natural order as morally superior to the social order, and in this respect Merton is closer to Thoreau than he is to Blake. When Czeslaw Milosz chided Merton for his uncritical approval of nature in a 1960 letter, Merton was forced to admit that "nature and I are very good friends, and console one another for the stupidity and the infamy of the human race and its civilization." Merton was not altogether consistent in his behavior toward nature, though. One remembers that in the evocative, natural setting of "Day of a Stranger" he recounts having killed a copperhead snake, presumably as luminous an example of natural order as any other.[15]

As in romantic literature generally, in Merton nature frequently serves as the agent of transcendental experience, as can be seen in a scene in *Conjectures of a Guilty Bystander* in which he found himself absorbed by a bowl of flowers in a monastery chapel:

> Beauty of sunlight falling on a tall vase of red and white carnations and green leaves on the altar of the novitiate chapel. The light and dark. The darkness of the fresh, crinkled flower: light, warm and red, all around the darkness. The flower is the same color as blood, but it is in no sense whatever "as red as blood." Not at all! It is as red as a carnation. Only that.

14. Merton, *Honorable Reader,* 11; Merton, *Raids on the Unspeakable,* 10; Merton, *Monastic Journey,* 150; Merton, *Opening the Bible,* 48–49.

15. Merton, *Literary Essays,* 426; Merton to Milosz, May 6, 1960, in Merton, *Courage for Truth,* 65; Merton, "Day of a Stranger," 216.

> This flower, this light, this moment, this silence: *Dominus est*. Eter-
> nity. He passes. He remains. We pass. In and out. He passes. We remain.
> We are nothing. We are everything. He is in us. He is gone from us.
> He is not here. We are here in Him.[16]

Holding fast to the flowers as reservoirs of the beauty of Creation, Merton
comes fortuitously into contact with their creator and equally fortuitously
experiences a temporary release from time.

As a Catholic writer Merton clung to the earth as the necessary route of
his salvation. As a romantic writer he clung to the earth in order to restrain
and to focus the imagination's headlong leap into the transcendental.
Although Merton, like Tate and Gordon, was wary of the abstract, his
view of nature is quite different from that of the southern agrarians, who
perceived the earth as an organizing reality by which to structure society
on a regional basis, an idea that does not initially mesh with Merton's
pronounced internationalism. In his writings Merton's encounter with
southerners does not generally reflect the regional interest and intimacy
one finds in Allen Tate, Caroline Gordon, Walker Percy, and Flannery
O'Connor but is instead an occasion for transcendental meditation—as in
the often-quoted passage in *Conjectures of a Guilty Bystander* in which on
a visit to Louisville he suddenly felt himself awakening from a monastic
"dream of separateness" to his spiritual unity with all human beings.[17]

Merton's ecstatic consciousness of the immanence of the divine was
not, strictly speaking, pantheistic since he attributed his conversion to
Catholicism to his realization of the presence of God as a distinct being
in *"this present life,* in the world and in myself," as he put it in *Conjectures
of a Guilty Bystander,* adding that his task as a Christian was to live in
"full and vital awareness of this ground of my being and of the world's
being." Dennis McInerny has argued that Merton's incarnational theology
underlay his belief that there was nothing that human beings could
perpetrate by way of "all-out evil" that could sink his optimism since that
optimism was not ultimately founded upon any "human capability." At
the same time, reflecting the hybrid nature of his thought as Christian
and romantic, Merton affirmed his being a *"part of nature,"* though a
"special" part, that which is "conscious of God." This ontological view was
continuous with, though not identical with, Merton's more theologically
conventional observation, stated in *New Seeds of Contemplation,* that for
those who believed in the Incarnation there should be no one on earth

---

16. Merton, *Conjectures,* 131.
17. Ibid., 140.

in whom one is not prepared to see, "in mystery, the presence of Christ." Indeed, typically in Merton's writings, particularly in the first half of his career, this view of the role of Christ, a perfectly orthodox one, was grafted, almost invisibly, onto the residual romanticism that he took with him into the monastery.[18]

Merton's interest in the primal matter of Creation attracted him to the unconscious, and in his writing there is a good deal of rapt attention given to dreams. Guided by his theological training, however, Merton did not look uncritically at the unconscious, but went so far as to urge the eradication of the "unconscious roots of sin" by exposing the darker side of the unconscious. Furthermore, Merton exhorted his readers to take command of the "mechanisms of natural instinct" instead of being swept away "blindly" by these subconscious forces.[19] Merton's wariness concerning the role of nature stemmed from what he perceived as threats to the freedom and sovereignty of human beings. Rather than confront the apparent contradiction between examples of his romantically optimistic and more pessimistic, theological interpretations of nature, Merton held to the center, upholding the need for human beings to celebrate the beauty and transcendental power of nature while cautioning against the dangers of its more threatening undertow.

It is a characteristic of Merton's thought that, frequently, when faced with contradictory polarities, his tendency was to work toward inclusiveness and unity. A salient example is his refinement of the theme of the inner versus the outer self. Rather than labor over the dangers presented by the external self, Merton warned against dealing too negatively with that external self, observing that though the outer self was relatively unsubstantial alongside the inner self, it need not thereby be despised, and paradoxically might even become a way of approaching God: "The mask that each man wears may well be a disguise not only for that man's inner self but for God, wandering as a pilgrim and exile in His own creation."[20]

Preoccupied with the genesis of the self's development in his famous autobiography, *The Seven Storey Mountain* (published in 1948), Merton selected from his early years those influences that most definitively shaped his inner search and destiny. Thus, in describing the village of St. Antonin, where he first attended school, Merton recalled that, like many French villages, St. Antonin was laid out so that every street "pointed more or

18. Ibid., 292–93; McInerny, "Thomas Merton and the Tradition of American Critical Romanticism," 173; Merton, *Conjectures*, 268; Merton, *New Seeds of Contemplation*, 296.
19. Merton, *Conjectures*, 98, 107.
20. Merton, *New Seeds of Contemplation*, 296.

less inward to the center of the town, to the church," a Catholic church that had been fitted into the landscape in such a way as to become the "keystone of its intelligibility."[21] In spite of the distrust of Catholicism that his American grandfather had passed on to him, the young Merton drank in the landscape that seemed everywhere to be crowned by old monasteries, and he was always to keep a sense of "those clean, ancient stone cloisters" (6).

Even in these early years his deep-seated egalitarian feelings, derived perhaps from the unconventional lifestyle of his father, drew him toward what he came to feel was the universality of Roman Catholicism. In particular, he held in retrospect an extraordinary, lifelong affection for a rural Catholic family with whom he lived briefly in the Auvergne, a family that humbly but firmly regarded themselves as in the true church and that regretted tenderly that their young Protestant visitor was not inside with them. Merton was drawn not so much to the tenets of their faith as to their warmth and stability, attractive qualities in the eyes of a motherless boy who never quite knew where he was going to move next. Moreover, the family gained luster in his eyes because of the ordinariness of their lives, "sanctified by obscurity, by usual skills, by common tasks, by routine" (56). In addition to Merton's gratitude at seeing the hand of God in the narrative of his life, memory is crucial, as in Wordsworth, in rescuing the fragments of lost youth and establishing a continuum with the present and older narrator.

Merton's narrative journey into the past in search of his identity (*The Seven Storey Mountain* can be read as a bildungsroman) included a pivotal visit to Rome. He had started out with the misconception that the real Rome was that of the ancients, whose gray, pitted temples were wedged in between the hills and the slums of the city. Fortuitously, he became interested in Byzantine mosaics, and their beauty led him gradually to study the religious subjects that they portrayed. Thus, without fully realizing what was happening, he became a "pilgrim" (108). The narrative is particularly delicate at this point in tracing the flow of unconscious urgings and conscious desires in the young man as well as in registering the gratitude of the older Merton in looking back at the mystery and fruitfulness of the direction that his life had taken.

In his attempt to unite himself spiritually with the world, whose divine pulse he felt so keenly, Merton found himself longing for the anonymity of the contemplative life and envying the cenobitic lives of those who

---

21. Merton, *Seven Storey Mountain*, 37, subsequently cited in the text parenthetically.

were "lost in the picture" (317). Finally resolved, Merton approached his destination with ecstatic anticipation. His impression, as he approached late in the evening the Kentucky monastery that would become his home, is conveyed in translucent prose:

> I looked at the rolling country, and at the pale ribbon of road in front of us, stretching out as grey as lead in the light of the moon. Then suddenly I saw a steeple that shone like silver in the moonlight, growing into sight from behind a rounded knoll. The tires sang on the empty road, and, breathless, I looked at the monastery that was revealed before me as we came over the rise. At the end of an avenue of trees was a big rectangular block of buildings, all dark, with a church crowned by a tower and a steeple and a cross: and the steeple was as bright as platinum and the whole place was as quiet as midnight and lost in the all-absorbing silence and solitude of the fields. Behind the monastery was a dark curtain of woods, and over to the west was a wooded valley, and beyond that a rampart of wooded hills, a barrier and a defence against the world. (320)

Set among the Kentucky hills, the Abbey of Gethsemani held the contemplative in close contact with nature, and Merton came to believe that his vocation was not only to the contemplative life but also to that very place. He felt that he had arrived at the "real capital" of the country, the "center" of the vitality in America and the "cause and reason why the nation is holding together," a significant claim in terms of the romantic quest for cosmic unity (325).

The spiritual role of nature is central to *The Seven Storey Mountain*, particularly the ending of the book, which is dominated by the cycle of the seasons and by the young monk's blissful entry into them and into contact with the God whom he felt to be matrix of all nature. The pace of the narrative slows in harmony with the procession of natural forms. Things settle into a soft light as the monks are portrayed going about their work in the fields, a work that is beautifully attuned to the events of the liturgical year. In Advent the monks are portrayed filing out with mattocks to dig up briars, and the trees are described as stripped bare, symbolically corresponding to the austerity of the penitential season. At Easter the cowled monks are pictured going out to the fields to plant peas and beans, paralleling the rebirth that is at that time symbolized in the Liturgy. In the warm months the monks are depicted going out with straw hats to hay, and then later on harvesting the crops in the early autumn of "bright, dry days, with plenty of sun, and cool air, and high cirrus clouds" when the trees have turned "rusty and blood color and bronze along the jagged hills" (399). The style is especially fervid in this section as Merton's consciousness and imagination settled serenely upon a world he found he had every reason to love. Merton focused on the beauty and power of nature, not entirely ignoring its Darwinian aspects but rather integrating these into a spiritual synthesis that emphasized a life-giving upwardness.

The delicacy of Merton's response to nature is an important source of the eloquence of his 1953 journal, *The Sign of Jonas*:

> Yesterday there was snow again and wind froze ribs on top of the drifts along the hillsides; sun shone through the copper grass that grew above the snow on Saint Joseph's hill, and it looked as if the snow was all on fire. There were jewels all over the junk the brothers dumped out there where the old horsebarn used to be. A bunch of old worn-out window-screens were lying about and they shone in the sun like crystal.[22]

As Merton had felt in his ruminations about art and the monastic calling, there was always the possibility that nature would seduce his attention with its inexhaustible fecundity and its suggestive ability to link up with other kinds of experience. A little locust tree, for example, which had died and "spilled all the fragments of its white flowers over the ground," became associated in his mind with the painting of Seurat (49). Winter mornings were especially suggestive, the sky filled with small high clouds that looked like "ice-floes, all golden and crimson and saffron, with clean blue and aquamarine behind them, and shades of orange and red and mauve down by the surface of the land where the hills were just visible in a pearl haze and the ground was steel-white with frost—every blade of grass as stiff as wire" (137). Merton turned the details of the landscape to contemplative use to achieve the elusive *inscape* that he admired in Hopkins, the tracing of the detail of the structure of natural objects under the pressure of an inspired intuition so that the spectator eased himself or herself into the center of the object being observed. In so doing, Merton wrote in an essay on the poetry of Edwin Muir, the contemplative tried not to disturb the integrity of the object seen, seeing it instead from the very point where it sprang from the "creative power of God."[23] The luminous quality that was always part of Merton's vision of nature was associated in his mind with nature's wildness and purity. The pristine character of the wilderness was a mirror of those same paradisal qualities and energies that he sometimes glimpsed in human beings, qualities that had atrophied, he felt, under the deadening effect of civilization.

22. Merton, *Sign of Jonas*, 317, subsequently cited in the text parenthetically.
23. Merton, *Literary Essays*, 30.

Similar to Thoreau and in contrast to Emerson and Whitman, Merton sometimes included in his writing a depiction of some of the harsher, predatory aspects of nature, as in the following scene from *The Sign of Jonas*. Having settled down after having been frightened by an eagle, a flock of starlings is described moving about on the ground, singing. Suddenly, a hawk swoops down, flying "straight into the middle of the starlings" just as they were getting off the ground. Rising into the air, Merton wrote, there was a slight scuffle on the ground as the hawk got his "talons into the one bird he had nailed" (274). Merton ponders the scene: "It was a terrible and yet beautiful thing, that lightning flight, straight as an arrow, that killed the slowest starling" (275). Merton does not overlook the violence of the scene, but shows the hawk in the field "like a king," taking his time in eating: "I tried to pray, afterward," Merton confides. "But the hawk was eating the bird." It is clear that Merton was not so much repelled as awed, feeling finally that the hawk should be studied by "saints and contemplatives; because he knows his business" (275). Although the episode might have spurred troubled thoughts about the creator of a Darwinian universe, there is no sign of such reflections. Merton accepts the mystery of nature, is stirred by its beauty as by its power, and piously leaves the answer of its inner riddle to God. Furthermore, though attracted to nature, he portrayed it as ultimately doomed. Consequently, he believed that the resourceful pilgrim would pass through nature to some other place so as to look not only at nature but also through it. Otherwise, Merton's symbolic episode implies, one would suffer the fate of the starlings.

In its marshaling of symbols Merton's writing frequently focuses on light and darkness, a pattern that is present both in romantic poetry and painting and in some of the great works of Christian mysticism, in Saint John of the Cross, for example, a favorite writer of Merton's. Underlying this motif in both romanticism and Christian mysticism is the Neoplatonic idea that the physical world with its superficial light constitutes a blindness, just as the hidden spiritual world is incandescent. A significant instance of this symbolic pattern in Merton occurs in the concluding section of *The Sign of Jonas*, "The Fire Watch." Here, Merton walks through his monastery as night watchman. The darkness bathes Merton's mind, awakening it to new life following the attrition of the day: "Baptized in the rivers of night, Gethsemani has recovered her innocence. Darkness brings a semblance of order before all things disappear" (349). The journey through the darkness is not only a journey into the mystery of being but also a journey within so that on his nocturnal rounds Merton finds himself face-to-face with his past and with the enigma of his life.

His journey through the darkness is not only through distance, therefore, but through time as well, as he encounters not only the phantoms of his own past but also those of his historic monastery, and he comes to feel "like an archeologist suddenly unearthing ancient civilizations" (354). The imagery reinforces the symbolism of darkness as a paradoxical source of vision. At a certain point, Merton notes, it was possible for the spirit to enter a lighted world where everything was "charged with intelligence, though all is night," a world in which the "holy cellar" of one's mortal existence opened into the sky. It was a "strange awakening," he added, "to find the sky inside you and beneath you and above you and all around you so that your spirit is one with the sky, and all is positive night" (339–40). Faith and imagination intertwine in Merton's theistic coloring of the scene, which resolves itself in a moment of sublimity in which God's "coming is recognized" (340).

Similarly, in "After the Night Office—Gethsemani Abbey" in *A Man in the Divided Sea*, published in 1946, Merton deftly brings out the heavenly paradox underlying the hidden, nocturnal lives of the monks. The scene is a "grey and frosty time," a time when the monastery barns "ride out of the night like ships" (*CP*, 108). Merton looks at the file of monks who, "bearing lanterns, / Sink in the quiet mist" and reflects that these contemplatives, who sank deeply into prayer during the night hours, had their "noon" before dawn. The coming of dawn transfers the flood of light from within the monks outward to the "lances of the morning" that shower "all their gold against the steeple and the water-tower." At this point the monks are pictured as moving out of themselves in order to do their work, and Merton concludes eloquently: "We find our souls all soaked in grace, like Gideon's fleece" (*CP*, 109).

In his 1949 *The Tears of the Blind Lions*, which won the Harriet Monroe prize for poetry, the poem "The Reader" exhibits water imagery in a manner that reflects Merton's Christian romanticism:

> And I sit hooded in this lectern
>
> Waiting for the monks to come,
> I see the red cheeses, and bowls
> All smile with milk in ranks upon their tables.
>
> Light fills my proper globe
> (I have won light to read by
> With a little, tinkling chain)
>
> And the monks come down the cloister
> With robes as voluble as water. (*CP*, 202)

The originality of the phrase "voluble as water," which is etched with spiritual connotations, draws attention to both its baptismal significance and as well to its romantic mysteriousness. This is natural as well as liturgical water, whose mystical purposes draw one toward a cosmic meaning that lies imprisoned within it, awaiting a paradisal consciousness to reveal it.

The Strange Islands, which was published in 1957, showed Merton moving toward a freer colloquialism, bringing him more into line with contemporary verse. Here, Merton made firmer poems than in much of the earlier work; these are less didactic, more objective poems, presenting objects for inspection without surrounding them with interpretive detail. He also experimented with different line lengths in order to build into the poems the hollows of silence that he felt were essential to poetry—in which the reader was compelled to stop, be silent, and to absorb the hidden meanings. In this way a number of the poems dramatize the creative fusion that resulted when Merton applied his imagination to nature. "In Silence" is an example, a poem that centers modestly on the speaker's perceptions of stones in a wall:

> Be still
> Listen to the stones of the wall.
> Be silent, they try
> To speak your
>
> Name. (*CP,* 280)

The lines were shortened and the progress of the poem made halting in order to trace the shape of individual stones as well as to create the pauses that would induce the sort of meditative reading that Merton wanted.

At one point the speaker's attempt to concentrate fails, and he finds himself questioning the "living" walls:

> Who are you?
> Who
> Are you? Whose
> Silence are you?
>
> Who (be quiet)
> Are you (as these stones
> Are quiet). (*CP,* 280–81)

The speaker's failure, brought about by the inquisitive fluttering of his mind, disturbs the tranquil mood of the poem but also creates dramatic interest. The speaker's perception of these stones has caught fire, a sign of that surcharging of the imagination that can be seen in Merton's poetry when the power and radiance of being are fully apprehended—even in blocks of stone:

> "The stones
> Burn, even the stones
> They burn me. How can a man be still or
> Listen to all things burning? How can he dare
> To sit with them when
> All their silence
> Is on fire?" (CP, 281)

Merton had always identified with the "burnt faces" of the prophets, seeing them in *The Sign of Jonas,* for example, as transformed and made great by the "white-hot dangerous presence of inspiration" (224). In the poem "Elias—Variations on a Theme," he focused on the period when the prophet had been "felled by despair under the juniper tree" while trying to find his way to Mount Horeb and God.[24] The juniper becomes a "blunt pine" that, along with the motifs of the fire and the bird, serves as the basis of the fugal arrangement:

> Under the blunt pine
> In the winter sun
> The pathway dies
> And the wilds begin.
> Here the bird abides
> Where the ground is warm
> And sings alone. (CP, 239–40)

The pattern of sound is divided between muffled and high-pitched vowels, paralleling the contrast between the rooted pine and the bird, which like the soul of the prophet wants to rise. Thematically, the bird recalls the use of that motif in a number of romantic poems, particularly by Keats and Whitman, in which birds appear as cosmic messengers.

In alternating images Elias's fiery chariot is compared to one of the abbey's farm wagons:

> This old wagon
> With the wet, smashed wheels
> Is better. ("My chariot")

---

24. Sister Therese Lentfoehr, "The Solitary," 65.

This derelict is better.
("Of fire.") (*CP*, 241–42)

Merton's homely wagon is presented as a suitable setting for spiritual growth because it is unlike the fiery chariots of technocracy ("Grand machines, all flame, / With supernatural wings"); instead, it resembles nature, which in its dilapidated state it will soon reenter (241).

As with Blake and the American transcendentalists of the 1840s, Merton's romanticism took on not only a contemplative but also a social form. Rooted in a privileging of individual consciousness over collective norms, the romantics tended to be anarchists politically, and this was true of Merton as well. There were also specifically Catholic influences upon the development of Merton's social ideas. In addition to the early influence of Dorothy Day and Catherine Doherty upon Merton, in the early 1960s, Daniel Berrigan, the Jesuit poet and peace activist, played an important role in the development of Merton's social thought. Unusual for their times, both Merton and Berrigan felt in the otherwise ebullient 1960s that they were witnessing the collapse of both church and state. In November 1961, Merton wrote to Berrigan that he felt that "we have about five years left to work in, and after that *venit nox*." In February 1964, Merton wrote that he often felt like an "alien in the Church," a sentiment echoed by Berrigan, who had recently been blocked from returning to teach at LeMoyne College because of his on-campus social activism. Both agreed that the church had been misled by what Merton called centuries of "triumphalist self-deception." Significantly, while both Merton and Berrigan continued to affirm the relevance of the church to the world, they abandoned the optimism of theologians such as Teilhard de Chardin, the Jesuit paleontologist who had maintained that humanity was on a path of evolutionary spiritual ascent.[25]

On the whole, Berrigan relied on Merton for the general picture without wanting him to plunge into the whirlpool of social activism. Exceptions occurred in 1968 when Merton was invited to be a witness at the trial where Berrigan was charged with destroying military draft files and later when he was asked to receive the draft cards of antiwar protestors, both of which invitations Merton quietly but firmly declined. If Berrigan encouraged Merton to feel responsibility for the fate of the world, Merton encouraged Berrigan to nourish the contemplative side of himself so as to balance

25. Merton to Berrigan, November 10, 1961; February 23, 1964; and June 30, 1964, all in Merton, *Hidden Ground*, pp. 71, 81, 83, respectively.

and deepen his social protest. In a letter written in March 1962, Merton emphasized the need for a "solitary, bare, dark, beyond-concept, beyond-thought, beyond-feeling type of prayer," characterizing this as the "secret, unknown stabilizer" and "compass" of the Christian life.[26]

In *Emblems of a Season of Fury*, published in 1963, Merton included a number of social-protest poems. The prosody shows a steady loosening and expansion in the lines and stanzas as well as a greater colloquialism in diction. Furthermore, with punctuation almost nonexistent, the lines flow freely. Much of the imagery in *Emblems of a Season of Fury* is made to flare, as in "The Moslems' Angel of Death," which is about the Algerian war of independence in the early 1960s. Death appears in the poem as a great honeycomb of bees, the armament of modern technocracies with a "million fueled eyes" (*CP*, 307). At the conclusion of death's visit there are only embers, "one red coal left burning / Beneath the ashes of the great vision" and one "blood-red eye left open / When the city is burnt out" (*CP*, 308). The poems seethe with urgency and discontent. Even the Greek myths, which had earlier been used by Merton as symbols of order in a chaotic world, seem hard-pressed to contain their volatile subjects, as in "Gloss on the Sin of Ixion." In that poem Ixion's fathering of the monstrous race of Centaurs, accomplished by a bizarre, onanistic union with a cloud, is made to symbolize the rape of the world by collective hubris, and in turn the giant "mechanical boys" (military technology) that issue from this rape are implicated in the ravishing of "sacred man" (*CP*, 314).

Other poems—such as "O Sweet Irrational Worship," which drew on the title of Cummings's well-known romantic poem "o sweet sponta-neous"—balance the poems of social protest and provide a touchstone of familiar reality that contrasts with the surrealism of the war poetry:

> Wind and a bobwhite
> And the afternoon sun.
>
> By ceasing to question the sun
> I have become light,
>
> Bird and wind.
>
> My leaves sing.
>
> I am earth, earth
>
> All these lighted things
> Grow from my heart. (*CP*, 344)

26. Merton to Berrigan, March 10, 1962, in ibid., 73.

The radical expansion of spacing, which also recalls Cummings, allows the stillness of the transcendental moment to be felt by the reader. Moreover, the poem as earth song, somewhat reminiscent of Emerson's "Hamatreya," conveys Merton's romantic consciousness of the ground of being, a basis upon which human beings could share their experience when they otherwise seemed consumed by their differences.

The contemplative and social sides of Merton's writing in the 1960s came together in his comparison of the figures of Christ and Prometheus in *Raids on the Unspeakable*, which he published in 1966. In contrasting the very different depictions of Prometheus by Hesiod and Aeschylus, Merton concluded that the Prometheus of Hesiod resembled Cain, whereas Aeschylus' Prometheus resembled "Christ on the Cross." Merton's Catholicism is evident in his perception that Prometheus' rebellion, if understood as a revolt against the circumstances of Creation, was wrongheaded. This was because, Merton observed, Prometheus already possessed what he rose in fury to wrest from God, his "divine sonship."[27] While Merton bristled at the human history of violence, he found himself unable, unlike Robert Lowell in "The Quaker Graveyard in Nantucket," to locate the source in nature. Rather, like Rousseau and Thoreau (and like Daniel Berrigan), he attacked the perversity of collective behavior, whose force and destructiveness, captured in Hesiod's Prometheus, threatened to extinguish individual consciousness that, along with an equally endangered nature, contained the spark of the divine. Merton's attack against collective consciousness was especially searing in his two long poems of the 1960s, *Cables to the Ace* and *The Geography of Lograire*, published in 1968 and 1969, respectively. In both poems parodied forms of social and academic discourse clog the paths of communication along which an individual mind and imagination, isolated and starved for meaning, might otherwise find relief.

In 1967, Merton again attempted to explain and reconcile the contemplative and social protest elements in his writing in his poem "The Originators":

> Because I chose to hear a special thunder in my head
> Or to see an occipital light my choice
> Suddenly became another's fate.
> He lost all his wheels
> Or found himself flying. (*CP*, 613)

---

27. Merton, *Raids on the Unspeakable*, 83, 84.

Through the use of the word *occipital* Merton alluded to the back of his skull, which contains no spaces for eyes, thus pointing to the eyes within. He refers specifically to his vocation in the poem by telling the reader that his ideas got "scarlet fever every morning / At about four" as "influence" went out of his windows (*CP*, 613). The image invites the reader to consider the paradox of the monk, at his desk before the morning light while the rest of the world sleeps, but who nevertheless plays a significant role in the lives of those sleepers, whose diurnal society lies beyond the monastery walls.

The most paradoxical part of the poem, however, has to do with the intensity of the poet's influence:

> And when the other's nerve ends crowed and protested
> In the tame furies of a business gospel
> His feeling was my explosion
> So I skidded off his stone head
> Blind as a bullet
> But found I was wearing his hat. (*CP*, 613)

The reciprocity between poet and reader, while paradoxical, is not especially novel in the case of someone like Merton. The poem's power derives rather from the surprising violence of the imagery, in particular the image of the bullet. The lines depict a spiral in which the words of the contemplative metamorphose into action—with this action in turn stirring the contemplative to further reflection, and so on. Through the poem's symbolic framework, Merton here acknowledged that, although he was a contemplative writing in the dawn, some of his writings might involve him in the radical actions of others, and he here consciously takes responsibility for this sort of effect. The poem does not signal a departure from Merton's commitment to nonviolence, as can be seen in the softened, culminating image of the circus, which permits the reader to visualize the earlier image of the bullet as having been fired from a circus cannon. Nevertheless, the poem asserts and even celebrates the open-ended, social, and potentially activist character of Merton's otherwise cloistered writing.

The Asian Journal of Thomas Merton, which appeared in 1973 following Merton's accidental death in Thailand, reveals a romantic and mystical consciousness in full flower, centering as it does on the ecstasy of transcendental awareness. One of the most enticing of these experiences was his view of the Himalayan peak Kanchenjunga: "There is another side of Kanchenjunga and of every mountain," he wrote, "the side that has never been photographed and turned into post cards," the only side, he concluded, "worth seeing."[28] On a tea plantation in the mountains of Ceylon, Merton looked back critically at his experience in India and decided that there had been too much " 'looking for' something: an answer, a vision, 'something other,' And this breeds illusion. Illusion that there *is* something else." It all led, he felt, to the old "splitting-up process," by which he presumably meant ratiocination, which he now thought of as "mindlessness" compared to the Zen-like "mindfulness" of seeing "all-in-emptiness and not having to break it up," presumably analytically, "against itself" (148).

Merton valued Asia's ability to give him fresh perspectives, as in a night walk along the shore in what was then Ceylon: "A hot night. Warm, rubbery waves shining under the moon. . . . A new strange feeling out there—westward nothing until Africa. And out there—to the south, nothing til Antarctica. . . . I was shocked to see Orion hanging almost upside down in the north" (214). Even the seductive Mount Kanchenjunga could be made finally to yield perceptions that one might trust. In spite of the shifting pantomime of the mountain's appearance with the changing of the light—white spiraling snow and cloud in the daytime and a few "discreet showings of whorehouse pink" in the evening—the full beauty of the mountain could be appreciated under certain conditions. Merton had to accept the fact that what he experienced contained a subjective reality in addition to an objective one. On rare occasions, though, when the mind settled into a quiet attentiveness, "the smoke of ideas" cleared, and the mountain was seen in itself (156–57).

The breakthrough in consciousness that Merton achieved at Polonnaruwa in Ceylon affected him with as much surprise as exhilaration. The huge stone Buddhas, one seated and the other reclining, both symbolized and made possible the sort of transcendental relationship with the world around him that his studies of Eastern religions had been preparing him for. The quiet smiles of the Buddhas were filled with "every possibility, questioning nothing, knowing everything, rejecting nothing, the peace not of emotional resignation but of Madhyamika, of sunyata, that has seen through every question without trying to discredit anyone or anything— *without refutation*" (233). He marveled at the pattern of the scene, the "clarity and fluidity of shape and line, the design of the monumental bodies composed into the rock shape and landscape, figure, rock and tree" (233). Aware of his tendency to transmute his aesthetic responses into mystical intuitions, he spelled out the exact nature of the experience:

28. Merton, *Asian Journal,* 153, subsequently cited in the text parenthetically.

"I don't know when in my life I have ever had such a sense of beauty and spiritual validity running together in one aesthetic illumination" (235). The illumination at Polonnaruwa represented the point of arrival in a book whose structure is that of a pilgrimage. Polonnaruwa symbolized Asia "in its purity," all that Merton felt he had been "obscurely" looking for. He had "pierced" the surface, passing beyond the "shadow and the disguise" (236).

The relationship between Merton's romantic/Zen vision in *The Asian Journal* and his Christianity is difficult to ascertain since his focus is on Asian religion. One is tempted to see this journal as Merton's ecumenical reconstruction of his religion, at least in its contemplative dimensions. This does not mean that Merton was thinking of abandoning his vocation, as Emerson had abandoned Unitarianism because of what he regarded as its narrowness; rather, Merton now perceived his vocation in a new and larger spiritual context in which he felt himself able, by relying on other religious traditions, to expand the experience and meaning of his own—even though he had also been troubled by the thought of Christian sectarianism, as can be seen in his later reservations about *The Seven Storey Mountain*, where his attention had been most ardently turned toward the Catholic Church. *The Asian Journal*, as with much of Merton's writing, expressed his ontological consciousness of and existential longing for the unity of all things, a characteristic of romantic thought more essential to it than to Christian eschatology, where a final judgment and consequently a division await all. *The Seven Storey Mountain* and indeed most of Merton's writings continue to be read by a large American and international audience representing a multiplicity of cultures and beliefs. Drawing upon both monastic Catholicism and romanticism, Merton attempted to question the aggressively active character of American culture by asserting the need on the part of all, not just those in religious communities, to be contemplatives.

Although the Catholic Church offers a vision to all of a world transfigured by the Incarnation of Christ, it also adopts a privileged view of reality, particularly of the operation of grace in the world, and thus conveys an expectation that those who share its view of reality will become formally part of it. While Merton valued being part of the church, what his lifelong attachment to romanticism made possible was an enhanced consciousness of the presence of God in the world both within the self and within matter—that is, nature—and this gave rise in his writings to a rapt perception of existence itself that both Catholic and other readers might share. More than any other Catholic American writer, Merton drew attention to our spiritual roots as human beings, thereby evoking feelings of unity in those who, like himself, sought to have the experience of God.

8

WALKER PERCY

(1916-1990)

ALTHOUGH HE WAS a convert to Catholicism, Walker Percy became an impassioned supporter of Catholic moral philosophy, especially that grounded in natural law and in Saint Thomas Aquinas, whose *Summa Theologica*, he once confided to correspondent Shelby Foote, he had read "cover to cover." For two of his most important novels Percy named his protagonist after Saint Thomas More, a hero of English Catholic history who was martyred for taking an uncompromising moral position in opposition to his monarch and whom Percy described in an interview as a man who "wore his faith with grace, merriment, and a certain wryness," a description that could apply to Percy himself.[1] Percy saw the sovereignty of technology in contemporary culture as particularly undermining of natural law, and he portrays technocrats as people whose dismissal of the world of Creation is both confident and myopic. While depicting a full range of human vanity and corruptibility, Percy's fiction and essays focus repeatedly on the hidden value of our created human nature at a time in our history when that value has frequently been seen to lack credibility.

In an essay titled "The Diagnostic Novel," Percy wrote that his training in pathology convinced him that even disease pointed to the existence of a

---

1. Percy to Foote, May 18, 1975, Percy Collection, Southern Historical Collection, Library of the University of North Carolina at Chapel Hill; Percy, *Signposts in a Strange Land*, 375.

teleological universe. Percy's distinctiveness as a Catholic novelist lies in his weighing of the effects of science and technology on modern American culture and in his apocalyptic dramatization of the cost of marginalizing religion in that culture. While Percy affirmed the role of science in ordering our perceptions of nature, he also noted its failure in dealing with philosophical questions connected with the purpose and meaning of life and regretted its destructive application in areas such as abortion, where Percy observed in an interview in 1987, "we kill more people than the Nazis did in all their death camps." With the ascendancy of science, Percy contended, humanity simultaneously expanded its objective view of the universe and alienated the self, which, he argued, could not be accounted for within an exclusively scientific view of the world. In this way, he contended in *Lost in the Cosmos*, the self became a "space-bound ghost" that roamed the cosmos it had come to understand so well. Furthermore, with the widespread collapse of religious belief in the twentieth century, people were left, Percy believed, in a moral vacuum. In this situation, Percy argued, as had Thomas Merton, the artist became a necessary interpreter, "naming what had heretofore been unspeakable, the predicament of the self in the modern world."[2]

Percy's focus as an artist interpreting the modern malaise is on the relationship between technology and abstractionism, the latter perceived as a Swiftian dividing of human behavior into alternating cycles of cerebral and animal activity, an affront to Percy's deeply ingrained incarnational outlook. In its comic form the syndrome can be seen in *The Moviegoer* (published in 1961), where Binx Bolling's father would have died because of his passion for reading and his neglect of eating had his wily wife not contrived a scheme to save him. In his 1971 *Love in the Ruins*, Art Himmelman (who is an infernal mischief-maker although his name means "man of heaven") seizes upon Tom More's "lapsometer" to effect an ostensibly utopian but actually diabolical transformation of human behavior.

Angelism of this sort, to use Allen Tate's phrasing, is defined by Tom More in connection with his behaviorist invention, the lapsometer, as the "abstraction of the self from itself," followed by bestiality, an "envy" of the "incarnate condition and a resulting caricature of the bodily appetites."[3] In both his personal and scientific roles in *Love in the Ruins*, Tom More epitomizes the pitfalls of angelism, alternating between abstract projections of

    2. Percy, "Diagnostic Novel," 40; Percy, "A Visitor Interview: Novelist Walker Percy" (October 1, 1987); Percy, *Lost in the Cosmos*, 13, 120.
    3. Percy, *Love in the Ruins*, 236, subsequently cited in the text parenthetically.

utopia on the one hand and on the other becoming involved in primitive skirmishes to keep and protect the three women he has herded into an abandoned motel. While the prized lapsometer attempts to correct the imbalance between angelism and bestiality brought about by twentieth-century life, it is made humorously apparent that home remedies are superior. When More has a male patient suffering from impotency, for example, he prescribes a long walk home through a swamp: "So it came to pass that half-dead and stinking like a catfish, he fell into the arms of his good wife, Tanya, and made lusty love to her the rest of the night" (37).

As in Tate's writing about the angelic imagination, Percy establishes a connection not only between science and abstractionism but also between romanticism and abstractionism. Thus, Moira is romantically stimulated by anticipation about the future and nostalgia about the past while re-maining quietly and utterly alienated from life in the present. She lives, as Tom More, puts it, for "rare perfect moments" (130). Analogously, Doris has adopted a religious form of abstractionism, seeing religion solely as spirit, as opposed to More, who, committed to a Catholic incarnational theology, recalls that it took contact with the "misty" interstate highways and "eating Christ himself" to make him "mortal man again" (254). More's commitment is to the empirical world, but not only to the empirical world. When the English spiritualist who runs off with More's wife offers to help More escape the laws of materialism that "straitjacket" modern science, More declines, adding that he believes in such laws and favors scientific objectivity (272). Throughout the novel More makes it abundantly clear that his battle is not with what science does but with the assumption that science can answer the larger philosophical and spiritual questions about life.

The theme of angelism is ubiquitous in Percy's fiction. In his 1987 *The Thanatos Syndrome*, for example, More's wife, Ellen, who has migrated from the Presbyterian to the Episcopal to the Pentecostal Church, is hor-rified by her husband's Catholicism and particularly by the Eucharist: "*Eating* the body of Christ. That's pagan and barbaric, she said. What she meant and what horrified her," More concludes, was the "mixing up" of body and spirit.[4] A particularly bizarre refinement on the theme occurs in *Love in the Ruins* where More recalls a monk who, owning nothing himself, coveted the monastery typewriter with a "jealous love" (307). In developing the associated theme of technological hubris, a form of angelism, Percy is acute in showing the effect of suffering on Tom More

---

4. Percy, *Thanatos Syndrome,* 353, subsequently cited in the text parenthetically.

when there is no technological remedy that will permit the suffering to be avoided. The death by disease of his beloved daughter, Samantha, (the father/daughter intimacy recalls Saint Thomas More's relationship with his daughter) leaves More emotionally defenseless, with only his lapsometer with which to strike back at the universe. Moreover, in romantic/angelic fashion he freezes the memory of his dead daughter, imbuing it with a value that no amount of compensatory happiness could assuage:

> did it break my heart when Samantha died? Yes. There was even the knowledge and foreknowledge of it while she still lived, knowledge that while she lived, life still had its same peculiar tentativeness, people living as usual by fits and starts, aiming and missing, while present time went humming, and foreknowledge that the second she died, remorse would come and give past time its bitter specious wholeness. (374)

Centering himself around a transfigured past, Tom More participates in the present in a mournful state that is only marginally offset by his scientific and erotic adventures. Similarly, Binx Bolling's Catholic mother in *The Moviegoer* insulates herself from the present by suppressing her emotions following the death of a favorite son: "No more heart's desire for her, thank you." After Duval's death she wanted everything "colloquial and easy, even God."[5] While suffering can awaken Percy's characters spiritually, it can also embitter them against the world, as is the case with Doris More in *Love in the Ruins*, who in the final stages of her daughter's grotesque and painful death bitterly remarks to her husband: "That's a loving God you have there" (72). After that, Doris gravitates toward a purely spiritual religion (angelism) while More veers in the opposite direction, becoming "coarse and disorderly" (72).

Tom More's intuitive response to the inconsolable grieving that has sapped his taste for life is to attempt suicide, an act that unexpectedly renews his interest in living: "Bad as things are still when all is said and done, one can sit on a doorstep in the winter sunlight and watch sparrows kick leaves" (97). More's discovery of the healing power of the physical world in *Love in the Ruins* parallels his experience in its sequel, *The Thanatos Syndrome*, where he reflects ruefully that it took two years in prison to enable him to "sit still, listen, notice his children" and "watch the sunlight on the ceiling" (43). Later, he finds solace in the

---

5. Percy, *Moviegoer*, 142, subsequently cited in the text parenthetically.

solitude of the Louisiana bayous in a lyrical scene that brings Thomas Merton's journals to mind: "The silence is sudden. There is only the ring of a kingfisher. The sun is just clearing the cypresses and striking shafts into the tea-colored water. Mullet jump. Cicadas tune up. There is a dusting of gold on the water" (57). Without drifting into romanticism, Percy depicts nature as the other, that which both frees the self from itself and allows it to look out upon creational beauty. Such a use of nature underlies the greenhouse setting in *The Second Coming* (published in 1980) and the nomadic excursions up the Natchez trace in *Lancelot* out into the "bright meadows" and the "pine-winey sunlight" against a background of "singing cicadas."[6]

Relief from the malaise of angelism is also provided by love in Percy's fiction, frequently in a paradoxical manner. In *The Last Gentleman* (published in 1966), for example, Will Barrett is struck by the fact that in order to love him, Kitty "has not to love" him, at least in an emotional sense, using her concentration instead to help him in a moment of faintness.[7] In this way, Percy prepares the reader for acts of love in a religious sense, including the sacrificial act of suffering that defined Christ's love. Percy's thematic emphasis is usually on balance, though, as in *The Moviegoer* where Binx Bolling cautions his sickly brother not to fast in Lent, even though this has been permitted by the boy's confessor; instead, Binx recommends the Eucharist as a more "positive" thing to do—to which Lonnie replies that the Eucharist was a "sacrament of the living," thereby revealing his wish to die (164).

In addition to developing the theme of the dangers of abstractionism on an individual level, Percy also skillfully brings out the social ramifications of his theme. In *Love in the Ruins,* for example, he depicts the political form of the malaise, as in the case of Professor Coffin Cabot, the leftist scholar from Harvard who confides that he believes in "creative nonviolent violence" in addressing cases of perceived social injustice (326). In the same novel, Will Barrett finds himself reading about World War I in which "white Christian Caucasian" Europeans, including "music-loving Germans" and "rational clear-minded Frenchmen" slaughtered each other abstractly "without passion" (47). Similarly, in *The Thanatos Syndrome,* Tom More reflects on the battles of the Somme and Verdun in which two million young men were killed in a clash of patriotic fervor that had "no discernible end" (86).

6. Percy, *Lancelot,* 118, subsequently cited in the text parenthetically.
7. Percy, *Last Gentleman,* 69, subsequently cited in the text parenthetically.

Angelism also underlies the social acceptance of euthanasia. In *Love in the Ruins,* Mr. Ives narrowly escapes the euthanasia clinic because of the intervention of Tom More, who undercuts the schemes of the allegorically named Dr. Buddy Brown, the quintessential technocrat. The following description by More of Brown is trenchantly relevant: "There is to commend him his health, strength, brains, and cleanliness. He is very clean. His fingernails are like watch crystals. His soft white shirt and starched clinical coat sparkle like snow against his clear mahogany skin. Burnished hairs sprout through the heavy gold links of his expansion band" (196). Even the hairs on Brown's skin, usually an animal sign, look metallic. The dehumanized vignette reflects Percy's characteristic mingling of comic, grotesque, and apocalyptic strains, not unlike Flannery O'Connor, although his is more pitched toward social criticism than her fiction tends to be.

In *The Thanatos Syndrome,* Father Smith's hospice is closed due to a lack of government funding, funding that had been transferred to the euthanasia clinics, all with the support of the local Catholic bishop who has other plans for both Father Smith and his hospice. While Percy's equating of the practice of euthanasia in a futuristic America with the Germany of the 1930s might strike some readers as straining credibility, he stresses that the practice was undertaken in Germany not by Hitler but by the doctors, and for the most well-intentioned reasons. The most blandly chilling part of Father Smith's recollections of Germany is the description of the room to which children, deemed suitable for euthanatizing, were led: "It was a very pleasant sunny room with a large window, but completely bare except for a small white-tiled table only long enough to accommodate a child. What was notable about the room was a large geranium plant in a pot on the windowsill to catch the sunlight" (253). The hygienic innocuousness of the killing room epitomizes Percy's theme of social angelism, the humane surface that conceals a horror.

Polarized with the euthanasia clinics in *The Thanatos Syndrome* is the genuinely humane hospice where Father Smith talks compassionately to the dying while seeing that they are also adequately treated for physical pain. All too aware of his own weaknesses and mortality, Father Smith enters almost gregariously into his work with the dying, aware that many of them, for perhaps the first time in their lives, find themselves relieved to be able to speak the truth about themselves as they approach the end. Percy's satiric attack against the eugenicists and social engineers in *The Thanatos Syndrome* becomes especially pointed in his reference to the *Doe vs. Dade* decision of the Supreme Court (a variation on the landmark *Roe vs. Wade* abortion decision) through which infants up to eighteen months are able to be legally euthanatized. Percy's naming the euthanasia clinics "Qualitarian centers" satirically recognizes the view of those for whom the quality of life is more important than the presence of life itself. In contrast, Father Smith welcomes to his hospice all human beings—"young or old, suffering, dying, afflicted, useless, born or unborn," whom others for the "best of reasons" wish to put out of their misery (361). As his phrasing carefully implies, Father Smith's response to the behaviorists rests upon his recognition of how imperceptibly tenderness can lead to the gas chamber.

Percy's handling of the issue of racism is integrated with the theme of angelism in *Love in the Ruins* where Tom More characterizes racism as the fall of the American Eden, an appropriate observation from someone who lives in a community called Paradise. As with euthanasia, racism is depicted as a moral darkness in otherwise well-meaning people. As Tom More says of Leroy Ledbetter, the "terror" comes from the "goodness," some fault in the "soul's terrain so deep" that "all is well on top and evil grins like good" (152). While Percy clearly abhorred racism, he did not shrink from showing the lure of angelism among blacks, as in his ironic portrayal of the black-power movement in *Love in the Ruins*. When one of the black-power leaders suggests that parts of the United States ought to be reserved for and administered by blacks, Tom More bluntly counters: "Look at Liberia. You've had Haiti even longer" (300).

What More disputes is the social angelism of the black-power advocates who want to abstractly impose order along the lines of race in an unconscious mirroring of white racism. To underscore the generalizing abstractness of the black-power movement, Percy depicts it as a northern phenomenon that never took root in the South with its more personal, localized culture in contrast to the dehumanizing technocracy of the North. Thus, in *Love in the Ruins,* Tom More suddenly prevents Lola from shooting Ely, recalling that Ely was the son of Ellilou Acree, a "midwife and a worthy woman" (287). Somewhat anachronistically, in the light of actual social reforms in the United States, Percy shows how black people might escape the poverty generated by racism by excelling in the angelism of higher education, a move made by Elgin in *Lancelot,* who in a single jump, Lancelot reflects, went from being a "Louisiana pickaninny playing marbles under a chinaberry tree" to a "smart-ass M.I.T. senior, leapfrogging not only the entire South but all of history as well" (92). Thus, while escaping poverty, capable blacks like Elgin are portrayed as ironically not only falling into the dehumanizing desert of technocracy but also giving up what Percy regards, in spite of its drawbacks, as one of the most humanizing environments in America—southern black culture.

In *The Thanatos Syndrome,* Percy extends his theme of the dangers of angelism by showing the use of medicine in social engineering. "They're treating everything in sight," John Van Dorn says to Tom More, "curing symptoms and wiping out goals" (219). With consummate irony Percy shows how the adding of chemicals to the water supply leads to a new kind of slavery in the South, symbolized, for example, by the prison farm where blacks pick cotton, the men "bare-chested," the women "kerchiefed" and singing a traditional Negro spiritual while armed horsemen patrol the levee (266). Percy also satirizes the pharmaceutical direction taken by psychiatry in contrast to the fruitful effects of the counseling employed by Tom More. Percy's objection to the behaviorist approach, which results in manageable patients, is that such an approach inhibits the quest for self-knowledge in both patients and physicians. In an interview in 1987, Percy declared that Jung was correct in encouraging his patients to believe that their anxiety and depression might be "trying to tell them something of value."[8]

Percy is particularly acute as a social analyst in distinguishing between the management of behavior and the spiritual alienation that often lingers behind such management. While the drugged citizens in *The Thanatos Syndrome* are cured of their fears and guilt, for example, they are also relieved of higher consciousness. Moreover, the scientific removal of fear, Percy reveals, may be rooted in the kind of false expectations disseminated by modern technocracies. An example is the fear of failure, whose ubiquitousness is obscured by film fantasies in which the producers not only hide the inherent tendency toward failure in most people's lives but also obscure their own failures by removing the many failed screen "takes" that precede a successful print. Thus, in *The Thanatos Syndrome,* Tom More, just out of prison and without any patients, thereby removed from the vortex of angelism, sails paper airplanes at a bird house and thinks of himself as a "failed but not unhappy" doctor (75).

The alienation that is the vapor trail of modern technocracy is the principal subject of *The Moviegoer, The Last Gentleman, The Second Coming,* and *Lancelot.* In *The Last Gentleman,* Percy skillfully uses the telescope as a symbol of a distanced relationship between the protagonist and the world around him. In *The Moviegoer,* Binx Bolling reaches a point where he cannot bear a newspaper headline announcing the gradual convergence of the physical and social sciences because he has come to associate such thinking with the causes of his own alienation. Earlier, Binx had felt the

---

8. Percy, "A Visitor Interview: Novelist Walker Percy" (November 8, 1987).

contrast between himself and a fellow student of science who seemed no
more aware of the mystery that surrounded him than a fish was aware of
the "water it swims in" (52). In *Lancelot* the protagonist observes that "interest or the lack of it" had replaced feeling (21). Indeed, Lancelot himself is
drawn by the "worm of interest" to track down the sexual immorality that
occurred in his own home, voyeuristically savoring it on videotape prior to
sweeping to his revenge (21). Victim of the angelism/bestiality syndrome
and of a concomitant alienation from the world around him, Lancelot
probes the sordid mysteries of his wife's and daughter's behaviors with a
relentless, prurient, yet analytical curiosity. His more profound curiosity,
however, is ontological; he is bent on establishing whether such a thing as
evil exists or whether human beings are simply cunning animals governed
by self-serving drives.

While Lancelot is involved in a pilgrimage that has evil as its holy
grail, Percy unobtrusively reveals that his wife's infidelity is related to his
angelistic division of her into two women—virgin and whore: "With you,"
Margot tells him at the end, "I had to be either—or—but never a—uh—
woman" (245). Lancelot's cerebralism results in an inner dividedness as
well, as when he discovers from his daughter's blood type that she could
not be his child. Comparing his family research to that of an astronomer,
he insulates himself from the outrage that finally explodes within him at
the end of the novel. Lancelot's cerebral/sensual polarization is apparent
throughout, as when he notes that there was no joy on earth like falling in
love with a woman and managing at the same time to keep just enough
perspective to "see her fall in love too" (122). Ironically, in order to bring
about the moral purging of society that would allow Lancelot to be able
to tell, as he puts it, the difference between a whore and a lady (his
name symbolizes an old-fashioned courtliness), Lancelot is prepared to
become a demagogue, as he indicates to the priest/psychiatrist who listens
patiently to him throughout the novel:

> There will be honorable men and there will be thieves, just as now, but
> the difference is one will know which is which and there will be no
> confusion, no nice thieves, no honorable Mafia. . . . The best of women
> will be what we used to call ladies, like your Virgin. Our Lady. The
> men? The best of them will be strong and brave and pure of heart, not
> for Christ's sake, but like an Apache youth or a Lacedemonian who
> denies himself to be strong. (178–79)

Reflecting a mixture of southern honor (pretended to but not lived up
to by his father) and pagan morality, Lancelot foresees a society in which
there will be no love and no suffering and, above all, no moral ambiguity, a

welcome change from what he calls the great "whorehouse and fagdom" of America (176). Lancelot's scorn for promiscuity arises from a cerebral discontent with the mixture of good and evil that, from Percy's point of view, is integral to human nature; it arises also from an aloof contempt for the physical world, including the sexual world, which he perceives as a Manichaean in spite of his avowed sensuality. Who else but God, Lancelot wonders bitterly, could have arranged that love should "pitch its tent in the place of excrement?" (238).

The powerful subconscious roots of Lancelot's feelings are dramatized late in the novel by a dream in which the figures of virgin and whore metamorphose, as suppressed memories of his mother's infidelity surface and confirm him in his resolve to kill the sexual/immoral. Given a bowie knife in the dream, his Arthurian sword, Lancelot moves to his revenge, resolved to avenge the stain not only on his own honor but, in southern fashion, that on his father's honor as well. Lancelot's assault is twofold, an assault upon an imperfect Christian incarnational reality on the one hand and a related (in terms of the theme of angelism) assault based upon a redolent, amorphous code of southern honor on the other. In carrying out his revenge, Lancelot ironically discovers that he failed, finally, to achieve his quest, the vision of what evil is. Why, he wonders, mystified, had he discovered "nothing" at the "heart of evil," not even, he reflects paradoxically, "any evil" (253)? Percy here registers a Thomist perception of evil as a negation, an absence of being that can simulate reality only by parasitically attaching itself to good.

In *The Last Gentleman*, Sutter parallels Lancelot in alternating between angelism and bestiality, a switch that is partly symbolized by his moving from psychiatry to pathology. The symbolism is more subtle here than it may appear, however, since both Sutter and Percy regard psychiatry as having degenerated into behaviorism, while pathology, which Percy himself specialized in at one point, at least had no social or psychological pretensions. Nonetheless, Sutter's sexual libertinism is directly linked to his abstract and alienated separation of himself from the world, including Will Barrett, who seeks his help. In *Lost in the Cosmos*, Percy observed that pornography generally resulted from an abstract view by males of themselves, which led to the abstraction and subsequent degradation of women (10).

What makes Sutter especially complex is his self-justifying converting of his bawdiness into metaphysics. Lewdness, he notes clinically in his journal, is the "sole concrete metaphysic" of the layperson in an age of science (279). While science is gnostic and abstract, divorcing human beings from their own experience, lewdness is concrete and immanent, even if only, as Percy shows, temporarily satisfying. Though called the "engineer" throughout the novel, a symbolic indication of his lack of personal identity, Barrett perceptively discerns that Sutter is a suicidal abstractionist because he cannot endure the agony of experience, including the impending painful death of Jamie in the face of which he as a physician is powerless. Percy shows, though, that Will Barrett *can* accept the suffering of Jamie's death because he has become attuned to suffering as a natural part of experience. Percy, incidentally, holds nothing back in describing Jamie's dying, which culminates in suffocation due to the accumulation of fluid in his lungs.

The climactic deathbed scene in *The Last Gentleman* includes some of Percy's best writing. The role created for the priest is fresh and paradoxical and is urbanely dramatized by Percy. Following noncommittal responses by Sutter and Barrett as to the reality of faith, Jamie puts the matter to the priest: "The priest sighed. 'If it were not true,' he said to Jamie, 'then I would not be here. That is why I am here, to tell you'" (404). The priest's odd impatience and apparently immutable faith contrast dourly with the desultory emotions that lie elsewhere in the room. While the death of Jamie is shrouded in ambiguity as far as his baptism is concerned, Percy shows clearly that a moral change has occurred in Will Barrett, who intercepts Sutter from a probable suicide attempt. Mysteriously transformed by the child's death and the priest's words, Will finds himself suddenly able to draw on strength that flowed like "oil" into his muscles so that he was able to run with "great joyous ten-foot antelope bounds" (409). The language reaches back into the novel's symbolism. Oil recalls the automobile imagery and the technological odyssey of the twentieth-century American nomad. The antelope image, however, cancels the technological connotations with its own attractive bodily associations and symbolically sets Barrett on the earth at last, freed from an isolation, which, unlike Sutter's, was not of his choosing.

Percy fills out the meaning of the novel's denouement by focusing on the character of Val, Jamie's older sister, who had become a nun. The characterization of Val is clothed in the symbolism of birds. As she recounts her religious conversion to Will Barrett at one point, she continues to carefully feed a hawk a packet of viscera. Percy's choice of a predatory bird for this scene is perhaps surprising. Nevertheless, it symbolizes in part both the nun's otherworldliness and her dynamic approach to faith as well as the unsentimentally viewed reality of the world that she must spiritually feed. She appoints Will to see that Jamie is baptized and does so with the same sangfroid with which she pockets all the money Will has on him. As in Flannery O'Connor's fiction, the obvious representatives of God in Percy's fiction are portrayed with a boldness that flows from their calling, ironically causing them to stand out against the passivity and relative uncommunicativeness of the surrounding society.

Another example of bird imagery occurs earlier as Barrett and Val converse at the Vaught estate. A towhee suddenly flies out of the azaleas, and Val uses the occasion of the bird's appearance to broach the difficult subject of Jamie's death. As she does so, her eye settles on the "tiny amber eye" of the towhee:

> "I don't want him to die without knowing why he came here, what he is doing here, and why he is leaving. . . ."
> "Why don't you tell him?" He was watching her as intently as the towhee watched her. There was no telling what she might do.
> She sighed and sat down. The towhee, released from its spell, flew away. "I have told him." (210)

Ingeniously, Percy uses the bird as a spring to dramatize the tension of the scene, releasing that spring as the bird flies off. The extra tension gives the passage an apt momentousness that heightens its crucial contents. The bird of course also conveys its residual symbolic value as coming from the air, a heavenly messenger, but this is secondary to its scenic use.

In *The Last Gentleman*, Percy not only focuses on angelism and alienation but also on the emptiness of the American dream. The most obvious American dream symbolism is that associated with Mr. Vaught with his immense automobile dealership, wealth, and castlelike home, which is set in an area that appropriately recalls Fitzgerald's descriptions of garish mansions in *The Great Gatsby*:

> The houses of the valley were built in the 1920s, a time when rich men still sought to recall heroic ages. Directly opposite the castle, atop the next ridge to the south, there stood a round, rosy temple. It was the dwelling of a millionaire who had admired a Roman structure erected by the Emperor Vespasian in honor of Juno and so had reproduced it in good Alabama red brick and Georgia marble. At night a battery of colored floodlights made it look redder still. (189)

The passage illustrates part of the lasting value of Percy's fiction, his impeccably civilized language and fine comic sense. In portraying the forlorn Will Barrett as the last gentleman, for example, Percy defers tactfully to Barrett's consciousness of clinging to an old-fashioned gentility in lieu of a self he can call his own, all the while, though, parodying the role Will has adopted for himself. Thinking about Kitty Vaught, for instance, Will resolves to court her in the old style: "I shall press her hand. No more grubby epithelial embraces in dogbane thickets, followed by accusing phone calls. Never again! Not until we are in our honeymoon cottage in a cottage small by a waterfall" (166). Echoing a popular American song of the 1940s, Percy incisively reveals both Will's mocking, trapped awareness of all that he feels alienated from yet also his underlying determination to cling to the love that has been offered to him. In terms of the American dream with its blandishments of luxury and comfort, Will reflects late in the novel that it was strange that "we are well when we are afflicted and afflicted when we are well" (240). Percy adds the further paradox that Jamie, the son of a millionaire, dreams of a life like that in a Russian novel where he could be a "refugee or a prisoner," traveling the whole length of Russia in a cattle car, "along with hundreds of others" (250).

In *The Second Coming*, Percy's sequel to *The Last Gentleman*, Barrett returns as a character alienated from his society, this time, though, following a successful career as a corporate lawyer. Though he is more conscious of his condition than in *The Last Gentleman*, Barrett is not only depressed by his own hollowness but also by the sight of a world that he has judged to be "in fact farcical."[9] Percy surrounds his central character's acedia with philosophical overtones, allowing Will to reflect early in the novel that peace was better than war only if peace was "not hell too." War, after all, "being hell, makes sense," he reflects (21). In a refinement on this theme, Will, overcome by déjà vu, reflects that nothing ever changed, that marriages, births, deaths, and terrible wars had occurred but had changed nothing. War, he concludes, was not a change but rather a "poor attempt to make a change" (52). More lucidly and assertively than in *The Last Gentleman*, Percy demonstrates that Barrett's alienation proceeds not from a failure in himself but from a failure in society to provide a meaningful environment.

Immersed in his solipsistic consciousness, Barrett, Percy imaginatively shows, has difficulty recognizing himself as a physical being:

> As he stepped out, he caught sight of a shadowy stranger in the mirror fixed to the door. But he quickly saw that the stranger was himself. The reason the figure appeared strange was that it was reflected by two mirrors, one the rearview mirror, the other the dark window-glass of the Mercedes door. . . . With two mirrors it is possible to see oneself briefly as a man among men rather than a self sucking everything into itself. (13–14)

9. Percy, *Second Coming*, 4, subsequently cited in the text parenthetically.

In a tense and startling scene Percy depicts Barrett snapping out of his solipsistic vortex by virtue of a poacher's bullet. Earlier in his life, it is made clear, Barrett had been temporarily lifted out of the haze that surrounded him by the death of his wife. Earlier still, in childhood, he had been hurled from a secure experience of life by his father's attempt to kill both his son and himself, a memory that more than all others saps Barrett's will to live. While Barrett is given a suicidal profile by Percy, based on family history, his metaphysical quarrel with the universe is at least as significant a factor in his decision to descend into the cave, perhaps forever. Driven to seek a God who alone, it would seem, could alleviate his pervasive feelings of alienation, Barrett finally abandons an interest in the Pascalian wager—the calculation that if there is a God one can only benefit by believing, and if not, one has lost nothing. Faced with such an abstract reckoning, Percy portrays Barrett as unimpressed by this sterile manner of coming to terms with divinity.

Establishing a symmetrical structure throughout, a pattern that appealed to Catholic writers such as Percy, O'Connor, and Powers, whose robust faith supported an absolute view of experience, Percy depicts Barrett's perilous descent into the cave, a symbolic death of the self, as followed by the arrival of new life. Significantly, in terms of Percy's interest in angelism and his incarnational theology, it is new life that arrives—a person, in fact—rather than new thought. The characterization of Allison Huger parallels that of Will Barrett in its focus on alienation. Alternating between silence and a cryptic speech, she seals herself off from the world. While her inhabiting of the abandoned greenhouse symbolically parallels Barrett's descent into the cave in some respects, it is obviously different in others, especially in its connotations of fertility. Like Barrett, though, Allison experiences life as emptiness. In her mother's words, she doesn't know how to live from "one Christmas to the next" (284).

Following the lines of Percy's symmetrical structure, one sees that while Barrett remembers everything and Allison remembers nothing, both extremes contribute to depression. Since he cannot forget, Will Barrett is haunted by the attempted murder/suicide and eventual suicide of his father; since she cannot remember, Allison is overwhelmed and terrified by those around her who encroach on the near vacuum that she has become. Rather than resisting this pressure, which she is not strong enough to do, Allison resorts, like Barrett, to disappearance, to reducing herself to near invisibility: "A red giant collapses into a white dwarf. Hard and bright as a diamond. That's what I was trying to do when my mother found me in the closet going down to my white dwarf" (90). The astronomical conceit neatly captures both the desire of Allison to escape the world and the emotionally frigid place that she sees the world as being.

While Percy in *The Second Coming* focused largely on characterization, a wider social perspective is established from time to time. Thus, Barrett concludes at one point that while death was the adequate symbol of his time, it was most visible in the "death people live" (271). Furthermore, in a rebuke of organized religion, he vows that death in the "guise of Christianity" would not prevail over him. If Christ brought life, he wonders, why do the churches "smell of death?" (272). Percy's portrait of religion in *The Second Coming*, the title of which resonates with apocalyptic overtones, is of a Christianity caught up in materialism. Similarly, in defining the post-Christian society in which he finds himself marooned, Binx Bolling in *The Moviegoer* reflects that being pagan would be an acceptable alternative to Christianity in a world in which everyone was "nicer" than Christians and "naughtier" than pagans (207). The euphemistic language echoes Percy's ironic perception that, without even the stability of a pagan hedonism, social mores in a post-Christian world would be anarchic at best, perverse at worst.

In *The Last Gentleman* the novel's opening epigraph from Romano Guardini's book *The End of the Modern World* expresses the prevailing view in Percy's fiction regarding contemporary post-Christian society. Guardini postulates a Western world that will live for a time on the interest accumulated by the moral capital of Christianity but speculates that eventually this will fade, leaving a society in which love will disappear from the face of the public world and in which Christians will experience a terrible loneliness. Such is the world depicted in *The Second Coming*, though one that is artfully disguised for most of the characters by the pleasantries of twentieth-century consumerism. In *Lancelot*, in contrast, the portrayal of society is more overtly apocalyptic. Lancelot angrily denounces his society, vowing that he will not "tolerate this age" and castigates the Catholic Church for having become a "part of the age" (157). Some insight into Lancelot's view can be found in *Love in the Ruins* in which Percy depicts an American Catholic Church divided into three contentious parts: a nationalistic church at odds with Rome; a church focused on social injustice rather than on God; and a remnant church, the church that Percy himself had joined, reduced to a marginal status.

In *The Thanatos Syndrome* religion in society is largely a peripheral phenomenon, whose sorry state is aptly symbolized by Ellen More's purchase of two iron convent beds, now fashionable, following the closing of a convent. Similarly, in the same novel, a bickering married couple, an ex-nun and ex-priest, attempt, ludicrously, to merge with their bizarre society.

Against the moral flaccidity of contemporary society, Percy focuses on a few, memorably anachronistic figures—Father Smith, Will Barrett, Allison Huger, Tom More. Quixotically isolated from their society, these characters attempt to find a refuge at least within their own consciousnesses, or in the case of the fortuitous circumstances of *The Second Coming,* within the life of another like themselves. In contrast to the spiritual desert that surrounds them, they appear to the reader in their vulnerability and solitude as fresh and vigorous as hardy green plants.

Stylistically, Percy is memorable for his lively, philosophical use of the picaresque, especially visible in novels such as *The Moviegoer* and *The Last Gentleman.* Moreover, Percy has a way of applying his imagination powerfully to particular moments so that they epitomize the whole of the narratives in which they occur. At the end of *Lancelot,* for example, the adulterous on-film activities of Margot and Merlin are made to seem demonically lurid by the defective filming, which reverses the colors so that their clothes are light and their faces dark. Equally effective, though in a comic vein, is the picture of Tom More in *Love in the Ruins* taking up the sword of Saint Michael, his heart thumping wildly, in order to become at last the hero his namesake had been, however absurd the difference in circumstances.

Percy's use of setting is no less imaginative. In *Love in the Ruins,* for example, as Will Barrett watches over the motel where he is attempting to protect the three women who have taken refuge there, he has a view from his high vantage point of the nearby television transmitter tower appearing to arise from the "dumpy silo of old Saint Michael's Church in the plaza" (12). The image instantly cements the identification between church and society that appears in much of Percy's fiction. Similarly, in *Lancelot* Belle Isle is described as a "small dark islet" hemmed in by "Ethyl pipery, Dow towers, Kaiser stacks, all humming away. Farther away, near the highway, gas burnoffs flared in the night as if giant hunters still stalked the old swamp" (56). The truncated phrases suggest a fragmented world of synthetic objects that have choked off the natural world, an objective correlative for the decadent inhabitants of Belle Isle.

Percy's handling of parody and burlesque is also impressive. In *Lancelot,* for example, Merlin is implicitly and derisively compared to the hunter Wilson in Hemingway's story "The Short Happy Life of Francis Macomber," Merlin being released finally by Lancelot to return to Africa to "find his youth. To see leopard" (201). Percy's use of burlesque is never better than in *The Thanatos Syndrome.* A vivid example is his Swiftian depiction of the drug-transformed school administrators, a transformation portrayed drolly through the eyes of two local African Americans:

Coach and Mr. Brunette are still in their "bachelor" postures of submission—Coach, head bowed, studying his palms, contenting himself with a single stomp of his running shoe; Mr. Brunette, one elbow crooked over his head, laying it over to allow Mrs. Brunette to groom him.

"Would you look at that woman," whispers the uncle to Vergil, the uncle at first rapt, then hopping and poking an elbow into Vergil's side.

But Vergil, arms crossed, eyes monitored, permits himself no more than a single, unsurprised shrug. There is no telling what white people—(319–20)

The satire is rich indeed. Two black men from a subjugated culture observe two white men acting like apes following the application of a sophisticated technology that would ordinarily have enhanced an attitude of white superiority. Once again in Percy, one has the sense of African Americans protected by the very poverty of their education and resources from a folly that has overtaken the rest of society, not that Percy approved of the poverty or the discrimination that underlay it. Percy's major theme is that the moral norms and behavior of the past, while far from perfect, nevertheless were being replaced by something worse, a technological quagmire in which good and evil cannot be adequately perceived and defined and in which the traditional, though not exclusively, Catholic morality that the end does not justify the means has been virtually ignored by contemporary society. In this respect, while Percy's fiction, not unlike Flannery O'Connor's, leans toward didacticism at times, it does so vividly within the bounds of narrative satire.

Percy's attraction to Christianity, and particularly to Catholicism, rested upon his sense that Christ had brought news from without, news that illuminated the human predicament in a way that human beings had been unable to do. With the slipping away of this inherited insight, Percy feared the worst. In particular, he feared the severing of the bond between the spiritual/intellectual and the physical worlds that had been held together by Catholic incarnational theology. With the abandonment of such an ideological model, Percy emphasized, love was reduced to personal feeling, while the state and the public world in turn hardened into a technological apparatus that was empty at the core. Percy's distinctive contribution as a novelist was to focus all these themes vividly within the compass of a scattering of memorable lives and places, most of them within easy reach of his semirural Louisiana home. Percy accomplished this by pinpointing the anxieties and depressions brought on by contemporary American culture and only then working back to the probable causes, which he attempted to show lay far beyond the scientist's power to rectify. What particularly enlivens Percy's fiction, though, is the gusty humor that blows through the novels, leaving the startled reader with a residue of sanity and wisdom that permit the thought that the world is a larger place than the weighty evils so brilliantly satirized by Percy would have led one to expect.

Dystopian novels such as *The Thanatos Syndrome* are not only techno-phobic but also attack what Percy perceived as the unscientific culture of science itself. In *The Thanatos Syndrome*, for example, Percy, through Father Smith, berates the scientific community for ignoring the implications of the big bang theory of creation that had otherwise won acceptance among physicists: " 'Even if the truths of religion could be proved to you, one, two, three, it wouldn't make much difference, would it? One hundred percent of astronomers have discovered that the universe was created from nothing. The explanation is obvious but it does not avail. Who can handle it? It does not signify. It is boring to think of. Ninety-seven percent of astronomers are still atheists' " (364).

In response to such a rebuff of religion, Percy offers a view of the Catholic Church that, as Anita Gandolfo has suggested, shows a church in "disarray."[10] The disunity in the post–Vatican II church in Percy's novels is all too apparent. At the end of *The Thanatos Syndrome*, Tom More and Father Rinaldo Smith form a saving remnant of sorts. Significantly, Father Smith exists outside of the formal administrative structure of his church as does Tom More, though each is fully Catholic in terms of belief and practice. As Tom More prepares to serve the Mass of the Epiphany for Father Smith, he utters the words of the pre–Vatican II Mass: "To God who gives joy to my youth" (363). For both Tom More and Father Smith, loyalty to the traditional church is perfectly consistent with Vatican II's emphasis on social justice.

Tom More's alienation from contemporary American society is implicit in the reference, albeit an ironic one, to Thomas Jefferson and to Jefferso-nian democracy in *The Thanatos Syndrome*. That reference occurs when Bob Comeau points proudly to the "yeoman farmer and yeoman craftsman" produced by his chemically induced utopia, although these farmers and craftsmen lack the essential Jeffersonian dimension of freedom (198). In an interview with Phil McCombs, Percy contended that once one ignored the "uniqueness and sacredness of the individual human" and set up "abstract" ideals for the improvement of society, then the "terminus was

10. Gandolfo, *Testing the Faith*, 41.

the gas chamber."[11] As an American Catholic of the old school, Percy had a respect for the sanctity of the individual that he felt both the social encyclicals of his church and the political idealism of his country supported. While in any practical sense the quixotic coming together of Tom More and the eccentric Father Smith cannot be said to represent, even symbolically, the beginning of a new American Catholic Church, it does represent the continuity of an ideology that in its balancing of individualism and communality is as old as both Jeffersonian democracy and early Christianity.

11. Percy, *More Conversations with Walker Percy*, 191.

9

ROBERT LOWELL

(1917-1977)

I N THE EARLY 1960s Robert Lowell told Frederic Seidel that his ostensibly secular poems of the 1950s and 1960s, while lacking the extensive Catholic framework and symbolism of the earlier work, nevertheless in some ways seemed more religious to him—though he added that he regarded his poetry as all of a piece, religiously speaking.[1] This surprising remark doubtlessly reflected a desire by Lowell to distance himself from Roman Catholicism, which he had abandoned in the late 1940s, at which time he was obtaining a divorce from his first wife, Jean Stafford, prior to marrying Elizabeth Hardwick. Moreover, his growing problem with manic-depressive behavior was also, he believed, exacerbated by intense ascetic episodes related to the practice of his faith. Nevertheless, Lowell's retrospective assessment invites one to take a second look at his Catholic poetry, which is largely contained in the two early volumes *Land of Unlikeness* and *Lord Weary's Castle* (published in 1944 and 1946, respectively), in order to examine the kind and strength of the poet's religious feeling. What one finds is a vigorous and passionate religious consciousness that contrasts markedly with the subdued and often sardonic approach to religion manifested in the later verse.

A number of critics, including Norma Procopiow and Sue Mitchell Crowley, have tended to agree with Lowell about the religious equivalency

---

1. Lowell, *Collected Prose*, 250.

of the early and later work. Others, such as Richard Fein, have argued that Lowell was chiefly indebted to Catholicism as a source of poetic subject matter. William Doreski has also observed that Lowell's "newfound" religious faith provided much of the "iconography, the structure, and the argument" of the poems of the 1940s. Similarly, Jay Martin described Lowell as having "explored" both Puritanism and Catholicism in his first two books before proceeding to "use" Western civilization and his "personal crisis" as "material" for his later poetry. This view has been most flatly set forth by Stephen Gould Axelrod, who concluded in an article on Lowell and Hopkins that language was always "central" and Catholicism "secondary" to Lowell.[2]

Some critics, on the other hand, have asserted the depth of Lowell's Catholicism in the early poetry, though sometimes, as in the case of Frank O'Malley, without being very detailed. Moreover, O'Malley at times seems to concede the case to the formalists by arguing that although the burden of Lowell's themes might be "darkling," Christ is really and finally the "Form of Lowell's poetry." The question of how much Lowell incorporates an incarnational theology in the early poems is a pivotal one in assessing the influence of Catholicism. Axelrod, for example, contrasts Lowell with Eliot in this respect, noting that while Eliot values both the still point and the turning world, Lowell disdains time and seeks to "abolish human history." Jerome Mazzaro, who makes the strongest case for the influence of Catholicism in Lowell's work, goes so far as to bridge the early and later poetry by postulating a shift from "contemplative love to human love" as if these were part of a single spiritual design. It was as if Lowell discovered that he had begun too high on the scale of love, Mazzaro wrote, and so took a "step backward" in the later work. In fact, the examples of love in Lowell's later poetry, such as they are, have little to do with religion. Similarly, Mazzaro's claim that even in *The Mills of the Kavanaghs* (written after Lowell's departure from the Catholic Church) Lowell focuses on the "peace of the truly Christian life" in his portrait of Mother Marie Therese seems far-fetched and out of touch with the bleakly ironic tone of that poem and volume.[3]

Critics such as Mazzaro and O'Malley have tended to overemphasize the influence of Catholicism in the early poetry, particularly in overlooking

2. Procopiow, *Robert Lowell: The Poet and His Critics*, 121; Crowley, "Mr. Blackmur's Lowell: How Does Morality Get into Literature?" 45; Fein, *Robert Lowell*, 31; Doreski, *The Years of Our Friendship*, 56; Martin, *Robert Lowell*, 20; Axelrod, "Robert Lowell and Hopkins," 58.

3. O'Malley, "The Blood of Robert Lowell," 6; Axelrod, *Robert Lowell: Life and Art*, 47; Mazzaro, *The Poetic Themes of Robert Lowell*, 91, 80.

the presence of Calvinistic elements. On the other hand, critics such as Philip Hobsbaum, Philip Cooper, and Sue Mitchell Crowley have emphasized the influence of Calvinism, sometimes to the near exclusion of the Catholic elements. Like Hugh Staples, Will Jumper has drawn attention to the anti-Calvinistic strain in Lowell's poetry of the 1940s. The truth is that Lowell was a hybrid, theologically (as can readily be seen in the greatest of the early poems, "The Quaker Graveyard in Nantucket").[4]

Lowell was raised in the Episcopalian Church, although he freely admitted that agnosticism prevailed within his family. However, even at Saint Mark's, the Episcopalian boarding school that he attended in Massachusetts, he showed a serious interest in religion and resented the contrast between the "poor chapel" and "magnificent fieldhouse" that he felt symbolized their relative status at the school.[5] In the light of his subsequent conversion to Roman Catholicism, it is noteworthy that Lowell's first published poem was titled "Madonna." It was Lowell's attachment to Allen Tate in the late 1930s, however, that spurred his interest in Catholicism, although Tate himself formally entered the Catholic Church only in 1950. It was also Tate who persuaded Lowell to adopt the formalism that is so characteristic of *Land of Unlikeness* and *Lord Weary's Castle*.

Lowell's early intellectual formation was also indebted to John Crowe Ransom at Kenyon College where Lowell excelled as a student of the classics. While he valued the civilizing features of Greek and Roman literature, however, Lowell indicated in some miscellaneous school notes written around 1940 that a classical education lacked "hierarchy," "orthodoxy," "intellectual spine," and a viewpoint that could be considered "instinctively moral or rational." In part because of his exposure to Thomist philosophy as a young man, Lowell felt strongly that reason and faith were compatible—as he argued in a letter to Robie Macauley in 1943.[6] In spite of this view, though, Lowell's Catholic poems are not markedly philosophical, as will be seen.

By July 1943, Lowell wrote to Peter Taylor that he didn't care about anything except writing and trying to be a "halfway decent Christian."

4. Hobsbaum, *A Reader's Guide to Robert Lowell*, 27; Cooper, *The Autobiographical Myth of Robert Lowell*, 22; Crowley, "Mr. Blackmur's Lowell," 35; Staples, *Robert Lowell: The First Twenty Years*, 69; Jumper, "Whom Seek Ye? A Note on Robert Lowell's Poetry," 53.
5. Lowell, "Moulding the Golden Spoon," 4, Lowell Collection, Houghton Library, Harvard University.
6. Lowell, "Miscellaneous School Notes and Prose," Lowell Collection, Houghton Library, Harvard University; Lowell to Macauley, 1943, quoted in Ian Hamilton, *Robert Lowell: A Biography*, 81.

Lowell also became friendly in the 1940s with two Catholic writers, Flannery O'Connor and J. F. Powers, in addition to his existing ties with Allen Tate and Caroline Gordon. Moreover, Lowell also cultivated an appreciation of Hopkins, whose life, he noted in a short essay called "Hopkins's Sanctity" in 1944, constituted a "continuous substantial progress toward perfection." Moreover, writing to his mother, Charlotte Winslow Lowell, in 1943 about *Land of Unlikeness*, Lowell confided earnestly that his poems were intended to help "recover our ancient freedom and dignity, to be Christians and build a Christian society."[7]

In spite of Lowell's later attempt to minimize the significance of the Catholic background of his early poetry, he conceded that Catholicism gave him both "subject matter" and a "kind of form," allowing him to begin a poem and "build it to a climax."[8] Thus, although a number of the early poems lack the sort of narrative, autobiographical underpinning that colors *Life Studies* and *For the Union Dead* (published in 1959 and 1964, respectively), they are enlivened in a formal sense by Catholic doctrine and imagery. A rather conspicuous example is the use of the doctrine of purgatory in "Napoleon Crosses the Berezina." A further example is the evocation of the doctrine of the community of saints with its bridging of this and the next world in the sonnet "The Soldier":

> Where is that Ghibelline whom Dante met
> On Purgatory's doorstep, without kin
> To set up chantries for his God-held debt?[9]

It is difficult to tell exactly how much religious feeling there is in either "Napoleon Crosses the Berezina" or "The Soldier," but on the whole the poet seems somewhat detached from the spiritual world he is describing. Allen Tate recognized as much in his introduction to *Land of Unlikeness*, when he observed that the Christian symbolism is sometimes rather intellectualized, a significant judgment from someone who was himself capable of cerebral writing on religious themes. One feels the same way about a number of the poems in which Lowell employs a metaphysical style, such as "The Bomber" and "On the Eve of the Feast of the Immaculate Conception 1942." In the latter poem, Mary's love is said

---

7. Lowell to Taylor, July 18, 1943, quoted in Hamilton, *Robert Lowell*, 101; Lowell, *Collected Prose*, 168; Lowell to Winslow Lowell, Lowell Collection, Hougton Library, Harvard University: bMS Am 1905 (1549).

8. Lowell, *Collected Prose*, 258.

9. Lowell, *Lord Weary's Castle*, 35, subsequently cited parenthetically in the text as *LWC*.

to be "burly," a startling image in connection with the Mother of God; Lowell later calls her a "Celestial Hoyden," an even bolder metaphor. Lowell's metaphysical poetic style at the time was more than a technical flourish, however, and more than an imitation of Tate and Eliot; rather, he believed that metaphysical poetry was useful in making the "miraculous explicit."[10]

In the early poems, rather like Tate, Lowell also attempted to interweave Catholic and classical allusions, thereby reflecting the most salient influences on his own intellectual formation. At times the effect of this merging of traditions is rather routine, and at times the classical allusions seem to mitigate the effect of the religious themes. An example is the poem "The First Sunday in Lent" in which those who fail to adopt a penitential attitude for the season are compared to the citizens of Troy who celebrate around the wooden horse that will be their undoing. The problem with the reference to Troy is that, contrary to Lowell's own reservations about the moral and rational limitations of classical literature, the pagan story is given a kind of moral equivalency, thus subverting the implied preeminence of the Christian reality. Similarly, in "The Drunken Fisherman," the old man reflects gloomily that the prince of darkness had stalked his "bloodstream to its Stygian term" (*LWC*, 32). Lowell's neoclassicism here, while consistent with the balancing of classical and Christian typology that one finds in Milton and other Renaissance poets, risks sacrificing the moral urgency that his relatively short lyrics on contemporary themes otherwise convey. Unlike Milton's, Lowell's poems are not primarily philosophical, not a justifying of the ways of God to man, but rather are a passionate attempt to divert those in the West from the precipice that in the early 1940s Lowell saw as lying before them.

For this reason many of the poems that incorporate Catholic themes within American locales have a greater immediacy and persuasiveness and more convincingly reflect the experience and feelings of the poet than the poems whose contents are suspended abstractly inside a web of Catholic and classical materials. "The Holy Innocents" is a good example. The biblical story of Herod's slaughter of the innocents, together with its moral application to modern Americans, is worked out against a vividly rendered New England setting:

> Listen, the hay-bells tinkle as the cart
> Wavers on rubber tires along the tar

---

10. Lowell, *Land of Unlikeness*, subsequently cited parenthetically in the text as *LU*; Lowell, review of *The World's Body*, by John Crowe Ransom, 59.

And cindered ice below the burlap mill
And ale-wife run. The oxen drool and start
In wonder at the fenders of a car,
And blunder hugely up St. Peter's hill. (*LWC*, 4)

The descriptive details—including the cindered road for winter driving, the burlap mill (a familiar part of the New England economy and landscape), and the naming of the hill after the Catholic church on top of it— all contribute tangibly toward the authenticity of the scene, which in turn lends realism to the atmosphere of menace that underlies the Christmas season. Through the subtle interaction of setting and lyric statement, a final, mordant theme gradually emerges in the poem to the effect that if Christ had escaped death at the hands of King Herod, he did not escape death in the America of 1945. For all of its conspicuous craftsmanship, the poem nonetheless convincingly conveys the religious alienation that arises from the juxtaposition of Christian ideology (St. Peter's hill) with the spiritual quagmire that Lowell felt his society had become.

The motif of spiritual quagmire is sharply registered in "Colloquy in Black Rock." Lowell lived in Black Rock, a Connecticut community in the Bridgeport area, while serving a sentence as a conscientious objector. In Black Rock, the speaker observes, immigrant workers "give their blood / For the martyre Stephen, who was stoned to death" (*LWC*, 5). Saint Stephen, the patron saint of Bridgeport (which has a cathedral dedicated to him), elicits a sacrificial love that is opposed to the clotted hedonism of contemporary America. Moreover, the fact that Saint Stephen, whose feast is celebrated the day after Christmas, was stoned to death is played off against the town's name. While the speaker characterizes the town disdainfully as Black Rock or Black Mud, a sign of its moral failure and materialism, the final stanza offers an alternative, supernatural view of the town's life and potential destiny:

On Corpus Christi, heart,
Over the drum-beat of St. Stephen's choir
I hear him, *Stupor Mundi*, and the mud
Flies from his hunching wings and beak—my heart,
The blue kingfisher dives on you in fire. (*LWC*, 5)

While the kingfisher image recalls Hopkins, its use in this fresh context renews it. The blue color enters the poem boldly against the grays and browns that otherwise prevail, a color that Lowell would have associated not only with the heaven-sent Jesus but especially with Mary, to whom Lowell had a special devotion.

In addition, the dynamic quality of the bird contrasts with the morose stagnancy of the scene, offering a moment of release from the seemingly endless predicament Lowell describes, including his own suffering as a prisoner of the state. The kingfisher is linked doctrinally to the rest of the poem through the allusion to Corpus Christi, the feast of the body of Christ, whereby, through the Incarnation and the Eucharist, human beings become incorporated into the divine. The biting use of the Latin phrase *Stupor Mundi* also links the poem's language, even if ironically, to that of the Mass and to the centuries-old church whose ancient pedigree had initially attracted Lowell to Catholicism.

Although the speaker indulges in some repetitiveness as he ponders his central themes and motifs, the poem is economical in its fresh use of these motifs with each reappearance; furthermore, the march of emphatic, end-stopped lines and violent images creates a counterpoint of tautness. Especially impressive is Lowell's layering of meaning and image, as in "Our ransom is the rubble of his death," a line that not only conceptually merges religious motifs with those of Lowell's Connecticut locale but also, through alliteration, generates an underlying unity. The alliteration seals the union of syllables for the ear so that the mind of the reader is prompted to return to the phrasing in order to discover additional unifying, thematic strands.

Although Lowell had originally volunteered for military service in World War II, only to be rejected, he gradually withdrew his support for the war because of the altered tactics of the Allied forces, particularly the destruction of huge civilian populations through the saturation bombing of large German cities. He told V. S. Naipaul that his subsequent refusal of induction sprang in large part from the fact that he was a Roman Catholic and had accepted the "very complicated" idea of the "unjust war" in Catholic thought. Before refusing military service, Lowell wrote to his maternal grandmother in 1943 and disclosed that he had talked at great length with his "priest in New York" about his intention to refuse the draft as well as written to the priest who had baptized him in Louisiana. Both, he added, told him to follow his conscience and to trust in God. "I have prayed for light and tried to persuade myself that I was mistaken," he added, but "I cannot."[11]

In retrospect, Lowell's stand can be seen as historically ironic in the light of the fact that, as Gordon Zahn has shown, very few American Catholics

---

11. Lowell, *Robert Lowell: Interviews and Memoirs,* 143; Lowell to Mary Devereux Winslow, October 13, 1943: bMS Am 1905 (1680).

refused to serve in the military during World War II. Nevertheless, in his later poem "Memories of West Street and Lepke," written when he was no longer a Catholic, Lowell explicitly identifies the stand he took at the time. While Lowell had been opposed to the war on Christian pacifistic principles, not dissimilar from those held by Thomas Merton and William Everson, he was moved to become a conscientious objector following the indiscriminate bombing of cities such as Hamburg, the subject of "The North Sea Undertaker's Complaint." The poem documents the destruction not only of German military installations but also of a Catholic priest, one of many "blue-lipped" priests the "hammer" of whose hearts were reduced to ashes by the phosphorous bombs (*LWC*, 33). The image of the hammer of the dead priest's heart deftly connects his death with the bell that tolls his funeral and in turn with the obliteration of that Christianity in whose name, in part, the Allied war machine had been dispatched.

The attrition of Christianity in Nazi-occupied Europe is seen to have issued not only from Allied bombing, though, but from more inherent causes as well. In "Cistercians in Germany" the monks are seen to have been evicted from their monasteries, a desperate situation that is nevertheless paradoxically offset at the end of the poem by a poignant appeal to their founder, Saint Bernard of Clairvaux:

> Yesterday pagan Junkers smashed our cells,
> We lift our bloody hands to wizened Bernard,
> To Bernard gathering his canticle of flowers,
> His soul a bridal chamber fresh with flowers,
> And all his body one extatic womb,
> And through the trellis peers the sudden Bridegroom. (*LU*)

These lines, some of the finest that Lowell ever wrote, rise unexpectedly from their sardonic context to a lyrical purity that permits one to momentarily overlook the intransigent fact that only through prayer and mysticism could a citizen in Nazi-occupied Europe escape.

Lowell's opposition to war eventually became wider in scope as he searched his religion to provide him with a conceptual and symbolic framework by which to understand the apocalyptic ramifications of the war that raged in Europe. Within the limelight of this broad, teleological approach Lowell found fault even with Britain's participation in the conflict, as can be seen in "Scenes from the Historic Comedy":

> Britain is wooden; gas
> Blows on the wind until her ghost is laid

> In Jacob's Well; her bastions break
> As the charred Angels blaze
> All manmarks from this world man never made,
> Armadas whelm the Roman Lake. *(LU)*

The British action in the Mediterranean became the focus for Lowell's perception that the war was destructive not only to the protagonists but also to a world, a creation, that had been given to human beings by a loving God. In these lines one notices the skillfulness with which Lowell employs sound, as in the plosive sounds of "break" and "blaze," which convey the violence of exploding shells. If this gives the poem an emotional urgency, phrases such as "Roman Lake" create a spacious and ageless perspective on human conflict into which the poem's biblical allusions can be interwoven.

The timelessness of war is the focus of the well-known poem "Christmas Eve Under Hooker's Statue":

> "All wars are boyish," Herman Melville said;
> But we are old, our fields are running wild:
> Till Christ again turn wanderer and child. *(LWC, 17)*

The end-stopped rhymes rather pointedly and emphatically project Lowell's religious beliefs, which at the time had all but absorbed his sensibility. Rejecting Melville's view of war, Lowell argues that the problem with the twentieth-century attitude to war is that we live in a historical and psychological cul-de-sac in which war is regarded as inevitable. What is required, the poem implies, is a fresh view, the child Christ's view, which Christmas after all provides us with.

The didacticism of a number of the poems in *Land of Unlikeness* and *Lord Weary's Castle*, it should be noted, was regarded by Lowell as consistent with the neoclassicist canons that he had accepted from John Crowe Ransom. Lowell wrote poems in the 1940s that unashamedly conveyed not only his passionate religious feelings but also religious dogmas, all embellished with the formal rhetorical resources of rhyme, rhythm, stanzaic arrangement, and the embroidery of poetic conceits. While Lowell, as opposed to someone like Allen Tate, is not fundamentally a poet of ideas, nevertheless he was attracted to the majestic exposition of reality offered by centuries of Catholic thought. Indeed, he was more attached to the long and august history of Catholicism than he was to the actual church that surrounded him in the 1940s. Thus, he tends to depict the Irish American Catholics in his midst with a condescension that at times borders on contempt. Similarly, he disapproved of Pope Pius XII's apparent aloofness from the war, as can be seen in "Dea Roma," where the pontiff is seen walking in the "waters of a draining Rome / To bank his catch in the Celestial City" instead of attending to the war that was consuming half the world (*LWC*, 49).

If "Dea Roma" is an acidic poem, some of the other poems of the 1940s can be described as prophetic, not unlike those written by Thomas Merton and Daniel Berrigan in the 1960s. A recurring symbol in these poems is the Leviathan, as is evident in these lines from "The Crucifix":

> How dry Time screaks in its fat axle-grease,
> As sure November strikes us through the ice
> And the Leviathan breaks water . . . *(LU)*

The arresting axle-grease image anticipates the ending of Lowell's cele-brated later poem "For the Union Dead," which also has a rather apoc-alyptic tone, confirming at least on this occasion Lowell's observation that a similar sort of religious feeling underlay all of his poetry. In the poem "Leviathan," Lowell considers the symbol in its Hobbesian sense, playing this derivative meaning off the biblical archetype. The result is a rhetorical questioning of the state's right to govern in ostensibly Christian countries when it abandons peaceful order in favor of factionalism and war. Given the widespread support for the war in America, and in Boston in particular, one can only assume that Lowell's position was based on deeply felt religious conviction.

Lowell's apocalyptic vision stemmed not only from the war but also from what he perceived as the morally turgid state of America, and specifically of Boston—as can be seen in "As a Plane Tree by the Water," whose title is taken from the Book of Revelations or what Roman Catholics in the 1940s called the Book of the Apocalypse:

> Darkness has called to darkness, and disgrace
> Elbows about our windows in this planned
> Babel of Boston where our money talks
> And multiplies the darkness of a land
> Of preparation where the Virgin walks
> And roses spiral her enamelled face
> Or fall to splinters on unwatered streets. (*LWC*, 47)

Recalling Eliot's view of London, Lowell's Boston is portrayed as a spir-itual desert in which its status as a modern-day Babel is only marginally offset by the image of the ubiquitous figure of the Virgin in Catholic churches. While the potentiality for change is present in the symbols of the roses and the Virgin, the environment is inhospitable—as is evident in the image of the Virgin's tears falling as "splinters."

From Lowell's point of view the usefulness of an apocalyptic vision lay in its capacity to generate fear, the only force strong enough, he had concluded, to precipitate the required spiritual awareness. At times this perception even leads him to modify his scriptural sources, as in the poem "To Peter Taylor on the Feast of the Epiphany." In that poem the three wise men are said to kneel at the crib in Bethlehem in "sacred terror" before distributing their gifts of gold, frankincense, and myrrh (*LWC*, 46). The evoking of fear in these poems arises not only through the adducing of intimidating symbols from the Book of Revelations but also from Lowell's surrealistic painting of his locales. In "Where the Rainbow Ends," for example, Boston is pictured unsettlingly as a city where "serpents whistle at the cold" (*LWC*, 69).

The generation of fear is one of the signs not only of the brimstone rhetoric that one encountered in Catholic homilies of the 1940s, but is also a telltale sign of a residual Puritanism in Lowell, the product of his ancestors' involvement in New England history and of Lowell's ambivalent identification with that history. At times his conscious dislike of the Puritans is quite evident, as in "Children of Light," in which he depicts the Puritans as fencing their gardens with the "Redman's bones" and planting in the New World the "Serpent's seeds of light" (*LWC*, 28). In the same poem the Puritans are seen as carrying within themselves the "landless blood of Cain," an ironic rebuke of both the Plymouth brethren and the nomadic strain in American culture.

Nonetheless, Lowell's Catholicism sometimes seems heterodox in spite of the fact that the tone of *Land of Unlikeness,* for example, was ascetically Catholic, the epigraph having been taken from Etienne Gilson's *Mystical Theology of St. Bernard.* The following lines from "The Wood of Life," however, appear to project a Calvinistic view of salvation:

> Dangerous and refulgent Tree,
> King's purple covers up your taint,
> What the worm and human want
> Wrung from the first man's extacy. *(LU)*

The image of Christ's "King's purple" covering up the "taint" of humanity's sin is redolent of Puritan poetry, of Edward Taylor, for example, who visualized salvation as a covering over of sin by God in contrast to the forgiving or removing of guilt, which is closer to Catholic theology.

On one occasion Lowell told the biographer Ian Hamilton that, after having immersed himself in both Calvinistic and Catholic writings in college, he did not regard the two as opposites but as united in their joint difference from modern secularism: "Catholicism notices things, the particular," he went on, while Calvinism studies the "attenuated ideal. I was too deep in that dogfight," he concluded, "to ever get out."[12] There are moments when Lowell consciously adopts Puritan typography, anticipating his later poetic studies of New England Puritans, as in the "Slough of Despond" section of "Scenes from the Historic Comedy." More typical, though, is the allegorical use of tropes in a manner that recalls the stark linguistic naïveté of Cotton Mather and Jonathan Edwards. In "The First Sunday in Lent," for example, Lowell describes Satan as looping his "cracking tail into a hangman's noose" (*LWC*, 15).

The mingling of Catholic and Puritan subject matter can be seen in a number of the poems of the 1940s, most notably in "The Quaker Graveyard in Nantucket." Sometimes the effect is jarring—if not, indeed, incongruous—as in "The Park Street Cemetery," where the inventory of names such as Mather, Franklin, and Adams is followed by the familiar Catholic formula *"in saecula saeculorum" (LU)*. A smoother integration of the two elements occurs in "At the Indian Killer's Grave," a poem about King Philip's War in which some of Lowell's ancestors, like those of Hawthorne, took part in a slaughter of American Indians with the blessing of the Puritan community. Lowell characterizes this war as ethically continuous with World War II, a subversion of the Edenic vision of the new world, whose "great garden" had become "rotten to its root" (*LWC*, 54).

Offsetting a completely dark view of the contemporary world, however, is the image of a freshly created garden where "Mary twists the warlock with her flowers" (*LWC*, 57). Lowell's appeal to Mary and, implicitly, to Catholicism is an entreaty to rescue the new world, which is depicted as having been scarred by the tradition of Calvinistic capitalism. Lowell turned particularly to the figure of Mary, the feminine principle in Catholicism, to balance the male and darkly violent side of the American Protestant tradition. A good example is the poem "In Memory of Arthur Winslow," in which Lowell describes the death from cancer of his maternal grandfather, an affluent and successful member of Lowell's family and an unbeliever. In the last days of his illness Arthur Winslow is depicted dryly as "less than dead," meaning both that he was not quite dead and that he was worse than dead in his final agony. His "wrestling with the crab" (cancer) is archly juxtaposed with the image of his "yachting blouse," a garment that is worse than of no use in that it measures not only the

12. Lowell, *Collected Prose*, 278.

suffering but also the fall from the only symbols of worth the old man believes in as, listening through the sick room window, he vacantly hears the *"resurrexit dominus"* of the bells on Easter (*LWC*, 19).

The opening stanza is one of Lowell's finest, joining a firm narrative setting to momentous religious themes that reach into the marrow of the speaker's soul as he measures both the intimacy and distance of his relationship with his grandfather. If Lowell, for example, differed from his grandfather in matters of religion, he yet seems curiously like him in terms of class consciousness, as is indicated in the condescending allusion to the "mid-Sunday Irish" who fish for "dusky chub" in the shallows of a nearby pond (*LWC*, 19). In terms of the Protestant/Catholic antithesis that characterizes many of these poems, sections 2 and 4 of "In Memory of Arthur Winslow" are polarized. In section 2, "Dunbarton," the name of the New Hampshire cemetery where Lowell's Winslow relatives had been interred for centuries, the Protestant service is marked by the "preacher's mouthings" that "Deafen my poor relations on the hill," a final state of poverty that will shortly overtake the otherwise well-to-do corpse of Lowell's grandfather. The atmosphere of this section is both cold and shabby, contributing to the sense that the vigor of the American Protestant tradition belonged to the past, a time in which the Puritans took lathes to "point their wooden steeples lest the Word be dumb" (*LWC*, 20).

Following Lowell's disaffected memory of the day of his grandfather's funeral, he moves unexpectedly in section 4 to a "Prayer for my Grandfather to our Lady," a part of the poem that produces something like the surprise of the "Our Lady of Walsingham" section of "The Quaker Graveyard in Nantucket." The invocation to Mary is connected to Catholic Liturgy when the speaker asks her to "run to the chalice, and bring back / Blood on your finger-tips for Lazarus who was poor" (*LWC*, 22). The Lazarus of the Gospels, who wondered whether his wealth would prevent him from entering heaven, is an obvious parallel to Arthur Winslow, who is reduced to a necessary poverty, not only by death but also by the speaker, who, free of bitterness at last, desires his grandfather to find salvation. In its unsentimental and profound mingling of family feeling and religious belief, "In Memory of Arthur Winslow" ranks as one of Lowell's most powerful poems—even if the metaphors are outlandish at times, as in the image of Mary's "thunderbreasts of love" (*LWC*, 22).

Mary figures prominently as well in Lowell's longish poem "Between the Porch and the Altar." Apart from giving the poem a formal, symmetrical structure, as the title implies, the poet relies on heroic couplets throughout all four sections. The formalism is further enhanced by the subject matter, which essentially compares four women—the speaker's mother,

Eve, the speaker's mistress, and Mary. In the first section, which is called "Mother and Son" and is part of the "porch" section, the speaker implicitly uses the symbol of the Ouroboras to describe his oedipal relationship with his mother. The lines abound with serpentine imagery, including that of a little golden snake that "mouths a hook"—or, seen in terms of the Ouroboras motif, its own tail. In addition to the evoking of oedipal feelings, the image captures the speaker's helpless and somewhat shamed sense of reverting to childhood in the presence of his mother. In this way, the relationship takes on a negative coloring, which will be contrasted later in the poem with the positive relationship with Mary as mother.

In the second section, titled "Adam and Eve," the speaker is with his mistress, and both of them are visualized under the symbol of the Fall, again seen here by Lowell in a sexual light. The scene is replete with guilt so that, even as he is unfaithful, the speaker's consciousness is flooded with images of his wife and children, and the serpentine motif becomes more insistent:

> When we try to kiss,
> Our eyes are slits and cringing, and we hiss;
> Scales glitter on our bodies as we fall.
> The Farmer melts upon his pedestal. (*LWC*, 42)

The allusion to the farmer points up an interesting aspect of Lowell's narrative technique. The speaker and his mistress, who have been quarreling, have been looking at a statue of a farmer in Concord, Massachusetts, on a hot summer day. The melting farmer is not simply an allegorical projection of the speaker's guilt and fear of hell, but is an external reality, a window of sorts on the adulterous relationship, although not a window through which God looks exclusively but still the sense of a world beyond ourselves by which we can be judged. The note of judgment is amplified by the rhyming of "fall" with the ever precarious "pedestal," an adroit repetition of and thus intensification of the Fall motif, both aurally and visually.

By locating the action in Concord, an idealized place-name in American history, Lowell suggests at least one external measure by which the couple might be judged. The poem, of course, goes on to adduce others. A significant aside, related to Lowell's Catholicism, occurs in section 2. The snake motif is associated by way of contrast with Saint Patrick, that "Colonial from Rome" who is said to have driven all the snakes out of Ireland. Ironically, though, the descendants of the Irish in Massachusetts are pictured as having erected a church with a "puritanical façade" in an aping of the Protestant establishment. In this sense they are seen to have lost touch with the powerful presence of Saint Patrick.

Section 3, "Katherine's Dream," is a dramatic monologue and opens like the beginning of a play, with Katherine, the speaker's mistress, saying offhandedly: "It must have been a Friday" (*LWC*, 43). In a dream Katherine is moved to seek forgiveness for her affair with a married man, and although she is not a Catholic she finds herself suddenly in a Catholic church named St. Patrick's, thus linking her with the preceding section of the poem:

> Black nuns with glasses smile and stand on guard
> Before a bulkhead in a bank of snow,
> Whose charred doors open, as good people go
> Inside by twos to the confessor. One
> Must have a friend to enter there, but none
> Is friendless in this crowd, and the nuns smile. (*LWC*, 43)

Lowell skillfully evokes the woman's feelings of apprehensiveness within the strange church yet at the same time her sense of spiritual community. Her attempt to obtain forgiveness is frustrated, however, by her consciousness that her lover, a Catholic, will have to accompany her through such a process.

The absence of the speaker in Katherine's dream is given enlarged significance in section 4, "At the Altar." While the foreground setting of Boston is palpable enough, the atmosphere of this section is markedly surreal, a reflection of the speaker's troubled yet determined intention to continue the adulterous affair. As he drives through the city with Katherine, however, the speaker passes by a "Gothic" church, which induces a recognition of his guilt until he is overwhelmed by a Gothic vision of his own funeral:

> The shocked stones
> Are falling like a ton of bricks and bones
> That snap and splinter and descend in glass
> Before a priest who mumbles through his Mass
> And sprinkles holy water; and the Day
> Breaks with its lightning on the man of clay,
> *Dies amara valde*. Here the Lord
> Is Lucifer in harness: hand on sword,
> He watches me for Mother, and will turn
> The bier and baby-carriage where I burn. (*LWC*, 45)

The surreal juxtaposition of the falling buildings and bones, mingled with the oddly realistic detail of the mumbled Mass (not uncommon in the

Latin Mass of the 1940s), gives way finally to the speaker's vision of himself as a damned soul claimed by Lucifer. While the last line (whose images of the bier and baby carriage recall Blake's "London") is anything but hopeful, nevertheless the figure of Mary, here retroactively merged with that of the speaker's mother—and indeed with those of all of the women in his life—suggests a possible redemptive path, even if one that the speaker is unwilling at the moment to choose. In this sense the speaker is suspended at the end, as the poem's title indicates, between the porch and the altar. As a piece of craftsmanship, "Between the Porch and the Altar," with its narrative undercarriage supporting the densely woven symbolism throughout, is very fine. While it is difficult to determine how autobiographical the poem is, certainly one is reminded of Lowell's relationship with his mother (a dominant personality) and of his marriage, which, at the time, had become increasingly tempestuous. In any case the rendering of the adulterous situation, both psychologically and spiritually, is chillingly convincing.

The long poem "The Quaker Graveyard in Nantucket" is the crowning achievement of Lowell's poetry of the 1940s and is one of the great poems of the twentieth century. It also incorporates most of the features of Lowell's writing that have been discussed: his formalism, his preoccupation with American history—especially Puritanism—his opposition to World War II, and his Catholicism. Ostensibly a rumination upon the death of Lowell's cousin following the torpedoing of his ship in the North Atlantic, the poem quickly evolves, through complex symbolic layering, into a study of America itself. What distinguishes "The Quaker Graveyard in Nantucket" from Lowell's other work is its epic character, which is evident not only in its lofty themes but also in its extensive literary allusiveness. Particularly noticeable are the echoes from Melville, Milton, and the Book of Genesis, in addition to those from Lowell's well-furnished larder of Greek and Roman archetypes.

The action of the poem is set against an epigraph taken from the Book of Genesis: "Let man have dominion over the fishes of the sea and the fowls of the air and the beasts and the whole earth, and every creeping creature that moveth upon the earth." The quotation envelops the poem to come by emphasizing a creation that had not been the work of human hands. Thus, the incessant warring that, from the poet's point of view, has marked human history is depicted as a scorning of the gift of life itself. The role of Warren Winslow, Lowell's cousin and presumably a consciously innocent young seaman, is subsumed into the larger drama of America of which he is a somewhat hapless though obedient representative. The epic dimensions of the poem eventually stretch from the creation of the world to World War II, focusing in between on a nineteenth-century America in which Lowell saw the moral direction of his country to have particularly gone awry. For this reason the most violent language in the poem occurs not in connection with the war but rather in connection with the carving up of whales by nineteenth-century Americans:

> In the great ash-pit of Jehoshaphat
> The bones cry for the blood of the white whale,
> The fat flukes arch and whack about its ears,
> The death-lance churns into the sanctuary, tears
> The gun-blue swingle, heaving like a flail,
> And hacks the coiling life out. (*LWC,* 12)

While Lowell's anger and horror recall Melville's, he is distinctive in turning the violence in the poem toward the mercy of God: "Hide, / Our steel, Jonas Messias, in Thy side" (12). The superimposition of the harpoon, the Roman soldier's lancing of the side of Christ, and the modern reader's holding of that lance leads to the further novel idea of contemporary humanity hiding within the wound of Christ. The sheltering motif reflected Lowell's Catholic spirituality with its emphasis on forgiveness in contrast to the harsh outlook dramatized elsewhere in the poem. The profound subject matter, here as elsewhere in the poem, is amplified by the march of pentameter end-stopped lines and a sonorous, tightly woven rhyme. The acute use of sound makes the poem unbearably painful at times—as in the above scene in which the whale's "fat flukes arch and whack about its ears;" here the sibilant *f* sounds, which convey the soft vulnerability of the whale, are poised against the sharp *k* sounds, which dramatize the savage cutting up of the whale.

Lowell focuses on a difference between the nineteenth and twentieth centuries in a scene involving a modern warship in target practice. In the scene Lowell emphasizes the gratuitousness of violence in the twentieth century:

> Guns, cradled on the tide,
> Blast the eelgrass about a waterclock
> Of bilge and backwash, roil the salt and sand
> Lashing earth's scaffold. (*LWC,* 10)

The lines vividly capture the ecological aspects of the assault on Creation, which in turn ironically cradles humankind, even as human beings perversely tear away at the base of that support.

Of the poem's seven sections only one is given a title, section 6, "Our Lady of Walsingham." This pivotal section, which focuses on a medieval

English shrine dedicated to Mary, catches the reader by surprise amid the somber Melvillian atmosphere that otherwise pervades the poem. Furthermore, the language in this section is comparatively bland and the tone neutral, if not dry, in contrast to the passion and outrage that appear elsewhere in the poem. The lines themselves are literally prosaic (a foretaste of some of Lowell's later work), having been lifted from a book on Catholic medieval culture that Lowell had been reading at the time, E. I. Watkins's *Catholic Art and Culture*. Watkins had outlined a decline in Western culture from the unity of medieval secular and religious life to the fragmentation of contemporary secular culture, a theme that T. S. Eliot had also taken up in his essays on Christianity and society.

The fact that Lowell changes the setting from America to England is also part of the surprise felt by the reader, who is thereby given another world, as well as another time, by which to judge American culture: "There once the penitents took off their shoes / And then walked barefoot the remaining mile" (13). The serene, yet penitential, language introduces an otherworldly scale against which to see the ageless struggle of human beings against themselves and against nature, a struggle that is suddenly and rather impossibly, it might have seemed, dwarfed by the figure of the Virgin:

> Our Lady, too small for her canopy,
> Sits near the altar. There's no comeliness
> At all or charm in that expressionless
> Face with its heavy eyelids. . . .
>   She knows what God knows,
> Not Calvary's Cross nor crib at Bethlehem
> Now, and the world shall come to Walsingham. (*LWC*, 13)

The mysticism of the passage is prepared for by the detail of the statue of Mary being too small for its canopy, a symbol of her humility and a sign that her abode is elsewhere. Nevertheless, through the doctrine of the Incarnation and the Mystical Body of Christ, she is accessible to humanity, especially, it would seem, to penitents. On the other hand, there would ironically appear to be few penitents in contemporary society or indeed within the nineteenth-century America portrayed by Lowell.

In the final section of "The Quaker Graveyard in Nantucket," Lowell synoptically recalls his principal motifs, the violence of the world and the silence of otherworldly. Of the seventeen lines in section 7, sixteen are dark and violent while one, the last, is piously hopeful, weighting the poem finally, it would seem, in the direction of failure and moral stagnancy. However, the language is brilliantly wrought to achieve the poem's dualistic and ambiguous outcome:

> Mart once of supercilious, wing'd clippers,
> Atlantic, where your bell-trap guts its spoil
> You could cut the brackish winds with a knife
> Here in Nantucket, and cast up the time
> When the Lord God formed man from the sea's slime
> And breathed into his face the breath of life,
> And blue-lung'd combers lumbered to the kill.
> The Lord survives the rainbow of His will. (*LWC*, 14)

The abruptness of Lowell's final line and the overall bleakness of the stanza make Jay Martin's observation that Warren Winslow is "transfigured in the image of the rainbow" seem a trifle superficial.[13] Implicitly recalling the extract from Genesis that opened the poem, Lowell considers the huge waves with their air-enclosed sleeves as the origin of human beings who would develop lungs and themselves "lumber" to the kill. In this sense it might be argued that God as Creator, if not as Redeemer, is darkly implicated in the unfolding violence of evolution even if the poet concedes humbly that God's will transcends our human understanding. An alternative reading, following on Lowell's consciousness of the power of Calvinism in his thinking, is that he perceived nature as having been corrupted by the Fall at an early stage of its development. In Catholic theology and philosophy, as has already been indicated, nonhuman nature— whether viewed in its evolutionary aspects or not—is viewed as having always been imperfect and thus potentially threatening from its inception just as it is regarded as incorporating some aspects of the beauty, grandeur, and even goodness of its creator. It is not, though, seen to be related to the Fall. In Catholic thought the Fall is linked to the moral and spiritual aspects of *human* behavior.

The last line of "The Quaker Graveyard in Nantucket" arrives with as much unexpectedness as the "Our Lady of Walsingham" section, seeming in every way incompatible with the lines that precede it, causing Paul Dolan to remark that if there is a resolution of the religious problem in the poem, it is a "strange" one.[14] It is delivered in the same neutral tone and seems logically unrelated to the images and ideas that precede it. Alluding to God's pact of peace with Noah and with humanity following the flood,

---

13. Martin, *Robert Lowell*, 17.
14. Dolan, "Lowell's *Quaker Graveyard:* Poem and Tradition," 180.

the line both recalls the retributive power of God and God's infinite capacity to forgive. Moreover, the word *survives* not only conveys the independence and mystery of God but also suggests, however remotely, the possibility of survival for mankind. Nevertheless, the asymmetrical division of the stanza into its largely pessimistic body and only briefly hopeful last line is another indication, along with the emotional disconnectedness between the section's two parts, of Lowell's division of the world into light and darkness, good and evil, a view that is at odds with the via media of Catholic incarnational theology. Because of this division and along with the Catholic devotion to Mary in the Walsingham section, the poem can be seen as something of a theological hybrid, although Lowell's conscious allegiance was clearly to Roman Catholicism.

Late in 1946, Lowell wrote to Jean Stafford that he was seeking a divorce and that he was no longer a Catholic. In spite of a temporary revival of interest in Catholicism in 1949, he essentially severed his ties with the church at the time of his divorce. In an unpublished letter written to George Santayana in 1948, Lowell announced formally that he was not a member of the Catholic Church any longer and that, although he believed Catholics held part of the truth, he did not believe that they possessed *the* truth.[15] Although there is one poem—"Mother Marie Therese"—in his 1951 *The Mills of the Kavanaghs* that appears to be a Catholic poem, Lowell's tone is detached and darkly ironic in spite of Jerome Mazzaro's belief that this was one of Lowell's last Catholic poems. Indeed, Lowell confided to A. Alvarez in 1961 that his stance in the poem was "non-Catholic" and "neutral." In November 1955 he rejoined the Episcopal church of his family and childhood. As one looks at the later poetry, it is evident that, although there are religious figures and themes, religious allusions are fewer, more subdued, and generally more sardonic than in the relatively zealous poems of the 1940s. Thomas More, adopted by Lowell as his patron upon entering the Catholic Church, is recalled approvingly in one of the poems in *History* (published in 1973) while a pope is caricatured in "Beyond the Alps" in *Life Studies* (published in 1959). A telltale reference in a poem about Saint Just in *History* reminds one of Lowell's Catholic past as the speaker reflects that the saint's "name seems stolen from the Missal."[16] The old apocalyptic vision revives on occasion in the later work, although in a more much more tempered form, notably in the title poem in

15. Lowell to Santayana, January 12, 1948, Lowell Collection, Harry Ransom Humanities Research Center, University of Texas, Austin.
16. Mazzaro, *Poetic Themes*, 80; Lowell, *Robert Lowell*, 79; Lowell, *Selected Poems*, 171.

For the Union Dead and in the sonnet "Words," from *History*. Nonetheless, apart from Lowell's historical interest in it, religion as such plays a far less prominent role in the later work than in the poems of the 1940s.

In some respects Lowell's poetry of the 1940s is similar in theme to that written by Thomas Merton and later by Daniel Berrigan. Both Lowell and Merton were converts, and all three were pacifists who had been influenced by the example of Dorothy Day. Although Lowell resembles Allen Tate in the introspectiveness of his religious journey, he was more emotionally dependent upon that journey than Tate, who approached Catholicism from a more steadying, philosophical vantage point. At the end of "The Quaker Graveyard in Nantucket," for example, the solace of Lowell's final line, so logically inconsistent with the despairing lines that precede it, is indicative of the trusting, rather simple faith that he then possessed.

Lowell's early poems arose from the tension issuing from his strong devotion to Mary—always a figure of refuge and compassion in his poetry—and a dark undercurrent in his poetry that separated goodness and humanity, an undercurrent that conflicted with the incarnational theology that he had ostensibly embraced in converting to Catholicism. Orthodox Catholic asceticism, recently reaffirmed in the new *Catechism of the Catholic Church,* has traditionally advocated self-denial in order to detach the soul from the seductions of the world, a different matter from rejecting the world as hopelessly evil, a stance that Lowell appears to take in a number of his early poems. That early poetry, so conspicuously Catholic, had as much in common with Jonathan Edwards, who so evidently fascinated Lowell in his later poetry, as with Thomas Aquinas. Harnessed to the tension created by these two voices, Lowell's fiery poems of the 1940s all but consume the poetic membrane that attempts to contain them.

10

J. F. POWERS

(B. 1917)

MORE THAN ANY other American fiction writer, J. F. Powers depicted the effect of the administrative organization of the Catholic Church upon its spirituality. In particular, he focused on the role of the priest as someone who is committed to two worlds in a way that most people "officially" are not, as he put it in an interview titled "The Catholic and Creativity" in 1960. While Powers wrote almost exclusively about the clergy, he told Donald McDonald that he had never seriously considered becoming a priest, having been put off not by the ascetic demands of the priesthood but by the need to talk to "old ladies on the sidewalk in front of church" and to persuade wealthy parishioners to contribute to the church. Underlying Powers's portrayal of ecclesiastical hierarchy lies the view that there was nothing "bigger, cruder, more vulgar in the world" than the Catholic Church, as he put it in "The Catholic and Creativity." Behind that view in turn lay Powers's belief that, vulgar as it was, the Catholic Church had been authorized to communicate to humanity the existence of theological realities and moral laws that were as "real as gravity," and that while those who achieved virtue might lose out in worldly terms, the "last round" would not be decided here.[1]

Although Powers did not himself become a priest, he had a number of clerical friends, and on one occasion attended a retreat for priests in

1. Powers, "Catholic and Creativity," 69; McDonald, "Interview with J. F. Powers," 88; Powers, "Catholic and Creativity," 74, 63–64.

Minnesota in 1943, the only layperson in attendance. On that occasion, in addition to learning a good deal about the problems and vices of the clergy, he was swayed toward pacifism by the retreat master, who reinforced the view that Powers had already begun to hold through his acquaintance with Dorothy Day and the Catholic Worker movement. Like Robert Lowell, William Everson, Thomas Merton, and Allen Tate (Powers became friendly with Lowell and Tate), he dissociated himself from World War II; instead of serving in the armed forces, he was permitted to work as an orderly in a Chicago hospital. In 1965 he reiterated his opposition to war and to what he characterized as the church's regrettable passivity on the issue, arguing in an essay that unless the church was willing to denounce *specific* wars, its moral authority could be expected to be marginal.[2]

Considering the forcefulness of Powers's moral vision, the rather prosaic nature of his characters and even of his writing style makes the reader wonder. Certainly he was opposed to narrative "huffing and puffing," as he put it in a laudatory review of Katherine Anne Porter's fiction in 1962. Furthermore, in a letter to Robert Lowell in February 1948 he said that, although he was attracted to the sort of impressionism employed by Conrad and Faulkner, he did not feel it a "legitimate" technique for a realistic writer like himself to use. In addition, although Powers as a reader (as he wrote to Robert Lowell in November 1948) preferred sustained writing, he felt constrained to write short or episodic fiction in order to make a living. The other formalist element that Powers emphasized in connection with his writing was economy; he confided in connection with *Morte D'Urban*, for example, that in writing it, he "cut, cut, cut."[3]

In his short stories Powers focused incisively on the ambiguity of the priestly role, nowhere more than in the title story of *Prince of Darkness* (which was published in 1951), his finest collection of stories. As with a number of Powers's clergy, Father Burner (whose name is appropriately infernal) has been corrupted by the materialism of the society around him. Powers once described that society, in language that parodied the U.S. Constitution, as "of, by, and for businessmen—and union men."[4] While these two groups might seem antithetical, Powers meant to indicate that they were both myopically concerned with power and materialism, to the exclusion of the needs of other Americans.

2. Powers, "Conscience and Religion," 91.
3. Powers, "She Stands Alone," 12; Powers to Robert Lowell, February 18, 1948, Lowell Collection, Houghton Library, Harvard University; Powers to Robert Lowell, November 29, 1948; Powers, "Catholic and Creativity," 67.
4. Powers, "Catholic and Creativity," 65.

While Father Burner is depicted as self-indulgent and mean-spirited, Powers does bring out the priest's glimmering moral consciousness of his failure. At the same time, driven by the humiliation of having been overlooked for promotion, Father Burner seeks advancement from the archbishop, who ironically demotes him in the hope that in his new appointment he will find "not peace but a sword."[5] While the archbishop's injunction provokes the shock and surprise that often conclude a successful short story, the careful reader will have noticed Powers's skillful preparation of the ending. Furthermore, the scene reveals Powers's superb handling of point of view. While the archbishop exhibits some of the suavity of Bishop Bloughram, for example, thereby catching Father Burner off-guard, he is shown to walk the line between knowledge of the world and detachment from it, as in his casual, urbane remark that in exchange for money, the church gave the rich "consolation" while making of the "eye of the needle a gate" (275). Had Father Burner been less obsessed with his own advancement, he might have noted the archbishop's irony, but certainly the reader has no such excuse. Moreover, the archbishop's observation that in contemporary society there were "few saints, fewer sinners, and everybody is already saved" betrays a deeper and more complex current of thought than Father Burner seems ready for (273). Finally, the ostensibly stray details of the scene, always crucial in Powers's fiction—the holes in the archbishop's slippers, the ancient typewriter—reveal a very different archbishop from the worldly figure of power whom Burner thinks he is facing, creating fine dramatic irony.

In surrounding Father Burner with the imagery of hell, as in his spontaneous rebuttal of a fellow priest with a "smoldering aside" (227), Powers uses the allegorical language to suggest a character who has lived his life in a two-dimensional fashion and who needs, as the archbishop implies, the deepening that suffering can bring—not merely the experience of failure, which has been habitual with Burner—but a sacrificial dedication to Christ and to his priestly vocation. It is noteworthy that, in this story at least, Powers locates worldly ambition not at the top of the ecclesiastical hierarchy but at the bottom, a sign of Powers's perception that the dangers of worldliness do not necessarily parallel authority.

Characteristically, Powers's narrative skill in the story is unobtrusively effective. There is the scene, for example, in which Father Burner and Father Quinlan discuss the alarming decline in the practice of the faith in

5. Powers, *Prince of Darkness and Other Stories*, 277, subsequently cited in the text parenthetically.

Spain, a distasteful topic for Burner, who generally eschews conversation with any hint of discomfort about it. Powers suddenly switches from the conversation to describing a nearby goldfish, which pauses to stare through the aquarium glass at the two priests, slipping then with a "single lob of its tail" into a "dark, green corner" (234). While the action seems inconsequential, it allows the reader to get outside of the characters in order to see them objectively for a moment, freed from the dominance of their point of view.

Powers uses setting with equal success in an earlier scene in the rectory in which Father Burner considers his surroundings with dismay: "He hated it, too. A fabulous brown rummage of encyclopedias, world globes, maps, photographs, holy pictures, mirrors, crucifixes, tropical fish, and too much furniture. The room reproduced the world, all wonders and horrors, less land than water" (216). Through Powers's subtle handling of point of view, what the careful reader is led to see here, apart from Father Burner's sense of tedium, is the challenge presented to a priest by the world, a challenge that in Father Burner's case goes unheeded.

If "Prince of Darkness" presents a favorable view of the hierarchical structure of the church, the same cannot be said of "The Forks," a tale in *Prince of Darkness* that pits a subordinate priest, Father Eudex, against his pastor. A local tractor company, which employs many Catholics, has been accustomed to sending the clergy annual checks in order, in part, it would seem, to discourage any clerical support for unions, thereby provoking a crisis of conscience in Father Eudex, who tears up the check sent to him, only to be chided by his pastor for doing so. Weighing the good uses to which his fellow priests might put the money against the classical ethical norm that the end does not justify the means, Father Eudex has further to weigh his obligation to obey his religious superiors. That obligation is tested severely.

His pastor, the Monsignor, is as worldly a priest as any described by Chaucer, and furthermore one who abuses his employees, notably his gardener, with all of the obliviousness that one would expect from the most ruthless of capitalists. The portrait is completed by the Monsignor's snobbery (he rebukes Father Eudex for demeaning himself in giving the gardener a hand) and fastidious table manners. The title scene involves the Monsignor's rebuke of Father Eudex for failing to use all of the cutlery that had been placed before him at dinner ("Father Eudex did not know the forks," 133). Powers's symbolism is telling. It is the Monsignor who does not know the "forks"—that is, the choices between this world and the next. Even more significant is the apparently parenthetical scene in which a widowed parishioner, ostensibly poor but in fact quite comfortable, comes to Father Eudex for financial advice. The initial shock felt by Father Eudex is intensified by his recognition that laypersons expected this service to be provided by the clergy and that the service was so provided in his own parish. Though less dramatic than the bribery by the tractor company, the episode is more quietly devastating in its implications about the corrupt state of the clergy and its effects upon the laity. Powers's use of such parenthetical techniques is one of the signs of his understated approach to narration and to satire, requiring the reader to be alert to the most mundane details in his fiction.

In "The Lord's Day," another of the stories in *Prince of Darkness,* the hierarchical relationship is between priests and nuns, specifically a small group of nuns who have to sacrifice their Sunday afternoons in order to count the collection while the parish priests take the afternoon off. The narration derives its piquancy from the governing point of view, that of the mother superior, who is divided between a respect for ecclesiastical authority and a sense of injustice at such a wasting of the Lord's Day. Powers underlines the plight of the nuns by constructing a sweltering summer setting, including a melting asphalt schoolyard, from which the autocratic pastor has ordered the removal of the only shade trees. Furthermore, while the clergy are depicted as materialistic and unreflective, the mother superior is shown to be pious, wisely humorous, and charitable. In this matter, one notices the skill with which Powers inserts meaningful detail, as in his description of the mother superior genuflecting in the "easy, jointless way that comes from years of it" (2).

In contrast to the casual and lethargic clergy who oversee her life, the nun is depicted as self-disciplined and honorable. While Powers deftly brings out feminist aspects of the Catholic Church's hierarchical structure, he doesn't, as compared with a writer like Mary Gordon, isolate feminist themes, but rather presents them as part of an overall decay that is as inimical to men as it is to women. Indeed, what gives Powers's fiction its distinctive effect is the tension between his support for the traditional, hierarchical church and his perception of the abuse that this structure all too often promotes. If those in positions of power are called by Christ to serve others, how, the mother superior wonders, can she work out her own salvation by leaving her nuns prey to a spiritually inferior clergy? Conscious of the fact that her passivity may in the present situation be a vice, she is also aware that she has not been able to bring herself to "make a stand against Father," in part, it is implied, because she believes in the hierarchical chain in which she herself administers authority (4). At such moments one becomes aware of the rich layers of psychological analysis that often imperceptibly deepen Powers's fiction.

The mother superior's position is painted with exquisite poignancy by Powers, who nonetheless never once intrudes upon his characters. With his satirical eye ever on the absurdity of the way in which his Catholic characters behave, as well as on the other world where a final judgment will be made, Powers incorporates in his descriptions details that reverberate with irony. An example is a gesture by the assistant pastor in the room where the nuns are counting the Sunday collection: "Father went over to the buffet. 'Like apples? Who wants an apple?' He apparently expected them to raise their hands but did not seem disappointed when no one did. He placed the bowl on the table for them. Three apples on top were real, but the ones underneath were wax and appeared more edible. No one took an apple" (8). While the phrasing "raise their hands" speaks volumes about the priest's condescension, the heart of the satire lies in the description of the apples. While the scene is not simply allegorical, the language introduces the idea of artificiality, which inevitably raises the related issue of falseness and hypocrisy, qualities that can be readily applied to the parish clergy.

In "The Valiant Woman," also in *Prince of Darkness,* the hierarchical relationship is between a priest and his housekeeper—except that here the balance of power is neatly and comically reversed. The satire derives in part from the fact that the role of housekeeper had become as institutionalized in the American church as that of the clergy. Ostensibly committed to celibacy, which among other things ought to confer a certain independence, Father Firman (who is anything but firm) is portrayed as a henpecked husband under the thumb of Mrs. Stoner. Unable to rid himself of this woman, who has poisoned the atmosphere of his parish and driven away his friends, Father Firman sinks back into the consoling thought that his housekeeper was, after all, a "clean" woman. Powers probes the psychological recesses of his character's plight in showing that, not only does he lack the will to act, but his irresolution is based upon self-interest; he fears that another housekeeper might be worse and, more revealing, he doesn't want to have to provide his present housekeeper with a pension.

While the characterization of Mrs. Stoner is held to a two-dimensional level, the comic surface of the story is given an added dimension by Powers's inclusion of a stray, prosaic detail that in hindsight expands the tale's significance. It is mentioned in passing that, sometimes during Father Firman's weekday masses, Mrs. Stoner is the only parishioner in attendance. Thus, the failure of Father Firman is unobtrusively portrayed as much more profound than a priest's skirmishes with a willful woman; unexpectedly, the fate of Catholic Christianity itself, one gradually realizes, hangs in the balance. While the subtlety of Powers's constructional ability and phrasing are frequently obscured by the mundane consciousnesses and conversations of his characters, they do finally have an impressive effect.

In "The Presence of Grace," the title story from Powers's second collection of stories, the hierarchical relationships portrayed are complex, involving both the relationship between an autocratic pastor and his assistant and that between aggressive laypersons and a diffident priest. This second plot involves a ploy by a Catholic widow who is in a compromising living arrangement with a man who is not her husband to regain respectability by having a priest to dinner. While the unwary priest, Father Fabre, the point-of-view character, attends, a woman named Grace, the standard of respectability in the parish, declines to do so, producing some droll, ironic inversions in terms of the theme of hierarchy.

Father Fabre's compliance incites a rebellion by the parish women's group that the pastor quells with an authoritative word, leading to a harmonious reunion of the widow with the other parish women. While the tale may be seen as an illustration of the value of compassion, Powers draws the reader toward deeper waters through some narrative subtleties. Whereas the pastor suppresses the acrimony of the women's group, for example, by denying that Mrs. Mathers is living in sin, he does so with a blithe lack of explanation, leaving his assistant and the reader unconvinced. "It was simple," Father Fabre reflects dryly, as "simple as when he, as priest, changed the bread and wine into the body and blood of Christ. But he had no power from his priesthood to deny the undeniable."[6] Here, as in the parallel story "A Losing Game," Powers touches on the primary source of the clerical abuse of power, the unwarranted transference of the charisma of their sacerdotal role to a more generalized use of authority. Powers adroitly underscores Father Fabre's consciousness of the pastor's error with an unobtrusive symbolic touch in that Grace is once again absent from the harmonious group of women in church at the end of the story. While the reader never meets Grace, either actually or allegorically, the shadow of her virtuous pressure suffuses the tale.

The story culminates in a significant merging of Father Fabre's viewpoint with Powers's: "Father Fabre, trailing the boys out of the sacristy, gazed upon the peaceful flock, and then beyond, in a dim, dell-like recess of the nave used for baptism, he saw the shepherd carrying a stick and then he heard him opening a few windows" (191). The detail of the harsh "stick" in connection with the shepherd's role accentuates the old priest's

---

6. Powers, *Presence of Grace*, 165, subsequently cited in the text parenthetically.

departure from the gentle, pastoral norms of the Gospel in favor of a peremptory and ultimately pernicious use of authority, one based upon the priority of order over truth. Having been absolved by her pastor before she is able to confess her sin, for example, Mrs. Mathers's consciousness of sin can do nothing but atrophy.

In "Dawn," also from *The Presence of Grace*, Powers wittily shows how clerical habits of highhandedness can rebound. An entrepreneurial priest, Father Udovic, attempts to ingratiate himself with his bishop by advancing the annual Peter's pence collection so that his bishop can bring a check with him when he goes to Rome. The scheme founders when an envelope from an uncooperative woman is dropped onto the plate, addressed to the Pope—personally. The subsequent turmoil shows Powers at his comic best, but at the end of the story when the woman is asked why she did not just mail the envelope with its paltry contribution to Rome, she exclaims bitterly: "Some flunky'd get hold of it! Same as here!" (22). In spite of the coarseness of the dialogue, it marks the most important turn in the story. Beneath the chilly and un-Christlike imposition of clerical authority on the laity, there beats not only the resignation of the laity but also its hostility and anger.

While most of Powers's short stories about clerical hierarchy tend to be bleak at bottom, two—"Lions, Harts, Leaping Does" from *Prince of Darkness*, and "Zeal" from *The Presence of Grace*—offer a trace of hope. In "Zeal" a sophisticated bishop, enjoying a period of solitude on a train, is accosted by a gregarious priest who is escorting a group of Catholics to Rome. While Powers focuses on the bishop's failed attempts to escape the zealous priest, a more serious narrative undercurrent shows the prelate slowly becoming part of the priest's persuasion. What changes him is the zealous priest's ingenuous and ill-fated attempt to prevent a young man from falling into sin. Reflecting upon his own passivity in the matter, the bishop is stirred by the thought of "Father Early still out there, on his feet and trying, which was what counted in the sight of God" (146).

As with many of Powers's stories, "Zeal" pits a relatively simple but more active character against a more sophisticated and reflective one, usually the point-of-view character. While Powers mines the comic potential of such meetings, he also shows how any crossing of this kind can provide an opportunity for change in the central character. Through the skillful planting of unobtrusive detail, Powers extends the technique by building up through narrative exposition a latent thematic energy that eventually competes with the pyrotechnics involved in the more active elements of the plot. In "Zeal," for example, it is gradually made clear through background detail that, although he is an agreeably sophisticated person, the bishop has over the years cultivated habits of detachment that are incompatible with his vocation and have sterilized his role as priest. The story's interest for the reader lies in the intersection between this gradual discovery about himself by the bishop and the wide cultural gap between him and the well-meaning priest who is his companion.

A similar sort of asymmetrical structuring of characterization can be found in Powers's highly praised story "Lions, Harts, Leaping Does." In its poetic impressionism the story is a departure from the author's customary stylistic astringency. Centering on the relationship between a dying Franciscan priest and the Franciscan brother who waits on him, the story has seemed to some to contrast the frigid asceticism of Father Didymus with the simple piety of Brother Titus. While such an interpretation may be possible following a cursory reading, it must be rejected upon consideration. What seems like Christian love in Titus turns out, under closer scrutiny, to more nearly resemble grudging acceptance. When Father Didymus suggests that Titus might like to accompany him on a winter walk, not expecting him to assent, for example, Titus responds with a parrotlike recitation from Thomas à Kempis' *Imitation of Christ*: " 'A good religious man that is fervent in his religion taketh all things well, and doth gladly all that he is commanded to do' " (37). While this would be an insulting response from an intelligent man, it is at best a servile response from Titus. Titus's response is a comically impassive one, at least from the reader's point of view, with the comedy of his rather blank life set off against the near tragedy of Didymus's.

Throughout, Powers develops the wintry setting of the story with unusual poetry and refinement, carefully preparing for the final scene in which the falling snowflakes, "for all their bright blue beauty as though struck still by lightning," caused Didymus to close his eyes, "only to find them there also, but darkly falling" (70). The outer darkness and cold, which have stalked Didymus throughout the story, here become the inner darkness. As has been suggested, though, the final encompassing darkness is foreshadowed even in the most apparently neutral scenes, such as that in which Didymus watches the winter light falling from his window toward the distant horizon, "which it sought to join" and was "still bright and strong against approaching night" (33). Powers's delicate choice of the word *still* evokes the underlying subliminal mood of expectation that pervades the story.

Contrasted symbolically with the winter setting is the blissful dream that Didymus has about the dead brother whom, in a shallow, renunciatory impulse, he had declined to visit. While the dream is impelled by guilt, it flowers in the pages of the story with a brightness and color that offset the encroachment of death. United in the dream as they were not in life, the brothers revel in an underwater heaven with an abandon that registers Didymus's relief, which in the dream he believes to be posthumous, that nature is no longer a problem for him. Significantly, with respect to the theme of nature, the brothers mistake the river that flows above them

> for an endless murmuring serpent. They considered unafraid the prospect of its turning in its course and standing on tail to swallow them gurgling alive. They sensed it was in them to command this also by a wish. Their visor hands vanished before their eyes and became instead the symbol of brotherhood clasped between them. This they wished. Smiling the same smile back and forth they began laughing: "Jonah!" And were walking murkily up and down the brown belly of the river in mock distress. Above them, foolishly triumphant, rippling in contentment, mewed the waves. (48)

Precipitated by Didymus's masochistic overnight vigil, the dream, rather like that of the little match girl in the fairy tale, brings a warmth that Didymus has denied himself for years, even though the vigil hastens his death.

Furthermore, with unsentimental thoroughness, Powers shows that what Didymus experiences following the dream more nearly resembles hell than heaven, as the blood vessels in his brain crack open and he experiences a terrifying disorientation: "The background of darkness became a field of varicolored factions, warring, and, worse than the landscape, things like worms and comets wriggled and exploded before his closed eyes. Finally, as though to orchestrate their motions, they carried with them a bewildering noise or music which grew louder and cacophonous" (52–53). While the terror of Didymus's waking dream intensifies the psychological suffering that he already feels, it also predisposes him toward death and sets his mind on his immortal journey so that he is finally able to pray, a sign that he has emerged from his despair, a despair that, theologically, could have cost him his place with God.

As a narrative of spiritual experience, what gives particular value to "Lions, Harts, Leaping Does" is the subtlety with which Powers depicts the evolution of Didymus's measured relationship with the world he will shortly leave. In particular, Powers shows Didymus weaning himself from an arid and somewhat perverse asceticism toward a more balanced relationship with the world, a world that, after all, had been created by God. Apart from the life-affirming symbolism of the dream, Powers uses animal imagery—indirectly in the title motif but also directly through the canary that becomes Didymus's companion—to soften his view of nature. At the same, there is some ambiguity about Didymus's release of the canary into the winter air. Although he thinks of himself as freeing the bird, he is, of course, consigning it to certain death, which is his subconscious desire for himself. The ambiguity, which may be a moot point for many readers, is probably not a sign of Didymus's reversion to a morbid asceticism but rather an indication of the mental confusion that has followed his stroke, a reflection of Powers's adamantine realism.

In the 1962 novel *Morte D'Urban,* a runner-up for the National Book Award, Powers focused again on the bifurcated nature of the role of the priest, portraying Father Urban not only as a successful fund-raiser for his order but also as a gifted preacher. The theme is not restricted to Father Urban. One of the most gravely ironic parts of the novel is that in which the provincial of the order, Father Boniface, anxiously awaits the legal script for the philanthropic gift of property that a benefactor makes to the order early in the novel. The scene shows drolly how easily a guileless and unworldly priest can quite unconsciously become attached to material things even when the beneficiary is his own religious order.

Taking advantage of the spaciousness of the novel form, Powers patiently fills in the background of his central character so that the reader begins to see the roots of Father Urban's attachment to the American dream. Brought up in a part of Illinois where Catholics were in the minority, a parallel to Powers's own background, the young Urban is placed outside the mainstream of American culture, though ambivalently so: "As a caddy at the country club, where his father was greenskeeper, he also knew that the best people, though Protestants, didn't always use the best language, or the best balls."[7] The passage, which in some respects recalls Fitzgerald's short story "Winter Dreams," silhouettes the position of the American Catholic as an outsider and the ironic role of the American dream of success in ensuring access to the national mainstream. At the same time, Powers carefully shows the genuine spiritual roots of Father Urban's vocation and in particular the powerful example of an admirable priest, Father Placidus, in stirring the young Urban's Christian idealism.

Powers's study in irony arises from the fact that, while his central character is firmly committed to Christianity and to his priestly role, he seeks to evangelize the world and to advance the church by the use of techniques that are germane to the materialistic society that surrounds him. With consummate irony Powers shows Father Urban, for example, unlike his saintly model, Father Placidus, traveling to Minnesota by train

---

7. Powers, *Morte D'Urban,* 77, subsequently cited in the text parenthetically.

in a comfortable compartment while his fellow priest is relegated to an uncomfortable journey by coach: "Jack, as he must have done on a thousand and one nights, sitting up in a day coach to save money, was weaving in sleep, banking as the train took a curve. Father Urban shook him gently with one hand, and with the other he hailed a blackamoor coffee boy" (35). In terms of Powers's handling of point of view, the choice of diction is exquisite—with the word *blackamoor* especially conveying both the expected urbanity of Father Urban in addition to an elegantly condescending racism.

For all of his reservations about impressionism, Powers uses point of view superbly in *Morte D'Urban*, as in the following scene: "The Provincial, a lean, pale, damp-looking Pole with a hairline winding up and around like the endless seam on a baseball, sat at his desk cleaning his fingernails with a letter opener. On the wall behind him, just as in their old quarters, hung a crucifix and part of the propeller from the airplane in which his brother, a chaplain in the First War, had perished" (26). With economy the passage projects the faint contempt of Father Urban as observer, and, particularly, of his ethnic bigotry, the very evil to which he felt vulnerable in his youth. Parenthetical as it is, the moment sharply reveals the ranking of American Catholics in terms of ethnic background, an affront to the moral universality claimed by the church in its official teachings. In addition, the baseball comparison quickly allows the reader to see that, if Urban is intelligent and energetic, his cultural horizon is, after all, limited. The homely details of the letter opener and, more symbolically, the propeller, cement Father Urban's dim view of his superior. They do more, though, for just as we are led to see the stagnancy that appalls Urban, so too do we become aware of a familial note that, however tasteless its expression, contrasts with Urban's lack of family and friends.

Powers builds up the complexity of his character from the earliest pages of the novel, depicting him, for instance, as modest enough to accept with good grace the menial and, from Father Urban's point of view, absurd tasks that have been assigned to him: "Father Urban was given a window, a block of wood, and a piece of sandpaper, and thus began the most difficult period in his life to date. Wilf showed him how to wrap the sandpaper around the block of wood. 'Always sand *with* the grain,' Wilf told him at the start, and a couple of times thereafter Wilf also told him to use *up* the sandpaper he had before taking a fresh piece" (85). The scene is perfectly played in that we hear the officious voice of his limited clerical colleague, Wilf, echoed through the skeptical but obedient mind of Urban, whose preference would be to raise money for tradesmen to do the work so that priests could get on with their own proper activity. Nonetheless, in genuine humility Urban determines that if "there was any purpose in his present situation, it would be revealed to them all, for better or worse" (94).

The subtlety of Powers's characterization lies in his portrayal not of a worldly priest but of a priest committed to raising the efficiency and success (quantitatively measured) of the church by enlisting the aid of affluent supporters whose values are only superficially those of the church while profoundly those of a materialistic America. Mrs. Thwaites is a salient example:

> In a room much larger than any bedroom at the Hill, Mrs. Thwaites sat in an overstuffed wheelchair, watching television on two sets. The only light in the room came from the sets, a dead light, so that Mrs. Thwaites's face showed up like a photographic negative: a little old woman with the face of a baby bird, all eyes and beak, but with a full head of bobbed white hair. One hand was wrapped in black rosary beads the size of cranberries, and the other gripped the remote control. A humidifier steamed at her feet. (145)

Seen through the lens of Father Urban's acute vision, Mrs. Thwaites emerges as an animated corpse with a birdlike intelligence, though far from innocent or harmless as the detail of the beak makes clear. Overcome by the heat that fills the darkness of the room, Urban can be forgiven if he feels that he has strayed into hell—which, symbolically, he has, in placing the welfare of the church in the hands of someone like Mrs. Thwaites.

Powers's telling use of Gothic description is also evident in his account of the conversion of Father Urban, which is precipitated by his having been struck on the head by the bishop's golf ball, an incident that, significantly, occurs on the infamous course that Urban had added to the order's retreat house. While the injury could be interpreted empirically, Powers leaves it open as to whether or not the ball was an instance of grace—of a divine reprimand, as it were. The conversion is the nub of Powers's tale, as he made clear in a comment about the title he had chosen: "All I wanted was the way Lancelot changed from the most famous knight, the most excellent knight, to a monk and priest."[8] It is worth noting that Powers's use of the Arthurian motif was not an indication of the author's nostalgia for the Catholic Middle Ages. This is made evident, for example, in a striking passage in which medieval and modern power politics are compared. Listening to Mrs. Thwaites, Urban suddenly has a bleak vision of late medieval life in which "kings and prelates were selling out right and

8. Powers, "Catholic and Creativity," 80.

left" (257). Billy Cosgrove's corrupt arrangement with Father Urban's order is also described as established on "rather medieval terms" (16). The Arthurian framework is not meant to draw the reader gratefully into the past but rather to silhouette a spiritual problem that the church has had since its inception: how to deal spiritually with a world that, in some respects, it depends upon for its survival.

The final temptation that Urban overcomes—that of the flesh—is deftly staged by Powers, as can be observed in the following scene involving Father Urban and Sally Hopwood:

> "Has it occurred to you that people might be disappointed by you and your reasons, and even more by you?"
> "I'm not sure I know what you mean," said Father Urban.
> "I mean you're an operator . . . and I don't think you have a friend in the world."
> Father Urban smiled. "Now you've gone too far."
> "Name *one*." (301)

What makes Sally Hopwood's seduction of Father Urban so effective is not just her attractiveness but her perceptiveness. She sees his hidden weaknesses and offers herself as a worthy companion to him all the same, an offer that in other circumstances he might well have welcomed. In a sense, she uncovers not just Father Urban's vulnerability but that of all the depicted clergy who, although they live in community, are portrayed as isolated and forlorn.

Gene Kellog has argued that a failure in *Morte D'Urban* is that once Powers has shown that American priests are "despiritualized," he seemed to have used up a "large part of what he had to say."[9] Apart from Kellog's unwarranted, dismissive tone, his judgment of the novel is simply inadequate. The focus of *Morte D'Urban* is not on a "despiritualized" clergy since a number of the clergy, such as Monsignor Renton, have a significant spiritual dimension. Indeed, the principal focus of the novel is not on the clergy in general but on one man in particular. *Morte D'Urban* is a study of character, registering the incremental changes in character and outlook that modify an expected destiny and that are finally, in the case of Father Urban, a definite sign of hope.

Wheat That Springeth Green, Powers's second novel, published in 1988, was almost twenty-five years in the making, a sign in part of Powers's fastidious revisions. Set in 1968, the novel, as with Ralph McInerny's fiction,

9. Kellog, *The Vital Tradition: The Catholic Novel in a Period of Convergence,* 178.

covers the post–Vatican II period, a period that Powers, like McInerny, had grave doubts about, as he told interviewer Mitch Finlay in 1989. For this reason, Powers's view of the church is darker in his second novel than in the first. As early as 1965, Powers expressed his wariness about some of the banality that characterized Catholic American spirituality in the 1960s, registering his antipathy to catchwords such as *"mystery, encounter,"* and *"commitment,"* and simultaneously stating his reservations about a church that had been simplistically reduced to making the world a "better place."[10] In some respects, Father Joe Hackett, the central character in *Wheat That Springeth Green*, feels somewhat stranded, as Powers did, by the aftermath of Vatican II, and some of the novel involves debate about controversial issues arising from it, such as clerical celibacy. Flanked by priests who looked forward to expected changes that would enable them to marry, Father Hackett suggests dryly that his clerical colleagues look at the problems that celibacy *doesn't* cause.

While Powers documents a whole series of abuses, including sexual abuses, that are committed by the younger clergy, he also exposes the spurious professionalism that purported to divide the virtue of the clergy from their functions as teachers. Father Potter tells Joe Hackett in connection with Father Conklin's teaching at the Catholic Institute: "What matters in teaching is a man's competence, not his private beliefs, or lack of same. And that applies to Scripture and theology, if they're teachable."[11] The conversation is far from theoretical. The celebrated cases of Charles Curran and Hans Kung in recent years, while not precisely parallel to Father Conklin's, have raised the question of the orthodoxy of those who teach at Catholic institutions. While Rome's answer has been to restate the requirements of faith and sanctity, the issue continues to fester in some quarters as American priests assert their rights not only as ordained ministers but also as American citizens.

Wheat That Springeth Green presents the familiar dilemma in Powers's fiction of the conflicting demands of the world and the spirit within the context of a study of ecclesiastical hierarchy. One of the most satirically barbed moments in the novel occurs when Father Hackett is in the barber shop and observes the archbishop "descending from his chair in the odor of witch hazel and talcum powder," then dropping his reading matter into Joe's lap: a copy of *Forbes* magazine (303). The role of the hierarchy in the spiritual malaise that Powers depicts is further underscored by Joe

10. Powers, "The Pesky Side of Paradise," 16.
11. Powers, *Wheat That Springeth Green*, 197, subsequently cited in the text parenthetically.

Hackett's description of the chancellor of the diocese, Father Toohey, as a "bottom feeder" (228). Strung out between the authoritarianism and materialism of the older clergy and the flaccid reasoning and hedonism of the new, Joe Hackett is portrayed as utterly alone. Joe's aloofness from the clerical generational struggle is captured by Powers when Joe reflects stoically that it wasn't the "singer, or even the song" that mattered but the "Cross" (210).

All the same, Joe's observant habits make it difficult for him to overlook much of what he sees, including the discrepancy between the pomp of those at the top of the ecclesiastical hierarchy and the poverty of those at the bottom, a parody of that secular American society from which the clergy had ostensibly separated themselves. Powers's gift for descriptive detail is particularly effective in this matter, as in his droll view of two rural priests who come to the diocesan retreat in an old Chevrolet, equipped with a "long waving aerial and an outsize bug screen" into which a "small yellow bird had flown and stuck as if mounted there" (207). The addition of the small yellow bird evocatively amplifies the atmosphere of shabby rusticity, a sign of Powers's meticulous evocation of setting.

The novel's denouement is precipitated by the demand that Father Hackett bring his parish into the Archdiocesan Renewal Fund, a slick, high-pressure fund-raising scheme approved by the archbishop. Powers constructs the novel in such a way that Joe's reluctance to go along is linked symmetrically to a traumatic event that had marred the beginning of his priestly life. Without any authorial comment, the reader is led to join the two halves of the novel together in order to understand Father Joe Hackett's rebellion. In the beginning of *Wheat That Springeth Green*, a newly ordained and idealistic Joe Hackett finds himself assigned as assistant to a demagogic priest, Father Stock, who, in order to increase the collection, insists that newly ordained priests, rather than laypersons, take it up. The requirement sparks a crisis of conscience in Joe, who argues that this would debase both the Mass and the priesthood.

The episode creates such revulsion in the young priest that he later devises a tithing scheme in his own parish. With ironical symmetry, however, Powers shows that in many respects Joe Hackett comes to mirror his old nemesis, Father Stock, by building himself an expensive rectory before even erecting a decent church. In asking for permission to build his expensive rectory, Father Hackett, commenting on the paltry office space in some rectories, asks rhetorically if this is "any way to carry on the most important business in the world?" (101). The words immediately and ironically recall Father Stock about whom Joe's mother had quipped that he successfully combined the careers of priest and businessman.

Joe's settling into the comfortable pew is mitigated to some extent by his subscription to the *Catholic Worker,* a sign of his lingering interest in social justice and Christian pacifism, a reminder of Powers's own stand. Reflecting bitterly about the church's inadequate denunciation of war, Joe reflects at one point: *"Dulce et decorum est pro patria mori!* How sweet and meet it is to die for my country! And to take a few with me, with ecclesiastical approbation" (251). In their unrelieved acerbity the reflections on war stand out from the rest of the novel:

> The just-war theologians would have a lot to answer for in the next world. In holding that conscripts could usually presume that their country was right, and if in doubt could prudently acquiesce because the civil and ecclesiastical authorities were probably right, and if wrong could not be blamed if acting in conscience, St Thomas and others had dated badly. . . . The Church, in playing footsie with the powers that be, from Constantine to LBJ, had been remiss. (252)

Graver and more idealistic than other parts of the novel, the passage rides resolutely over the welter of events—the manipulation, dismay, and betrayal of vocation—that mark Powers's depiction of the clergy.

The eruption of Joe Hackett's moral outrage over the abandonment within his church of an adequately Christian outlook on war points obliquely to the idealism embedded in the novel's title. Taken from a nineteenth-century English carol, which was in turn derived from a French medieval carol, the title with its Christmas associations evokes the picture of a birth out of the darkness. In this sense the novel is parallel, in its patient documenting of the process of moral conversion, to *Morte D'Urban.* Father Hackett accepts his final appointment to the significantly named Holy Cross parish as altogether fitting, reflecting wryly that the position should properly be taken by someone like himself who was *not* eager to "go among the poor" (173). While Powers depicts some egregious clerical vices, he constructs his novel in such a way that one sees the need for parish priests like Joe Hackett to keep at least one foot in the world. To this end Powers includes a chapter on the disaster that can overtake a parish when it is administered by a contemplative, as in the case of Father Van Slaag, who among other absurdities tolerates a bullying housekeeper and her vicious dog as a means of personal mortification.

Powers's use of symbolism in *Wheat That Springeth Green* is a little less obtrusive than in *Morte D'Urban.* Probably the most effective symbol is the weather ball that emerges as part of the bedrock of the setting rather than being imposed from without like the Arthurian motif in *Morte D'Urban.* Designed to promote a Congressional bill that would fund a new missile and thereby help a local company, the illuminated weather ball seems to Joe Hackett, who sees it as infernal, to be "red as fire" (110). Significantly, however, although Father Hackett is unalterably opposed to the local campaign and the church support it has received, he doesn't go as far as Thomas Merton or Daniel Berrigan would have gone in condemnation, instead reminding his parishioners that they are to pray for the "things that lead to salvation" and for temporal things only "insofar as they conduce to that end" (111). Unlike Thomas Merton and Daniel Berrigan, Joe's role is pastoral, rather than prophetic; he doesn't want to stir up and divide his parishioners on a specific issue not directly related to his pastoral care of them.

The point is a moot one, and is related, perhaps, to Julian Moynahan's observation that Powers is elusive in deciding whether or not Father Joe Hackett is an "extraordinary or an ordinary man." The same sort of comment might well be made about a number of Powers's protagonists, whose lives tend to skirt the mundane. What lifts figures like Father Joe Hackett and Father Urban from oblivion is difficult to say, partly because of Powers's minimalist diction. As John Hagopian observed, however, in all of Powers's fiction the "theology is there. It is not dogmatic or mystical, but ascetic, moral, natural, or pastoral."[12] As has been illustrated, Powers tightly packs his phrasing so that every word carries more than its usual load. Apart from these stylistic considerations, however, the question of the depth and range of his characters' consciousnesses is a fair one to put. In general, his characters, even his central characters, are portrayed as existing within a relatively narrow cultural framework, and their only claim to significance arises from their spiritual struggles, which all too often are diminished by self-doubt and by doubt about the sanctity of the Catholic Church.

Just as Powers is excruciatingly persuasive in portraying the spiritual torpor of his clerical protagonists, though, so too is he convincing in showing the pale light that occasionally but decisively enters their lives. Apparently resolved never to exaggerate a favorable change of heart in his characters, Powers, by the same token, seems determined not to exaggerate the gloom that pervades his studies of Catholic clergy. It is for this exactitude in measuring the religious and moral value of his characters that the reader may feel grateful—a measuring that at the end of complex novels such as *Morte D'Urban* and *Wheat That Springeth Green* finally yields a glimpse of the ineffable. At that point Powers's characters

12. Hagopian, *J. F. Powers*, 121.

become "extraordinary," caught up in a drama whose proportions enlarge the scale of their otherwise prosaic lives. Powers's accomplishment as a novelist lies in his ability to trace the monotony and disappointment of priestly lives, vitiated by individual and institutional vices, to a vanishing point involving the action of grace where there are changes wrought that satisfy yet transcend, however faintly, a purely realistic reckoning.

11

DANIEL BERRIGAN

(B. 1921)

ALTHOUGH THEY CAME from different backgrounds and followed very different lifestyles, Thomas Merton and Daniel Berrigan shared a common outlook regarding the need to balance the roles of contemplation and action. Furthermore, throughout the 1960s, when their relationship was at its strongest, each played a role in helping the other to achieve the desired balance. Both Merton and Berrigan had been influenced by Dorothy Day and the Catholic Worker movement, which long before Vatican II had stressed the ordinary Christian's responsibility not only to aid but also to stand up for the oppressed and the poor—if need be against the political and even the ecclesiastical establishment. A further bond arose from the fact that both Berrigan and Merton were internationalists, perceiving the world as a whole as their proper sphere of action and thus helping to break down what they regarded as the rather stifling nationalism of the American Catholic Church. Merton had spent much of his early life in Europe, and Berrigan had been transformed by a sabbatical year in France in 1953, a year in which he had associated with the worker priests, who, much to his dismay, were suppressed by Rome shortly thereafter.

Berrigan began writing to Merton in 1948, having been impressed by the recently published *The Seven Storey Mountain,* but the relationship came to life only in the 1960s after Berrigan read a piece by Merton that had appeared in the *Catholic Worker* on the roots of war. Both were in agreement that the traditional Augustinian morality of the just war no longer applied in a nuclear age and under conditions in which huge civilian casualties were unavoidable. Moreover, both Berrigan and Merton had struggled during the 1950s and 1960s against ecclesiastical authority; in each case this was related to their attempts to preach and to live the social gospel. While Merton met resistance because of his writings on peace, Berrigan's high-profile antiwar activities drew fire from the powerful prelate Cardinal Spellman, who persuaded Berrigan's religious superiors to remove him from the New York diocese for a time during the early 1960s.

Berrigan is distinct as a Catholic writer in conflating his writing and his work as a social activist in an attempt to infuse avant-garde Catholic social thought into the American body politic. The trajectory of Berrigan's thought and social activism began with the vigorous groundwork provided by the theologians of the 1950s, including Karl Rahner, Yves Congar, and Teilhard de Chardin. Their consciousness of the church's relationship to history led these theologians to feel that Catholics needed to be extricated from the defensive and isolating posture that had followed the Counter Reformation and in particular, the Council of Trent, four hundred years earlier. Berrigan's personalist approach convinced him that history was made by significant individuals acting against stagnant institutions and reactionary traditions. Strongly attracted to the Catholic Church's incarnational theology, Berrigan stressed in a book of essays about the church, which was called *The Bride*, the significance of history and of time itself as a hidden and unexpected treasure for the church: "Time is to her a perpetual springtime, with unlimited opportunity for the planting; time is a perpetual autumn, with labors and harvest to try her energies to the utmost." The lyricism of this passage arose from Berrigan's belief that the intervention of Christ definitively transformed history into a process whereby the mind of God became incrementally revealed within matter and time. Moreover, he argued, in coming to know the mind of God through an assiduous study of the paradigmatic life of Christ, human beings would also in time come to know themselves spiritually as human beings. In *The Bow in the Clouds*, published in 1961, Berrigan described Christ as "universal man" with history being perceived as a "controlled release of the energies of the risen Christ." Time is visualized as a spiral through which humanity ascends as consciousness enlarges, a view that reflected Berrigan's debt to Teilhard de Chardin at the time.[1]

---

1. Berrigan, *The Bride: Essays in the Church*, 142; Berrigan, *Bow in the Clouds*, 167, 168.

Looking, however, at the disarray in the actual order of history, Berrigan stressed the importance of asceticism—a joyful asceticism—in restoring the world to its pristine unity and harmony. In Berrigan's view, the prophets, like the saints, approached the beautiful things of the world with a penetrating sense of their underlying spiritual reality and thus escaped being seduced and captivated by them. Berrigan did not advocate an asceticism that disparaged the material universe, but rather envisaged a love of God that was "nourished by a love of creation."[2] One is impressed by the exquisite balance of Berrigan's thought in this matter. The world within and without, he observed, will be restored when we are able to regard material things transparently, with a full, even sensuous, appreciation of their value yet also with a sense of their significance as emblems of the divine and of our own spiritual nature.

As he was a poet as well as a theologian, it was natural that Berrigan should place a good deal of emphasis on the role of the imagination in the history of religious experience. Recalling that pre-Christian religions had grounded substantive matters of belief in resonant images and motifs, Berrigan argued that Christianity's understanding of itself had drifted in later centuries in the direction of an overly rational, desiccated tendency toward verbal formulation. In this way, he argued, Christianity, and particularly Catholicism, had ignored and thereby failed to awaken the imaginative and subconscious riches of the souls of its adherents. In an essay published in 1962, Berrigan observed that humanity should be regarded by the religious artist as "one in origin and destiny." For this reason one of the prominent themes developed in *They Call Us Dead Men* (published in 1966) is that the church must be open to the world. Berrigan repeatedly alludes to the social nature of religious activity and to the "supreme value of relationships" in discovering one's own direction and in extending religious consciousness into the world at large. This involves a willingness, Berrigan added, to "incarnate relationships, to ground ourselves firmly in other lives, to give visible form to the mystery of Christ's brotherhood and, in the process, to extend the mystery itself, to make it apparent, palatable, attractive."[3]

Gradually, Berrigan came to feel, as in *Consequences: Truth And . . .* (which was published in 1967), that the web of experience was too subtle for the sort of a priori thought he had cultivated during his theological and

---

2. Berrigan, *Bow*, 128.
3. Berrigan, "The New Spirit of Modern Sacred Art," 32; Berrigan, *They Call Us*, 103, 113–14.

philosophical studies in preparing to become a Jesuit priest, and he called on religious and other intellectuals to become more closely involved in the social phenomena they attempted to describe: "Logically, the first man to the block, or on the picket line, or to prison in social crisis," he wrote, "ought to be the intellectual." Berrigan's shift toward social activism in the mid-1960s was based not only on moral considerations but also on an empirical sense that truth would likely emerge existentially from the ground up: "Truth that descends only from the top eventually ceases to flow at all. It becomes glacial or sterile, or both."[4]

At the same time, Berrigan went out of his way, as in his 1970 *No Bars to Manhood*, to detach himself from the prevailing liberalism of the 1960s, contending that many liberals tended to inhibit change "at exactly that point where change is needed, which is to say at the depths" of the human spirit.[5] The problem with liberalism, Berrigan believed, was that it focused on particular evils rather than on the spiritual malaise that underlay these evils. In the essay "Bonhoeffer: God Is Neither Here Nor There," Berrigan concluded that the failure of liberalism derived as well from its attempt to accommodate all sides in a dispute. In so doing, he maintained, it absorbed the complexities of an issue to such an extent that it became worn down, with little achieved.

From the beginning of his life as a priest Berrigan wrote and published poetry, and from the beginning, as was the case with Thomas Merton, a tension existed between his priestly vocation and his calling as an artist. The dilemma was not a philosophical one, as it had been for Merton, but rather a conflict about which career had a greater claim on his time and energy. While, in one sense, the matter of Berrigan's dual calling is not extraordinary, since most poets give a good deal of time to other occupations and to their families, nevertheless, increasingly, Berrigan would devote himself to causes that would leave little time for the sort of intellectual concentration required for the craft of poetry. There is no doubt that some of the poetry written by Berrigan at the height of his life as a priest/activist suffered from a lack of creative time, some of it having been written when he was on the run. On the other hand, what is remarkable is the overall quality of the poetic canon, which includes some ten volumes in addition to a number of separately published poems.

While Berrigan attached a priority to his roles as priest and social activist, he did not view his poetry as wholly distinct from these other

4. Berrigan, *Consequences*, 54, 24.
5. Berrigan, *No Bars to Manhood*, 76.

roles. For one thing, as he indicated in an essay about religious art in 1961, he perceived art not only as a mirror of experience but also as a shaper of the reader's sense of reality. When an observer looks at religious art, for example, he is invited to become what he has contemplated with "mind and heart and imagination" in order to bring about the "assimilation of the ikon to human life." In Berrigan's view all art merges at its deepest levels with religion since, like the priest, the artist could "untangle the raveled skein of cause and effect that wound all men into its inescapable circle"— not by means of metaphysical analysis but, as Berrigan put it in *The Bride*, by the "force of creation." Similarly, when commenting upon the effect of African art on modern aesthetics, Berrigan emphasized not merely the stylistic influence of this type of art but its ineluctable spiritual dimension as well. The stark African mask reminded the viewer, he noted, that life was an "arena of powers and dominations" in which moral choices were constantly creating the "soul."[6]

Time without Number (published in 1957) was a formidable success for Berrigan, winning the Academy of American Poets' Lamont Prize and receiving a National Book Award nomination. The book, which went into three printings, had been recommended for publication by Marianne Moore, whose praise for it was unreserved. The book was also well received by critics, attracting qualified praise, for example, from respected poets such as Galway Kinnell.[7] Broadly speaking, the poems are compact meditations on a few central themes, which are in turn clustered about the motif of time. Correlative symbols—notably that of trees—reinforce the focal subject of time in a series of variations. The perspective is distant and the tone somber, as is reflected in archetypal titles such as "The Crucifix," "The Moon," "The Workmen," and "The Men on the Hill." The mood is contemplative and tranquil, quite unlike the restlessness and passion that would characterize the activist poems of the 1960s and 1970s.

Also typical of Berrigan's earlier writing is the optimistic depiction, derived in part from the ideas of Teilhard de Chardin, of the mind's graceful ascent through matter, as in "Lightning Struck Here." In another of the poems in *Time without Number*, Berrigan views, with similar trust and serenity, the migration of the heron, a majestic bird "powerfully steered by its lodestone, its perfect heart."[8] One of the most evocative instances in these poems of the immanence of mind within the natural world occurs

6. Berrigan, "The Catholic Dream World and the Sacred Image," 550; Berrigan, *Bride*, 6–7; Berrigan, "Africa: A People's Art," 22.

7. Kinnell, "Four First Volumes," 183.

8. Berrigan, *Time without Number*, 8, subsequently cited in the text parenthetically.

in "our very heart" where, following the shedding of its leaves, a naked tree is depicted as "clothed" by the first snow, a "luminous cloud of thought" (22).

In a few of the poems the mood is bleaker, as in "The Crucifix," which centers on a roadside crucifix that Berrigan had seen when traveling through Quebec. Time and weather had eroded the already agonized features of the figure on the cross so that it seemed an emblem of defeat:

> What time had done, breaking the bones at knee and wrist,
> washing the features blank as quarry stone,
> turning the legs to spindles, stealing the eyes
>
> was only to plant forever its one great gesture
> deeper in furrow. (2)

Lashed by the elements, the figure on the cross is nonetheless a symbol of endurance, as can be seen in the concluding lines in which the weathered body on the cross "took punishment like a mainsail / bearing the heaving world onward to the Father" so that the villagers in the pious Quebec countryside went to sleep at night knowing that "in the clear lovely morning he will be there" (3). Implicit in the imagery of this and of many of the poems in *Time without Number* is Berrigan's durable view that life is both harvested beauty and necessary ordeal.

In *Encounters*, published in 1960, Berrigan's poetic powers were at their acutest in tracing the frontiers of the eternal and the finite. A ubiquitous symbol in *Encounters*, one related to the intersection of time and eternity, is the stone. In "Chartres" the flying buttresses of the medieval cathedral are portrayed as wings of a "blackened stone giant" chained to the earth and waiting to rise at evening—"bearing in talons an uprooted planet."[9] Registering the power of great religious art to transcend time and space, the imagery also implies that the church, which lifts the world, is also indissolubly part of it. Generally in this collection, stones embody the intransigence of death and time, as in "Lazarus" and "Saint Ann," as well as symbolize the power of God in being able to unlock energy from something as inert as stone. Berrigan uses the symbol with considerable innovation and skill in the self-portrait of Stephen, the first martyr, who was stoned to death and about whom little else is known: "I stood them to a cairn," Stephen relates, "and died / unknowable" (32). The image of the cairn is a masterful touch since the stones that pile up around

---

9. Berrigan, *Encounters*, 70, subsequently cited in the text parenthetically.

Stephen in killing him also make him a sign or marker, a guide for other Christians.

For Berrigan, Christ, above all others, epitomized the heroic, symboliz- ing an unexpected potency in suffering that contrasts, for example, with the aggressive simplicity of the earlier Greek heroic archetypes. In the poem "Tasks," for instance, Orpheus is enjoined to "remember Christ," while Hercules is pitied for having experienced nothing but a hopeless sorrow for the "dolorous dead" (67). In another poem Atlas is urged to "take up the cross" (59). Compared to Caroline Gordon, who in her fiction also considered the relationship between classical and Christian heroism, Berrigan is much more emphatic in stressing not merely the completion of heroism in Christ but the paradox of Christ's servantlike triumph as well. In *Encounters,* Berrigan focused not only on heroism but also on the higher purpose for which this reserve of strength exists, as in the poem "Radical Strength," where the flutist's playing serves a higher beauty in the muscular flexure that issues at its apex in "one / crucial delicate finger at the flute stop" (64). Proximately, the image captures the sublimation of strength into sensitivity and beauty; implicitly as well it records the tribute of a natural gift to a higher purpose.

In his 1962 *The World for Wedding Ring,* Berrigan's support for the life of action surfaced amid the political tumult of the 1960s and the stir within the church created by the Second Vatican Council. In these poems Berri- gan proclaimed: "Truest credo is event" and "Events are orthodoxy."[10] Furthermore, as Berrigan became more and more committed to social ac- tivism, particularly in opposing the Vietnam War, the poems became more direct in phrasing and more disaffected in tone. In the autobiographical poem "A Fortieth Year," for example, Berrigan reviewed developments in American society over the four decades of his life, and what he saw was a river of blood released by a series of wars largely sanctioned by his own church:

> Doctrinaire, red with zeal
> men drown the human in a sacred stream
> and generate, row on row, eyeless faces
> out of this world. (9)

As in the poetry of Robert Lowell the war dead are viewed as doubly dead because they died in the act of killing their fellow human beings so that, from the point of view of eternity, they "rot, not rise" (9).

---

10. Berrigan, *World for Wedding Ring,* 5, subsequently cited in the text parenthet- ically.

While still essentially ruminative, the tone of the poems in *The World for Wedding Ring* is increasingly heavy with concern in contrast to the earlier volumes. While there are some poems in which Berrigan delighted in the play of language—as in "Sun" with its bold puns—on the whole there appears to have been little time for such verbal playfulness. Even the usually innocuous subject of style is given unexpected portentousness when projected in the negative image of the "long shadow" a man's style casts "at evening," isolating "all he is not" (20).

Nominated for the National Book Award in 1967, the poems in *No One Walks Waters,* which was published one year earlier, registered Berrigan's increasingly troubled and dejected perception of history. In a poem titled "Astonishment" the speaker wonders about a God who appears to regard history impassively while human beings are repeatedly broken "in the kiln, on the wheel."[11] Against such misery and such divine aloofness, Berrigan questioned the value of a traditional piety of patience:

> What use
> the tarrying savior, the gentle breath of time
> that in beggars is contentious and unruly,
> that in dumb minds comes and chimes and goes
> that in veins and caves of earth
> sleeps like a tranced corpse, the abandoned body
> of violated hope? (31)

Inevitably, Berrigan's thematic focus on this world led to a growing naturalism, even in his treatment of religious themes. In "Last Day," for example, the speaker undercuts the general Christian expectation about the end of the world so that, instead of a cosmic conflagration, he laconically forecasts an ordinariness that would cause "preachers" to cry like "frogs":

> Not a sleeper's hair turned, not one.
> Where the living dwelt, He took breath; where the dead
> lay cold as stones, or stood, long stones on end,
> He troubled none alive. They were safe from Him.
>
> Not one
> dull standing autumn weed denied
> its windless hour, warmth and seed. (45)

What gives these poems their emotional edge is the tension between Berrigan's growing belief in the apparent, de facto detachment of God

---

11. Berrigan, *No One Walks Waters,* 30, subsequently cited in the text parenthetically.

200 THE CATHOLIC IMAGINATION IN AMERICAN LITERATURE

from human affairs and his continued emphasis on the divine intervention of Christ in human history. Indeed, if in Berrigan's early work God is seen to have entered human history, in the later writings it seems as if history had come perilously close to swallowing God. The new emphasis on contemporary actualities tested Berrigan's belief in Teilhard de Chardin's spiritual evolutionism, and he came to regard contemporary Western culture as all but collectively unredeemable in its intellectual pride and moral indifference. Thus, Berrigan's increased naturalism, which stemmed from his belief that matter had been transformed by Christ and therefore must be known and valued, differed from the increasing secular naturalism in American culture, whose philosophical horizons were essentially Darwinian.

Against such a wall of indifference Berrigan found his church, to say the least, unprepared. In the poem "In Memoriam," an elegiac and yet not uncritical poem about a Jesuit professor of philosophy at Fordham who had died at forty, Berrigan contrasts the professor/priest's remoteness with the teeming scene in the Bronx, "hemmed in by trucks and tumbrels," which lay just beyond the university gates (28). On the other hand, for those in the religious life who had plunged into the problems of their society, there was a different danger, that of losing all sense of direction. Berrigan resolved the dilemma between clerical detachment and engagement in the poem "Talisman" where the silver scapular medal worn by the priest exhibits the face of Christ, "incised / in the year's acid" (37). Imaginatively balancing the monetary against the spiritual value of the silver medal, Berrigan indicates through the image of acid that the life of suffering will make of the priest's life a likeness of Christ.

In the 1960s, Berrigan came to regard his poetry as the shadow cast by his life. This intimacy between social dissent and art was sketched in the envoi to *No One Walks Waters,* a poem titled "This Book." The speaker begins by noting that, as his life goes by, "poems follow close," the "mind's dark overflow, the spill of vein / we thought red once, but know now, no" (78). The internal rhyming skillfully captures the transmutation of the blood of life into the blood of poetry. Eventually, the poem moves through a series of analogies in which the pattern is reversed and in which the life of Berrigan is perceived as a book of verse composed by a divine hand that someday would disclose

> the last, first line,
> the shadow rise,
> a bird of omen

snatch me for its ghost

and a hand somewhere, purposeful as God's
close like two eyes, this book. (78)

In the best poems in *No One Walks Waters,* such as "Dachau is Now Open for Visitors," there is an underlying composure and restraint that allows for the intertwining of complex feeling, idea, and use of language:

The arabesque scrawled by the dead
in their laborious passage,
leaf and flower mould of their spent bodies,
faces frost touches gently and coldly
to time's geometric— (55)

The elegiac interfusion of aesthetic detail and the moral reverberations of the death camp gives the poem a carved intensity that is reminiscent of Allen Tate's "Ode to the Confederate Dead." On the other hand, some other poems in *No One Walks Waters,* such as the "Year of Our Lord (Algeria, 1961)," in which the war between Algeria and France became the occasion for a surrealistic vision of human violence, exhibit a blunt, arresting intensity that prefigures the poems of the 1970s:

World spins like a headless top,
butchers put up their shutters,
Caesar in dreams sucks red thumbs clean. (41)

False Gods, Real Men—a 1969 collection of poems that came out as Berrigan awaited at Cornell the outcome of his judicial appeal following the Catonsville, Maryland, draft card–burning case—is experimental and diverse in form compared to his earlier verse. The collection, which is Berrigan's strongest and included a number of poems previously published in prestigious publications such as *Poetry* and the *New Yorker,* traced the outline of his life through the late sixties, including his exile to Latin America, his trip to Hanoi, and his life in New York as a partially deinstitutionalized urban priest. The false-gods motif evidently referred, at least in part, to the waywardness of the historical church. In one of the poems composed during his exile to Latin America, for example, Berrigan ruefully accepted the caustic vision of the church portrayed in the murals of the Mexican painter Diego Rivera. In one of Rivera's scenes, following the torture of certain Indians by the Spanish conquistadors, Berrigan remembered "monkey-faced monks" complaisantly holding before the dying Indians "the lying crucifix." With mordant irony Berrigan paradoxically depicts the Spanish priests themselves as prisoners within the Roman collar.[12]

Fashioning elliptical and fragmentary lines, Berrigan in a number of poems in *False Gods, Real Men* adopted an Eliotian perspective in which he depicted contemporary culture as a surrealistic procession of the dead, as in "The Clock in the Square":

> Ineffectuals
> chained, reined to time's beaten track—
> simulacra all, strangers to action, passion
>
> strike the hour, lurch away
> pale as linen
> the pharaohs of long refusal. (29)

Subjugated by the deadening habits of their culture, the characters resemble the hollow men of both Eliot's and Lowell's poetry. Distinctive in Berrigan's poem, however, is the metaphorical flourish of the "pharaohs of long refusal," the sardonic breaking of the surface of despair by the poet, who insists on the need to recognize the moral freedom of his otherwise catatonic protagonists.

Those poems in *False Gods, Real Men* that grew out of Berrigan's trip to Hanoi in 1968 are terse repositories of compressed themes. An example is the poem Berrigan composed while waiting in Vientiane for the shuttle plane to Hanoi:

> The birds of dawn are crying, drawing
>   the great sun into conflict
>   a contested light
> the bloody challenge taken, the spurred leap, roof
> after roof.
>
>   SUN
>   who alone cocks eye (eyeing that cock)
>   and not
>   burns his socket blind; from his
> intolerable equinox, seeing in the sea
>   himself rampant, eye to eye
>   lives in that cry nor turns to stone
>   nor no, shall die. (11)

The superimposition of the fierce cock's eye and the aggressive sun arises appropriately out of the steamy, war-torn Asian setting. So does an

---

12. Berrigan, *False Gods, Real Men*, 72, subsequently cited in the text parenthetically.

unquenchable penchant for survival, which is also symbolized by both sun and bird. The poem mirrored Berrigan's state of mind as he prepared to move through the charnel house of war toward the possibility of a modified human consciousness on the other side. The air-raid shelters in Hanoi figure in a number of the poems. In "Bombardment," for example, the speaker disappears into the shelter like a "blown match," lamenting the loss of "sun and moon / and one other face"—while above the gases of war "flare on the world's combustible flesh" (15).

"The Pilots Released" plays on the classic theme of American innocence. Thinking about the three downed American pilots who had been released by the North Vietnamese, Berrigan reflected wryly:

> When I think of you it is always (forgive me)
> of disposable art; 50 designs drawn from the damp woodcut
> of 50 States, the physiognomy of camp. (21)

Following the woodcut motif, the speaker provides a portrait of the release of the youngest of the pilots on the journey out of Vietnam in the shuttle aircraft:

> In the old moth-eaten plane (one-eyed—heroic
> as a pirate carp) the youngest pilot
> lived it over and over   roped like an animal
> to the water wheel   drawing up
> buckets water blood honey spleen
> lug and tug 104 days in solitary
> loneliness near madness interrogations
> brainwashing of that brain already
> hung high and dry as a woodcut
>
> of himself by himself; *Our Boy; Spit, Polish,
> Literal Death.* (22)

Steeped in the die-cast outlook of his military school, the young pilot is incisively portrayed by Berrigan, whose tone is not unsympathetic, as helplessly immune to the possibilities of change that are implicit in his suffering at the hands of the outraged Vietnamese. Brilliantly, the poem's vortex of ideas and feelings is crystallized in the image of the decrepit plane, which metamorphoses into the forlorn picture of a blind carp, the nadir of the poem's themes of blindness and obduracy.

The new poems in *Selected and New Poems*, published in 1973, are shards of time stretching back to the late sixties, barely rescued moments in a life that was in a process of high acceleration. For this reason they are especially remarkable for their sharply realized clarity and composure.

An example is the poem "Flew to New York," in which Berrigan recounts a furtive trip to the city to perform a baptism, even though his movements at the time had been restricted by a federal prosecutor. Stopping briefly at his apartment, he finds a note and a spring flower left by a friend:

> So took up the flower, common as our fate,
> $\qquad\qquad\qquad$ tomorrow's
> discard. Filled a stem glass,
> placed the flower, a prima donna, in a box seat.
> Let tomorrow wane. The flower
> blooms like Tolstoi's ripe riposte,
> $\qquad\qquad$ her naked shoulders
> taking time in stride,
> $\qquad\qquad$ one white wing, then another.[13]

The image of war, implicit in the allusion to Tolstoy, induces a hushed, fearful consciousness by Berrigan of his imminent fate, the weight of which is suddenly and fortuitously lifted by the petals of the flower gift. Moreover, through the use of irregular spacing in the final lines Berrigan generates an image of flight that simulates the raising of his leaden spirit in the period prior to his imprisonment.

In their visual arrangement the poems of the late 1960s and early 1970s that were included in the *Selected and New Poems* reflect a freedom and movement that matched the pace of Berrigan's life, especially his position at the center of the antiwar movement at Cornell. In "Autumn, the Streams Are Heavy," for instance, the confluence of rain from above and water from below in the Cornell gorges gave rise to the following startling, stanzaic configuration:

> $\qquad\qquad\quad$ sudden
> air $\qquad\qquad\qquad\qquad$ water
> $\qquad$ conjoin (255)

The emphasis on spacing and movement reflected not simply Berrigan's attraction to open-form poetry but also the fact that he had begun to formulate a theology of movement. In commenting on Pasolini's film *The Gospel of St. Matthew*, for example, he noted that, as opposed to most sacred art, Jesus was portrayed as "always in motion," thereby epitomizing the kinetic quality inherent in life itself, a "forward movement of awareness,

---

13. Berrigan, *Selected and New Poems*, 257, subsequently cited in the text parenthetically.

of consciousness, of love" in which the followers of Christ cannot "remain static and hope to grasp what He is about."[14]

During the late sixties, when Berrigan was associate director of Cornell's United Religious Work, he focused on the university as a poetic subject in a sensitive and densely structured poem titled "The Gorges." Employing the central symbols of water, sun, and light, Berrigan posits absolutes of wisdom both above the earth—where God is pictured in the Greek style as a "waylaying cloud above / waters he struck open"—and below in the still pools of the gorges, whose "cold, untouchable / wisdom" is unvisited by the passing sun. The sun, the active principle in the poem, symbolizes the diurnal world of consciousness, which is fertilized by the university—"intelligence, panoply of artists, / genius, entelechy" (254). While bracing and exciting, the intellectual ferment associated with the university is nonetheless depicted as subject to the alternating laws of thermodynamics, which are represented in the poem by the piling of stone upon stone—the venerable university buildings themselves—and by the entropic falling away of water—the cataracts that fed the gorges beneath Cornell.

The speaker in the poem feels himself to be a link between the kinetic world of intellectual endeavor associated with the campus and the ontological pools of absolute wisdom associated with the gorges. He passes through the landscape like a nocturnal animal, moving in "footless" silence over the gorge bridge. The bridge is softly illuminated by the moon, as opposed to the harsh, dissecting light of the sun, which is visualized at one point as an ax, a symbol of the professional and competitive activities of the university. In part the poem mirrors Berrigan's consciousness of his distinctive role at Cornell, his calling of attention to the deeper pools of wisdom that could easily go unobserved amid the burgeoning of ideas within that community. In its originality and thematic and structural density the poem represents a high level of achievement in Berrigan's poetry.

The conditions under which Berrigan wrote the *Prison Poems* (which were published in 1973) were obviously far from optimal as he revealed in a free-verse sonnet in which he described himself as scribbling lines with difficulty, "lights out, at a barred window. / Snow filigrees the April green."[15] The poems, which are tinted by the gray walls of the federal prison in Danbury, Connecticut—where Berrigan had been sentenced as a

---

14. Berrigan and Thich Nhat Hanh, *The Raft Is Not the Shore*, 138.
15. Berrigan, "O Danbury, To What Shall I Compare Thee?" *Prison Poems*, 22, subsequently cited in the text parenthetically.

result of his involvement in an antiwar protest in Catonsville, Maryland—give one a convincing impression of the abrasiveness of prison routine. Berrigan's candor strengthens the prison poems by bringing out some of the underlying ambiguities of his situation. The sense of alienation he sometimes instinctively felt toward many of his fellow inmates, for example, undercut his hopes for kindling a sense of community within the prison walls. Helpless at his own ambivalence, Berrigan and his brother, Philip, began study groups at Danbury in an effort to transform the prison world that successive government bureaucracies had cobbled together. In addition, even the most fleeting contact with nature in these prison surroundings poignantly exposed Berrigan's buried life. In "Tulips in the Prison Yard," for example, he wistfully compared his response to the flowers with that of the great romantic poets: "Yeats, Wordsworth would look once / breathe deeply, sharpen their quills / with a flourish pluck you from time" (23). By way of contrast the tulips at Danbury were not presented as a symbol of perennial freedom, but were "jail-yard blooms," born in prison and destined to die there. Moreover, instead of being an emblem of hope, they were perceived as a harbinger of revolution, a "first flicker in the brain's soil, the precursor / of judgment" (23). The symbolic import of the flowers, then, was not that they offered an escape from the harsh enclosure of prison but rather that they revealed that even there life could be transformed.

Following a decade that included an enervating prison term and a tempestuous involvement in antiwar protests, Berrigan in 1984 issued *May All Creatures Live,* which was published privately and whose proceeds went to the peace movement. In this collection Berrigan incorporated his belief about the social and political import of poetry, as in the following lines:

> When the poet recanted
> they hacked off his fingers
> and gave him a signet ring
>
> The poet recanted.
> They tore out his tongue
> and crowned him their laureate.[16]

Berrigan believed that academic poets in particular risked being emasculated by the state that employed them, a compounding of a moral danger already implicit in their physical remoteness.

---

16. Berrigan, "I Hope and Pray This Doesn't Happen to Me," *May All Creatures Live,* 88, subsequently cited in the text parenthetically.

In "Ignorance Is Like a Sourdough Starter," Berrigan reflexively considered his lengthy involvement in social dissent. In a letter to the author on June 7, 1986, he explained that the word *ignorance* in the poem referred to a kind of humility, "at once modest and yeasty, that I consider a prelude to such knowledge as ends up not inert." In a more precise sense the poem is a candid reflection of Berrigan's sorties into social action, which were sometimes taken with a minimum of knowledge but which were also followed by a rising of consciousness as mind interacted with event and as inert knowledge sprouted into deed. Stylistically, the poem is typical of the poems in *May All Creatures Live* for its bold imagery and phrasing. An example is the depiction of the sterile knowledge that Berrigan associated with much academic poetry as unleavened dough, a "death's head" that "squats / stares at the phantom tit" (59).

In a few of these poems Berrigan considered his problematic relationship with the officialdom of the Catholic Church. In "O Catholic Church," for example, he pictured himself as a trapeze artist performing under the "tent's navel," but nonetheless anchored by the church. Though his tone is essentially conciliatory, he vividly registers his objection to the church's institutionalized heaviness, its compulsion to regiment every detail of its religious vision instead of

> a word
> from a starry mouth
> heard softly here and there
>   with authority too
>
>   —a forefinger pointing
>   —a voice saying 'north'
>
> We could infer the other directions. (22)

Noticeably in these poems from the 1970s the beauty of nature became a consolation at a time when Berrigan had become increasingly conscious of aging, in part due to the attrition inevitable in a life spent in the resistance movement. As his own energy ebbed, he clung to signs of vitality in the world at large, and this accounted in part for a gradual shift in mood from the somber, apocalyptic scenarios of the 1970s to the consoling landscapes of the 1980s. Nevertheless, even in these landscapes, death hovers, though with an oddly reassuring quality. Thus, in poems such as "Ambition" and "Consolation," Berrigan initiates a colloquy with the dead, whose voices are like "winds in empty / branches" (13). The analogies are apt; like the wind in the branches and the stars seen through the winter trees, the voices of the dead, though marginally perceptible, are a felt presence.

The serene poems in his 1985 *Block Island* grew out of Berrigan's grateful use of a summerhouse owned by his friend William Stringfellow. The island off the coast of Rhode Island in Long Island Sound served Berrigan as a haven from the stress of life in Manhattan and as a location in which to write. Relaxed and affectionate in tone for the most part, the untitled poems in *Block Island* flow easily into each other. Sharing a single location and cast of characters, the poems offer an unhurried and undated view of experience. Rustic and windblown, life on Block Island is portrayed as elemental and domestic, a change from Berrigan's highly socialized existence on the mainland. The mood of the poems, which develops cumulatively, alternates between a mournful feeling of loss and a modest assertion of survival. Death occurs as naturally and implicitly on the island as life. At one point, Anthony Towne, the writer who shared Stringfellow's house on Block Island, dies alone—with Stringfellow away in Canada at the time and Berrigan teaching at Berkeley. Upon their return the two bury the ashes of their friend beneath a huge rusting anchor, both of them shivering under a "driving downpour, prayer books dissolved / to illiterate oatmeal."[17]

In the *Block Island* poems the interlaced motifs of life in death, death in life, were heightened by the fact that while he wrote within the dispensation of timelessness bestowed by the island, Berrigan awaited the final judicial decision on his action as a member of the Plowshares Eight group, which had broken into a nuclear weapons factory, a decision that he believed could entomb him for the rest of his life. The emotional calm of the poems in *Block Island* arises from the limpid depths of the perspectives offered by the island, as in a view of the distant stillness of a cargo ship. Similarly, life on the mainland, though never really forgotten, feels remote, so much so that the sorting of his mail feels to Berrigan like "tugging distant nets ashore" (48). The poems are given structural unity by the recurring motifs of sea, bird, and house, the latter being the most prominent and elaborate symbol. The house is important not only as a symbol, though, but also as a literal reality, a stable residence among people whom Berrigan regarded as family, a refuge from a nomadic life in which the nearest a "Jesuit knows / of dwelling place" is the communal "long house" (6). Released from the need to strenuously shape reality in the light of ideological goals, Berrigan's mind slipped into a more passive mode in which the ordering of things could be accomplished by others, even by the rustic house itself:

---

17. Berrigan, *Block Island*, 9, subsequently cited in the text parenthetically.

> The little house
> all eyes, saw for me. I peered through windows
> that colored nothing dank or rosy, saw
> a waxy bush billowing like a sail; or hunched
> face downward, a buffalo riding storm.
> No. A mere bush, no burning bush. (14)

Implicit in the rejection of the biblical burning bush is a sense of release from the pressure of an allegorical reading of the world and a consequent resting instead against the concreteness of being.

Indeed, Berrigan extracted from his sojourns on Block Island a sense of well-being that allowed the house and island to pass for an experience of heaven:

> Be not astonished
> if, on stroke of midnight,
> stroke of noon—
> table, porch, fundament, roof
> pots and pans, with great clatter
> levitate in the blue.
> Dumb clapboards strike alleluia!
> Blue nail heads burn like glass!
> Shingles—feathers of birds of paradise!
> an angel's shoulder nudges the house, no weightier than
> balloon and basket—up, up
> into the Presence. (45)

The irregular, shifting lines, which mimic the loosening and rising parts of the house, reflect the sustained airiness of the poems. Even the elegiac passages are frequently infused with a lightness of touch that keeps afloat the pervasive theme of a community of the blessed. On the whole, the poems in *Block Island* registered the compensatory, contemplative side of Berrigan's spirituality that he insisted had to balance and indeed nourish the life of social activism.

More than any other twentieth-century American Catholic writer Daniel Berrigan emphasized the church's necessary involvement in history as a corollary to the doctrine of the Incarnation of God in the world through Christ. More than any other Catholic writer Berrigan also illustrated the unity that can exist between the artist, the religious contemplative, and the social activist. The quality of Berrigan's poetry varied enormously with the fluctuations that accompanied his active life as a spiritual leader and social protestor. This was not simply an inevitable, unsought effect but one that reflected Berrigan's determination to give his energies to the work that seemed to him most compelling at the time. Nevertheless, it would be misleading to suggest that his best poems were those written in the relatively tranquil periods of his life, as in the academic years when he taught at LeMoyne College in Syracuse. While the poems of those early years exhibit a fastidiousness in phrasing and artifice that would not, on the whole, be repeated in the later work, nevertheless his most stimulating and distinctive writing was done in the mid to late 1960s, in volumes such as *No One Walks Waters* and *False Gods, Real Men,* when his imagination, energy, and social commitment were all at their peak.

Berrigan liberated many American Catholics from an uncritical patriotism that stemmed from their desire to be part of the cultural mainstream. In addition, in eloquently questioning the church's historical habit of respecting political authority in the hope of ensuring its own survival, Berrigan sharpened Catholics' allegiance to individual conscience, particularly with respect to war, and thereby helped cause the American Catholic resistance to the Vietnam War to swell in the 1960s. Somehow, against the thunder of his presence on the political scene, Berrigan's poetry, some of it of high quality as has been suggested, has been largely ignored by the critical establishment. As was the case with Thomas Merton, the unevenness of Berrigan's poetry can be daunting. Nevertheless, a new selected edition of his poetry is long overdue and should help to establish him as one of the formidable poets of the sixties. While Berrigan's poetry was generally not as polished or as recondite as, say, Robert Lowell's, it did, more than Lowell's, trenchantly depict the white flame of ideological engagement. Far from leading him into the cloister, Berrigan's religious faith drew him into the center of his society and of his time. In this sense he demonstrated convincingly that to be Catholic in America meant, after all, to be *catholic.*

12

FLANNERY O'CONNOR

(1925-1964)

W HILE FLANNERY O'CONNOR once said, in an essay titled "On Her Own Work," that her role as a writer was to describe the action of grace, she added that such action occurred in a world "held largely by the devil." O'Connor's sensibility was formed within the largely Protestant and Fundamentalist South from which she drew most of her characters. Indeed, she declared in "The Catholic Novelist in the Protestant South" that she felt a "good deal more kinship with backwoods prophets and shouting fundamentalists" than she did with mainstream Protestants or Catholics for whom the supernatural had become an "embarrassment" and for whom religion had become a "department of sociology or culture or personality development." She identified with the Southern Fundamentalist's knowledge of and deference to Scripture, distrust of the abstract, and emphasis on the pervasive reality of evil. As for the Southerner's religious consciousness in general, O'Connor observed in an essay called "The Grotesque in Southern Fiction" that in the South the "general conception of man" was still, "in the main, theological."[1]

It is likely that the radically polarized view of good and evil in O'Connor's fiction, her emphasis on the spiritual value of suffering, and her

1. O'Connor, *Mystery and Manners*, 118, 207, 44.

avoidance of sexuality sprang as readily from her Irish Catholic culture, with its Jansenistic tendencies, as from her absorption of Southern Fundamentalism. From either side, though, O'Connor believed that the strong religious emphasis in southern culture, a view shared by her friends and fellow southerners Allen Tate and Caroline Gordon, aided it in culturally surviving the Civil War. In this matter O'Connor once wrote dryly, in an essay called "The Regional Writer," that southerners were "doubly blessed, not only in our Fall, but in having means to interpret it." O'Connor believed that the sting of defeat experienced by the South was its badge of spiritual awareness, its consciousness of mortality and imperfection (as opposed to the hubristic North), and hence of its need for God. In "The Grotesque in Southern Fiction," O'Connor related her attraction to allegory, which writers in the Calvinistic tradition have been especially fond of, to her admiration for Hawthorne, who was himself absorbed by the traditions of American Puritanism and whom O'Connor defended for his use of the allegorical romance form.[2]

From O'Connor's point of view, what both Catholic and Protestant writers had in common was an audience largely composed of nonbelievers who put "little stock either in grace or the devil." In the same essay, "On Her Own Work," in connection with her novel *Wise Blood*, O'Connor maintained that while many unbelieving readers hoped that the protagonist managed to escape the inner voice that called him to his vocation as a prophet, his "integrity" lay in his not being able to elude that destiny.[3] As has been intimated, O'Connor's view here seems to conform much more readily to Calvinistic theology—particularly the doctrine of election—than to Catholic theology, which emphasizes the universal accessibility of grace through the sacraments and the church.

While O'Connor wrote in "Novelist and Believer" that she doubted that there would be great religious fiction until the coming of a "happy combination of believing artist and believing society," she formulated a strategy, a successful one as things turned out, for presenting religious fiction to a secular readership. In the same essay O'Connor observed that this involved the dramatizing of religious events such as baptism with sufficient "awe and mystery" to jar the reader into an "emotional recognition" of their significance. In addition to other techniques, O'Connor's use of the grotesque in order to bring about this jarring effect has been widely commented on. As is indicated in an essay titled "The Fiction Writer and

2. Ibid., 59, 38–39.
3. Ibid., 118, 115.

His Country," O'Connor's view of the grotesque is many-sided in the sense that she not only uses it to provoke religious consciousness but also to illuminate moral "distortions" that secular readers were accustomed to regarding as "natural." While O'Connor's use of the grotesque recalls southern writers such as Faulkner who are part of an implicitly Protestant tradition, she is Catholic in her insistence upon the theological importance of the physical world. The more a writer wishes to make the supernatural apparent, she has contended, the more "real he has to be able to make the natural world." Furthermore, as an assiduous reader of Saint Thomas Aquinas, O'Connor argued in "On Her Own Work" that the Catholic fiction writer was provided with a complete cosmology and metaphysics and was thereby drawn to observe the world with heightened attentiveness: "Open and free observation," she wrote in "Catholic Novelists," was founded on "our ultimate faith that the universe is meaningful, as the Church teaches."[4]

O'Connor's use of the grotesque is partly allegorical—as in her silhouetting of Mr. Head's tubelike face in "The Artificial Nigger," a face whose grotesqueness mirrors the self within. O'Connor tends to highlight the physical plainness of her characters as a basis for them to feel their unworthiness and hence their need of God, as in the sour child observer in "The Temple of the Holy Ghost" (from the 1955 collection *A Good Man Is Hard to Find*), whose sense of her own worth appreciates when she hears the theological phrase that gives the story its title and feels as if "somebody had given her a present."[5] While there are moments of beauty in O'Connor, for the most part nature, both in its human and in its nonhuman manifestations, is neutral at best and frequently threatening. The river that baptizes Harry Ashfield, for example, also kills him in a grotesque, baptismal parody of the death of the old self preceding the birth of the new.

Both O'Connor's ascetical Catholicism and her techniques for addressing a secular audience can be seen in *A Good Man Is Hard to Find*, especially in the title story. The story is constructed of a number of antitheses: the old and new South, Catholic and Protestant theology, appearance and reality, rationalism and religion, to name a few. In terms of the story's theological tenor the reader cannot help but feel the tide of determinism that underlies the unfolding of events, here as elsewhere in O'Connor's

4. Ibid., 168, 162, 33, 116, 178.
5. O'Connor, *Good Man*, 88. Quotations from the stories in this collection are subsequently cited in the text parenthetically.

fiction. Indeed, the chain that binds Bailey's family to its fate is so tight and somber and the characters are so ineluctably led to their doom by their evil inclinations that the story seems a rather un-Catholic allegory. On the other hand, the ending, even though it involves an encounter between an atheist and an old-fashioned, Protestant, southern gentlewoman, seems comparatively Catholic in its emphasis upon the power of the individual to change morally. Not only does the grandmother bring about a change in the Misfit's destiny, predisposing him to become the prophet he was meant to become, but, as O'Connor has noted, the grandmother alters her own fate at the last minute in a compassionate gesture that converts her religious "prattling," as O'Connor put it, into something of substance.[6]

While O'Connor respected the moral and religious traditions of the South, she was rather reserved about southern racism, and was not delighted with what appeared to her to be a counterproductive political pressure from the North for immediate racial integration. Nevertheless, her portrayal of race frequently undermines the pretensions of racist characters—as in Mr. Head's startled recognition of the wealth and personal status of the coffee-colored man on the train in "The Artificial Nigger" and in Nelson's unnameable longing for a mother, which ironically surfaces in his encounter with a black woman. Typically, race is one of the many sources of complexity in O'Connor's characters. Though O'Connor satirizes the grandmother's implicit racism in "A Good Man Is Hard to Find," for example, she honors the grandmother's respect for manners. While the grandmother's manners are flecked with vanity, she is the only one in the family to reprimand the children for their insolent behavior at Red Sammy's. Ironically, with respect to manners, it is the Misfit who most resembles the grandmother. Even in ordering the sequence of killings, his voice is subdued and his phrasing extremely polite. While O'Connor abhors what the Misfit does, she does appear to admire his self-control, even if this is of a repressive sort. At a profound level of her characterization of the Misfit, O'Connor reveals the Misfit's use of verbal etiquette as a way of containing the explosive anger that smolders just below the surface. On the other hand, as opposed to the vacant consumerism of both Bailey's family and the people at Red Sammy's, the Misfit is the only one in the story, other than the grandmother, with anything like a philosophical and moral consciousness. Indeed, he kills the grandmother—the only time in the story when he is out of control—

6. O'Connor, *Mystery and Manners*, 112–13.

expressly in order to protect his nihilistic philosophy, which has suddenly been threatened by the grandmother's instinctive, compassionate gesture. Although there is a perceptible alteration in the moral standing of the Misfit and the grandmother, the story as a whole is shrouded in its title and its corollary: if a good man is hard to find, a bad one is hard to avoid, a tacit underlining of O'Connor's Calvinistic or perhaps Jansenistic vision of the sovereignty of evil in the world.

In her handling of narrative O'Connor straddles allegory and realism, as can be seen in her withholding of personal names from the grandmother and the Misfit. She does the same sort of thing in "The Artificial Nigger," another of her studies of determinism and free will in *A Good Man Is Hard to Find*. The central character in that story, Mr. Head, is named allegorically, a reflection of his narrow obsession with power:

> He had a long tube-like face with a long rounded open jaw and a long depressed nose. His eyes were alert but quiet, and in the miraculous moonlight they had a look of composure and of ancient wisdom as if they belonged to one of the great guides of men. He might have been Vergil summoned in the middle of the night to go to Dante, or better, Raphael awakened by a blast of God's light to fly to the side of Tobias. (103)

The contrast between the grotesque face or head and the elevated epic allusions creates an allegorical burlesque that is typical of O'Connor.

Myth is also assimilated into allegory in a number of stories in *A Good Man Is Hard to Find,* as in "A Circle in the Fire," in which Powell, barred forever from the Eden of his youth and thus from hope, sets fire to the woods. The blaze, which readers are intuitively led to associate with hell, metamorphoses suddenly under the author's touch into an image of the prophets in the fiery furnace of the Book of Daniel. Myth also dominates the ending of "The Temple of the Holy Ghost," where the setting sun is pictured as a blood-drenched Host so as to register the theme of betrayal by Christians—in this case by Christian clergy—of Christ in the world, here present in the form of a hermaphrodite. A similar thrust of mythic energy occurs when O'Connor has the priest in "The Displaced Person" identify Mr. Guizac with Christ, in this case a Christ who came, as did the original, as a stranger into the world.

What saves O'Connor's fiction from didactic ponderousness is her unstinting realism, her fine eye for dramatic irony, and her vividness. Regarding the latter, Caroline Gordon observed perceptively in a 1952 letter to Walker Percy that O'Connor focuses the spotlight on her characters as a "burglar plays the safe he is cracking. You don't see anything else in the room."[7] An example is the plaster figure in "The Artificial Nigger," which draws all the elements of the story to itself. Once encountered by the reader, the figure becomes accepted as both allegorically and dramatically appropriate. The image crystallizes the fact that everything about the relationship between Mr. Head and Nelson has been artificial. Furthermore, the figure with its look of misery is oddly referred to as a "monument to another's victory" (128). The language is astonishing, if instructive. What possible victory can be referred to? Obviously not that of black Americans. The scene is all the more puzzling in that it brings Nelson and Mr. Head together in mutual sympathy. What is monumental about the statue, and in a sense thereby liberating, is the fact that the misery embodied in the figure is externalized and frozen, an expression of the suffering, guilt, and fear that Nelson and his grandfather have experienced but have been unable to conceptualize or express. The story, which ends with the Edenic allusion of the serpent, is typical of O'Connor's welding of the elements of allegory and myth.

Enveloping the narratives in *A Good Man Is Hard to Find* is O'Connor's acute moral insight and, in particular, her complex awareness of the difficulty of virtue. In a story such as "The Displaced Person," for example, not only does she arouse the reader's awareness of the moral tragedy that turns all the major characters literally into displaced persons at the end of the story, but she also illuminates the difficulty faced by a resourceful woman such as Mrs. McIntyre in coping with a man intent upon overlooking racial separation in an attempt to save European refugees. O'Connor is effective in allowing us to see, not without sympathy, the perplexed and impossible position Mrs. McIntyre feels herself to be in. Unlike the visionary world inhabited by the old priest who brings Mr. Guizac into her life, Mrs. McIntyre inhabits the actual world of social and financial contingencies. Thus, characteristically, O'Connor places her allegorical dramas squarely in the context of convincingly realistic settings that act as largely failing backdrops to the richly allegorical dramas that beckon them to a higher good.

The freshness and profundity of O'Connor's moral insight are felt everywhere in *A Good Man Is Hard to Find*. An example is her well-known story "The River." Ostensibly a story about a neglected child who is rescued for a day by a well-meaning religious woman, the story's theme goes much deeper than its baptismal symbolism. What O'Connor

---

7. Gordon to Percy (1952), Percy Collection, Southern Historical Collection, Library of the University of North Carolina at Chapel Hill.

incrementally reveals through her description of the parents' careless lives is not simply their neglect of their child's physical and emotional needs but also, and more crucially it turns out, the cost of ignoring the child's innate spiritual nature. What the story finally and disturbingly reveals is that the ignoring of the inherent spiritual character of human beings is not only an act of omission but quite possibly—as in this case—an act of destruction.

If in much of her collection O'Connor depicts the theme of *felix culpa,* the dependence of good on evil, in "Good Country People" she also portrays the paradoxical dependence of evil on good. The one-legged woman, the story's protagonist, can bring about the evil she intends only if the Bible salesman is in fact the good person he claims to be. Similarly, he in turn depends upon the grain of trust in her in order to outwit and exploit her. A devoted reader of Saint Thomas Aquinas, O'Connor presents evil as a negation that parasitically feeds on good in order to survive. The fact that evil *appears* so vivid in O'Connor's fiction is due, in a philosophical sense at least, to its setting ablaze the realities that only a good existing world can provide. Thus, in "The Life You Save May Be Your Own," for example, O'Connor provides the ironic codicil of Mr. Shiftlet's conversation with the hitchhiking boy following Shiftlet's betrayal of Mrs. Crater and her daughter. Following his successful duping of Mrs. Crater, Shiftlet is unaccountably restless when he should be buoyant. Unconsciously (and following the noblest created tendencies in his nature from O'Connor's point of view), he seeks goodness and therefore contact with being—an escape from his own emptiness—in picking up the hitchhiker. Ironically, what he gets is someone who, though more honest, is as separated from goodness and being as he is himself.

O'Connor's second collection of short stories, *Everything That Rises Must Converge* (published in 1965), revealed her interest in the implications of the doctrine of the Incarnation. In this respect, in his introduction to this collection, Robert Fitzgerald pointed out that the title came from Teilhard de Chardin, whose triumphant evolutionary vision O'Connor rejected because, rather like Father Flynn's in "The Displaced Person," it tended to sidestep the Crucifixion and the awkward necessities of the actual world. Like Daniel Berrigan, O'Connor was skeptical about the subjectivity of de Chardin's synthesis of science and religion.

In "The Enduring Chill," O'Connor satirizes the excessive subjectivity of the protagonist's vision. Although Asbury Fox rejects Christianity, he is open to all manner of occult theories and finally, as O'Connor satirically depicts, even to the suggestiveness of a water stain on the wallpaper in his bedroom. At the end of the story, seeing the stain as a large bird with an icicle in its mouth, he follows its descent, which will mark his own death:

> The fierce bird which through the years of his childhood and the days of his illness had been poised over his head, waiting mysteriously, appeared all at once to be in motion. Asbury blanched and the last film of illusion was torn as if by a whirlwind from his eyes. He saw that for the rest of his days, frail, racked, but enduring, he would live in the face of a purifying terror. A feeble cry, a last impossible protest escaped him. But the Holy Ghost, emblazoned in ice instead of fire, continued, implacable, to descend.[8]

The symbolic confluence of the wallpaper bird—part of the subjective fear of the protagonist's childhood—and the descent of the Holy Ghost, is parodied by the fact that, while in the New Testament the Holy Ghost descended in a revivifying fire, here the descent occurs in ice. Fox has wasted his life on a willful narcissism and with subconscious justice consigns himself at the end to a spiritual death. Furthermore, even in the midst of his flight from religious orthodoxy, he unconsciously mimics that orthodoxy, a pattern that is repeated over and over again in O'Connor's fiction.

If "The Enduring Chill" dramatizes the effects of excessive subjectivity, "The Lame Shall Enter First" depicts the sterility of empirical rationalism. In that tale Sheppard is rejected by Norton, finally, because he draws his view of Rufus Johnson solely from the social sciences, ignoring the spiritual dimension that attracted the delinquent youth to the reading of Scripture. Johnson's clubfoot radicalizes his vision so that he can see past the conventional psychological commonplaces that circumvent a recognition of his spiritual nature: "When I get ready to be saved," Rufus exclaims, "Jesus'll save me, not that lying stinking atheist" (189). Here, as elsewhere in O'Connor, the grotesque is portrayed as a stimulus for perception beyond the conventional. Ironically, in trying to protect Rufus from what he regards as the dangerous doctrines of religion, Sheppard, rather like Rayber in *The Violent Bear It Away*, frustrates the latent hope in Rufus (as well as that in his son, Norton) that there is help for humanity beyond the empirical.

Sheppard, whose name suggests a pastoral role, is ironically compared to a priest at one point: "Sheppard's office at the reformatory was a narrow closet with one window and a small table and two chairs in it. He had never been inside a confessional but he thought it must be the same kind

---

8. O'Connor, *Everything That Rises*, 114. Quotations from the stories in this collection are subsequently cited in the text parenthetically.

of operation he had here, except that he explained, he did not absolve. His credentials were less dubious than a priest's; he had been trained for what he was doing" (149). Paradoxically, Rufus will not accept explanations of his behavior that omit forgiveness or the need for it. Reflecting traditional Catholic thinking in this matter, O'Connor implies that, rooted in the soul, is both a moral consciousness and an orientation toward God that cannot easily be suppressed by relatively shallow neoscientific interpretations of behavior.

Nevertheless, with fine comic aplomb, in the story "Revelation," O'Connor shows that visions of the eternal can arise unexpectedly from a jolting contact with the everyday world. Lulled into a false complacency by spiritual vanity, Mrs. Turpin's narcissism is abruptly overthrown by a tongue-lashing administered by the young woman in the doctor's office: " 'Go back to hell where you came from, you old wart hog,' she whispered. Her voice was low but clear. Her eyes burned for a moment as if she saw with pleasure that her message had struck its target" (207–8). The outburst ironically becomes Mrs. Turpin's "revelation," the external cue needed to correct her vision, and significantly she does so, at a subconscious level at least, as is indicated in her culminating vision of heaven:

> There were whole companies of white-trash, clean for the first time in their lives, and bands of black niggers in white robes, and battalions of freaks and lunatics shouting and clapping and leaping like frogs. And bringing up the end of the procession was a tribe of people whom she recognized at once as those who, like herself and Claud, had always had a little of everything and the God-given wit to use it right. . . . They alone were on key. Yet she could see by their shocked and altered faces that even their virtues were being burned away. (217–18)

While Mrs. Turpin's vision is a subjective one and while it was sparked by the ravings of a mad woman, it paradoxically promotes an overdue humility. The moral wisdom achieved is that which, from O'Connor's point of view, Mrs. Turpin latently possessed, having been implanted in her soul by God.

O'Connor interweaves motifs of vision and the grotesque in the story "Parker's Back." Here, with her eye ever on the Incarnation, O'Connor attacks the Albigensian heresy that construed God to be pure spirit, a view expounded by Parker's infuriated wife who, upon seeing the Byzantine Christ tattooed on his back, cries out angrily:

> "God don't look like that!"
> "What do you know how he looks?" Parker moaned. "You ain't seen him."

"He don't *look*," Sarah Ruth said. "He's a spirit. No man shall see his face." (244)

O'Connor slants the characterization of Sarah Ruth so that her abstract perception of God parallels her cold and spiteful temperament. Parker, on the other hand, is pricked into moral awareness by the penetrating eyes of Christ in the tattoo: "Parker sat for a long time on the ground in the alley behind the pool hall, examining his soul. He saw it as a spider web of facts and lies that was not at all important to him but which appeared to be necessary in spite of his opinion. The eyes that were now forever on his back were eyes to be obeyed" (241). The deliberate ambiguity of the word *forever* brackets both the indelibility of the tattoo and Parker's fresh awareness of the longevity of the soul.

If the stories in *Everything That Rises Must Converge* demonstrate O'Connor's Catholic, incarnational vision, *Wise Blood* (published in 1952), her first novel, focused, rather Calvinistically, on the theme of God's rescue from damnation of the chosen soul. Hazel Motes's desperate flight from God, and particularly from the call to be a preacher, is set off against an all but deterministic series of events that lead him inexorably to his divinely appointed destiny. O'Connor underlines the strong connection between Hazel's Fundamentalist beliefs and the Old Testament in which human beings chosen by God for particular roles are pursued until they either accede or damn themselves. Divine intervention acquires added force in *Wise Blood* when it reaches out not only to Hazel but also to those who are seconded by God, as it were, to bring Hazel around. Such is Enoch Emery, who is given a parodic role as a John the Baptist awaiting his messiah. Harboring the secret of the shrunken mummy, Enoch reflects that he could not show the mystery to just anyone: "Who he had to show it to was a special person. This person could not be from the city but he didn't know why. He knew he would know him when he saw him."[9] In Enoch's room is a tabernacle-like cabinet that was meant to contain a slop jar. Since Enoch does not own a slop jar, he leaves the space empty since he has a "reverence" for the "purpose" of things (131). This otherwise bizarre narrative detail underlines Enoch's openness to the intuited voice of God in contrast to Hazel, who flees that voice. At a more philosophical level the phrasing recalls O'Connor's reading of Aquinas, who emphasized the purposefulness that had been incorporated in Creation.

While O'Connor's characterization in *Wise Blood* appears deterministic, her conception of free will included the convergence of a number of

---

9. O'Connor, *Wise Blood*, 81, subsequently cited in the text parenthetically.

conflicting wills in one person, as she put it in the author's note to the second edition of the novel in 1962. In this sense the divine will, though potently felt by Hazel, competes with his own will and with the wills of others—such as Asa Hawks's daughter, who lures Hazel toward a quite different destiny than that which finally claims him. Furthermore, O'Connor sketches a determinism of a naturalistic kind in showing the impact of Hazel's parents and grandparents on him. When Hazel goes into the army, for example, he takes only two things with him, a black Bible, which recalls his grandfather, and a pair of spectacles that had belonged to his mother. Even the car, which eventually becomes so central to Hazel's thinking, recalls the automobile that his grandfather had used in preaching. At times Hazel becomes conscious of the influence of the past in his life—as when he has the feeling that everything he saw was a "broken-off piece of some giant blank thing that he had forgotten had happened to him" (74).

The weight of the past is given concrete expression in the novel by the recurring coffin symbolism, which, among other things, reminds the reader of Hazel's isolation following the deaths of all the members of his family. His recollection of the deaths of his two younger brothers is particularly revealing in terms of the novel's symbolic structure. When one of the small coffins was closed, Hazel ran to open it in the fear that his brother might have been mistakenly shut up alive in it. Thus begins Hazel's nightmarish fear of being buried alive, a theme that pervades the novel. Related to this is Hazel's memory of his father's coffin and his father's ludicrous scheme for avoiding being buried alive. In reality, Hazel sees that his father, dropped into the grave, "flattened out like anybody else" (20). Thus, all escape routes for Hazel are closed by O'Connor, except one, that through Christ, which corresponds with the voice of God that has been calling him.

The novel is full of coffins, like the one at the carnival that contained a woman who was too long for it, a further variation on the buried-alive motif. While somewhat comic, as was the statement of bravado by Hazel's father about keeping the coffin lid from being closed, these scenes are also prophetic in a Christian sense. While human beings are mortal, they are not, following the Resurrection of Christ, in O'Connor's view, finally meant for death. Touching on this theme, in a fine interweaving of conscious and subconscious elements, O'Connor portrays Hazel having a flashback of the trip to the carnival when his parents were still alive and when his mother hit him across the legs with a stick and said, "Jesus died to redeem you," to which Hazel replied: "I never ast him" (63).

Hazel's resistance to the Word of God is paralleled by his attraction to Asa Hawks, which is in turn parallel to Enoch's instinctual attraction to Hazel. Hazel's attraction to Hawks continues until he discovers that Hawks is a charlatan and can physically see. He is thus led by deflection however, through the false gate of Hawks's religion to the true gate of Christianity. Hazel's resistance stemmed from his feeling of having been buried alive by the fundamentalist Christianity of his grandfather and mother and by the deaths of his immediate family members. Burying himself through his own inverted version of religion, Hazel ironically and umbilically copies the very Christianity he rejects, another indication of O'Connor's natural theology.

The coffin motif is interwoven with the theme of vision throughout the novel. Sometimes the vision is of a subconscious sort, like the dream that Hazel has of his mother's death when he lies in the coffinlike upper berth on the train. Sometimes the vision breaks fearfully through to consciousness as in Hazel's clairvoyant picturing of his mother's death after his visit to the tent carnival. Hazel's vision is thus related symbolically to blood, as the title suggests, since an authentic Christian vision in O'Connor's view inexorably involves sacrifice and suffering. Hazel's blinding of himself physically in order to see spiritually is consistent with O'Connor's linking of vision and suffering. The link is indirectly made by Hazel himself when he says to his landlady at the end: "If there's no bottom in your eyes, they hold more" (222). In this sense Hazel's self-punishment in the final pages of the novel is meant to atone for his earlier willful blindness but also to open up his intuitiveness to a vision of transcendental reality, a gnostic touch apparently approved by O'Connor.

The theme of vision is ubiquitous in the novel, often in an ironic form. Early on, for example, Asa Hawks taunts Hazel for his lack of vision: "I can see more than you!" the blind man yelled, laughing (54). The truth is that Asa *can* see better than Hazel since Asa only pretends to be blind whereas Hazel pretends that he can see. Hazel's eyes become an object of interest in the novel from the very beginning, foreshadowing their later prominence in the plot: "They were the color of pecan shells and set in deep sockets. The outline of a skull under his skin was plain and insistent. . . . his eyes were what held her attention longest. Their settings were so deep that they seemed, to her, almost like passages leading somewhere" (10). The description of Hazel's eyes here is in conflict with his last name, which is drawn from Christ's famous description of spiritual blindness. The conflict is what animates Hazel as a character and propels him beyond the straits of the allegorical.

Because Hazel is determined to find the truth, his rebellion against the encroachment of the past eventually leads him to Christianity. Even Sabbath Lily Hawks, who is fascinated by Hazel's eyes, says that they

" 'don't look like they see what he's looking at but they keep on looking' " (109). Hazel rejects, for example, Enoch's absurd worship of the shrunken mummy, O'Connor's hilariously grotesque symbol of secular humanism. Moreover, in his fierce pursuit of the truth he runs over the false preacher, Layfield, precisely because he sees him as knowingly purveying falsehood. While murder might strike most readers as a more heinous offense than lying, Hazel is a grotesque precisely in his radical valuing of the truth above the ordinary conventions of life and morality. In this respect O'Connor, as with Bishop's death in *The Violent Bear It Away*, seems curiously aloof from the fates of those of her characters who are not themselves caught up in the drama of salvation. Perhaps her own lifelong affliction with degenerative disease made her impatient with those who were oblivious to the religious dimensions of their existence. While her sympathy can be elicited by her characters' sinning, it is not easily awakened by their indifference or even, it would seem, by their ignorance.

Hazel's pursuit of the truth reaches its climax following the moment when the policeman pushes his old car over the cliff, thereby psychologically disenfranchising Hazel, who had pinned his final hopes on materialism. Gazing out over the cliff, he realizes that all the roads he has followed have now been blocked: "His face seemed to reflect the entire distance across the clearing and on beyond, the entire distance that extended from his eyes to the blank gray sky that went on, depth after depth, into space. His knees bent under him and he sat down on the edge of the embankment with his feet hanging over" (209). While some critics have regarded this as a conversion scene, it is equally plausible as a scene of despair. Nevertheless, O'Connor does show Hazel's conversion as beginning here with the humiliation of self-doubt. The subsequent blinding of himself with quicklime parallels Hazel's violent dealing with Layfield, a gesture of radical impatience on the part of one who, even at the end, exhibited a restless face with a "peculiar pushing look," as if it were going after something it could "just distinguish in the distance" (214).

In addition to coffins, the novel is awash in animal imagery, a feature of all of O'Connor's fiction. "Take off your hat, king of the beasts," says Sabbath Lily Hawks in the act of seducing Hazel (170). Hazel's hat, the symbol of his calling as a preacher, is indeed what inhibits him from becoming an animal, as the girl recognizes in snatching it and flinging it across the room. The presence of animal imagery is so dense in the first half of the novel that one sees the characters as straining to raise themselves above it in order that their human visages might be seen. Enoch Emery has a "fox-shaped face" and the expression of a "grinning mandrill" (38–39).

A woman who approaches Asa Hawks on the street is described as having two bright "flea" eyes (55). Hazel has a nose like a "shrike's bill" (10), and on the train he is seated with three young women who were dressed like "parrots" (15). While one of the women has a bold "game-hen" expression, the dining car steward in turn resembles a "crow," darting from table to table (15). Hazel's grandfather is pictured as a "waspish" old man who drives over three counties with "Jesus hidden in his head like a stinger" (20). If, as O'Connor believed, the Incarnation of Christ involved the taking on of human nature by God, that nature in O'Connor's fiction, prior to religious conversion, is latently animalistic.

Paradoxically, however, animals themselves in the novel free the mind of the reader, if not the characters, to contemplate their creator. While Enoch Emery hates the animals in the zoo, for example, he does so in the belief that everything should have a use. Enoch's puritanical repressiveness about the body is captured when he voyeuristically watches the women at the swimming pool. While O'Connor avoids descriptions of sexuality in her fiction, she is aware of its power, as can be felt in the scenes between Hazel and Sabbath Lily Hawks and between Hazel and Leora Watts. Furthermore, her own depiction of animals is serenely humorous, as in the genteel depiction of the two black bears in the zoo who sat facing each other like "two matrons having tea, their faces polite and self-absorbed" (93). For O'Connor the body, while created by God, is as often as not a source of comedy, a sign that human beings are destined for something better. In spite of the Catholic Church's emphasis on the final resurrection of the body, O'Connor generally portrays it unerotically and as a sorry thing indeed in comparison with the soul, thereby cutting a considerable swath between herself and Catholic writers such as Walker Percy, Ralph McInerny, Mary Gordon, and William Everson.

A Pentecostal, and rather anti-Catholic, atmosphere surrounds the setting of *The Violent Bear It Away* (published in 1962), O'Connor's second and last novel. In that novel the minister's wife perceives the Roman Catholic Church as a place where minds were still "chained in priestly darkness."[10] Given this setting, O'Connor's imagery is nevertheless sometimes curiously Catholic, as in Rayber's memories in watching the family of preachers: "He felt the taste of his own childhood pain laid again on his tongue like a bitter wafer" (130). The reference to the Communion Host is strangely incongruous within the contexts of Pentecostalism and Rayber's Fundamentalist upbringing.

---

10. O'Connor, *The Violent*, 128, subsequently cited in the text parenthetically.

Once again, as in *Wise Blood*, a character has felt himself elected by God for a particular mission, an election that comes straight to the individual, young Tarwater, and that strikes home like a thunderbolt at times, as in his first sight of Bishop:

> He did not look into the eyes of any fiery beast or see a burning bush. He only knew, with a certainty sunk in despair, that he was expected to baptize the child he saw and begin the life his great-uncle had prepared him for. . . . His black pupils, glassy and still, reflected depth on depth his own stricken image of himself, trudging into the distance in the bleeding stinking mad shadow of Jesus, until at last he received his reward, a broken fish, a multiplied loaf. (91)

Young Tarwater tries to wriggle out of his vocation because he fears the world's contempt for Christianity, a recognition that undermines his self-esteem and youthful ambition.

The force of the subconscious hold by old Tarwater and by the divine will on young Tarwater is expressed at the end when young Tarwater baptizes Bishop in the very act of drowning him, a curiously Catholic act in a religious culture where adult voluntary baptism was the norm. As with the aforementioned image of the Host, this lapse suggests the ease with which O'Connor sometimes drew on material alternately either from Catholicism or Protestantism in accord with her purposes. Her latitude in this respect reflected her not altogether ecumenical assumption that the best of Protestantism was Catholic at heart. For this reason she declared, in a letter written to William Sessions in 1960, that old Tarwater, being a genuine prophet, "not a church-member," was a "natural Catholic."[11] While this pronouncement might seem at odds with O'Connor's valuing of the spiritual harvest of southern Protestantism, her view of that in turn was that evangelical Protestants as individuals frequently adhered to the divine will more closely than Catholics did either corporately or individually.

Following the murder/baptism, Rayber sees himself as moving through the "black forest toward a violent encounter with his fate" (203). The phrasing recalls the title of the novel with its assumption that at least part of the work of salvation will be accomplished by those who have been violent turning toward God. The image of the black forest, which recalls Hawthorne, is here used as an allegorical allusion not only to secular society but also to the pit of evil within Tarwater himself.

11. O'Connor to Sessions, September 13, 1960, in O'Connor, *Habit of Being*, 407.

O'Connor makes it clear that, while Tarwater will be a very minor prophet indeed, he will at least have met the requirements of his divinely appointed destiny. In underscoring the eventual incline of Tarwater's will toward that destiny, O'Connor contrasts him with Rayber, who flouts his vocation as a preacher. In spite of her depiction of the power of the divine calling of an individual soul, O'Connor shows through the characterization of Rayber, who is used as a foil, that the call can be refused. Centering her novel on the soul's response to grace, O'Connor depicted a humanity so free that with its "last breath" it could still "say *No*."[12] Beneath the surface of Rayber's consciousness lies a divided self, with one part of him inclining toward rationalism and the other toward an involuntary emotional life in which he is able to love his son without reservation, a love "without reason, love for something futureless, love that appeared to exist only to be itself" (113).

Like young Tarwater, Rayber is subject to unaccountable longings that undercut his conscious resolve, an "undertow in his blood dragging him backwards to what he knew to be madness" (114). Nevertheless, Rayber pits his will against the destiny that old Tarwater had envisaged for him and in his dedication to rationalism plots the death of his beloved child, an act that young Tarwater, resolved to assert his own identity, tragically carries out. The characterization of Rayber is a test of sorts of Frederick Asals's comment that the middle ground in O'Connor's fiction is always mediocre, a "condition ultimately of illusion" in a world where only extremes have "genuine existence."[13] Certainly Rayber's story is subordinated to that of young Tarwater and of young Bishop. At the same time, Rayber does attract a welcome, if relatively uncommon, measure of the author's sympathy in his tortured emotional contradictoriness regarding his son.

While the relationship between Rayber and young Tarwater is dramatically centered on Tarwater, the tangle of conscious and subconscious elements in Rayber's dreaming increases the reader's sense of his significance as a character:

> He had waked up after a wild dream in which he chased Tarwater
> through an interminable alley that twisted suddenly back on itself
> and reversed the roles of pursuer and pursued. The boy had overtaken
> him, given him a thunderous blow on the head, and then disappeared.
> And with his disappearance there had come such an overwhelming

---

12. O'Connor, *Mystery and Manners*, 182.
13. Asals, *Flannery O'Connor: The Imagination of Extremity*, 3.

feeling of release that Rayber had waked up with a pleasant anticipation that his guest would be gone. He was at once ashamed of the
feeling. (139–40)

At a subconscious level Rayber recognizes the impending failure of his
attempt to root out religion from young Tarwater. The sense of relief,
though, is clearly directed not only at young Tarwater but also at his
own habitual need to suppress his own intuitions, emotions, and religious
memories.

As with most of O'Connor's fiction *The Violent Bear It Away* is a mingling
of allegorical, satiric, and realistic elements. Some of the scenes are vividly
allegorical, as in the partially clad Rayber sticking his head through the
window of the Pentecostal church while the rest of his body stands outside,
a tableau of his inner dividedness. Also strongly allegorical is the motif of
food in connection with young Tarwater, an insatiable hunger that only
God can fill. At one point young Tarwater stops in front of a bakery with
a look on his face like someone who, starving, sees a "meal he can't reach
laid out before him." The bakery window, it turns out, is empty, except
for a loaf of bread "pushed to the side that must have been overlooked
when the shelf was cleaned for the night" (122). While the loaf of bread
is symbolically linked to the motif of Tarwater's mysterious, insatiable
hunger, it is also a Eucharistic and, again, a rather Catholic symbol, an
implicitly sacramental sign of Christ appealing to young Tarwater.

Allegory mixes with grotesque realism at the end of the novel in the
scene in which a diabolical homosexual rapes young Tarwater. The scene
occurs in a dark forest, and the rapist is given the features of a vampire.
"His delicate skin," O'Connor writes, "had acquired a faint pink tint as if
he had refreshed himself on blood" (231). The allegorical role of the devil
in O'Connor's fiction is again consistent with her Thomist portrayal of
evil as a negation, vicariously feeding on a living good world in order
to generate an impression of its own existence. Furthermore, O'Connor's
use of the devil, an aspect of her Catholic traditionalism, was based upon
the theme of *felix culpa*, which is evident everywhere in her fiction. In "On
Her Own Work," O'Connor remarked in connection with the ending of
The Violent Bear It Away that Tarwater's "final vision could not have been
brought off if he hadn't met the man in the lavender and cream-colored
car." Evil, she observed in the same essay, is thus often the "unwilling
instrument of grace."[14] O'Connor's unflinching inclusion of the devil in

14. O'Connor, *Mystery and Manners*, 117, 118.

her fiction is another of the bonds between herself and the Fundamentalist Protestants among whom she lived and is clearly different from the gradual disappearance of the devil from Catholic rhetoric, if not from Catholic doctrine, in the second half of the twentieth century.

The role assigned to the devil by O'Connor not only includes evil actions like those of the rapist, but also involves the weakening of faith through the promotion of skepticism. In the evocative scene in which Bishop rushes toward the park fountain, for example, the light seems to descend on him like the descent of the dove on Christ in the New Testament: "The sun, which had been tacking from cloud to cloud, emerged above the fountain. A blinding brightness fell on the lion's tangled marble head and gilded the stream of water rushing from his mouth. Then the light, falling more gently, rested like a hand on the child's white head. His face might have been a mirror where the sun had stopped to watch its reflection" (164). While the scene may be interpreted allegorically or symbolically, it can more properly be described as sacramental since, like a sacrament, it effects what it signifies; in other words, it transforms the observer, young Tarwater. At the same time, he is attacked from within by the voice of his "friend," the devil, a voice of doubt that O'Connor also attributes to the reader: "Well, that's your sign, his friend said—the sun coming out from under a cloud and falling on the head of a dimwit. Something that could happen fifty times a day without no one being the wiser" (165). Significantly, the voice of skepticism, which is analogous to the sort of narrow rationalism exhibited by Rayber, is identified by O'Connor with evil; and the case for a faith that transcends reason is put neatly in terms of the novel's polarities of good and evil. As an avid reader of the philosophy of Saint Thomas Aquinas, O'Connor was not dubious about the value of reason. Rather, she perceived reason in twentieth-century culture as frequently used not to lead to a faith in the creator of reason but rather in a self-sufficient agnosticism. Motivated by a disapproval of this contemporary use of reason, O'Connor liked to portray the sterility and helplessness of reason when it is turned narcissistically in on itself.

O'Connor's settings are also rather allegorical, with Powderhead representing an Edenic world that is contrasted with the dehumanizing city. The lake in which Bishop is drowned is an intermediate locale, combining, as Robert McConn has suggested, symbolic characteristics of the other two. At the same time, with its connotations of violence, the word *Powderhead* has an obvious connection with the novel's title. The connection is paradoxical because of the isolation of Powderhead from the rest of the world, a place that was "not simply off the dirt road but off the wagon track and footpath, and the nearest neighbors, colored not white, still had to walk through the woods, pushing plum branches out of their way to get to it" (12). Powderhead is thus a retreat in which the prophet prepares a subsequent encounter with the world, a place of quiet in which the violence associated with converting the world is contemplated.

The detail of the black characters living closer to Powderhead than the whites is important. O'Connor portrays these black characters as more fertile ground for Christianity than the technocratic white culture in the city, whose indifference to religion is symbolized by the shabby Pentecostal church. It is noteworthy that it is a black person who buries old Tarwater and a black woman at the general store who berates young Tarwater for not burying his great-uncle: "There was all knowledge in her stony face and the fold of her arms indicated a judgment fixed from the foundations of time. Huge wings might have been folded behind her without seeming strange" (225). The archetypal characterization reflects both young Tarwater's point of view and O'Connor's modulating of characterization, which can range from caricature to epic, sometimes in the case of the same individual.

While the paradoxical title motif of violence is appropriate to young Tarwater's life, it is also enacted in a scene involving Rayber. When Rayber's wife wants to institutionalize Bishop, claiming that she could not adequately care for him, though it was plain from the look of him, his father reflects, that he "thrived like an air plant" (182), Rayber instinctively knocks his wife down, as surprised at himself as he is enraged that the child he secretly loved and to whose death he would later contribute should be so abused. The scene reinforces the impression that, among Catholic American writers, O'Connor seems the most open to violence as a defense against evil.

Structurally, while the novel centers at times on violent or grotesque incident, it also incorporates a meditative format in which the characters reflect upon the significance of a given action. While the novel opens abruptly with the death and flight of young Tarwater, for example, it is only at the end, when the meaning of that event has been explored, that the reader is made aware of how the old man was buried. In spite of the graphic depiction of such spikes of violence, the style of *The Violent Bear It Away* is even more fluid, impressionistic, and figurative than in *Wise Blood*. The most prominent symbolic patterns in the novel are those associated with fire and water, and each is given both positive and negative connotations. It is in fire, for example, that old Tarwater ironically perishes, his own blood having been "burned dry" (6). Fire is earlier framed in a more positive way by old Tarwater, who tells young

Tarwater that the mercy of the Lord can burn, presumably by purging the soul of its egotism (20).

A similar symbolic association links fire, cleansing, and vision in the scrawled message left on the outside of a magazine in Rayber's house. The motif of fire as a purifying agent reaches its zenith at the end of the novel when, through a series of fires, young Tarwater literally burns up his past, starting with the piece of ground where he was raped. The reflexive nature of the fires is made evident in the allusion to Tarwater's "scorched eyes," which looked as if they had been touched with a "coal like the lips of the prophet" (233). The eyes that had been cavernous were now filled with vision. In igniting the area around Powderhead, he had, he conceives, made a "rising wall of fire between him and the grinning presence" of Satan (238). Finally, in the image of the fiery tree, reminiscent of the burning bush in the Book of Exodus, Tarwater has his vision of God and therefore of his own birth as a prophet.

Fire symbolism merges with the hunger motif at the end of the novel, as young Tarwater, mystified by the fact of his uncle's burial, imagines his great-uncle in heaven being fed directly by Christ, his hunger finally relieved by a food that, as Tarwater finally acknowledges, "nothing on earth would fill" (241). Water symbolism, like that of fire, is pervasive in the novel, merging with the food motif, for example, to indicate a spiritual thirst that no natural water can fulfill. After killing Bishop and when he is en route to Powderhead, young Tarwater draws water from a well by a black man's shack, drinking until he begins to feel dizzy. Subsequently, he stares down into a gray clear pool to where "two silent serene eyes were gazing at him" (223). The eyes are clearly not his since his are anything but serene; they are, obviously, Bishop's eyes, the eyes of innocence, now immortal. While the scene, as is so often the case in O'Connor, can be explained in realistic terms (Tarwater has not eaten for a long time and is possibly hallucinating), the religious suggestiveness of the moment lingers on the page. The ambiguity of the water symbolism reaches its nadir at the lake, where Tarwater uses water to both murder and baptize in the same instant. The scene reflects O'Connor's focus on the split-second moral freedom of her characters to create and/or destroy.

While Flannery O'Connor is one of the most conservative Catholic American writers in the twentieth century, she has also, paradoxically, been one of the most widely read, in part, perhaps, because she appeals not only to Catholic but to Protestant readers as well. In O'Connor's emphasis on the freedom of God in choosing to directly confront the individual soul, she manifested not only her respect for Protestantism but also her sense that within the irreligiousness of contemporary culture God might not have any other choice. Similarly, although Marshall Bruce Gentry has argued that in some unobtrusive ways O'Connor tries to bring her characters finally into a state of community, one has to admit that the institutional church, particularly the Catholic Church, plays little role in the lives of her protagonists. O'Connor's appeal is obviously wider than these considerations would imply, though. Apart from her consummate artistry, she is most universal in revealing the spiritual hunger of her characters and in her conviction, shared by writers such as Walker Percy, that the problem of evil will never be dealt with adequately by social scientists.

What most distinguishes O'Connor as a writer of fiction is a gift she shares with Hawthorne for creating bold allegorical scenes and memorable tormented characters who are propelled by radical psychological and spiritual forces that enlarge the canvas on which their otherwise insignificant dramas are played out. Furthermore, as in Hawthorne, the religious dimension of the fiction is bolstered by a subtle moral probing that can be of interest to even the most intractable religious skeptic. What makes O'Connor Catholic is her sacramental view of reality, her sense that experience and time are always edged with spiritual opportunity and with the possibility of religious discovery and decision—no matter how unpromising the circumstances of her characters' lives. Embracing a vigorous Catholic natural theology in her fiction, O'Connor portrays the beckoning hand of God as located, if not within the church, society, or even nature, then certainly in the human heart, where, whatever the secularism of the surrounding society, she implicitly argues throughout her fiction, a restless hunger for God has been implanted. This is evident, for example, in the bitter tale of Hulga (in "Good Country People") whose atheism can survive only in a world in which she assumes others are believers and in which her own nihilism is soon broken by a God-given need to trust and to love. Thus, frequently within the shabby and violent web of the temporal world that O'Connor provides for them, a number of her characters collide with a transcendental order of experience that had previously been encountered only abstractly. Because, as has been indicated, O'Connor emphasized the ironies and complexities of this conversion experience, she managed to offset some of the latent didacticism in her writing. Nevertheless, having felt freed by her Catholic faith to look patiently and hard at the modern world, she did so, only to find that underneath its waywardness it had, after all, an orthodox heart.

As Frederick Asals has pointed out, there is a gulf between the natural and the supernatural, between the "hylic and the numinous, between the less than human and the more than human" in O'Connor's fiction.[15] The effect of this tension is to stretch the doctrine of the Incarnation almost to the breaking point. Furthermore, more than any other Catholic American writer, O'Connor explores the tension between the Hellenistic, rational side of Catholicism and the nonrational side. Accustomed herself to daily reading of the philosophy of Saint Thomas Aquinas, O'Connor nevertheless chose to dramatize the lives of characters who seem far removed from philosophical rumination, characters who are instead opened to the salvatory lightning strikes by God into their lives.

Unsnared by the beauty of the world, though far from unconscious of it, O'Connor characteristically moves her characters toward a shock and pain that conspire to push them toward a dissatisfaction with the world they live in—except in those inspired instances when that world is electrified by the swift and dramatic intervention in their lives by the God who made them. More than in any other of the writers considered in this study, in Flannery O'Connor the Catholic doctrine of the Incarnation wears the face of suffering. The result of this is that her characters turn gratefully away from the natural world—like the child in "The River"—with a sense that at last their lives, while no less unlovely, have been given the greater gift of purpose.

15. Asals, *Flannery O'Connor*, 93–94.

13

Ralph McInerny

(b. 1929)

P ERHAPS BECAUSE HE is also a popular mystery writer, Ralph McInerny has been overlooked as a Catholic novelist. Moreover, some of McInerny's writings, such as *The Search Committee* and *The Noonday Devil,* are literary hybrids, part detective story, part novel. Nevertheless, three of his novels, *The Priest, Gate of Heaven,* and *Leave of Absence,* are significant examples of contemporary Catholic fiction and deserve more critical attention than they have received. Leavened by satiric panache and moral acuity, these novels focus on the American church in transition from the 1950s to the present. What distinguishes McInerny's fictional review and analysis of this period is his focus on the confusion in the post–Vatican II church and his implicit setting of the question of whether or not the Catholic Church will survive—no matter what happens in the rest of American society.

McInerny's attempt to make his chronicle of the American Catholic Church representative is indicated in a variety of ways. In *The Priest* (published in 1973), for example, the diocese of Fort Elbow, which is the novel's setting, is described as the "nation writ small," since the citizens reflect "almost to the decimal point, the national figures."[1] Furthermore, McInerny centers on issues that confronted all Catholics during

---

1. McInerny, *The Priest,* 51, subsequently cited in the text parenthetically.

the 1960s, such as the widely publicized controversy that surrounded the encyclical *Humanae Vitae*, which appeared in 1968. In connection with this controversy, Father Frank Ascue, the central character in *The Priest*, reflects dispiritedly at one point that as a "citizen of what has been called a contraceptive culture," he heard the "head of his Church, the Bishop of Rome, the successor of Saint Peter, the vicar of Christ on earth" declare that contraception was "in and of itself immoral" (349–50). More than Powers or Percy, McInerny was concerned with theological exactitude. The phrase "in and of itself" in the above passage, for example, is theologically crucial in preventing Father Ascue (whose name signals a fundamental weakness in character) from construing the ban on artificial contraception as merely an ecclesiastical regulation. The comedy in the passage arises from Father Ascue's hypnotic inventory of the pope's titles, the verbal excess drolly symbolizing the weight of Rome pressing down upon his shoulders.

Like the novelist J. F. Powers, with whom he has much in common, McInerny portrays an American church dominated by an Irish hegemony that had not only perpetuated itself for generations but also set itself up as a model for the laity. This can be seen in *The Priest*, for example, in the case of the rectory housekeeper, Mrs. Ryan, who, in spite of her German American background, had turned herself into an "aging colleen" (15). McInerny's subject matter is the friction between the new and old guards, which are roughly divided by the Second Vatican Council. He depicts the old guard as strongly hierarchical—as can be seen in the depiction of Bishop Caldron (most of McInerny's character names are similarly barbed), who epitomizes the old regime through his habit of tallying the number of priests in his diocese like a "prince in Tolstoy counting serfs" (15). The capriciousness of Bishop Caldron is shown when he arbitrarily decides to appoint Father Ascue, who has just returned from Rome (following advanced training in moral theology), not to a teaching position in the seminary but to a rundown, inner-city parish.

Also representative of the old guard is Father Ewing, the seminary's incumbent lecturer in moral theology, who, on the verge of retirement, has the autocratic habit of teaching for forty-five minutes, allowing no questions (11). Father Ewing's condescension toward his students and toward the world in general proceeds from orthodox certitude and intransigence, as is shown in his shunning of theological conferences and post–Vatican II books and journals. Late in life, the man becomes indistinguishable in action from his cast of mind—as McInerny brings out in a number of sharply drawn scenes. At one point Father Ewing is shown sidestepping a "chalky fried-egg-like besmirchment that formed on the walk before him," at which point he lifts a wary eye toward a "burgeoning but fortunately now birdless branch above him. A passing covey of seminarians tipped their birettas and the priest returned the courtesy" (9–10). Elegantly constructed, the passage captures the military significance of the salute offered by junior to senior ranks; furthermore, the image of the covey precisely etches the priest's point of view in which the untidy birds of the natural world are associated with the callow students (as Father Ewing thinks of them) who attend his classes.

In addition to its passion for hierarchy, the pre–Vatican II church is represented as supporting a virile asceticism, such as that represented by the founder of the order of Saint Brendan in *Gate of Heaven*, which was published in 1975. Eschewing such comforts as air conditioning, the founder, a heroic turn-of-the-century Irish missionary, builds up a considerable religious establishment in the New World, including a college and seminary, only to see them dwindle away under the impact of a weakened American church. Under the founder and in earlier times, standards, it is made evident, had been higher. Seminarians, for example, had been forbidden from plagiarizing their homilies from prepared texts and had been compelled to generate sermons from their own reflection, reading, and experience, blending "instruction and exhortation, history and dogma."[2]

Condescension toward the laity and especially toward women is associated with the old guard, as can be seen in *The Priest* in McInerny's portrayal of Father Entweder (whose name means "either" as opposed to his colleague, Father Oder, whose name means "or"). In Father Entweder's seasoned view, women were always sure of themselves though "seldom right" (175). The intellectual horizons of the pre–Vatican II clergy are depicted as circumscribed by such solid prejudices, including the omniscient status accorded to Saint Thomas Aquinas as *the* Catholic philosopher.

Although a notable Thomist scholar himself, McInerny manifests an ironic awareness of the philosophical provinciality of Catholic culture in the 1950s, as in his portraits of Vera Halloran and Andrea Bauer in *Leave of Absence* (published in 1986): "If Andrea could lay claim to Hopkins, Vera countered with Claudel. She had tried Dante at first, but Andrea had convinced her that Scotus as well as Aquinas had influenced the great Florentine. They traded the verses from the *Paradiso* . . . what fun that had been, snug and comfortable within the cocoon of Catholic culture yet feeling in tune with what unabashedly they would call the Western Tradition."[3] In addition to exposing the insulation of American

2. McInerny, *Gate of Heaven*, 223, subsequently cited in the text parenthetically.
3. McInerny, *Leave of Absence*, 35, subsequently cited in the text parenthetically.

Catholicism in the 1950s, McInerny portrays this older Catholicism as breeding a childlike reliance on the church for all the answers to life's questions. Sheila Rupp, for example, observes in *The Priest*: "Isn't it strange that when a Catholic gets into trouble and asks what it all means the answer is always right there on the tip of the tongue, some answer learned a long time ago that has just been lying in wait for the question?" (205).

While McInerny's respect for the orthodoxy and asceticism of the pre–Vatican II church is evident enough, especially in contrast to the instability of the church of the 1960s, he does not hesitate to point up the absurdities of the older generation of American Catholics. Sometimes he does so in a way that brings out their pathos as well—as in his characterization of Miss Simpson in *The Priest*, who, dying of cancer, dabs herself with Lourdes water every day, and then dies in despair anyway, feeling that her life has been without value. Also rather childlike is Vera Halloran in *Leave of Absence* who, desperately wanting to become pregnant and unaware that her husband is sterile, prays to God to send her a child, a prayer that is ironically undermined by her contrite memory of the spiritual "bouquets" she had offered for her parents as a schoolgirl, bouquets that had been likened by a nun at the time to "heavenly bankbooks" (127). In spite of such gaucheness, McInerny clearly approves of the disciplined piety of the traditional churchgoer, as can be seen in the case of Andrea Bauer's mother, a woman who attended Mass daily on cold mornings, her stride "stiff-legged and very fast," a babushka pulled over her head, and her chin set into the "rabbit-fur collar of her chocolate-colored cloth coat" (41). While the descriptive details suggest a life of privation, a habit of going without—in addition to a want of taste—Mrs. Bauer exemplifies an unsentimental piety that has the author's respect.

In McInerny's fiction the post–Vatican II American church contains a diversity of types: the remnants of the old guard, the new breed of liberals, and a number of rather bewildered-looking in-betweens. Typical of the new liberalism is Lydia Donovan in *The Priest*, who suddenly found herself regarded in the Catholic media as a noteworthy lay theologian on the basis of a few journalistic articles that served in lieu of a doctorate in theology. Her husband, a failed Ph.D. student, similarly drifts into prominence as a Catholic newspaper editor in spite of the thinness of his background. Another example, in McInerny's view, of the absurdity of the liberal post-1960s church was the stampede of Catholic clergy to abandon their vocations in order to marry. In *Gate of Heaven* a religious superior dryly considers one such defection within his fold: "Father Fogarty's note informing the father superior that he was eloping with Miss Liczenski was typewritten and Father Faiblesse wondered if the prospective bride had done it" (240). With quiet wit the passage depicts the supplanting of one kind of servitude by another.

The apogee of McInerny's satirical survey of the new breed is Father Phil Floeck (in *The Search Committee*), whose ludicrously exaggerated response to Vatican II's emphasis on the unity of clergy and laity as the people of God led to his saying Mass in an Indian blanket surrounded by half a dozen women wearing "some sort of vestment," women who were "indistinguishable from Floeck except for the Indian blanket."[4] Apart from the satirized New Age features of Floeck's ministry, McInerny's wariness about feminist intrusions into the Mass is evident. Where he perceives no threat to orthodox belief and practice, however, McInerny can be sensitive to a female, if not a feminist, perspective. An example is Sheila Rupp's perception in *The Priest* of the raw neck of a female duck at the zoo: "Knowing the cause of that raw used neck, the effect of the drake's pinning the object of his attention, Sheila wished that they had stopped at one of the benches just inside the park entrance" (153).

On the whole, however, McInerny's fiction, in contrast to that of Mary Gordon, offers little succor to Catholic feminists and little as well to those who espoused Vatican II's emphasis on social justice. In *Connolly's Life* (published in 1983), for example, while the dissident theologian who gives the novel its title contends that his writings had little to do with the Second Vatican Council, implying that he simply used the liberalism unleashed by the council to pursue his own agenda, nonetheless in repentance he finds himself no longer interested in "what the Church should do in the modern world," a departure from the direction taken by the council.[5] In McInerny, one feels the loss of traditional private practices such as prayer, meditation, and the sacrament of Confession, which, like the Mass, had tended to give way to more open and communal practices in the 1960s and 1970s. More significant, McInerny mourns the loss of the sense of the transcendental in Catholic worship as well as of the consciousness of sin. Typical of this sort of change is Vera Halloran, who recalls having at one time gone to Confession every two weeks prior to the new liturgical language that followed in the wake of Vatican II: "There was talk of reconciliation rather than penance, with the suggestion that soon there would be general absolution given to all as to soldiers going into battle," there being no need to go "groveling to the priest" (6).

4. McInerny, *Search Committee*, 84, subsequently cited in the text parenthetically.
5. McInerny, *Connolly's Life*, 205, 182.

All in all, McInerny's depiction of the church in transition is of a church in decline, whether with respect to the loss of vocations, the secularization of Catholic colleges, or the abandonment of high moral expectations of conduct. Typical of what McInerny depicts as the weakness of the newer clergy is the reaction of Father Hoyt, in *Gate of Heaven*, who, noting wistfully the steady decline in attendance at Mass, adjusts his standards ever downward. Rationalizing his way through life, Hoyt foresees a church in which regular Sunday worship will eventually disappear: "Better," he reflects, Mass three or four times a year, "praying with sincerity, than a weekly drudgery done under duress and half asleep" (204–5).

While Father Hoyt represents one rather bleak end of McInerny's ecclesiastical spectrum, the dramatic interest in McInerny's fiction centers around those characters who are caught between the old and new orders, such as Father Ascue. Aware of the shifting surfaces and divided state of his church, Father Ascue, a balanced and reasonable young man, attempts to get his bearings. Formed within a stable and even confident Catholic culture, he feels the ebbing of vitality within the institution to which he has pinned his fate, yet he is determined not to become hidebound though he is reluctant to challenge the hierarchy. Estranged in some respects from the traditional church, he ponders how on earth he could begin to discuss the subject of miracles, for example, with a contemporary audience. At the same time, he is unimpressed with the attention given by the new clergy to sexuality, reflecting on one occasion that the trouble with a romanticized theory of sexuality was that it seldom matched what people found in marriage, no matter what the "disgruntled celibate" imagined. Moreover, he muses, both celibacy and the ban on artificial contraception at least had the merit of reminding both clergy and laity that they were called to "something higher than secular comfort" (269).

The Priest is a novel of initiation, the testing of a relatively inexperienced, promising young priest in the roiling waters of the American Catholicism of the 1960s. Aware of how anachronistic his priestly vocation appears to others in the sixties, including his sister, Charlotte, who asks how young men can be expected to pledge themselves to a celibate priesthood for the rest of their lives, Father Ascue replies that one could make the same argument against people marrying in their twenties, ostensibly for life. Although Father Ascue is inexperienced with women and to some extent with life—as is shown by his surprise in meeting the mousy woman who had become sexually involved with the university chaplain—he maintains his chastity in spite of the efforts of an attractive woman to become involved with him.

While his habits of self-discipline see him through this sort of personal temptation, however, he finds himself more at sea as a spiritual counselor, largely because of the muddy waters of controversy within his church. Prior to Pope Paul VI's unexpected reimposition of the ban against artificial contraception, for example, Ascue finds himself in the confessional permitting an apparently honest and deserving woman to start taking the birth control pill. Later, when *Humanae Vitae* appears, he has to live not only with his decision but also with his own uncertainty, echoed by many theologians, about the wisdom of the encyclical. A further stage in Father Ascue's initiation comes when he is asked by his auxiliary bishop to compose, along with the Catholic newspaper editor Frank Donovan, a dissenting response to *Humanae Vitae*. Although Donovan boldly and unethically publishes a dissent under the bishop's name without consulting either Father Ascue or the bishop, Ascue later reflects ruefully that he had been too timid in responding to an earlier draft of the letter. His reflection is an apt mirroring of character. Eager not to give offense to either side in his divided church, he is portrayed by McInerny as sinning by omission.

A final test comes when Father Ascue's unmarried niece becomes pregnant and is scheduled by her mother, who suddenly drops the veil on a life of tireless commitment to her church, for an abortion abroad (prior to *Roe vs. Wade*). Stunned by the behavior of his sister, but also immobilized by his own protective, emotional feelings toward his niece, Father Ascue fails to speak out against the abortion, thereby precipitating a crisis with respect to his vocation. As befits a novel of substance, the crisis is as much a crisis of character as of belief. With a discerning novelistic eye McInerny portrays Father Ascue as the victim of his own diffidence. "Dear God," Ascue laments, "he did not want to be a judge, a spectator, the bureau of standards of the acts of mankind. Was it distaste for that burden, more than the itch of the flesh, which accounted for men leaving the priesthood?" (507). Probing still further, McInerny shows the reader (without disclosing it to Father Ascue) that the young priest felt the need to be loved by everyone, a perilous weakness. Thus, while Father Ascue clings marginally to his vocation at the end, it would be a mistake to interpret this as a sign of hope. What began as an honorable vocation is skillfully shown to have failed, not only because of the tempestuous state of the church but, more important, because of significant character weaknesses in the protagonist, weaknesses that McInerny deftly portrays as part of Father Ascue's trustworthiness and charm at the beginning but that evolve into aspects of his tragedy at the end.

McInerny's fine handling of point of view throughout *The Priest* can be seen in his meticulous tracing of the steps of Father Ascue's troubled journey and growing uncertainty—as can be illustrated in the following extract:

> he thought of the surface of the globe, crisscrossed with the paths men make: a point of origin, travels to and fro making lines upon the earth which intersected other lines, and the intersections like the lines themselves might so very easily not have been. Eventually, the paths stop, grow faint, disappear. There had to be a vantage point on the lives of men which lifted them above such finite tracings of absurdity. (100)

Through a sophisticated handling of point of view, McInerny reveals to the reader, though, once again, not to Father Ascue, that it is precisely Ascue's acute consciousness of absurdity that ultimately undermines his priestly vocation. Writers such as Merton and Berrigan freely conceded the absurdity of the role of the priest; indeed, they insisted upon it as a way of distinguishing that role from the norms of secular society. Father Ascue, though, appears caught within the web of his need to reconcile the claims of all competing parties. Moreover, his inability to make a leap of faith, to surrender his perplexed awareness of unfathomable complexity to the word and vision of God is a troubling sign of the paleness of his religious beliefs.

McInerny's use of setting in *The Priest* is no less admirable. For example, there is the moment at the end when the Franciscan priest who has described the ruinous state of the American church to Frank Ascue suddenly turns and points toward the sky where a hawk is being harassed by two blackbirds. Without any need for further comment the scene captures the divisive state of the church. In addition, McInerny's descriptive language is generally pithy and memorable, although there is a tendency toward caricature at times. Furthermore, the phrasing is generally arch and polished, as can be seen in the depiction of Charlotte Nygaard, who liked to think of the members of her family as a well-organized team, each with an allotted task, moving through the day in an "allegro of camaraderie" (12). The final phrase, with its connotations of an irrepressible, lifting rhythm, is perfectly suited to the character, a woman of movement and action rather than of reflection and deliberation.

McInerny shows the wider dimensions of Father Ascue's drama by allowing the reader to see that at the periphery of the priest's story is a recognition that while the church after Vatican II strove to relate itself to society, ironically society simultaneously found the church to be increasingly irrelevant. In an evocative passage Father Ascue reflects that the relics of the past were "scattered in the present century, in monuments and mottoes, in our language if not in our hearts. Like the altar Paul found in Athens, they spoke of an unknown God, a forgotten God" (349). A similarly desolate vision is rendered in blackly comic form in *Gate of Heaven* in the figure of Father Stokes, who in order to feel needed by society lurks about the airport, prominently displaying his Roman collar in the desperate hope that he will be called upon to minister to the dying or to those in distress. Pathetically, in order to generate business, Father Stokes has himself paged on the loudspeaker so that a migrant public would realize that there was a priest nearby.

In *Gate of Heaven*, McInerny's second most important novel, the church in transition is again the focus as the founder of a religious community lies dying while his successors try to decide whether or not to give up a seminary building that a nominally Catholic college wants to turn into a residence for female students. Once again, there is a clash between the pre– and post–Vatican II church with the central character given the apt name of Father Tumulty. Apart from the vivid struggle for power that forms the dramatic nucleus of the novel, much of what is valuable in *Gate of Heaven* arises from McInerny's illuminating moral dissections of his characters. As a religious and moral study the novel centers on the virtue of humility, which certain characters have in abundance while others appear to have little or none. Father Faiblesse, for example, the superior of the order, has long espoused humility under the guise of passivity. He reflects dourly at one point that, if it was true that he had been used by others more "self-willed" than himself, nevertheless there were worse things. He might, he considers gratefully, have "used others" (217). At the end of the novel, though, Father Faiblesse emerges with unaccustomed boldness from his cocoon of passivity in order to dismiss a Machiavellian college president, and although it is far from evident that this dismissal will end the scheming of Father Hoyt, nonetheless, from the vantage point of the novel's moral norms, Father Faiblesse, a dying man, has been saved at last.

Implicit in the novel's complex moral design is the suggestion that, contrary to Father Faiblesse's case, there are other times when one should abandon action in favor of forbearance, give up interfering in the world even when one foresees a deteriorating future for the church. Such is the advice of the dying founder and of his successor, Father Garrity. Moreover, the central narrative interest hovers over a sophisticated priest who, while sensitive enough to appreciate the wisdom of spiritual detachment, nevertheless sees the danger of not acting. Comparable in some respects to J. F. Powers's Father Urban, Father Tumulty is attracted to decisiveness even while becoming increasingly hamstrung by moral complexity and ambiguity. Furthermore, McInerny unobtrusively reveals Tumulty's fear of death to be based upon his instinctive view of it as a humiliating, final state of inaction. In this connection, throughout the novel McInerny shows Father Tumulty's discomfort about the indignities of aging, both in the founder, who had been a vigorous model, and in himself. The force of McInerny's probing of Father Tumulty depends in part on the reader's ability to see that it is not Tumulty's desire to act that is wrong but rather his habitual and understandable belief that everything depends upon his readiness to act. What the novel demonstrates is that no matter how prudently and energetically Father Tumulty commits himself to action, the outcome lies in the hands of others, and especially of God, who, in McInerny's fiction, frequently moves others to act unexpectedly.

McInerny skillfully weaves his tale so that the foreground conflict, which revolves around the sale of a building, eventually casts a light on some unexpected spiritual depths. This larger spiritual drama looms before the reader at significant moments in the narration, as in the searching of Father Tumulty's consciousness during the funeral Mass for the founder: "For a moment, listening to the burial liturgy, looking over the rows of the society's dead, Michael Tumulty had an intimation of what matters and what does not and he knew a fugitive peace" (293). While Father Tumulty is attracted to control for its own sake and is eventually made aware of this weakness in himself, the peace he experiences here does not issue from a resolve to forgo the desire to manage but rather stems from a momentary perception of the ideal.

The lines of symbolism in *Gate of Heaven* tend to divide into the combative (the struggle between the old and the new orders) and the Edenic (a spiritual transcendence of the aforementioned struggle). The figurative language that generates an atmosphere of embattlement is easily enough located—in Father Phelan's point of view, for instance, as he looks from a distance at the old seminary building that had become an object of dispute: "It came as almost a relief to see that the Little Sem still stood. The crane was still there, too, the wrecking ball dropping like a plumb line from its arm. It looked like an Erector set. Destructor set" (107). The image sets into perspective the juvenile machinations of those attempting to decide the fate of the building, just as the novel's pastoral images, which radiate about the quaint figure of Father Ucello, introduce a counterpoint of Edenic consciousness. In one scene Father Ucello is set off from those around him by his Franciscan charisma with birds (as his name implies) and animals, a striking contrast to the prewar chaplain, who had been unsuccessfully trying to feed the squirrels at Porta Coeli, the order's retirement home. The scene, one of McInerny's best, is recorded by Father Faiblesse's chauffeur:

> Mr. Nickles noticed that the trees about were now alive with birds; they darted and swooped and fluttered to the ground at Father Ucello's feet. Absent-mindedly he scattered the contents of his pockets upon the lawn. A pair of bluejays tried to monopolize the food but Ucello stepped into the fray and restored peace. A magnificent redbird alighted on his unoccupied shoulder. The prewar chaplain's face was a mask of rage. (99–100)

With its final flourish of antagonism the scene becomes a microcosm of the novel as a whole in which men of God become embroiled acrimoniously in a battle over a building that had not been used for any substantive religious purpose for years.

Father Ucello's second important symbolic appearance occurs when he questions the strenuous efforts of retired priests such as Father Phelan to save the old seminary building:

> "Why won't Leo settle down?" Ucello asked. "Doesn't he realize our lives are over? We are here to prepare for death."
> "We must not despair."
> Trask spoke as one who had kept vigil at the deathbed of hope. What a crazy quilt his life would seem when it was over. It seemed so now. The patient had survived though the operation was a failure. Maybe Ucello was right. *Lasciate ogni speranza.*
> Ucello looked at him with surprise. "I said nothing of despair." (182)

Although Father Ucello is presented as an absurd figure at times—as when he loosens the lids of garbage cans so that he can attract raccoons—he represents a joyful, otherworldly vision that contrasts with the forced austerity of others and with the unacknowledged and un-Christian fear of death felt by the central character, Father Tumulty.

In *Leave of Absence*, McInerny once again explores the church in transition, this time from the viewpoints of two women who had been molded by the post–Vatican II church. The plot turns on an ironic symmetry whereby a nun and a married woman exchange roles. The ironic reversal arises not only from internal changes in the women themselves but also from the changes in the post–Vatican II church, which in many respects seemed to Andrea Bauer, the nun, to have definitively altered its character. Attracted to the contemplative discipline of a traditional religious order, Andrea looked on in disbelief as the reforms of the 1960s were applied, sometimes in a bizarre fashion, in American convents. When the time came that some nuns were using makeup, she decides at one point that it was no longer necessary to devise complex, justifying arguments: "Change soon gained such momentum that it swept everything before it" (108).

In a wistful exchange between Andrea and Vera Halloran, who were old school friends, Andrea says bitterly:

> "there aren't any convents or nuns or peace or quiet anymore."
> "No one kneeling in chapel saying prayers for the rest of us?"
> "No." (147)

While in some respects an innocuous bit of dialogue, the passage nonetheless points up the changes in the traditional Catholic model of the community of saints in which certain individuals and groups specialized in forms of spiritual activity—such as prayer—that were viewed as a benefit to the whole church, including the living and the dead. In the post–Vatican II church such specialization, particularly if it involved a physical separation from others, tended to be downplayed in favor of a more active involvement with a world whose needs cried out for attention.

Completing the pattern of inversion, McInerny shows that while Andrea moves from the nunnery into a relationship with Vera's husband, Edward (a relationship in which she eventually loses interest), Vera moves out of marriage, in shock at first, but then in relief at her newfound independence and privacy. In her backward motion toward the source (the traditional Catholic Church), Vera becomes a Thomist and searches for a religious order that resembles those she was accustomed to seeing in her youth. Eventually, she comes across a Carmelite convent in Illinois that had taken as its patron Edith Stein, the formerly Jewish Carmelite nun who had been killed at Auschwitz. While Vera's conversion to the contemplative ideal fills her with a sudden spiritual longing, McInerny skillfully shows her state of mind to have resulted from an incremental process involving small but significant alterations in attitudes and values. For example, in retrospect, Vera (whose name conveys something of the authority of her viewpoint) recalls the unexpected importance of a chance remark by Andrea, still a nun at the time, about God's ubiquitousness:

> The thought of God's hanging around Dayton's Tearoom told Vera how little she and her friend still had in common. Thank God Andrea had not gone on about it. Yet it was that remark that had stayed with her through the years, to recur with particular urgency since her divorce, though the Andrea who had spoken of prayer across the luncheon table in Minneapolis no longer existed. . . . That there is a

God who is everywhere is already improbable enough. That there is
anything whatever is the most improbable thing of all. (75–76)

With a fine stroke of irony McInerny shows in Vera's final reflection her
surprised consciousness that, given the evidence of the existing universe,
not to believe in a creator paradoxically required an act of faith.

Vera's attraction to the transcendentalism of traditional Catholicism
is convincingly registered by McInerny as she wanders about Europe
in search of God. Drawn inexplicably to a Parisian shrine where the
preserved heart of Saint Vincent de Paul is on display in a reliquary at the
side altar, Vera is struck by the plaques commemorating favors received in
answer to prayers. While momentarily skeptical about what she sees, Vera
asks herself what she knew that prevented God from intervening in the
lives of human beings. Observing the crowds in the chapel along the rue de
Bac, "Frenchmen and foreigners, young and old, poor and rich," she comes
to realize that it was what "they knew that she craved to learn" (175).

Completing his cycle of irony and reversal, McInerny shows not only
the illusoriness of Andrea's hopes about love and marriage but also the
impossibility of Vera being permitted to become a contemplative nun.
Blocked by the simple, technical impediment that she remains a married
woman in the eyes of the church, Vera slowly and reluctantly turns back
toward a probable reunion with Edward: "She wanted to be a saint, a
heroine, someone like Edith Stein. But she had Edward and vice versa. She
sat in a pew and closed her eyes, holding back the tears. Prayer is getting
in touch with God. But what is God? *Todo y nada*, according to John of the
Cross. Everything and nothing." (210) The passage recalls the tempered
morality of *Gate of Heaven* in which limitations on one's capacity to act
and on one's happiness are regarded as the norm by the author, although
this is not perceived as a cause for despair. Indeed, Vera's perception
that God is all or nothing frees her to find God, as the earlier episode in
Dayton's Tearoom had foretold, even in the midst of her desultory life.
Without permitting her, finally, to escape the insipid circumstances of her
marriage to Edward, Vera's thoughts allow her to develop a contemplative
existence, even within marriage, in which every particle of existence can
be made to yield, she comes to understand, a glimpse of the divine. The
passage exemplifies McInerny's unsentimental and disciplined approach
to religious consciousness.

The ethic of renunciation is pervasive in McInerny's fiction, as the
ending of *The Search Committee* (published in 1991) attests. In that novel,
Matthew Rogerson, in spite of his antifeminist outlook, attracts an ardent
academic colleague who is every inch a feminist:

> By all rights she should have hated him. But she loved hearing heresy
> from his lips. She could disagree with him on everything and some-
> how feel more affinity with him than with Peter and Laplace and
> Handel and all the wimps who championed Women's Studies as
> much as she did. There was condescension in their agreement whereas
> Rogerson, no matter his theory, treated her as an equal. . . . Rogerson
> was everything she should not like—traditionalist, gallant, Catholic,
> against every social cause that stirred her blood. (72–73)

Although Rogerson, by arguing with Sylvia Woods in the way he does,
treats her as an equal, a compliment whose significance she is sensitive
enough to appreciate, and although he is obviously attracted to her sexually, he gives her up, perhaps fearing that the gulf in their values would
eventually doom the relationship. In any case, his final thoughts are those
of renunciation: "Winter was his season and snow his element. Rogerson
did not find this a difficult truth to accept" (243). Here, one is reminded of
the ending of *Gate of Heaven* with its interwoven themes of death and hope.

Set against the outer world of secular American society, Rogerson's
renunciation appears anomalous indeed, a reactionary gesture within
a religious framework that has become more and more marginalized.
The outline of the larger society is brought home to the reader by such
outlandish figures as the university chancellor, Herbert Laplace, who,
rather like one of the born-again Watergate conspirators, sets off into the
evangelical media circuit with a new religion that attempts to convince
people that they are better than they think they are. In this respect Laplace
resembles a number of characters in the fiction of Flannery O'Connor,
especially those in *Wise Blood* who attempt to promulgate a similar travesty
of Christianity.

If, in McInerny's view, Catholicism had deteriorated fundamentally
following Vatican II, this deterioration was regarded as nothing compared
to the horrors promulgated in the name of other religions in post-Christian
American society. There is Amanda Davis, for example, who murders two
of Rogerson's colleagues and tries to murder a third under the influence of
a Zen-like mind-set in which the individual soul, so prized within Rogerson's Catholic theology, is set at naught. Amanda confides to Rogerson at
one point:

> "I prefer mysticism. Do you know Zen?"
> "Do you know Teresa of Avila?"
> She had never heard of Saint Teresa but her mind was filled with
> oddments of Eastern mysticism. She doubted the body was real and
> that people are meant to be individuals.
> "In the end we'll all end up as one." (205)

In the vacuum created by the departure of Christianity, McInerny foresees a clutter of religious practices and beliefs juxtaposed with an underlying moral chaos in which the ideal of a vigilant respect for individual human life will be increasingly eroded.

Given the implicit pessimism of McInerny's point of view, which at times recalls that of Walker Percy, one is struck by the liveliness of his plots, the verve and charm of his characters, and the wit and grace of his narrative style. The conjunction of these rich novelistic resources and his underlying pessimism can be explained, perhaps, by what one might think of as McInerny's rearguard sanity, his latent assumption that even if Catholicism was moving through a period of obvious decline, it was always there to be retried—as Vera Halloran discovers in *Leave of Absence*.

For all of their entrenched traditionalism, *The Priest, Gate of Heaven, Leave of Absence,* and *The Search Committee* are exceedingly well-written novels, and certainly deserve a wider and more serious reading audience than, possibly because of their backward glance, they have so far received. In addition to being discriminating studies of character and social change, McInerny's novels are, finally, novels of ideas, one of the ways in which his fiction differs from Powers's. Perhaps reflecting his years as a philosophy professor at Notre Dame, McInerny takes obvious enjoyment in placing his characters in animated debate with each other and in seeing them attempt to unravel the limited, and sometimes not so limited, enigmas he sets before them. On the whole, the novels reflect a balance between Thomist rationalism and transcendental vision, since inevitably in McInerny's fiction there remains at the end the intractable mystery of the divine shadow that crosses the human soul from time to time.

Mary Gordon

(B. 1949)

I N HER FICTION Mary Gordon has epitomized the dilemma of a contemporary writer who feels drawn toward a feminist image of freedom and autonomy yet feels a lingering attachment to the church. Gordon's position as both Catholic and feminist is certainly more ambiguous than that of writers such as Mary Jo Weaver, who has described herself as a "convinced feminist who is decidedly Catholic." Nevertheless, Gordon's Catholicism is as evident in her fiction, particularly in the early novels, as is her argument with it. Furthermore, while she has been critical of the treatment of women within the traditional Catholic Church, Gordon has also been dismayed at the post–Vatican II church for its low aesthetic standards and for its loss of the deeper spiritual and psychological appeal that she experienced as a young Catholic—although she has endorsed the contemporary church's enlarged social consciousness. In this respect, in an interview with Annie Milhaven, Gordon has described the post–Vatican II church as operating on relatively superficial levels of activity as opposed to those that, related to prayer, involve contact with "beauty, reflection, and a kind of race memory."[1]

In her fiction Gordon reflects the views of most Catholic feminists, including the Canadian writer Mary Jo Leddy, that the church's attempt

1. Weaver, *New Catholic Women*, xi; Milhaven, *The Inside Stories: Thirteen Valiant Women Challenging the Church*, 109.

to accommodate feminist ideals in recent years amounts to "tokenism." Gordon also echoes the views of Catholic feminists such as Rosemary Radford Ruether that the problem for women in the church arises from the expanding possibilities for women in society at large as contrasted with those in the church. Ruether has characterized the role of women in the Catholic Church as that of "permanent dependents, the lowest class in a hierarchy of clergy over laity, men over women." Both Ruether and Leddy also link the low status of women in the church to the too literal valuing of the maleness of Christ and of God the Father. As the American feminist and theologian Anne Carr has put it, in the name of the "son and his father in heaven, wives have been subject to husbands and fathers, told to be silent, blamed for sin, denied the fullness of the image of God, and burned for witchcraft, even as they were told they share a glorious equality through baptism in the community of faith."[2]

While Carr's view seems close to that embodied in Gordon's first novel, *Final Payments*, Gordon departs at times from the usual feminist writing about the church in tracing her own feminism to the fact that in being brought up a Catholic she was given "images of heroic women," as she put it in an essay titled "Getting Here from There: A Writer's Reflections on a Religious Past," adding that this was "not so frequently the case in other religious traditions." In 1991 Gordon confided to an interviewer that she would not have become a feminist if it had not been for her early training as a Catholic. "I was brought up to take issues of justice very seriously," she added. "And what is feminism except a desire for universal justice not bounded by gender roles?"[3]

A number of Catholic feminists have emphasized the role of Mary in connection with female empowerment within the church. Mary Jo Weaver, for example, has characterized Mary as the image of creativity without "male intervention." Gordon has emphasized not only the importance of Mary, the mother of Jesus, but also the examples of female saints, female doctors of the church, and the founders of great religious orders for women who had in some cases defied popes and bishops. As a Catholic girl, Gordon has said, she was used to seeing women in the church as authority figures. Moreover, Gordon has on a number of occasions cited the opportunity for women to exist in the church within a community

2. Leddy, Roo, and Roche, *In the Eye of the Catholic Storm*, 45; Ruether, foreword to Milhaven, *Inside Stories*, vi; Carr, *Transforming Grace: Christian Tradition and Women's Experience*, 176.

3. Gordon, *Good Boys*, 169; Gordon as quoted in Eleanor Wachtel, ed., *Writers and Company*, 272.

of women, without the encumbrances of marriage, as a liberating model of sorts, historically speaking. Gordon, who in her younger years had considered becoming a nun, was attracted by the lives of female religious, who, independently of men, she told Eleanor Wachtel, "operated in the world" on their own. On the other hand, she told interviewer Trisha Gorman that she was appalled at how difficult it was for women to be leaders within the church without appealing to a male authority—in particular, priests—whom she described as having a "hidden magical potency" that was both "sexually inaccessible and directly connected to spiritual ritual and the mystical."[4]

Gordon's feminism not only issued from her recognition of female authority figures in the Catholic Church but also ironically derived to a great extent from the encouragement given her by her father, who empowered her by nourishing her intellect as a child, teaching her languages, and talking to her about serious intellectual matters: "He never said to me," Gordon recalls, "that there are things that you can't do because you are a girl." At the same time, Gordon was aware, up to the time of her father's untimely death when she was seven, that she was her father's rather than her mother's child. Nevertheless, Gordon has acknowledged her debt to her mother, who brought her up and provided a living for her following the death of her father. She has also said that her mother tuned her ear as a writer to the spoken language around her.[5]

Both of Gordon's parents were Catholics, her mother of Irish Italian background, her father a converted Jew. Although Gordon was raised in the Irish American Catholic tradition and was not exposed to Judaism in her youth, she believes that her assertiveness as a writer stemmed from the Jewish part of her. In her short story "Temporary Shelter" she has also celebrated her Jewish roots in the characterization of Dr. Meyers. Nonetheless, her upbringing was thoroughly Catholic, and she has expressed her gratitude for this formation in shaping her as a novelist, especially for the inspiration of the Mass with its dramatic sweep and rich lodes of rhetoric, which led to a consciousness of the ineffable. Similarly, the majesty of the service of Benediction stirred Gordon's creativity, as has the recollection of her First Communion, which for "utter purity and lightness and singleness," she told Peter Occhiogrosso, could not be duplicated outside the church. At its best, she added, the church has

4. Weaver, *New Catholic Women*, 206; Wachtel, *Writers and Company*, 267; Gorman, "Interview with Mary Gordon," 225.
5. Milhaven, *Inside Stories*, 117; Gordon, *Good Boys*, 151–52.

been a source of high aesthetic and ethical idealism that one doesn't find elsewhere.[6]

Gordon's relationship to Catholicism as an adult has been more problematic. Noting that her connection to the institutional church had become more tenuous, she nevertheless declared to Occhiogrosso in 1987 that she was still a Catholic, if not necessarily one who observed the Mass and the sacraments punctiliously. She declared to Eleanor Wachtel in 1991 that when she attended Mass, she liked being in a place where people, whom she felt on the whole to be very different from herself, all had their "hearts tilted toward one thing which, at its best, I find very beautiful."[7]

In her essay "Getting Here from There," Gordon indicated that her objection to certain aspects of the church arose not so much because it was dominated by a male clergy, but rather by a celibate clergy, whom she regarded as having had a "history of hatred and fear of the body." In this respect Gordon is in the mainstream of Catholic feminist writing. Ruether, for example, has lamented the oppressive effects of Catholic sexual morality upon women by celibate males who claim to "know better." While bridling against the Jansenistic asceticism of Irish American Catholicism, Gordon has nevertheless praised that same tradition for its unsentimental pointing up of human failure measured against Christian ideals, permitting one to see the human condition in its "clearest, most undiluted colors, to feel its starkest music in the bone," as she put it in an essay in *Good Boys and Dead Girls*.[8]

Gordon's ambivalence toward the asceticism of Irish American Catholicism—particularly its fear of sexuality—ironically stems from her attachment to the Catholic Church's incarnational theology:

> Abstraction I define as the error that results from refusing to admit that one has a body and is an inhabitant of the physical world. Dualism, its first cousin, admits that there is a physical world but calls it evil and commands that it be shunned. I'd venture to say that these two "sins"—dualism and abstraction—are the cause of at least as much human misery as pride, covetousness, lust, envy, hatred, gluttony, and sloth.[9]

Apart from the Jansenism that she perceives in Irish American Catholicism, Gordon, like Joyce, identified masochistic tendencies as well. These

6. Occhiogrosso, *Once a Catholic*, 72–74.
7. Ibid., 74; Wachtel, *Writers and Company*, 272.
8. Gordon, *Good Boys*, 161; Ruether, foreword to Milhaven, *Inside Stories*, vi; Gordon, *Good Boys*, 206.
9. Gordon, *Good Boys*, 160.

have been vividly portrayed in stories such as "Mrs. Cassidy's Last Year," which was included in *Temporary Shelter* (published in 1987). In that story, which subsequently evolved into the opening chapter of Gordon's fourth novel, *The Other Side* (which was published in 1989), a newly married man gives a sacred promise to his wife that he will see that she is allowed to die in her own bed rather than in the care of strangers, a promise that becomes an ordeal to keep after his wife becomes demented. Mr. Cassidy's reflections on his torment are revealing in terms of Gordon's thesis about masochism since he feels that his wife is punishing him—"though he had kept his promise."[10] The story "Eileen," also in *Temporary Shelter,* further illustrates masochistic aspects of Irish American Catholicism. From Gordon's point of view the celibate, antisexual, and masochistic elements in Irish American Catholicism have an especially deleterious effect on women, who, on the whole, are perceived by Gordon as at the bottom of the power structure in the church.

The problem of the powerlessness of women in the church has been compounded, Gordon believes, by the anti-intellectualism of American Catholicism. She regards this distrust as directed against secular learning in particular and as based upon a fear that such learning will undermine religious faith. Allied with the Irish Catholic American church's distrust of secular learning, from Gordon's point of view, has been the low value given to aesthetics, a matter of singular importance to her as a writer of fiction. Ironically, it is with the post–Vatican II church that she has had the greatest difficulty in this respect. Gordon has lamented the lack of aesthetic standards in the contemporary Catholic Church's Liturgy and in its rhetoric, in particular the loss of the sense of solemnity that she treasured from her youth. Ironically, the most beautiful liturgical music to be evoked in Gordon's fiction is created by a cantor in a synagogue in the title story from *Temporary Shelter:* "The winding music, thick and secret. . . . The music that traveled to a God who listened, distant and invisible, and heard the sins of men and their atonement in the darkness and in darkness would forgive or not forgive. But would give back to men the music they sent up, a thick braid of justice and kept promises and somber hope" (14–15).

In addition to her elegiac sense of the aesthetic failure of the contemporary Catholic Church, Gordon has regretted the overlooking of what she has termed the mythic appeal of the church. In particular, she has

---

10. Gordon, *Temporary Shelter,* 197. Quotations from the stories in this collection are subsequently cited in the text parenthetically.

felt the loss over time of a sense of contact with the sacred. At the same time, Gordon has supported the post–Vatican II church's intensified social commitment, which has been informed, she observed, by a "very high ethic of love," adding that she has especially admired the priests and nuns working "with the homeless and the poor and the imprisoned" in developing countries, performing the "corporal works of mercy in a very pure way."[11] Gordon has identified not only with peace activists such as Daniel Berrigan, who have operated within the church, but also with the Catholic women who have challenged the church's opposition to abortion, which she, along with most feminists, links with the issue of the empowerment of women.

At the same time, Gordon told Annie Milhaven that she associated the fortunate emergence of law and of formal systems of justice in Western civilization with the male-dominated societies of Athens and Jerusalem. Gordon's liberalism is more tempered than that of many feminists, and tempered in a way that reflects her Catholic background. At the base of Gordon's moral thinking is a belief in the irreducible and tenacious existence of evil, a belief that inevitably implies limits on what can be accomplished through social reform. Moreover, in an interview called "Growing Up Catholic and Creative," she associated the idea of progress and the euphemisms surrounding it with Protestantism rather than Catholicism. Furthermore, although Gordon is critical of the Jansenistic asceticism in Irish Catholicism, she indicated to Milhaven that she does not regard nature as a benevolent force: "Nature is very bleak; nature does not protect the weak." In the same interview, she noted that although women have been the victims of long-standing structural injustice, she does not think that women should approach justice solely in a gender-related manner, noting at one point that the cruelest people in her family were women. On the other hand, she has argued that society lost a lot of its "connection to the earth, and to nature, and to the moral unconscious" because of the subordination of women in Western society.[12]

Gordon's first novel, *Final Payments* (published in 1978), is an attempt to record the process of female victimization within both American society and the Irish American Catholic church. While the most odious character in the book is a woman, Margaret Casey, nonetheless the central conflict focuses on the dangers inherent in a male-dominated church and Catholic family structure. Gordon has commented that Margaret Casey's guilt is

11. Occhiogrosso, *Once a Catholic*, 77.
12. Milhaven, *Inside Stories*, 110; Gordon, "Growing Up Catholic"; Milhaven, *Inside Stories*, 110.

mitigated to some extent by her institutional subordination as a woman within the Catholic Church, adding that because women have a smaller "area of power," their cruelty is more "pointed."[13]

In *Final Payments*, Gordon centers on the evil that results from the repressive influence of a celibate clergy on the church and especially on women. The weight of this element in Isabel Moore's plight is evident in her commitment to give up her life to care for her father: "The Church exists and has endured for this, not only to preserve itself but to keep certain scenes intact: My father and me living by ourselves in a one-family house in Queens. My decision at nineteen to care for my father in his illness."[14] From a moral point of view Gordon complicates her tale by showing the incestuous roots that underlie Isabel's decision to have her father dismiss Margaret Casey as his housekeeper. Isabel eventually recognizes this moral ambiguity in reflecting later that, if she had sacrificed a normal life as a young woman, she had done so for the "person I most loved, with the passion of mind and soul that he reserved for God" (40). This incestuous undercurrent, which in some ways recalls Gordon's closeness to her own father, is so apparent that Isabel's friend Liz Ryan is moved to remark that no one will ever love Isabel with the intensity shown by her father. Late in the novel the controlling role played by Professor Moore in the development of incestuous feelings finally filters through Isabel's consciousness as she recalls her father's passionate words to her when she was only six: " 'I love you more than I love God. I love you more than God loves you' " (251).

The power of Professor Moore over his daughter is abetted by priests who always seem to be about his house, eating and drinking, while debating theological niceties and taking for granted the young woman who served them. Isabel's depiction of these clerics is wryly memorable: "They argued about baptism of desire, knocking dishes of pickles onto the carpet in their ardor. They determined the precise nature of the Transubstantiation, fumbling for my name as I freshened their drinks" (3). Some of Gordon's most memorable writing can be found in her acidic portraits of the clergy, as in Isabel's reflection that Father Mulcahy was "clean as a piglet bathed in milk" (60). While the clergy in Gordon's fiction may be pampered by the laity, they are not villainous. Their ugliness lies in their unquestioned authority, an authority that is exercised over women above all others.

13. Milhaven, *Inside Stories*, 113.
14. Gordon, *Final Payments*, 4, subsequently cited in the text parenthetically.

While Isabel's father attempted to instill Catholic orthodoxy in his daughter, he did so (as did Gordon's father) so that she would do something remarkable in the church. Isabel recalls her father saying that he intended to raise a Teresa "of Avila, not a Thérèse of Lisieux, someone who would found orders and insult recalcitrant bishops, not someone who would submit to having dirty water thrown on her by her sisters in Christ and die a perfect death at twenty-four" (28). Furthermore, although Isabel's father might be construed by some readers as a hidebound traditionalist, his objections to the banality of the post–Vatican II church's liturgical practices and his consciousness of the loss of the old solemnity and majesty in the church are matters upon which he, Isabel, and Gordon were in agreement (101).

Where Isabel does finally take issue with her father, even if only after his death, is on the question of suffering, the value of which she sees her father as affirming above all others. Somehow, in her father's and her own twisted asceticism, Isabel regards every good received as an installment in future, compensatory suffering, thereby echoing the novel's bitter title. The novel's title reflects the pervasiveness of a twisted spirituality that encompasses, for example, Isabel's grotesque attempt to compensate for her earlier wrong to Margaret Casey and her later masochistic behavior as she prepares to became sexually active. Even though her faith has ebbed, Isabel is portrayed with persuasive irony as administering punishment to herself out of habit. The greatest irony of the book, though, is certainly Isabel's anticipated return to Hugh Slade, who, even if he is not as assertive as her father had been, is certainly a domineering male. While Slade is clearly a better companion than Margaret Casey, the reader is left to conclude that Isabel has been conditioned to end up with such a man and that her sense of her own identity remains precarious to the last.

The matter of identity is raised squarely in connection with Isabel's Catholic education. She remembers a nun cautioning her, as a member of the high school debating team, to remember what she represented: "What did it mean, to represent? It meant you were not yourself but something larger. Only you were not the thing itself; you were the parts of you that were like the thing you represented. It meant being connected to something so strongly that people could not think of you without thinking of that thing. What if you represented nothing but were only yourself?" (158). The question of identity touches on Isabel's rebellion at its deepest level. She simply feels no sense of identity within the context of a divine, transcendent, and universal love, as is implied in the inset quotation from Auden's "September 1, 1939," which states that what each of us craves is not "universal love / But to be loved alone" (224). While Auden's poem raises some interesting theological questions—the relationship between sainthood and individuality, for example—it must be said that Gordon squanders this sort of exploration of human versus divine love in an affirmation of hedonism. Isabel reflects rather meanly at one point, for example, that inevitably, in sacrificing for others, one "liked them less" (169). "We must not try to second-guess death," she muses later in the novel, by refusing to love individuals in favor of the "anonymous poor" (289). Such a simplistic resolution falls beneath the intellectual horizon visible earlier in the novel, involving the taut conflict between Isabel's right to her identity and her father's possessive love and need of her. Furthermore, because the reader is restricted largely to Isabel's point of view, Gordon leaves it unclear as to whether Isabel's final circumstances represent an ironic and shallow escape from the past or a maturation of character. Seen as an ironic form of escape, the ending is acceptable in resolving the antithetical forces that have been at work in the novel (institutionalism versus individual identity)—although only just so.

In *The Company of Women*, published in 1980, Gordon contrasts the communal consciousness of her central female characters with the brooding and isolating asceticism of male clergy. In this respect Gordon parallels the thinking of other Catholic feminists—including Mary Jo Leddy, who has criticized the traditional hierarchical structure of the church for failing to "create a community."[15] *The Company of Women* is in every respect a more complex and accomplished novel than *Final Payments*. The title gives rise to the central paradox of the novel: If it is true that the group of women focused on are all subject to Father Cyprian, it is also true that they provide "company," support, not only to this alienated priest, but, significantly, to themselves as well. Thus, although he is superior in one sense, in another, Father Cyprian is shown to be helplessly dependent upon women to give him a context, a society of sorts in which to exist.

This dependency is nowhere more evident than in Cyprian's intense love for Felicitas, Charlotte's daughter, a quasi-oedipal love that recalls Isabel Moore's father's platonic but psychologically incestuous passion for his daughter in *Final Payments*. When Cyprian fears that Felicitas might have perished in a car accident in which he was at fault, he reflects that, if the child died, so would he: "He had left father and mother, but the child was his. In the sty of the world, she shone like diamonds for him."[16] As with Professor Moore, Cyprian tries to form the mind of the young

15. Leddy, Roo, and Roche, *In the Eye*, 69.
16. Gordon, *Company of Women*, 52, subsequently cited in the text parenthetically.

woman so that it will resist speciousness either within or outside of the
church, cautioning Felicitas at one point to be beware of pious rumors
and to shun superstition. The difference between Felicitas's education and
that of Isabel Moore is that Felicitas emerges as a more sophisticated and
independent thinker, particularly with respect to the subordination of
women in the church. In this connection Anne Carr noted that the more
educated a Catholic woman is, the more likely it is that she will be a
feminist.[17]

Like Professor Moore, Cyprian attempts to instill a spirit of renunciation
in Felicitas, making it impossible for her to lead an ordinary life. Cyprian's
Jansenistic rejection of even the natural beauty of the world is not only
rebelled against by Felicitas, in a way that reveals the damage already
done to her soul, but is of a sort that would have been refuted by Catholic
writers such as Thomas Merton who clung to the visible world in their
search for God. Cyprian tells Felicitas dourly that the beauty of nature can
easily be mistaken for God, that natural beauty has no meaning in itself.
With considerable acuity Cyprian perceives the temptation to worship
nature as a particularly American error, implicitly challenging the sort of
fusion of religion and romanticism that had been embodied in the work
of writers such as Emerson and Merton.

Cyprian trains Felicitas, and for that matter the other women in his
charge, to be virgin martyrs. Thus, he cautions Felicitas against being
"womanish"—by which he means feminine, in an old-fashioned, mawk-
ish sense: "It was womanish to carry pastel holy cards and stitched novena
booklets bound with rubber bands. It was womanish to believe in happiness on earth. . . . The opposite of womanish was orthodox. The Passion
of Christ was orthodox" (44). In contrast to the sort of insipid femininity
scorned by Cyprian, Felicitas, who hears her name read out as one of the
virgin martyr saints at each Mass she attends, is formed by Cyprian for
heroic deeds. Cyprian's orthodoxy is portrayed as tending toward the
legalistic, not because he is superficial but because he seeks exactness and
because he is polemical. All the same, as she matures, Felicitas comes to
realize the limits of what she takes to be the narrow maleness of Cyprian's
intellect, at one point paralleling the relationship between Cyprian and
herself with that between Carlyle and Margaret Fuller: " 'I accept the
universe,' said Fuller, expressing stupidly a genuine intellectual problem.
'By gad, you'd better,' said Carlyle, winning himself an audience through
his wrong-headed wit. For he was wrong. Fuller was speaking of volition,

17. Carr, *Transforming Grace*, 17.

of the central human struggle to place oneself in relation to the absolute"
(264).

In becoming aware of Cyprian's compulsion to achieve not only intellectual precision but also certitude, a necessary concomitant to the kind
of orthodoxy he holds, Felicitas becomes conscious of her own emphasis
on the volitional, an area of experience that Cyprian would regard as
inchoate. For Felicitas, the volitional element is at least as important as
the cognitive. What Felicitas is open to explore is the relationship between
individual consciousness, supernaturalism, freedom, and happiness. In
contrast, Cyprian's "orthodoxy" is portrayed as so regimented that it
would shackle even the sovereignty of a soul that chose to give itself
to God. Under Cyprian's tutelage Felicitas comes to experience religion
as a sort of prison, a place of emotional starvation, and in this respect she
resembles Isabel Moore in *Final Payments.*

The Company of Women is structured in such a way that we build up a
portrait of Cyprian cumulatively as he is refracted through the viewpoints
of the women who place themselves in his care and who in turn care for
him. In each case we see his strengths and weaknesses, as in the case of
Mary Rose, whom Cyprian extricates from a disastrous marriage, only
to argue stringently, but probably erroneously, that she cannot obtain an
annulment. Clare in turn mirrors Cyprian's cool managerial ways, which
correspond to her own attempts to suppress the affective parts of herself
as a woman. She is also indebted to Cyprian for his bringing of order and
meaning to her existence with his passionate insistence that life was far
more than "simple breathing" (22).

The most paradoxical of Cyprian's vestal virgins is Elizabeth, whose
warm and communal understanding of her faith stands in such clear
contrast to his own austere vision. Elizabeth, more than any of the other
characters, is able to fill out Felicitas's humanity and to demonstrate
the place of ordinary human affection within the Catholic community.
If Elizabeth reflects a female sense of the immanence of God in ordinary
human life, Cyprian expresses the transcendence of God, as can be seen in
his response to Felicitas's pregnancy, which he argues loftily might have
been permitted by God to spare her greater sin. The irony here is that not
only does Cyprian not know of Felicitas's attempt to have an abortion,
but his transcendental perspective conceals, even from himself, his selfish
hope that the pregnancy will likely lead to Felicitas's remaining within his
care. At the same time, with admirable balance, Gordon brings out the very
real help—physical, psychological, and spiritual—that Cyprian provides
for the women in his care. Avoiding the uniform mood of barrenness
that characterized *Final Payments,* Gordon achieves a superior view of her

characters in *The Company of Women*, based upon a more discriminating awareness of their richness as characters.

Nevertheless, in spite of Felicitas's recognition of the quixotic tenacity of Cyprian's life, she approaches the idea of a transcendent God with wariness, reflecting in the final pages of the novel that if she could "see the face of God as free from all necessity," she would "look for Him" (265). Her final reluctance is based in part upon a rational reserve, ironically derived from the rigorous intellectual training given her by Cyprian. It is also, however, experiential; she is determined not to have a supernatural faith of the sort set forth by Cyprian in order to avoid blighting the ordinary human life of her child as she feels her own life had been blighted. At the end she insists that the faith that filled her youth either accommodate itself to the full circumstances of her life as a woman—or risk being discarded. In this respect she is completely opposed to Cyprian's outlook, which demands that life be disciplined to fit the requirements of a transcendent, renunciatory vision.

Gordon's theme could not be clearer. The sort of orthodoxy in which both she and Felicitas grew up diminishes women particularly, with their communal consciousness and affective sensitivity, into virgin martyrs who are the projections of male minds and a male church. Thus, the novel ends in a stalemate, with Felicitas viewing herself, not without a profound sense of loss, as the only one of the women around her who lacks a spiritual life. On the other hand, with her eye on relationships and community, on "company" if not on doctrine, Felicitas has determined—Gordon's final irony—that her child will be raised a Catholic.

Although *Men and Angels*, which was published in 1985, is not primarily devoted to religious themes, it reflects a development in terms of Gordon's exploration of feminism and the church. In contrast to her earlier two novels, in this novel Gordon explores the moral arena created by women when they are freed from a position of powerlessness within society and within the church. As was the case with Gordon's earlier novels, *Men and Angels*, in spite of its title, is even more a novel about women. Indeed, significant male figures are either kept offstage, as with Michael Foster, or are shown to be at the mercy of women, as is the case with Caroline Watson's son, Stephen. In addition, Ben Hardy can hardly be described as a strong male figure. The only influential male in the novel, though his role is peripheral, is Caroline Watson's father, who insists that Stephen Watson remain in America rather than being raised in Paris by his mother.

There are three main approaches to religion set forth in the novel: the psychotic Fundamentalism, later blended with charismatic Catholicism, of Laura Post; the wariness toward religion exhibited by Anne Foster;

and the Anglo-Catholicism practiced by Jane Watson, which is portrayed sympathetically by Gordon. Laura Post's perversion of Scripture into a creed of human alienation is depicted as both pathetic and terrifying. As with Stephen Watson's suicide, her suicide is the culmination of an emotional process that began with her mother's rejection of her. In this sense, religion is merely a means to an end, the replacement of a life of rejection with one in which *she* is able to do the rejecting. Reviewing her life, Laura reflects that she had been "misunderstood, unwelcomed, asked to leave places." Jesus, she comforts herself by remembering, had said that "this would happen to the chosen."[18] While fundamentalist Christianity offers Laura a battlement of sorts, Gordon depicts it as failing to provide her with a community of believers whose support is adequate to overcome the anguish of her loneliness. In fact, the kind of Christianity Laura espouses allows her to harbor violent subconscious feelings toward others, even in moments of religious fervor.

Laura Post would appear to be at the center of the question raised by the novel's title and epigraph, which is taken from Saint Paul's epistle to the Corinthians: "Though I speak with tongues of men and angels, and have not charity, I am become as sounding brass, or a tinkling cymbal." In some ways, however, she is the least eligible character to be considered under this piece of Scripture since it is made evident that her life has largely been determined by the actions of others, particularly by her mother. The same sort of comment, though to a much more limited extent, can be made about most of the other characters, whose lives have been determined by parental rejection or by compelling attraction, as in the relationship between Caroline Watson and Jane. The overall effect of the characterization is to deny the freedom required to adhere to the moral imperative issued by Saint Paul. Indeed, if the novel through its epigraph purports to contrast instinctive love and the sort of idealized, spiritual love articulated in the Pauline epistle, it is difficult to see what room, if any, there is for spiritual love.

Even Anne Foster appears to fail in overcoming her instinctive antipathy to Laura, which is not surprising, perhaps, given her commitment to instinctual affection: "Some deep encoded pattern drew her to her children and made her circle them: her body itself was a divide between them and the rest of the human world" (68). Although Anne's instinctualness is challenged by Caroline Watson's abandonment of her son and dedication of her life to art, thereby taking herself "out of the way of her own body"

18. Gordon, *Men and Angels,* 3, subsequently cited in the text parenthetically.

(50), Anne comes to realize as time passes that Caroline Watson had room in her life for a child, though not the child she bore.

That Anne's own life is grounded in the instinctual is symbolized in the images of the natural and animal world that are incorporated into her point of view, as in her reflection that her children's "spirit" flickered briefly within the "thick forest of their animal lives" (100). In addition, psychologically speaking, her own life appears as a forest of sorts at one point, containing a small warm lake in which she swam and whose bottom "had always been muddy; leaves and twigs, weeds, gray-green and shapeless" (107). Similarly, when she becomes suspicious that her husband had been unfaithful, Anne feels as if a "dark fish" had come between them, possessed of "rows of clever teeth, not yet visible" (135). Finally, when she believes that Laura has endangered her children's lives, the animal imagery deployed by Gordon silhouettes the primitive side of Anne's psyche: "Rage rose up in her: a loud clatter of dark wings. The wings flew, blocked the light. They twisted, they became involved in a tremendous whirring circle. She heard nothing, could see nothing but a circle of confused wings, whirring horribly, and the sharp beak somewhere about to strike" (202). The passage is important in narrowing the thematic distance between Laura and Anne, which is difficult to accomplish, given Laura's grotesqueness and Anne's ostensible reasonableness and charm.

Transcendental spirituality enters the novel through Jane Watson, whose guilt over the suicide of her husband moves her to seek forgiveness outside of the human community. "I turned to faith," she tells Anne, "because it showed the possibility of forgiveness for the unforgivable" (167). As opposed to Anne, Jane presupposes moral consciousness and therefore assumes moral responsibility when she marries Stephen in order to be close to his mother. Nevertheless, Jane's religious faith cannot shield her from the mystery of suffering: "As I believe in a loving God," she confides to Anne, "it is much more difficult to understand" the "dark cruel face" that looks on while "His children suffer" (230). At the same time, however, Jane places her hope in an incarnational Christianity that will rescue someone like Laura Post from a merely obsessive life, observing that the "love of God means nothing to a heart that is starved of human love" (231). The transcendentalism articulated by Jane Watson represents the Catholic theology Mary Gordon grew up with in its purest form. Its relation to Gordon's underlying feminist perspective in *Men and Angels* is that, instead of arising amid a conflict between dominant males and suppressed women, here it emerges from a social order in which women are in control of their fates and in which men play relatively minor roles in the scheme of things. It is as if Gordon has freed her women from a pattern of historical bondage in order to have them enact the fall from grace on their own terms.

Somewhat the same can be said of Gordon's fourth novel, *The Other Side* (published in 1989), although that novel is only incidentally concerned with religion, being primarily an artistic rendering of social history. In *The Other Side*, Gordon presents a new image of Catholic males, a more self-effacing and loving image than that found in her earlier fiction while she retains her portrayals of women who are subordinated within and angry at the church. Gordon's altered rendering of Catholic men recalls the observation by the theologian Anne Carr that men become more acceptable Christians when the paradigm of Christ's death and resurrection is balanced by other, gentler Christological symbols, such as those of "servant and sacrifice."[19]

Catholicism permeates *The Other Side* as it did Gordon's first two novels. The Irish American characters have simply been so immersed in Catholic culture that it reveals itself at every turn—as in Dan MacNamara's ironic reflection that Disney World, where he periodically took his daughters, was the "Lourdes of divorced fathers."[20] As in *Men and Angels*, the men in this novel play relatively passive roles, though they are much more developed as characters than in the earlier novel. In general, however, it is the female characters who are the protagonists: Ellen, Cam, and even Sister Otile Regan, who turns an inert piece of church property into a refuge for the aged and for battered women and their children.

Although Ellen MacNamara, for example, grew up in Catholic Ireland under a tyrannical and immoral father and although she suffers all her life from the trauma of this upbringing, she is nevertheless portrayed by Gordon as having a stronger personality than her husband, Vincent, though she recognizes that he can be formidable if aroused to anger. All the same, she makes a number of important family decisions without consulting him, such as taking in the neighbor's children and deciding which school her grandchildren, Cam and Dan, will attend. Significantly, when she becomes demented, Dan, moving about her house, feels that the rooms are meaningless without her "governance" (32). Similarly, Cam reflects in passing that if she wanted the truth of something, she would go to Ellen; she would go to Vincent, on the other hand, for emotional comfort, a neat reversal of traditional gender typing.

19. Carr, *Transforming Grace*, 177.
20. Gordon, *Other Side*, 177, subsequently cited in the text parenthetically.

At the same time, it is implied that Ellen could have had a significant career in politics, had her society been open to such a role for women and had she been freer to leave her family to pursue such a career. Such restrictions do not impinge upon Cam, but she seems not to share her mother's burning reformism. Similarly, while Ellen reacts with fury at what she sees as the passivity of the Catholic Church—as is dramatized in the episode of the bees in Ireland—Cam, in a much younger generation, feels insufficiently engaged by the church to react angrily.

Excluding the rather pathological example of Theresa, Vincent represents the strongest religious consciousness in the novel, but in a benign and loving fashion, as opposed to Professor Moore and Father Cyprian in Gordon's earlier novels. In this way the shaping of the MacNamara children and grandchildren takes on a more balanced and healthier form than in Gordon's earlier fiction. While Cam, for example, acquires a love of life from working alongside Vincent in his garden, she also inherits an anger, which she treasures, from Ellen, an anger that leads her to separate her own identity as a human being and as a woman from people and issues she wants not to be linked with. Not unlike Emily Brontë's symmetrical arrangement of the generations in *Wuthering Heights*, it might be said that whereas Ellen is to Vincent, as Cam is to Dan, there is nevertheless a perceptible softening and blending of sensibilities in the younger generation. In the three generations represented in the novel, though, the ascendancy of female power is manifest and seems to parallel a decline both of the influence of males and of the church. On the other hand, Vincent's piety is treated respectfully by Gordon. He is depicted as living in the light of an incarnational theology in which supernaturalism combines fruitfully with moral consciousness, as in his struggle for the rights of working people and in his unconditional love of other human beings.

In 1993 Gordon published *The Rest of Life*, a collection of three novellas, one of which, "Immaculate Man," focuses on Catholic themes. Narrated by a non-Catholic, divorced woman who has entered into a clandestine affair with a priest, "Immaculate Man" sensitively documents the woman's and the priest's plight against the background of a church that had lost an enormous number of its clergy since the 1960s and that appeared to be drifting. In this respect the atmosphere of the story is distinctly elegiac. Gordon's subtle, oblique rendering of the priest's situation is acutely and poignantly registered by the woman who loves him and who in a sense has come to love the priest in him and in fact counts on his holding to his vocation to secure her own place in his life. On one occasion, for example, she observes with admiration that a priest can "say anything as long as it's the truth. He never has to worry if it's his place to say it: every place is his place, since he has no place of his own."[21] "Immaculate Man" is thus, as its title suggests, not focused on the argument for married clergy but is rather a study of inner dividedness both in the priest and in the narrator. Significantly, the narrator rarely refers to Father Clement by his secular name, Frank, tacitly including herself among those who perceive his chosen religious name as an integral part of his identity.

What gives the story additional depth and dramatic interest is that the narrator realizes at one point that while she is attracted to Father Clement, she is also different from him in some fundamental ways, so much so that she cannot bring herself to think of marrying him. She sees in his priestly point of view an uncompromising and potentially fierce nature that makes her anxious about her children's happiness, noting at one point that, unlike Clement with his otherworldly norms, her children had "never believed that their lives were at stake" (53).

Declaring that her children seemed to her to have been "born good," a view that Clement would have rejected, the narrator nonetheless concedes that they were, after all, quite capable of evil—in their gratuitous cruelty toward Clement's dog, for example. Nevertheless, she values the ordinary, domestic kindnesses that her children are capable of and sees that these would never be enough for Clement. The differences in vision and belief are focused in the story through the narrator's imaginative rendering of Clement's and of her own divergent conceptions of eternity. While she characterizes Clement's idea of eternity as a state of rest following a life of sacrifice, self-denial, and even heroism, her own vision of eternity is bleak and chilling:

> I could easily see myself, I have always been able to, spinning and spinning through millions of light years of emptiness, the others I have loved spinning millions of light years away in their own emptinesses, none of us with anything to recognize, anything to attach to, nothing to stop any of us, no reason to go one way or the other, one place or the other, since there is no place or placement and no stopping, only emptiness and motion, senseless motion, hurtling toward nothing, to and with no end. How, then, could I dream of eternity since what I can't see or even hope for is the face at the end of motion, the embracing arms. (70)

This loveless vision of eternity captures not only the narrator's desolate insecurity, which is evident everywhere in the story, but also her sense

21. Gordon, *Rest of Life*, 41, subsequently cited in the text parenthetically.

that there is a gulf between Clement's austere theology and the anthropomorphic realities that she values. Why exclude from heaven, the narrator implicitly wonders, the loving relationships that brightened and gave value to one's life on earth? While the narrator's view underestimates the Catholic Church's vision of heavenly happiness, which incorporates the doctrine of the communion of saints, it is nonetheless based on what she has learned from a priest whose life had been useful and, up until his affair with the narrator, honorable. Reflecting the sort of feminism found in other of Gordon's novels, the narrator's view in this respect is clearly portrayed as part of her womanhood, just as Clement's is, once again, perceived as a view developed and espoused by a celibate, male culture.

A critic of Gordon's work, Carol Iannone, has contended that Gordon's books are not about love but rather about the "monumental self-centeredness released by the collapse of orthodoxy," a self-centeredness that, Iannone argues, finds expression in feminism.[22] There can be no doubt that Gordon has attracted a good deal of critical attention because of her censorious portrayal of American Catholicism and that feminism is a large part of this stance. In this sense it may take a while before the artistic merits of Gordon's work become separated from her role as a feminist ideologue. Whatever the springs of her motivation as a writer, however, she has vividly characterized the lives of some contemporary Catholic American women so that one witnesses not only the individual dramas but also something of the generalized predicament that can confront Catholic women within their church. Moreover, for Gordon the strong female figures in the Catholic Church, such as Mary, the Mother of Jesus, and Teresa of Avila, challenge the stereotype and to some extent the authority and history of Catholicism as a patriarchal church.

Gordon represents many in the current generation of American Catholics who, having been somewhat marginalized by ethnic isolation in the past, are now drawn toward the mainstream of American life. American Catholics, long-schooled in civil dissent, have been loath in recent years to give up their democratic freedoms in approaching their church. On the other hand, it is clear that in Gordon's rendering of post–Vatican II American Catholicism there has occurred a significant loss of belief in the transcendental aspects of religion. These aspects are undoubtedly the most definitive aspects of religion, and, as has been seen, Gordon herself mourns their passing. While Gordon is generally effective in portraying the demeaning effects of ecclesiastical authoritarianism, she deals with

22. Iannone, "The Secret of Mary Gordon's Success," 66.

some moral issues—notably euthanasia and abortion—in a rather cursory and superficial manner. Gordon's strength lies in her powerful depiction of the perversion that can overtake certain kinds of Christian asceticism. Similarly, she has convincingly, often with a sharp, satiric eye, depicted the folly of an uncritical submissiveness that can be confused with the virtues of humility and piety. One misses in her work, though, any sense of the sublimity possible within a theistic framework, as in J. F. Powers's "Lions, Harts, Leaping Does" or in Paul Horgan's fiction about the Southwest.

While Gordon's dismissive approach toward sacrificial love is sometimes too simplistic to merit credence, especially in *Final Payments*, her characterization of Ed Corcoran in *Men and Angels* and Vincent MacNamara in *The Other Side* suggests a welcome change in direction. Significantly, both of these characters are male, a sign, perhaps, that Gordon's female characters remain wary of a spiritual love that may risk their empowerment. Ellen MacNamara's bursts of generosity, for example, tend to be portrayed as more instinctive than sacrificial, unlike Vincent's willed return to his wife's house at the end of the novel, for example.

Whereas Gordon's depiction of contemporary American religion tends to focus on the mundane and the unheroic, it is evident from both her essays and her fiction that the images of her youth—the consecration at midnight Mass, the hallowed silence of First Communion, the heroism of the church's saintly women—still have the power to stir her imagination. However, the banality of the liturgical and some other aspects of post-1960s American Catholicism, as exemplified by characters such as Sheilah and Bob Gallagher in *The Other Side,* is not a hopeful sign. To some extent, Gordon's fiction is the story of how she cannot go home again; it is also, however, a challenge to the contemporary church to show that it has the power to engage the sensibilities of sophisticated Catholics like Gordon with the beauty and compassion of its vision of transcendental reality. Regarding this possibility, Gordon, rather like Felicitas at the end of *The Company of Women,* would appear to be still waiting.

THE CATHOLIC LEGACY

THE WRITERS INCLUDED in this study were born before Vatican II and thus experienced the atmosphere of the preconciliar church, a formation that, though giving rise to diversity, also produced an underlying unity of outlook that is now more difficult to identify in the increasingly fragmented American Catholic Church. Even the novelist Mary Gordon, the youngest and most disaffected of the writers considered, in conversation with Eleanor Wachtel recalled the church of the 1950s as having an austerity and "richness of form and language and sensuality" that provided "wonderful training" for an artist by establishing a high standard of "aesthetic formality." Apart from the increased rate of departure of Catholics from the church during and after the 1960s, which has been noted by James Hennesey and other historians, and the steep decline in the numbers of seminarians and candidates for female religious orders—factionalism, particularly between traditionalists and liberals, has contributed to divisiveness within the church in recent years, especially in the area of sexual ethics. Furthermore, according to sociologist James O'Kane, many Catholics have continued to practice their faith on their own terms, attending Mass and receiving the sacraments, for example, while violating the church's prohibition against artificial contraception.[1]

1. Wachtel, *Writers and Company,* 265; Hennesey, *American Catholics,* 329; O'Kane, "A Sociological View of United States Catholicism," 26.

Opinion surveys suggest that American Catholics feel free to differ with their church on certain moral issues, primarily involving sexuality, while remaining more or less contendedly Catholic. As Andrew Greeley succinctly put it in the context of one such survey: "They *like* being Catholic." Commenting on the willingness of American Catholics to identify with their religion while acting autonomously in matters of conscience, the American theologian John Langan has linked this phenomenon to the fact that Catholicism in recent years has become "thoroughly integrated" into a highly "pragmatic and pluralistic" American society. The effect has been an assimilation of the ideology of American individualism into American Catholic culture with unprecedented force, leading the critic Anita Gandolfo to predict that the "overriding spirit of individualism" will have to be accounted for in any new model of the Catholic Church in America. Gandolfo cautions, however, that Catholic writers continue to object to an "unbridled individualism" that could give rise to an "idiosyncratic Catholicism that has little relation to the Church of history and tradition." Support for individual dignity and rights has come not only from American political idealism but also from the social encyclicals of the last hundred years, beginning with Pope Leo XIII, encyclicals that played a prominent role in Vatican II with its strong social emphasis. The problem that writers such as Walker Percy, Mary Gordon, and Ralph McInerny have called attention to in their fiction is the reuniting of the social apostolate of the church with its transcendental consciousness and life through its sacraments and liturgy in particular.[2]

Though still affirmed by Rome and by the Catholic philosophical and theological establishment, Thomism, which provided the intellectual underpinning of the Catholic Church in America over the last hundred years, has become somewhat less influential since Vatican II. The reason has to do, at least partly, with the empirical character of the age in which Catholics, and perhaps American Catholics in particular, have participated. An example of this sort of change can be seen in a letter to the editor written in the summer of 1992 by the Catholic ethicist A. W. Richard Sipe, who, in refuting the Vatican's characterization of homosexuality as an "objective disorder," pointed out that this view was not based on "any reliable scientific foundation, psychological or biogenetic."[3] The effect of this sort of skepticism and restiveness toward not only the legislative but also the teaching authority of the church has been to create uncertainty

2. Quoted in Paul Gray, "The Catholic Paradox," 54; Langan, "Is This a Catholic Moment?: 4: Out of the Ghetto," 1309; Gandolfo, *Testing the Faith*, 208.
3. Sipe, "The Homosexual Person," 1071; Gleason, *Keeping the Faith*, 174.

about what precisely the faith is and what exactly it implies for everyday life, as Philip Gleason has pointed out. In his groundbreaking book *Insight*, the Catholic philosopher and theologian Bernard Lonergan attempted to expand Thomist thought so as to include the findings and methods of modern science and philosophy, but, in spite of the continued interest in Lonergan among some Catholic intellectuals, his influence on the church as a whole at this point would have to be described as marginal.

It goes without saying that historically significant changes have occurred over the last forty years in the American Catholic Church, even with respect to fractious issues such as the role of women. If the Catholic Church has been intransigent on some aspects of the issue of women in the church in recent years, official pronouncements from Rome about the dignity and equality of women contrast sharply with the obduracy of the nineteenth-century church in which Orestes Brownson attacked the supporters of women's rights for trying to "reverse the laws of nature."[4] Furthermore, in part through the achievement of the American Catholic writers considered in this study, there is far less evidence now to support a wholesale charge of anti-intellectualism in American Catholicism such as that brought by John Tracy Ellis in an influential essay in the Jesuit quarterly *Thought* in 1955.

Also significant has been the ability of American Catholicism and of Catholic American writers in particular to adapt themselves to many different types of environments. Unlike the Puritans of the seventeenth century, who were associated with a particular region and culture, American Catholics and American Catholic writers have exhibited an almost chameleon-like ability to adapt to diverse surroundings, as can readily be observed in the very different environments lived in by writers such as Flannery O'Connor, Thomas Merton, and Paul Horgan. Furthermore, those differences might be expected to multiply in the case of writers who converted to Catholicism as opposed to those who grew up in the faith. Such is the view of Paul Giles, who argued that converts tend to experience Catholicism in a much more "self-consciously theoretical way, as a cerebral rather than subliminal phenomenon."[5] While generalizations of this sort are precarious, one can certainly assent to Giles's view in the case of writers such as Robert Lowell, Allen Tate, Caroline Gordon, and even Walker Percy and William Everson. Certainly these writers turned toward Catholicism with its lucid, systematic theology and philosophy as a haven

4. See James Kenneally, *The History of American Catholic Women*, 18.
5. Giles, *American Catholic Arts and Fictions*, 527.

against the perceived fragmentation of contemporary culture. Moreover, the momentousness of their conversions fertilized their imaginations as creative artists in addition to giving them a fresh and stimulating subject matter with which to work. Writers who had been brought up in the faith, on the other hand, such as J. F. Powers, Daniel Berrigan, Mary Gordon, Ralph McInerny, and even Flannery O'Connor were perhaps more likely to focus on the friction that attended day-to-day life in the church, having spent a lifetime experiencing it.

In spite of the diversity of experience manifested by Catholic American writers, however, what is remarkable about them is the way in which they register, over and over again, a broadly similar approach to experience. Primarily, this took the form of a sacramental view of the world, an approach that, in Flannery O'Connor's words, involved a penetration of matter until "spirit" was "revealed in it," a phrasing that, oddly enough, recalls the erotic mysticism of William Everson, who is otherwise a radically different writer from O'Connor.[6] Nevertheless, the sacramental view of nature and of human experience generally exhibited by the writers in this study should not be confused with romanticism—even in the case of those Catholic writers who were heavily influenced by romanticism. What distinguishes Catholic sacramentalism from romanticism is both the separate transcendental nature of God in Catholic theology and the role of the Crucifixion, the way of the cross. In work after work Catholic American writers have demonstrated the necessary role of suffering, which results from the friction between the natural and the supernatural, in drawing humanity upward to God through the resistant flesh and ego. This is a ubiquitous theme in Catholic American writing, though one emphasized more in a writer such as Flannery O'Connor than in, say, Thomas Merton.

Central to Catholic belief is the doctrine of the Incarnation, wherein human experience and the natural world are perceived as both flawed and redeemed. The doctrine of the Incarnation can be seen as the axis on which Catholic American literature in general rests and from which variances between particular authors can be measured. For Catholic writers the optimism implicit in the doctrine of the Incarnation, together with their inherited American political consciousness, allowed them, even though they were not part of the American mainstream, to identify with a Jeffersonian and an essentially Protestant political idealism that privileged the dignity of the individual. Counterpointing this emphasis on the individual, though, are the doctrines of the church as an intermediary between

6. O'Connor, *Presence of Grace,* 130.

God and humanity and the belief in the community of saints, both of which doctrines, in concert with that of the Incarnation, gave Catholic writing a communal and prophetic dimension aimed at the whole of American society.

In particular, what these Catholic American writers—notably writers such as Allen Tate, Robert Lowell, and Walker Percy—had to say to American society was that the United States had become a meretricious, scientistic wasteland that ignored the differences between ends and means insisted upon in Catholic philosophy and that dismissed the spiritual and religious dimensions of human experience as illusory. What these writers depict is the human cost of this proclivity in twentieth-century American culture. At the same time writers such as J. F. Powers, Caroline Gordon, Paul Horgan, Thomas Merton, Daniel Berrigan, and Ralph McInerny silhouetted both the prophetic insights and moral weaknesses of the American Catholic Church as that church struggled within the web of time and timelessness, thereby becoming—to Powers and Berrigan in particular—a complex symbol of both virtue and ineptitude.

Most of the Catholic American writers considered in this study wrote between 1940 and 1980, and most of them, including both Everson and O'Connor, were inspired by the originality and holiness of Dorothy Day. Furthermore, many of them were published by Robert Giroux, either when he was an editor at Harcourt, Brace, or when he assumed control of his own publishing house. Moreover, as one looks at the correspondence of Catholic American writers in university libraries, it is immediately evident that these writers were stimulated by each other's work and initiated a rich correspondence based on their mutual interests as Catholics and artists.

At the same time, one cannot avoid the question of the universality of Catholic American literature. Apart from the respect accorded the writers included in this study due to their technical mastery, what is the value of their religious vision for the non-Catholic or nonreligious reader? Touching on this subject, Flannery O'Connor observed that one of her basic problems was trying to communicate her religious vision to an audience to whom that vision was increasingly meaningless. Nonetheless, she added, she could communicate with the reader on the "level of truth" in which case her overriding concern was not to falsify reality. An example of this sort of effect is the fiction of J. F. Powers, which, although focused on the plight of Catholic clergy caught up in the baroque hierarchy of the church, nevertheless connects with other scenarios in which individuals are ground beneath the wheels of institutions. In fact, Powers was stung when he read reviews of *Morte D'Urban* that suggested it was a book "about Catholics, for Catholics." Responding to one such reviewer, he asked irritatedly: "Would you say that *The Wind in the Willows* is a book for animals?"[7]

Reflecting on the place of religious belief in literature in a 1929 essay on Dante, T. S. Eliot noted that, while the reader cannot avoid Dante's philosophical and religious beliefs, he or she is not required to accept these beliefs in order to give the work "poetic *assent*." In a subsequent essay on Goethe (published in 1955), Eliot qualified his earlier pronouncement, arguing that the philosophical or religious beliefs in question had to be "tenable," that a poem that contained religious beliefs that struck the reader as "vile" would not succeed as a poem.[8] While the words *tenable* and *vile* obviously beg the question, Eliot added that what drew the reader who was not of the author's religious persuasion was the presence of wisdom in the work, a view that is strikingly similar to that set forth by Jacques Maritain in his attempt to formulate a Catholic aesthetics.

In a somewhat similar vein the critic M. H. Abrams, in an essay titled "Belief and the Suspension of Disbelief," disputed the idea that the reader accepted ideas in literary works only in a provisional manner, contending that in *King Lear,* for example, we take sides, based upon our assent to the morality that Shakespeare incorporated into the play. Turning toward Dante, as Eliot had done, Abrams contended that Dante's narrator, whose eyes took in heaven, purgatory, and hell, was nevertheless someone with whom the twentieth century reader could identify, specifically with the "terror, the anguish, the incomprehension, the divided mind and emotions of the finite and temporal intelligence which is forced to look upon the universe under the aspect of eternity." Taking the issue one step further, Douglas Bush, in an essay titled "Tradition and Experience," maintained that the reader, in order to value a literary work, is not forced to translate a religious viewpoint into nonreligious terms, but rather the religious novelist or poet succeeds by creating common ground for reader and author both to stand on. In particular, Bush observed, the successful religious writer will set forth a compelling "vision of earth," which in turn embraces a vision of "perfection" whose origins lie beyond the earth.[9] Part of the general appeal of writers such as those considered in this study is their sensitivity to the beauty of the world in both its human and nonhuman aspects, a beauty whose face is captured even by writers as intent upon conveying the presence of evil as Flannery O'Connor. For Catholic writers the beauty of the world is the sign of the surviving art

7. O'Connor, *Conversations*, 87; Powers, "Catholic and Creativity," 68.
8. Eliot, "Dante," 257; Eliot, "Goethe as the Sage," 225–26.
9. Abrams, *Literature and Belief,* 20, 23; Bush in ibid., 49.

of the Creator and therefore of the continuing goodness of at least part of Creation.

In an essay called "Twentieth Century Gothic: Reflections on the Catholic Novel," Albert Sonnenfeld took the position that Catholic fiction flourished on "desecrated soil," that it arose as a reaction to disorder in periods of rapid and severe social change during which the values of Catholic thought were abandoned. The Catholic novel began, Sonnenfeld wrote, as a reaction to the "secular and materialistic doctrine of progress which dominated the thinking of nineteenth century Europe." As a group, Catholic writers have been loath to adopt the idea of progress. Furthermore, enveloped in a system of belief that at least up to the Second Vatican Council appeared to answer all questions that could be put to it, Catholic writers have tended to think holistically about the world, and, furthermore, are ill at ease with nominalism even if they have learned to live with scientific empiricism. This comprehensiveness in Catholicism has been commented on by Mary Gordon in her essay "Getting Here from There," where she recalled that being a Catholic in "Protestant America" meant sharing assumptions about everything from the "appropriate postures for kneeling to the nature of human consciousness."[10]

While Mary Gordon was somewhat resentful about the claustrophobic aspects of such an upbringing, she, and indeed virtually all of the writers in this study, assertively, if sometimes self-consciously, projected their imaginations and sensibilities into the American mainstream. Some—including Walker Percy, Thomas Merton, and Daniel Berrigan—wanted not only to register their Catholic outlook but also to reshape American society according to Catholic philosophical and moral norms. In this light there seems little point in arguing, as Sally McFague TeSelle did in her book *Literature and the Christian Life* that literature, unlike religion, explored "possibilities for contemplation" rather than "programs for action."[11] Even if Walker Percy's novel *The Thanatos Syndrome*, for example, does not advocate immediate action, it obviously elicits social reform at some point. The same sort of thing might be said either in an individual or social context about the poems of Robert Lowell, William Everson, and Daniel Berrigan and about the religious fiction of Caroline Gordon and Flannery O'Connor.

What is distinctive about the Catholic vision is not only its ontological comprehensiveness and self-sufficiency but its overall balance as well. In the fiction and essays of a writer such as Walker Percy, who in many ways

10. Sonnenfeld, "Twentieth-Century Gothic," 388; Gordon, *Good Boys*, 164.
11. TeSelle, *Literature*, 189.

epitomizes the Catholic imagination, the world is portrayed as craven and manipulative, selfish and blind, but not without goodness and never without hope, a world that, with all of its endemic evil, is capable of being transformed by the example of those who, like Father Smith in *The Thanatos Syndrome*, manage to stir its laconic heart. Indeed, the narrative role of Father Smith, a man who embodies the intercessory role of the church, is as salient an example as any of the depiction of the Catholic view of the communal action of grace.

Approaching the world emblematically and with a sense of its mysterious depths, the Catholic artist, both as Catholic and artist, savors the riches of nature, including human nature, perceiving the imagination not as a source of distraction from God but, potentially at least, as a path to God. In this light all the things of the world become eligible symbols of divine largesse and hence of the discovery of the holy as well as the beautiful. As Kathleen Raine suggested in *The Inner Journey of the Poet*, the holy and the beautiful, while harmonious, are not identical—though the differences are subtle. As opposed to beauty, Raine maintained, the holy is not definable in terms of form. Also, while it is possible to appreciate beauty coldly, "as if external to ourselves," the numinous includes "at once the object and the beholder." Reflecting on the force of the holy on her imagination when she was growing up, Mary Gordon said that she was not supposed to be simply a "good girl" or even a "lady," but rather a "saint."[12] While the depiction of the pursuit of the holy might seem the most ineffable aspect of Catholic American writing, the reader who encounters sanctity in the image of Mary in Robert Lowell's poems or in the figure of Catherine Pollard in Caroline Gordon's novel *The Malefactors* cannot help but recognize it and be moved by it.

Balanced against this heightened view of experience in the Catholic world picture is the adumbrated assumption of the intractability of evil, which is ubiquitous in the fiction of Caroline Gordon, Ralph McInerny, and Flannery O'Connor and in the poetry of Allen Tate, Robert Lowell, and Daniel Berrigan. Catholic American literature has tended to focus on moral rather than physical evil and suffering, leaving the thorny question of physical evil to the mystery of God. What Catholic American writers have in common is a belief that no amount of scientific knowledge and social planning will obviate the power of evil within the human soul, no matter what structural improvements occur in society. Nonetheless, perceiving matter in part in its sublimated, Christological form, Catholic

12. Raine, *Inner Journey*, 179–80; Gordon, *Good Boys*, 167.

writers such as Walker Percy, Thomas Merton, and Daniel Berrigan vigorously and eloquently sought the transformation of the actual, flawed world. A number of Catholic writers, such as J. F. Powers and Paul Horgan, at times located the marrow of evil within the church itself. In this way, there was created the sort of dramatic tension between ideology and experience that leavens art.

The relationship between American Catholic writers and their church is not only problematic at times, but is of the essence of their identities as Catholics. The reason for this is that the sacramentalism that informs their vision of the world preeminently encompasses the church itself as the fount of doctrine and grace. In a sense this is a distinctively Catholic dilemma since the Catholic Church has attributed to itself such an imposing, intermediary role in what theologians call the economy of grace. Even those who satirize the church (such as J. F. Powers) believe themselves inextricably tied to it, not only as a system of belief but also as an indispensable source of contact with the divine. In spite of this privileged position occupied by the church, the writers considered in this study, extending themselves by the process of art beyond the perimeters of their church community, have generally presented a vision not of exclusivity but of inclusivity, grounded in the belief that there is nothing on earth that is inaccessible to God's mercy.

The crisis in identity experienced by American Catholics in recent years can be seen in microcosm in a recent study of the Catholic university in America edited by Theodore Hesburgh, the former president of Notre Dame University. In *The Challenge and Promise of a Catholic University*, Hesburgh and a number of faculty members from Notre Dame examine, among other issues, the present state of Catholic awareness and identity. Hesburgh, who presided over the transformation of a sectarian (used in a neutral sense) Catholic university to one that has attracted large numbers of non-Catholic faculty and students, notes in his introduction: "We do not require the Catholic, or even Christian, faith of everyone in the community. We think that most must have this faith or at least respect it, if the vision is to be real, not fictional." Though hospitable, these words strike the reader as extremely tenuous and bland as far as any statement of religious faith might be concerned. In an attempt to account for such amorphousness, Wilson Miscamble, an associate professor of history, observes nostalgically that the collapse of neoscholasticism as the intellectual nexus of Catholicism in the 1960s has not been replaced by any other source of "intellectual coherence" by which reason and Catholic faith might engage with each other. The Notre Dame historian Philip Gleason notes that after Vatican II "Catholic belief was not nearly so clear as it had been." Another professor of history, Marvin O'Connell, writes wryly about Notre Dame that now that "we have in the name of pluralism become like everybody else, we seem to have confirmed the adage that tragedy evolves into farce." David Leege, a professor of government, traces the problem of Catholic identity to the process of assimilation whereby many Catholics "swallowed the whole American dream" so that a confusion developed between being a "faithful Catholic" and a "good American."[13]

Ironically, though they are on different sides of the American Catholic Church's political spectrum, recent writers such as Mary Gordon and Ralph McInerny exhibit a high energy that contrasts with the comparatively subdued tenor of the Notre Dame deliberations. Furthermore, the Catholic Church's ability to attract significant writers is evident in the recent entry into the church of Annie Dillard, who in 1994 was awarded the Catholic Book Club's Campion Medal. With a similar appreciation of the vitality of the church, the Catholic theologian Tina Beattie recently announced that she had come to feminism *through* the writings of Catholic women theologians. Beattie also described a recent, large meeting of Catholic theologians that she had attended as manifesting a remarkable "love for and commitment to the church."[14]

It was that love of the Catholic Church in an ideal sense that kindled the imaginations of the writers considered in this study. All of these writers were stirred by the church's ability to evoke a sense of the sacred by visualizing the sacramental presence of God in the world and by the church's summons to sainthood. Furthermore, the church attracted these writers through the authority of its historical continuity and through the comprehensiveness and perceived self-sufficiency of its philosophical and theological interpretation of reality. The conditions that underlay the rich harvest of Catholic literature between 1940 and 1980 undoubtedly depended, at least in part, on the relatively insular state of Catholic culture in a period when, while Catholics were gradually preparing to enter the mainstream, they yet bore the marks of a distinct subculture. What distinguished the Catholic literature of the past fifty years was the centrality of religion in the thinking of these writers—even in the case of someone such as Robert Lowell, whose Catholicism burned fiercely for a limited time. It was this religious passion—a passion *for* religion as much as a passion for life that stemmed from religion—that marked the

13. Hesburgh, *Challenge and Promise*, 8, 215, 99, 241, 132.
14. Beattie, "A Step on the Royal Road," 1128, 1127.

work of these writers and that continues to provoke the imaginations of contemporary readers.

The outlook for Catholic American literature is difficult to foresee at the present time. In recent fiction by certain writers with a Catholic background, such as Alice McDermott, for example, Catholicism has been portrayed with historical detachment rather than through the eyes of faith. Anita Gandolfo has suggested that recent American Catholic fiction writers have been unable to propose a "viable new paradigm." Similarly, in his book *Tomorrow's Catholics, Yesterday's Church,* Eugene Kennedy observed that the institutional church would not recover the sense of supernatural mystery, the "essential component of religion," until it once again believed in, and freed, its own "imaginative powers." In this respect it could be argued that in its informalizing of the Liturgy and in its increased structural awareness of social and political problems, the church in the 1960s unintentionally overlooked the ways in which it was *not* like the rest of society.[15]

More than ever, recent Catholic writing reflects the place of Catholics who no longer perceive themselves in a dominantly Protestant culture but rather in a thoroughly secular culture that is dismissive toward religion in general. For this reason the salient atmosphere of recent Catholic writing has been that of the diaspora. In such an atmosphere the characters in novels by Catholic writers have generally had a new set of preoccupations. Less concerned about their transgressions from ecclesiastical practice and authority and considerably less focused on the church's role in transforming society, they are instead self-conscious about their upbringing as Catholics and tenuous about their beliefs as adults in a society inclined to scoff at the persistence of religious belief. The effect has been, on the whole, to shift the drama of that belief ever more toward the psychological and ever less toward the spiritual. Furthermore, the emphasis has shifted to the experiential matrix out of which belief might grow rather than focusing on the transmission of the faith through the church and through time. What makes the present situation distinctive is the widespread tendency among post–Vatican II American Catholics to individually and autonomously select and modify the doctrines that constitute their faith and morality. Not all Catholic writers have viewed the decline of Christendom with dismay. Walker Percy, for example, thought that in becoming detached from particular cultures, especially in the West, the Catholic Church might

---

15. Gandolfo, *Testing the Faith,* 210; Kennedy, *Tomorrow's Catholics, Yesterday's Church,* xi.

provide an imaginative stimulus by its very marginality. It would become, Percy ventured to say, what it was in the beginning, a "saving remnant, a sign of contradiction, a stumbling block, a transcultural phenomenon, a pilgrim church."[16]

The atmosphere of the diaspora has been vividly registered in Kit Reed's novel *Catholic Girls*, a work that in its broader outline recalls Mary McCarthy's celebrated novel *The Group*. Centering on a crisis that overtakes a group of four Catholic women who had gone to convent school together, the book documents their gradual slide away from girlhood principles of faith and morality. While the plot, which focuses on the effects of adultery, seems somewhat hackneyed, Reed is effective in capturing the wilting faith of these brittle women and their nostalgic remembrance of the certainties of their youth. Not only had adulthood with its moral complexities and ambiguities overtaken them, not only had their society turned away from religion, but their church had with its new mood of uncertainty and political infighting left them stranded. Georgia Kendall, the point-of-view character in *Catholic Girls*, sees contemporary Catholicism thusly: "Certain parts were still immutable, but it was getting harder to figure out exactly how many, or where or how to draw the line."[17]

Furthermore, in line with the writing of Mary Gordon, in recent Catholic fiction there has been a continuing depiction, either implicitly or explicitly, of the erosion of transcendentalism. In the title story of Philip Deaver's collection *Silent Retreats* (published in 1988), for example, the protagonist, Martin Wolf, stares at a contemporary picture of Christ that was an "ordinary picture of a man, only Martin knew it was Christ because of how the guy was holding his hands. When had they stopped painting halos," Martin reflected, "so you knew who was holy?"[18] The story's edge arises from its author's satiric depiction of the odyssey of Martin Wolf to find in the gregarious atmosphere of the contemporary church something like the old silent retreats, which a person could "go to and think" (7). Instead, the desperate man finds himself closeted in a rectory with a sympathetic but inadequate priest to whom Martin says ironically: "Are we gonna start sharing now?" (23)

In Deaver and others Vatican II continues to be the great divide for fictional explorations of the church's significance in contemporary society. If in Deaver there is the impression of the church's hasty and oblivious

16. Percy, *Signposts*, 319–20.
17. Reed, *Catholic Girls*, 88.
18. Deaver, *Silent Retreats*, 23, subsequently cited in the text parenthetically.

betrayal of its own past, in Starkey Flythe Jr.'s short story collection *Lent: The Slow Fast* (published in 1990), that past is rejected as ineffectual in the present social environment. An example is the acerbic tale "The Point of Conversion," a skillfully written story in which a devout, old-fashioned Catholic woman cares for a young, pregnant woman, all the while hoping that the young woman will convert. When the young woman becomes baptized outside the Catholic Church and marries outside that church, the older woman, Clemmie, sinks into depression wondering what it would take to bring about a conversion. Such a simple and sectarian understanding of her role as a Christian toward others is clearly at odds with Flythe's view of the challenge facing the contemporary church. Also found to be at fault in the old church is its legalistic manner of dealing with offenses toward others, as can be seen in Alfred Alcorn's novel *The Pull of the Earth*, which was published in 1985. In an apparently innocuous but revealing passage in that novel Janet Vaughn reflects upon her cruel treatment of an orphan boy, related to her husband, who had come to live with them: "She had beat him bloody about the mouth that time; knocked out a tooth. You should not administer corporal punishment in anger, Father Fahey told her, giving her a whole rosary to say for penance."[19] The fact that the priest says nothing about Janet's need to make up to the boy or even to love him identifies the priest as a sterile icon of the pre–Vatican II church, someone who might easily have fitted into the fiction of J. F. Powers or Paul Horgan.

Alcorn's second novel, *Vestments* (published in 1988), is a boldly imaginative and stylistically elegant story of a man who begins to dress as a priest in order to secure an inheritance. The book is a narrative tour de force that combines realistic psychological analysis, fantasy, and satire. Immersed in the diaspora of modern materialism, the central character, Sebastian Taggart, a lapsed Catholic and a "passive agnostic," ironically finds himself growing spiritually into the vestments that he had spuriously put on in order to impress his dying aunt.[20] Initially haunted by the sacrilegious nature of his imposture, Sebastian finds not only that his interest in the inheritance wanes, but he finds himself unexpectedly wanting his aunt to live:

> She was visibly shrinking, giving up the borrowed matter of her body, literally disappearing. She would be gone soon. The thought startled him: the most real thing in the world, which is another person, would

19. Alcorn, *Pull of the Earth*, 9
20. Alcorn, *Vestments*, 70, subsequently cited in the text parenthetically.

soon cease to exist, would disappear absolutely. It made him think
that death was as radical, as mysterious, as miraculous, as life itself.
It nearly made him disbelieve in death as final and total. He could
almost believe in a soul. (59)

The passage is typical of the novel's moral and psychological sensitivity.
Pained at last by his aunt's imminent death, he catches a glimpse of the
gulf between the depth of the woman who raised him and the coming
dissolution of her body. Rather than being drawn to despair, though,
Sebastian, guided intuitively by his submerged Catholic beliefs, considers
the absurdity of the immensity of the woman's character and life being
subsumed by her body. The telltale word *borrowed*, in connection with
her body, reveals Sebastian's lingering belief about immortality both to
the reader and—quite suddenly, Alcorn's narrative deftly indicates—to
Sebastian himself.

Propelled by a series of ironies, many of them substantive, the plot leads
Sebastian to the point where he abandons money and searches for faith,
a faith that ironically will not come. Plunging himself desultorily into
work that is comically unsuited to him but that he hopes will lead to faith,
Sebastian gropes his way up the unlit stairs of his life only to be given faith,
miraculously it would seem, at the very moment when he had given up
hope of gaining it. While the theology is evident enough—we must want
faith but only God can give it—the novel's vitality lies in its droll study
of religious awakening in a culture apparently immune to the value of
such an event. Alcorn skillfully captures the many-sidedness of religious
consciousness in such a culture by having his character inch toward faith
from within the maw of a secular culture with which at the beginning he
seems entirely in harmony. In this sense, novels such as *Catholic Girls* and
Vestments are representative of the tendency in contemporary Catholic
writing to existentially have the faith of the characters grow out of their
lives instead of the other way around.

Apart from its structural and thematic strength, *Vestments* is very fine
stylistically, in part because of its multiplicity of rhetorical effects. At times
the style is antithetical and epigrammatic—as in Sebastian's reflection
about a half-hearted attempt at seduction as involving "Catholic guilt for
having tried and American guilt for having failed" (87). Descriptive detail
is knitted into characterization with unobtrusive expertise as in the scene
in which Sebastian feels relief in recovering his old car, a moment that
causes him to clear away the snow remaining on the windshield as if
"wiping the face of a loved one" (250). Here, descriptive detail transcends
itself in impressionistically evoking the larger spiritual drama portrayed
in the novel.

Not all recent Catholic writing portrays Catholics as all but over-whelmed by the diaspora of contemporary American pluralism. Certainly Jon Hassler, one of the most important Catholic writers of this genera-tion, does not. Whereas in writers such as Alcorn and Reed, faith itself, marginalized by contemporary American culture, becomes the issue, in Hassler it is the living of faith that is the issue, and in this respect he is part of a continuum that reaches back into the earlier Catholic writing of this century. What Hassler maintains in his fiction is the reality of the community of the church as the ordinary vehicle through which God's grace passes. As with the earlier writers considered in this study, for Hassler the Catholic community exists as a subculture within the whole, even though the Catholic Church is now seen to be in a state of decline, as is indicated by the ubiquitous references in his fiction to the closing of seminaries and parochial schools.

Rooted in rural Minnesota, Hassler and his characters are sheltered from some of the effects of ecclesiastical attrition in the United States by the stability of their setting. Furthermore, as in writers such as Powers, whose work Hassler's resembles in some ways, Hassler's attachment to the rural small town is fundamental. The following description from *Dear James* (published in 1993), which focuses initially on the Badbattle river, is a case in point:

> the Badbattle was dark and light in irregular masses like the hide of a Holstein—black in the swift places where it hadn't yet frozen, white with snow-covered ice. The tree line along the far bank was purplish-black against the dying pink light in the sky. . . . warm lamplight glowed in the windows of the houses belonging to the Wempners, the Koenigs, the Simpsons, and the Jacobsens. Blinking Christmas lights were draped in trees and strung along rooflines. In front of the hospital a spotlighted company of lifesize figures in garish robes—Mary, Joseph, and the Wise Men—were gathered in the snow and gazing down into the snow-filled manger.[21]

Hassler's Christmas figures are set against a background that is as timeless as they are. The timelessness of small-town community life envelops the action of the community of saints, which reaches its fullest expression in characters like Janet Meers in *Dear James,* who, having been befriended by Agatha McGee, is seen by both Agatha and the novelist as having inherited the older woman's distinctive spirituality of toughness and charity.

While some of Hassler's earlier fiction is flecked with implausible incidents and an intrusive humor reminiscent of Sinclair Lewis—as in

21. Hassler, *Dear James,* 133.

the Gothic episode of the burial of a woman's leg in *Simon's Night*—
the later novels dissect small-town life with meticulous realism. The
characters are more fully developed than in the early work and a good
deal more plausible, particularly in their motivations. Thus, in *Dear James*,
Imogene Kite's ostensibly thoughtless but essentially evil exposure of
Agatha McGee's correspondence with James O'Hannon is depicted by
Hassler as forging an ugly chain of events that Hassler follows with
patient, intelligent, and finally hopeful, interest.

In order to extend his narratives of the community of Catholics beyond
the increasingly secular culture of the United States, Hassler developed
the stratagem of taking his characters to Ireland, the virtual home of
American Catholicism and a bastion of Catholic culture. Thus, a number
of characters—such as Agatha McGee—find themselves located in what
Hassler depicts as a compatible and parallel religious setting to that of the
Catholic communities in Minnesota that are the American settings of his
novels. Rome plays an even more heightened role as setting in *Dear James*.
The effect of these Catholic European settings is to offset the increasing
mood of decline and fragmentariness that had become attached to contemporary Catholic America and to suggest that if dialogue is no longer
possible between Catholicism and American culture—as Tate, Merton,
and Berrigan had believed it was—nevertheless by its very universality
the lamp of Catholicism would always be burning in some part of the
world. Such at any rate is the religious perspective that underlies the
foreground action in the 1985 *A Green Journey* and in *Dear James*.

Hassler's portraits of strong Catholic women are one of the ways in
which he is more contemporary in sensitivity than novelists such as J. F.
Powers or Walker Percy. Also different is his acceptance of some of the
more admirable features of the post–Vatican II church. An example arises
in the case of Father Frank Healy in *North of Hope* (published in 1990),
who reflects ruefully about the time when priests in the confessional were
expected merely to "admonish people and dole out penances ('"Ten Our
Fathers and ten Hail Marys and make a good Act of Contrition"') like a
judge consulting a sheet of sentencing guidelines. Well, that oversimple
time was dead and gone, and good riddance."[22] Dubious about the trendi-
ness and aberrations that have marred some aspects of contemporary
Catholicism—exemplified in his portrait of Sister Judith in *Dear James*—
Hassler nevertheless views the great continuum of the church's history
and teaching as working through and beyond Vatican II for better and for

22. Hassler, *North of Hope*, 336.

worse. On the other hand, it must be admitted that the strongest Catholics in Hassler's fiction are from the generation of Catholics that was formed in the pre–Vatican II period.

In novels such as *A Green Journey, North of Hope,* and *Dear James* Hassler focuses on the difficulty of celibacy, a choice of narrative situation that some readers might initially perceive as a narrow and worn subject. The story of Father Frank Healy in *North of Hope* is illustrative. While the origin of Frank's vocation to the priesthood is eventually discovered to have been based on a deception, and while he goes against his own nature in separating himself from Libby Girard, he grows into the role of priest in a period of history when that role is accorded less and less respect and authority, finally choosing the priesthood for the good that it is capable of doing both for others and for himself. Thus, the novel is only incidentally about the celibacy requirement and more centrally about the unexpected value to others and to oneself of such a way of life. Hassler shows the eventual spiritual worth Frank has for Libby as a priest even as both of them realize at every moment of their lives the ill-founded choice that had initially and irrevocably separated them.

In a thoughtful article about Jon Hassler's fiction, C. W. Truesdale suggested that Hassler is not so much interested in whether "ideas are true or real, or not, so much as he is in the ways they affect and shape the lives of the characters."[23] In this respect Hassler has much in common with writers such as Mary Gordon, Philip Deaver, Starkey Flythe Jr., and Alfred Alcorn. Hassler is distinctive among recent Catholic American writers, however, in unequivocally affirming the religious faith that in turn shapes the lives of his characters. While Hassler, whose reputation is growing steadily, will appear a traditionalist to many—and thus be approached warily by some—he is significant among recent Catholic American writers in representing the vigorous survival of Catholic American literature on the eve of the next millennium, a vigor that is as remarkable, perhaps, as it was unforeseen.

23. Truesdale, "The Novels of Jon Hassler," 57.

BIBLIOGRAPHY

Abrams, M. H., ed. *Literature and Belief.* New York: Columbia University Press, 1958.

Alcorn, Alfred. *The Pull of the Earth.* Boston: Houghton-Mifflin, 1985.

———. *Vestments.* Boston: Houghton-Mifflin, 1988.

Aquinas, Saint Thomas. *On the Truth of the Catholic Faith: Summa Contra Gentiles.* Ed. Vernon J. Bourke. Garden City, N.Y.: Hanover, 1956.

Asals, Frederick. *Flannery O'Connor: The Imagination of Extremity.* Athens: University of Georgia Press, 1982.

Axelrod, Stephen Gould. *Robert Lowell: Life and Art.* Princeton: Princeton University Press, 1970.

———. "Robert Lowell and Hopkins." *Twentieth Century Literature* 31 (1985): 58.

Balthasar, Hans Urs von. *Seeing the Form.* Vol. 1 of *The Glory of the Lord: A Theological Aesthetics.* Edinburgh: Clark, 1982.

Bartlett, Lee. *William Everson: The Life of Brother Antoninus.* New York: New Directions, 1988.

Beattie, Tina. "A Step on the Royal Road." *Tablet* (September 10, 1994): 1127–28.

Berrigan, Daniel. "Africa: A People's Art." *Jesuit Missions* 41:1 (January–February 1967): 22–27.

———. *Block Island.* Greensboro, N.C.: Unicorn, 1985.

———. *The Bow in the Clouds.* New York: Coward-McCann, 1961.

———. *The Bride: Essays in the Church.* New York: Macmillan, 1959.

———. "The Catholic Dream World and the Sacred Image." *Worship* 35 (1961): 549–60.

————. *Consequences: Truth And . . .* New York: Macmillan, 1967.

————. *Encounters.* Cleveland: World, 1960.

————. *False Gods, Real Men.* New York: Macmillan, 1969.

————. *May All Creatures Live.* Nevada City: Berliner, 1984.

————. "The New Spirit of Modern Sacred Art." *Critic* 20:7 (July 1962): 30–33.

————. *No Bars to Manhood.* Garden City, N.Y.: Doubleday, 1970.

————. *No One Walks Waters.* New York: Macmillan, 1966.

————. *Prison Poems.* Greensboro, N.C.: Unicorn, 1973.

————. *Selected and New Poems.* Garden City, N.Y.: Doubleday, 1973.

————. *They Call Us Dead Men.* New York: Macmillan, 1966.

————. *Time without Number.* New York: Macmillan, 1957.

————. *The World for Wedding Ring.* New York: Macmillan, 1962.

Berrigan, Daniel, and Thich Nhat Hanh. *The Raft Is Not the Shore.* Boston: Beacon, 1975.

Bishop, John Peale, and Allen Tate. *The Republic of Letters in America: The Correspondence of John Peale Bishop and Allen Tate.* Ed. Thomas Daniel Young and John J. Hindle. Lexington: University Press of Kentucky, 1981.

Blake, William. *Complete Writings.* Ed. Geoffrey Keynes. London: Oxford University Press, 1966.

Brinkmeyer, Robert H. *The Art and Vision of Flannery O'Connor.* Baton Rouge: Louisiana State University Press, 1989.

————. *Three Catholic Writers of the Modern South.* Jackson: University Press of Mississippi, 1985.

Brownson, Orestes. *The Works of Orestes A. Brownson.* Ed. Henry F. Brownson. 20 vols. New York: AMS Press, 1966.

Carr, Anne E. *Transforming Grace: Christian Tradition and Women's Experience.* San Francisco: Harper and Row, 1988.

Cooper, Philip. *The Autobiographical Myth of Robert Lowell.* Chapel Hill: University of North Carolina Press, 1970.

Crowley, Sue Mitchell. "Mr. Blackmur's Lowell: How Does Morality Get into Literature?" *Religion and Literature* 19:3 (1987): 27–47.

Davidson, Donald, and Allen Tate. *The Literary Correspondence of Donald Davidson and Allen Tate.* Ed. John Tyree Fain and Thomas Daniel Young. Athens: University of Georgia Press, 1974.

Deaver, Philip. *Silent Retreats.* Athens: University of Georgia Press, 1988.

Dolan, Jay P. *The American Catholic Experience.* Garden City, N.Y.: Doubleday, 1985.

Dolan, Paul. "Lowell's *Quaker Graveyard:* Poem and Tradition." *Renascence* 21:2 (1969): 171–80.

Doreski, William. *The Years of Our Friendship*. Jackson: University Press of Mississippi, 1990.

Dupree, Robert S. *Allen Tate and the Augustinian Imagination*. Baton Rouge: Louisiana State University Press, 1983.

Eco, Umberto. *The Aesthetics of Thomas Aquinas*. Trans. Hugh Bredin. Cambridge: Harvard University Press, 1988.

Eliot, T. S. "Dante." In his *Selected Essays*, 237–77. London: Faber, 1934.

————. "Goethe as the Sage." In his *On Poetry and Poets*, 207–27. London: Faber, 1957.

Ellis, John Tracy. "American Catholics and the Intellectual Life." *Thought* 30 (1955): 351–88.

Everson, William. "The Artist and the Religious Life." Typescript. Bancroft Library, University of California, Berkeley, 1960.

————. *Birth of a Poet: The Santa Cruz Meditations*. Santa Barbara: Black Sparrow, 1982.

————. "A Conversation with William Everson." Expanded version of *Right On* interview. March 1975. Ts. Berkeley collection.

————. *Earth Poetry*. Ed. Lee Bartlett. Berkeley: Oyez, 1980.

————. *The Excesses of God*. Stanford: Stanford University Press, 1988.

————. "Is the Modern Sensibility Defective?" Typescript, n.p. Berkeley collection.

————. "Letter on Clerical Celibacy." 1958. Typescript, n.p. Berkeley collection.

————. Letters. Typescript. Bancroft Library, University of California, Berkeley.

————. *On Writing the Waterbirds and Other Presentations: Collected Forewords and Afterwords, 1935–1981*. Ed. Lee Bartlett. Metuchen: Scarecrow, 1983.

————. "Poetry and the Dark Night of the Soul." Typescript, n.d., n.p. Berkeley collection.

————. *Prodigious Thrust*. Santa Rosa: Black Sparrow, 1996.

————. "Prodigious Thrust." 1956. Ts. Berkeley collection.

————. "Rhetoric and the Poetry of Protest." 1979. Typescript, n.p. Berkeley collection.

————. *The Veritable Years, 1949–1966*. Santa Barbara: Black Sparrow, 1978.

————. "Whitman's Mysticism." Ts. Berkeley collection.

Fein, Richard. *Robert Lowell*. 2nd ed. Boston: Twayne, 1979.

Finlay, Mitch. "Author J. F. Powers: An Entertainer, Not a Thinker." *Our Sunday Visitor* (January 1989): 5.

Fletcher, John Gould. *The Autobiography of John Gould Fletcher*. Ed. Lucas Carpenter. Fayetteville: University of Arkansas Press, 1988.

Flythe, Starkey, Jr. *Lent: The Slow Fast.* Iowa City: University of Iowa Press, 1990.

Fraistat, Rose Ann. *Caroline Gordon as Novelist and Woman of Letters.* Baton Rouge: Louisiana State University Press, 1984.

Frye, Northrop. *The Double Vision: Language and Meaning in Religion.* Toronto: University of Toronto Press, 1991.

—————. "Humanities in a New World." In his *Four Essays,* 15–29. Toronto: University of Toronto Press, 1960.

Furst, Lilian. *Romanticism in Perspective.* 2nd ed. London: Macmillan, 1979.

Gandolfo, Anita. *Testing the Faith: The New Catholic Fiction in America.* New York: Greenwood, 1992.

Gelpi, Albert. "Everson/Antoninus: Contending with the Shadow." In *The Veritable Years, 1949–1966,* by William Everson, n.p. Santa Barbara: Black Sparrow, 1978.

Gentry, Marshall Bruce. *Flannery O'Connor's Religion of the Grotesque.* Jackson: University Press of Mississippi, 1986.

Giles, Paul. *American Catholic Arts and Fictions.* New York: Cambridge University Press, 1992.

Gish, Robert. *Paul Horgan.* Boston: Twayne, 1983.

Gleason, Philip. *Keeping the Faith: American Catholicism Past and Present.* Notre Dame: University of Notre Dame Press, 1987.

Gordon, Caroline. "The Art and Mystery of Faith." In *Newman Annual,* University of Minnesota (December 1953): 55–62.

—————. "Cock-Crow." *Southern Review* 1 (1965): 554–69.

—————. *The Collected Stories of Caroline Gordon.* New York: Farrar, Straus, and Giroux, 1981.

—————. *The Glory of Hera.* Garden City, N.Y.: Doubleday, 1972.

—————. Letters. Percy Collection, Southern Historical Collection, Library of the University of North Carolina at Chapel Hill.

—————. Letters. Tate-Gordon Collection, Manuscripts Division, Department of Rare Books and Special Collections, Princeton University Libraries.

—————. "Letters to a Monk." *Ramparts* 3:12 (1964): 4–10.

—————. Literary and theological notes from Caroline Gordon to her grandson, Allen Tate Wood, 1969–1978. Tate-Gordon Collection, Manuscripts Division, Department of Rare Books and Special Collections, Princeton University Libraries.

—————. *The Malefactors.* New York: Harcourt, Brace, 1956.

—————. "Some Readings and Misreadings." *Southern Review* 61 (1953): 384–407.

————. *The Southern Mandarins: Letters of Caroline Gordon to Sally Wood, 1924–1937.* Ed. Sally Wood. Baton Rouge: Louisiana State University Press, 1984.

————. *The Strange Children.* New York: Scribner's, 1951.

Gordon, Mary. *The Company of Women.* New York: Random House, 1980.

————. *Final Payments.* New York: Random House, 1978.

————. *Good Boys and Dead Girls.* New York: Viking, 1991.

————. "Growing Up Catholic and Creative." *U.S. News and World Report* (October 5, 1987): 74.

————. *Men and Angels.* New York: Random House, 1985.

————. *The Other Side.* New York: Viking, 1989.

————. *The Rest of Life.* New York: Viking, 1993.

————. *Temporary Shelter.* New York: Random House, 1987.

Gorman, Trisha. "Interview with Mary Gordon." In *Contemporary Authors,* ed. Frances Locher, 225. Vol. 102. Detroit: Gale, 1981.

Gray, Paul. "The Catholic Paradox." *Time* (October 9, 1995): 53–56.

Greeley, Andrew. *The Catholic Myth.* New York: Scribner's, 1990.

————. *An Ugly Little Secret: Anti-Catholicism in North America.* Kansas City: Sheed, Andrews, and McMeel, 1977.

Hagerty, Cornelius. *The Problem of Evil.* North Quincy, Mass.: Christopher, 1978.

Hagopian, John V. *J. F. Powers.* New York: Twayne, 1968.

Hamilton, Ian. *Robert Lowell: A Biography.* New York: Random House, 1982.

Happel, Stephen, and David Tracy. *A Catholic Vision.* Philadelphia: Fortress, 1984.

Hassler, Jon. *Dear James.* New York: Ballantine, 1993.

————. *A Green Journey.* New York: Morrow, 1985.

————. *North of Hope.* New York: Ballantine, 1990.

Hebblethwaite, Peter. "How Catholic Is the Catholic Novel?" *Times Literary Supplement* (July 27, 1967): 678–79.

Hennesey, James. *American Catholics: A History of the Roman Catholic Community in the United States.* New York: Oxford, 1981.

Hesburgh, Theodore, ed. *The Challenge and Promise of a Catholic University.* Notre Dame: University of Notre Dame Press, 1994.

Higgins, Michael. "A Study of the Influence of William Blake on Thomas Merton." *American Benedictine Review* 25:3 (1974): 377–88.

Hobsbaum, Philip. *A Reader's Guide to Robert Lowell.* London: Thames and Hudson, 1988.

Horgan, Paul. "The Abdication of the Artist." *Proceedings of the American Philosophical Society* 109:5 (1965): 267–71.

————. *Approaches to Writing*. New York: Farrar, Straus, and Giroux, 1968.

————. Campion Award acceptance speech. May 2, 1957. Yale Collection of American Literature, Beinecke Rare Book and Manuscript Library, Yale University.

————. *A Certain Climate: Essays on History, Arts, and Letters*. Middletown: Wesleyan University Press, 1988.

————. "Critical Essay." In *Selected Poems*, by Witter Bynner. Ed. Robert Hunt. 2nd ed., rev. New York: Knopf, 1943.

————. *Everything to Live For*. New York: Farrar, Straus, and Giroux, 1968.

————. *Humble Powers*. Garden City, N.Y.: Doubleday, 1954.

————. Introduction to *Maurice Baring Restored*. Ed. Paul Horgan. London: Heinemann, 1970.

————. Introduction to *N. C. Wyeth*, by Douglas Allen. New York: Crown, 1972.

————. Letters. Yale Collection of American Literature, Beinecke Rare Book and Manuscript Library, Yale University.

————. "Reflections on the Act of Writing." *Reflection: The Wesleyan Quarterly* 5 (1968): 2–6.

————. *The Saintmaker's Christmas Eve*. New York: Farrar, Straus, and Cudahy, 1955.

————. *Things as They Are*. New York: Farrar, Straus, and Giroux, 1964.

————. *The Thin Mountain Air*. New York: Farrar, Straus, and Giroux, 1977.

————. *Whitewater*. New York: Farrar, Straus, and Giroux, 1970.

————. "A Writer's Discipline." *Critic* 21:5 (1952): 34–35.

Iannone, Carol. "The Secret of Mary Gordon's Success." *Commentary* 79:6 (1985): 62–66.

Jumper, Will C. "Whom Seek Ye? A Note on Robert Lowell's Poetry." *Hudson Review* 9:1 (1956). Reprinted in *Robert Lowell: A Collection of Critical Essays*, ed. Thomas Parkinson, 53–62. Englewood Cliffs: Prentice-Hall, 1968.

Jung, Carl Gustav. *Memories, Dreams, Reflections*. Ed. Aniela Jaffe. New York: Vintage, 1965.

Kellog, Gene. *The Vital Tradition: The Catholic Novel in a Period of Convergence*. Chicago: Loyola University Press, 1970.

Kenneally, James. *The History of American Catholic Women*. New York: Crossroad, 1990.

Kennedy, Eugene. *Tomorrow's Catholics, Yesterday's Church*. New York: Harper and Row, 1988.

Kilcourse, George. *Ace of Freedoms: Thomas Merton's Christ*. Notre Dame: University of Notre Dame Press, 1993.

Kinnell, Galway. "Four First Volumes." *Poetry* 92 (1958): 183.

Langan, John. "Is This a Catholic Moment? :4: Out of the Ghetto." *Tablet* (October 15, 1994): 1308–9.

Leddy, Mary Jo, Remi de Roo, and Douglas Roche. *In the Eye of the Catholic Storm*. Toronto: Harper Collins, 1992.

Lentfoehr, Sister Therese. "The Solitary." In *Thomas Merton, Monk*, ed. Brother Patrick Hart, 59–77. New York: Sheed and Ward, 1974.

Lowell, Robert. *Collected Prose*. New York: Farrar, Straus, and Giroux, 1987.

————. *Land of Unlikeness*. Cummington, Mass.: Cummington Press, 1944.

————. Letters. Houghton Library, Harvard University.

————. *Lord Weary's Castle*. New York: Harcourt, Brace, and World, 1946.

————. "Miscellaneous School Notes and Prose." Lowell Collection, Houghton Library, Harvard University.

————. "Moulding the Golden Spoon." Lowell Collection, Houghton Library, Harvard University.

————. Review of *The World's Body*, by John Crowe Ransom. *Hika* (October 1938): 59.

————. *Robert Lowell: Interviews and Memoirs*. Ed. Jeffrey Meyers. Ann Arbor: University of Michigan Press, 1988.

————. *Selected Poems*. Rev. ed. New York: Farrar, Straus, and Giroux, 1977.

Maritain, Jacques. *Art and Scholasticism and the Frontiers of Poetry*. Trans. Joseph Evans. Notre Dame: University of Notre Dame Press, 1974.

————. *Creative Intuition in Art and Poetry*. New York: Pantheon, 1953.

————. *The Rights of Man and Natural Law*. Trans. Doris Anson. New York: Scribner's, 1947.

Marshall, Bruce. "The Responsibilities of the Catholic Novelist." *Commonweal* 50 (May 27, 1949): 169–71.

Martin, Carter W. *The True Country: Themes in the Fiction of Flannery O'Connor*. Nashville: Vanderbilt University Press, 1968.

Martin, Jay. *Robert Lowell*. Minneapolis: University of Minnesota Press, 1970.

Mazzaro, Jerome. *The Poetic Themes of Robert Lowell*. Ann Arbor: University of Michigan Press, 1965.

McConn, Robert, S.J. "The Education of a Prophet." *Kansas Magazine* (1962): 73–78.

McDonald, Donald. "Interview with J. F. Powers." *Critic* 19:5 (1960).

McInerny, Dennis. "Thomas Merton and the Tradition of American Criticial Romanticism." In *The Message of Thomas Merton*, ed. Patrick Hart, 166–91. Kalamazoo, Mich.: Cistercian, 1981.

McInerny, Ralph. *Connolly's Life*. New York: Atheneum, 1983.

———. *Gate of Heaven*. New York: Harper and Row, 1975.

———. *Leave of Absence*. New York: Atheneum, 1986.

———. *The Priest*. New York: Harper and Row, 1973.

———. *The Search Committee*. New York: Atheneum, 1991.

———. *St. Thomas Aquinas*. Boston: Twayne, 1977.

Merton, Thomas. *The Asian Journal of Thomas Merton*. Ed. Naomi Burton, Brother Patrick Hart, and James Laughlin. New York: New Directions, 1973.

———. *Bread in the Wilderness*. New York: New Directions, 1953.

———. "The Catholic and Creativity." *American Benedictine Review* 11 (1960): 197–213.

———. *The Collected Poems of Thomas Merton*. New York: New Directions, 1977.

———. *Conjectures of a Guilty Bystander*. Garden City, N.Y.: Doubleday, 1966.

———. *The Courage for Truth: The Letters of Thomas Merton to Writers*. Ed. Christine Bochen. New York: Farrar, Straus, and Giroux, 1993.

———. "Day of a Stranger." *Hudson Review* 20 (1967): 211–18.

———. *The Hidden Ground of Love: The Letters of Thomas Merton on Religious Experience and Social Concerns*. Ed. William Shannon. New York: Farrar, Straus, and Giroux, 1985.

———. *Honorable Reader*. Ed. Robert Daggy. New York: Crossroad, 1989.

———. *The Literary Essays of Thomas Merton*. New York: New Directions, 1981.

———. *The Monastic Journey*. Ed. Brother Patrick Hart. Kansas City: Sheed and Ward, 1977.

———. *Mystics and Zen Masters*. New York: Farrar, Straus, and Giroux, 1967.

———. *New Seeds of Contemplation*. New York: New Directions, 1961.

———. *Opening the Bible*. Collegeville, Minn.: Liturgical Press, 1970.

———. *Raids on the Unspeakable*. New York: New Directions, 1966.

———. *The Seven Storey Mountain*. New York: Harcourt, Brace, 1948.

———. *The Sign of Jonas*. New York: Harcourt, Brace, 1953.

———. *Zen and the Birds of Appetite*. New York: New Directions, 1968.

Meynell, Hugo. *Is Christianity True?* Washington, D.C.: Catholic University of America Press, 1994.

Milhaven, Annie, ed. *The Inside Stories: Thirteen Valiant Women Challenging the Church*. Mystic: Twenty-Third Publications, 1987.

Millgate, Michael. "An Interview with Allen Tate." *Shenandoah* 12 (spring 1961): 27–34.

Moynahan, Julian. "Waiting for God in Inglenook." *New York Review of Books* (December 8, 1988): 51.

Nogar, Raymond. *The Lord of the Absurd*. New York: Herder, 1966.

Occhiogrosso, Peter, ed. *Once a Catholic*. Boston: Houghton-Mifflin, 1987.

O'Connor, Flannery. *Conversations with Flannery O'Connor*. Ed. Rosemary Magee. Jackson: University Press of Mississippi, 1987.

———. *Everything That Rises Must Converge*. New York: Farrar, Straus, and Giroux, 1965.

———. *A Good Man Is Hard to Find*. New York: Farrar, Straus, and Cudahy, 1955.

———. *The Habit of Being*. Ed. Sally Fitzgerald. New York: Farrar, Straus, and Giroux, 1979.

———. Letters. Lynch Collection, Yale Collection of American Literature, Beinecke Rare Book and Manuscript Library, Yale University.

———. *Mystery and Manners*. Ed. Sally Fitzgerald and Robert Fitzgerald. New York: Farrar, Straus, and Giroux, 1969.

———. *The Presence of Grace and Other Book Reviews*. Ed. Carter W. Martin. Athens: University of Georgia Press, 1983.

———. *The Violent Bear It Away*. New York: Farrar, Straus, and Giroux, 1960.

———. *Wise Blood*. New York: Farrar, Straus, and Cudahy, 1952.

O'Kane, James. "A Sociological View of United States Catholicism." In *Teaching the Catholic Faith*, ed. Eugene V. Clark. New York: Fellowship of Catholic Scholars, 1991.

O'Malley, Frank. "The Blood of Robert Lowell." *Renascence* 2:1 (1949): 3–8.

Orwell, George. "Inside the Whale." In *Collected Essays, Journalism and Letters of George Orwell*, ed. Sonia Orwell and Ian Angus. Vol. 1. London: Secker and Warburg, 1968.

Pasquiariello, Ronald. *Conversations with Andrew Greeley*. Boston: Quinlan, 1988.

Percy, Walker. "The Diagnostic Novel." *Harper's Magazine* 272 (June 1986): 39–45.

———. "Herman Melville." *New Criterion* 2 (November 1983): 39–42.

———. *Lancelot*. New York: Farrar, Straus, and Giroux, 1977.

———. *The Last Gentleman*. New York: Farrar, Straus, and Giroux, 1966.

———. *Lost in the Cosmos*. New York: Farrar, Straus, and Giroux, 1983.

———. *Love in the Ruins*. New York: Farrar, Straus, and Giroux, 1971.

———. *The Message in the Bottle*. Farrar, Straus, and Giroux, 1975.

———. *More Conversations With Walker Percy*. Ed. Lewis Lawson and Victor Kramer. Jackson: University Press of Mississippi, 1993.

———. *The Moviegoer*. New York: Knopf, 1961.

———. *The Second Coming*. New York: Farrar, Straus, and Giroux, 1980.

———. *Signposts in a Strange Land*. Ed. Patrick Samway. New York: Farrar, Straus, and Giroux, 1991.

————. *The Thanatos Syndrome*. New York: Farrar, Straus, and Giroux, 1987.

————. "A Visitor Interview: Novelist Walker Percy." *Our Sunday Visitor* (October 1, 1987): 5; (November 8, 1987): 7.

Powers, J. F. "And of the Author as a Responsible Storyteller." *New York Times Book Review* (May 12, 1989): 3.

————. "The Catholic and Creativity." *American Benedictine Review* 15:1 (1964): 63–80.

————. "Conscience and Religion." *Commentary* 40:7 (1965): 91–92.

————. Letters. Lowell Collection, Houghton Library, Harvard University.

————. *Morte D'Urban*. Garden City, N.Y.: Doubleday, 1962.

————. "The Pesky Side of Paradise." *New York Herald Tribune Book Review* (May 23, 1965): 5, 16.

————. *The Presence of Grace*. Garden City, N.Y.: Doubleday, 1956.

————. *Prince of Darkness and Other Stories*. Garden City, N.Y.: Doubleday, 1951.

————. "She Stands Alone." *Four Quarters* 12:11 (1962): 56.

————. *Wheat That Springeth Green*. New York: Knopf, 1988.

Procopiow, Norma. *Robert Lowell: The Poet and His Critics*. Chicago: American Library Association, 1984.

Raine, Kathleen. *The Inner Journey of the Poet*. London: Allen and Unwin, 1982.

Reed, Kit. *Catholic Girls*. New York: Donald Fine, 1987.

Rexroth, Kenneth. "San Francisco Letter." *Evergreen Review* 1:2 (1957): 5–14.

Rudman, Mark. *Robert Lowell: An Introduction to the Poetry*. New York: Columbia University Press, 1983.

Simpson, Eileen. *Poets in Their Youth*. New York: Random House, 1982.

Sipe, A. W. Richard. "The Homosexual Person." *Tablet* (August 29, 1992): 1071.

Sonnenfeld, Albert. "Twentieth Century Gothic: Reflections on the Catholic Novel." *Southern Review* 1 (1965): 388–405.

Sparr, Arnold. *To Promote, Defend, and Redeem: The Catholic Literary Revival and the Cultural Transformation of American Catholicism*. Westport, Conn.: Greenwood, 1990.

Spivey, Ted R. *Flannery O'Connor: The Woman, the Thinker, the Visionary*. Macon, Ga.: Mercer University Press, 1995.

Squires, Radcliffe. *Allen Tate: A Literary Biography*. New York: Pegasus, 1971.

Staples, Hugh. *Robert Lowell: The First Twenty Years*. New York: Farrar, Straus, and Cudahy, 1962.

Sullivan, Walter. *Allen Tate: A Recollection*. Baton Rouge: Louisiana State University Press, 1988.

Tate, Allen. "Christ and the Unicorn." *Sewanee Review* 63 (1955): 175–181.

————. *Collected Essays*. Denver: Swallow, 1959.

————. *Collected Poems, 1919–1976*. New York: Farrar, Straus, and Giroux, 1977.

————. *The Forlorn Demon*. Chicago: Regnery, 1953.

————. Letters. Tate-Gordon Collection, Manuscripts Division, Department of Rare Books and Special Collections, Princeton University Libraries.

————. *Memoirs and Opinions, 1926–1974*. Chicago: Swallow, 1975.

————. *The Poetry Reviews of Allen Tate, 1924–1944*. Ed. Ashley Brown. Baton Rouge: Louisiana State University Press, 1983.

————. *Reactionary Essays on Poetry and Ideas*. New York: Scribner's, 1936.

————. "Religion and the Intellectuals." *Partisan Review* 17:3 (1950): 250–53.

Tate, Allen, and Caroline Gordon, eds. *The House of Fiction*. New York: Scribner's, 1950.

Teiser, Ruth. "Brother Antoninus: Poet, Printer, and Religious: An Interview." William Everson Collection, Bancroft Library, University of California, Berkeley, 1966.

TeSelle, Sally McFague. *Literature and the Christian Life*. New Haven: Yale University Press, 1966.

Tracy, David. *The Analogical Imagination: Christian Theology and the Culture of Pluralism*. New York: Crossroad, 1981.

Truesdale, C. W. "The Novels of Jon Hassler." *South Dakota Review* 32:1 (1994): 47–87.

Wachtel, Eleanor, ed. *Writers and Company*. Toronto: Knopf, 1993.

Weaver, Mary Jo. *New Catholic Women*. San Francisco: Harper and Row, 1985.

Wood, Ralph C. *The Comedy of Redemption: Christian Faith and Comic Vision in Four American Novelists*. Notre Dame: University of Notre Dame Press, 1988.

Wuerl, Donald. *The Catholic Catechism*. Huntingdon, Ind.: Sunday Visitor, 1986.

INDEX

Abrams, M. H., 272; "Belief and the Suspension of Disbelief," 272
Aeschylus, 129
Alcorn, Alfred, 279, 281, 283; *The Pull of the Earth*, 279; *Vestments*, 279–80
Alvarez, A., 171
American political ideology: and Catholicism, 2, 9, 10, 13, 270–71
—in Catholic writing: Berrigan, 210; Brownson, 21–22; Horgan, 81–82; Percy, 150–51; Powers, 174, 187; Tate, 54, 71
Anderson, Sherwood, 56
Antoninus, Brother, 3, 92, 99. *See also* Everson, William
Aquinas, Saint Thomas, 5, 6, 9, 16, 17, 20, 51, 97, 112, 133, 172, 213, 217, 228, 232; *Summa Theologica*, 133. *See also* Thomism
Aristotle, 5
Arnold, Matthew, 53
Art: and Catholicism, 7–8, 13–18, 272–74
—view of, in Catholic writers: Berrigan, 194–96; Brownson, 24; M. Gordon, 248; Merton, 117, 122
Asals, Frederick, 231
Auden, W. H., 255; "September 1, 1939," 255
Augustine of Hippo, Saint, 51, 65, 77
Axelrod, Stephen Gould, 153

Balthasar, Hans Urs von, 8
Baring, Maurice, 73
Barth, Karl, 114
Bartlett, Lee, 109
Beattie, Tina, 276
Belloc, Hilaire, 30
Bernanos, Georges, 35
Berrigan, Daniel, 3, 9, 11, 22, 26, 42, 49, 77, 93, 127, 129, 161, 172, 190, 192–210, 217, 240, 253, 270, 271, 273, 274, 275
—works: "Ambition," 207; "Autumn, the Streams Are Heavy," 204; *Block Island*, 208–9; "Bombardment," 203; "Bonhoeffer: God Is Neither Here Nor There," 195; "The Book," 200; *The Bow in the Clouds*, 193; *The Bride*, 193, 196; "Chartres," 197; "The Clock in the Square," 202; *Consequences: Truth And . . .* , 194; "Consolation," 207; "The Crucifix," 196, 197; "Dachau Is Now Open for Visitors," 201; *Encounters*, 197–98; *False Gods, Real Men*, 201–3; "Flew to New York," 204; "A Fortieth Year," 198; "The Gorges," 205; "Ignorance Is Like a Sourdough Starter," 207; "In Memoriam," 200; "Last Day," 199; "Lazarus," 197; "Lightning Struck Here," 196; *May All Creatures Live*, 206–7; "The Men on the Hill," 196; "The Moon," 196; *No*

CREDITS

P ARTS OF THE chapters about William Everson, Thomas Merton, Robert Lowell, Ralph McInerny, and Mary Gordon have appeared in the following journals: "Sexuality and Mysticism in the Poetry of William Everson," *Christianity and Literature* (fall 1994); "Merton and the American Romantics," *Merton Annual* (1997); "Reassessing Robert Lowell's Catholic Poetry," *Renascence* (winter 1995); "An Overview of the Fiction of Ralph McInerny, *Canadian Catholic Review* (April and May 1995); "Women and the Catholic Church in the Fiction of Mary Gordon," *English Studies in Canada* (June 1996).

Acknowledgment is gratefully made to the following: to Nancy Tate Wood and to the Manuscripts Division, Department of Rare Books and Special Collections, Princeton University Libraries, for permission to quote from the Allen Tate/Caroline Gordon correspondence; to Thomas B. Catron III and to the Yale Collection of American Literature, Beinecke Rare Book and Manuscript Library, Yale University, for permission to quote from the Horgan manuscripts; to William Hotchkiss and the Bancroft Library, University of California at Berkeley, for permission to quote from the Everson manuscripts; to the Houghton Library, Harvard University, for permission to quote from the Robert Lowell manuscripts; to the Southern Historical Collection, Library of the University of North Carolina at Chapel Hill, for permission to quote from the Walker Percy papers; to Farrar, Straus, and Giroux for permission to quote from *Collected Poems, 1919–1976,* by Allen Tate, and *Things as They Are,* by Paul Horgan; to Black Sparrow Press for permission to quote from *The Veritable Years, 1949–1966,*